ATI TEAS: Full Study Guide, Test Strategies and Secrets

Copyright © 2024 Smart Edition Academy.

All rights reserved. No part of the material protected by this copyright notice may be reproduced or utilized in any form or by any means, electronic or mechanical, including photocopying, recording or by any information storage and retrievable system, without written permission from the copyright holder.

To obtain permission(s) to use the material from this work for any purpose including workshops or seminars, please submit a written request to

Email: info@smarteditionmedia.com

Library of Congress Cataloging-in-Publication Data

Smart Edition Academy.

ATI TEAS 7: Full Study Guide, Test Strategies and Secrets/Smart Edition Academy.

ISBN: 978-1-949147-81-0

1. ATI TEAS 7.
2. Study Guides.
3. TEAS
4. Nursing
5. Careers

Disclaimer:

The opinions expressed in this publication are the sole works of Smart Edition Media and were created independently from ATI Nursing Education, or any National Evaluation Systems or other testing affiliates. Between the time of publication and printing, specific standards as well as testing formats and website information may change that are not included in part or in whole within this product. Smart Edition Academy develops sample test questions, and they reflect similar content as on real tests; however, they are not former tests. Smart Edition Academy assembles content that aligns with exam standards but makes no claims nor guarantees candidates a passing score.

Printed in the United States of America

ATI TEAS 7: Full Study Guide, Test Strategies and Secrets/Smart Edition Academy.
ISBN: 978-1-949147-81-0

How To Access Online Timed Practice Tests

Thank you for your purchase of the SE Nursing ATI TEAS 7 study guide! Included with your purchase is access to 4 online timed practice tests that will simulate the real exam. You can access the online resources both on our website and on the mobile app.

To access the online resources first use the QR code below to sign up for the practice test that comes with your book. You can also access it by going to:
https://www.smarteditionacademy.com/courses/ati-teas-7-book/

Mobile App

After you have registered your book on the website use the QR codes below to download the mo-bile app in the Apple app store or the Android store.

Bonus Offer To Create The Ultimate Study Package

50% off the Smart Edition Nursing TEAS 7 Online Course and Mobile App

This book is a great start on your journey to prepare for the TEAS 7 exam. Smart Edition Nursing also offers a comprehensive online course with materials and resources that go far beyond what can be offered in a book and we want to make sure it's something you can add to your resources to get the most of your study time.

We're excited to offer you 50% off the first month of the online course **when you use the code: BOOK15**

Use the QR code below to access and purchase the course, purchase directly in the mobile app you have already downloaded or visit:

https://www.smarteditionacademy.com/ati-teas-online-course

ATI TEAS 7 Online Course Includes

- 8 Timed Practice Tests
- 60 + lesson modules for every topic
- 100+ video lessons
- Flashcards for every topic
- Study Planner

- Question banks with over 1,000 practice questions organized by each topic on the test
- Video explanations for every practice question
- AI Tutoring Assistant 24/7 chat
- Mobile App and laptop/computer access

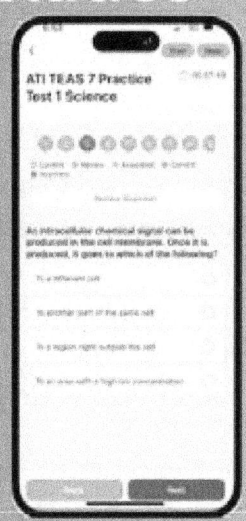

INTRODUCTION

TEAS Overview

The Test of Essential Academic Skills (TEAS) is a standardized exam that is published by Assessment Technologies Institute (ATI) Nursing Education. It is used as part of an overall assessment of qualifications for individuals when applying to a nursing school or an allied health school. Professionals already working in the health science industry may also take this exam while embarking on the path to advanced certification. The exam is administered weekly at PSI testing centers, as well as at nursing and allied health schools throughout the United States and Canada.

About This Book

This book provides you with an accurate and complete representation of the Test of Essential Academic Skills (TEAS) standardized exam and includes all four sections found on the exam: Reading, Mathematics, Science, and English Language and Usage.

The reviews in this book are designed to provide the information and strategies you need to do well on all four sections of the exam. The full-length practice test in the book is based on the TEAS and contain questions similar to those you can expect to encounter on the official test. A detailed answer key follows each practice quiz and test. These answer keys provide explanations designed to help you completely understand the test material. Each explanation references the book chapter to allow you to go back to that section for additional review, if necessary.

- 209 minutes
- 170 questions

Reading
- 45 questions
- 55 minutes
- Key Ideas and Details
- Craft and Structure
- Integration of Knowledge and Ideas

Mathematics
- 38 questions
- 57 minutes
- Numbers and Algebra
- Measurement
- Data Analysis

Science
- 50 questions
- 60 minutes
- Human Anatomy and Physiology
- Biology
- Chemistry
- Scientific Reasoning

English and Language Usage
- 37 questions
- 37 minutes
- Conventions of standard English
- Knowledge of Language
- Using Language and Vocabulary to Express Ideas in Writing

TABLE OF CONTENTS

Introduction vii
The Smart Edition Study Program ix
How to Use This Book viii

Section I Reading 1
Chapter 1 Key Ideas and Details 3
    Lesson 1.1 Main Ideas, Topic Sentences, and Supporting Details 3
    Lesson 1.2 Summarizing Text and Using Text Features 7
    Practice Quiz 11
Chapter 2 Craft and Structure 15
    Lesson 2.1 Tone, Mood, and Transition Words 15
    Lesson 2.2 The Author's Purpose and Point of View 18
    Lesson 2.3 Evaluating and Integrating Data 21
    Practice Quiz 25
Chapter 3 Integration of Knowledge and Ideas 27
    Lesson 3.1 Facts, Opinions, and Evaluating an Argument 27
    Lesson 3.2 Understanding Primary Sources, Making Inferences, and Drawing Conclusions 31
    Lesson 3.3 Types of Passages, Text Structures, Genre and Theme 35
    Practice Quiz 40

Section II Mathematics 43
Chapter 4 Numbers and Basic Operations 45
    Lesson 4.1 Basic Addition and Subtraction 45
    Lesson 4.2 Basic Multiplication and Division 50
    Lesson 4.3 Decimals and Fractions 56
    Lesson 4.4 Addition and Subtraction of Fractions 63
    Lesson 4.5 Multiplication and Division of Fractions 67
    Lesson 4.6 Ratios, Proportions, and Percentages 71
    Practice Quiz 75
Chapter 5 Algebra 77
    Lesson 5.1 Equations with One Variable 77
    Lesson 5.2 Solving Real-World Mathematical Problems 82
    Lesson 5.3 Powers & Exponents, Roots & Radicals, with Polynomials 85
    Practice Quiz 89
Chapter 6 Measurement and Data 91
    Lesson 6.1 Standards of Measure 91
    Lesson 6.2 Interpreting Graphics 96
    Lesson 6.3 Similarity, Right Triangles, and Trigonometry 104
    Lesson 6.4 Circles 109
    Practice Quiz 112

ATI TEAS: Full Study Guide, Test Strategies and Secrets

Section III Science 115
Chapter 7 Human Anatomy and Physiology: Organization of Systems 117
- Lesson 7.1 Organization of the Human Body. 117
- Lesson 7.2 The Cardiovascular System 123
- Lesson 7.3 The Respiratory System 132
- Lesson 7.4 The Gastrointestinal System 137
- Lesson 7.5 The Reproductive System 142
- Lesson 7.6 The Urinary System 147
- Practice Quiz 154

Chapter 8 Human Anatomy and Physiology: Support and Movement 156
- Lesson 8.1 The Skeletal System 156
- Lesson 8.2 The Muscular System 162
- Lesson 8.3 The Integumentary System 169
- Practice Quiz 175

Chapter 9 Human Anatomy and Physiology: Integration and Control 177
- Lesson 9.1 The Nervous System 177
- Lesson 9.2 The Endocrine System 186
- Lesson 9.3 The Lymphatic System 193
- Practice Quiz 199

Chapter 10 Life and Physical Sciences 201
- Lesson 10.1 The Scientific Method and Designing an Experiment 201
- Lesson 10.2 The Foundations of Biology 207
- Lesson 10.3 Cell Structure, Function, and Type 214
- Lesson 10.4 Cellular Reproduction, Cellular Respiration, and Photosynthesis 219
- Lesson 10.5 Genetics and DNA 227
- Practice Quiz 232

Chapter 11 Chemistry 233
- Lesson 11.1 Scientific Notation 233
- Lesson 11.2 States of Matter 241
- Lesson 11.3 Properties of Matter 246
- Lesson 11.4 Chemical Bonds 252
- Lesson 11.5 Chemical Solutions 261
- Lesson 11.6 Acids and Bases 267
- Practice Quiz 273

Section IV English and Language Usage 275
Chapter 12 Conventions of Standard English 278
- Lesson 12.1 Spelling 278
- Lesson 12.2 Capitalization 281
- Lesson 12.3 Punctuation 284
- Practice Quiz 287

Chapter 13 Parts of Speech 289
Lesson 13.1 Nouns 289

Lesson 13.2 Pronouns 292
Lesson 13.3 Adjectives and Adverbs. 295
Lesson 13.4 Conjunctions and Prepositions 298
Lesson 13.5 Verbs and Verb Tenses 300
Practice Quiz. 303
Chapter 14 Knowledge of Language 305
Lesson 14.1 Subject and Verb Agreement 305
Lesson 14.2 Types of Sentences 308
Lesson 14.3 Types of Clauses. 313
Lesson 14.4 Formal and Informal Language 315
Practice Quiz. 317

Chapter 15 Vocabulary Acquisition 319
Lesson 15.1 Root Words, Prefixes, and Suffixes 319
Lesson 15.2 Context Clues and Multiple Meaning Words 323
Lesson 15.3 The Writing Process 327
Practice Quiz. 331

Section V Full-Length Practice Exams 333

TEAS Practice Exam 1 Answer Sheet 334

TEAS Practice Exam 1 335
Section I. Reading 335
Section II. Mathematics. 346
Section III. Science 352
Section IV. English and Language Usage 358
Answer Key with Explanatory Answers 362

HOW TO USE THIS BOOK

Studies show that most people begin preparing for exams approximately six to eight weeks before their test date. If you are scheduled to take your test in sooner than eight weeks, do not despair! Smart Edition Media has designed this study guide to be flexible to allow you to concentrate on areas where you need the most support.

Whether you have eight weeks to study—or much less than that—Smart Edition Media can help you make the most of your time.

How This Book Is Organized

Take a look at the Table of Contents.

- Notice that each **Section** in the study guide corresponds to a subtest of the exam.
- These sections are broken into **Chapters** that identify the principal content categories of the exam.
- Each chapter is further divided into individual **Lessons** that address the specific content and objectives required to pass the exam. Some lessons contain embedded example questions to assess your comprehension of the material "in the moment."
- All lessons contain a bulleted list called **Let's Review.** Use this list to refresh your memory before taking a practice quiz, test, or the actual exam.
- A **Practice Quiz**, designed to check your progress as you move through the content, follows each chapter.

Whether you plan on working through the study guide from cover to cover or select specific sections to review, each chapter of this book can be completed in one to two study sessions. If you must end your study session before finishing a chapter, try to complete your current lesson to maximize comprehension and retention of the material.

THE SMART EDITION STUDY PROGRAM

The educators at Smart Edition Media have created this study program to help you manage your time and organize your efforts as you prepare for your exam.

On page xi, you will find a checklist that will take you through our study program in six weeks. Notice that, while the assignments are organized by week, we have not listed the days on which you should study. Recognizing that every student is different, we have left that part up to you.

Our experts tell us that most students retain more information when they study in frequent, short study sessions. They suggest that it is preferable to dedicate 1–2 hours per day for 4–5 days/week than working straight through a 6-hour study session two days/week. However, feel free to work through the content at your own pace according to your schedule.

The routines in our study program are designed to create the foundation for your study habits over the next few weeks as you prepare for your exam.

- The **Lesson Routine** utilizes the instructional lessons in this book along with online resources, such as flashcards and videos, that can be found on the Smart Edition Media website.
- The **End of Chapter Routine** assesses your understanding of new skills with short quizzes and helps to reinforce learning.
- The **End of Section Routine** builds on the mastery of skills by assessing the subject area as a whole. This test is the actual subject test that appears on your exam.

STUDY ROUTINES

Take a Diagnostic Test

The purchase of this book includes a selection of online Practice Exams. You will find instructions on how to access the online site at the front of this book.

1. Access the companion website and select the "Diagnostic Test" in the Practice Tests section. Once you have completed the test, you will receive a detailed report of your results. This report includes: a listing of your submitted answers with the correct answers indicated, detailed answer explanations for each question, and reference lesson topics to help you identify areas of strength and weakness.

2. The results of your diagnostic test can be used to create a study plan that suits your study habits and time frame. If you are short on time, look at your diagnostic test results to determine which subject matter could use the most attention and focus the majority of your efforts on those areas. While this study guide is organized to follow the order of the actual test, you are not required to complete the book from beginning to end, in that exact order.

Lesson Routine

For each lesson you complete, you should:

- Skim through the pages of the lesson.
  - Read the introduction and Let's Review section to obtain the main ideas.
- Complete the lesson by reading the instructional content and working through any practice questions.
  - Pay close attention to any graphics, illustrations, or other "call-outs" along the margins or within the lesson. These contain snippets of valuable information that will help you with your exam!
  - Take notes! If you have purchased this book, highlight it, write in the margins, annotate it in a way that helps you. If this is a library book, you can still take notes—use a separate notebook or paper!
- Utilize the Smart Edition Media online resources, such as the flashcards and videos, to supplement and reinforce understanding of concepts, as needed.

End of Chapter Routine

- Read the Let's Review section for each lesson.
- Complete the Practice Quiz at the end of the chapter.
- Review the answers and rationales.
  - Pay close attention to rationales for incorrectly answered quiz questions.
- Utilize the Smart Edition Media online resources, such as the flashcards and videos, to reinforce understanding of concepts, as needed.

End of Section Routine

- Use a Practice Test, either from the book or online, for this End of Section Routine. You will complete only the portion of the test for the section you have just studied. You will complete other sections of this Practice Test as you work through your study guide.
- Once you have completed the section test, review the detailed report of your results.
  - Pay close attention to rationales for incorrectly answered test questions.
- Utilize the Smart Edition Media online resources, such as the flashcards and videos, to reinforce understanding of concepts, as needed.

☑ **Week 1: Reading**	☑ **Week 4: Science – Foundations of Science**
Let's Get Started!	Chapter 10: Life and Physical Sciences
☐ Take a Diagnostic Test	☐ Complete lessons 10.1 – 10.5
☐ Score the Diagnostic Test and analyze results	☐ End of Chapter Routine for Chapter 10
Chapter 1: Key Ideas and Details	Chapter 11: Scientific Reasoning
☐ Complete lessons 1.1 & 1.2	☐ Complete lessons 11.1 – 11.6
☐ End of Chapter Routine for Chapter 1	☐ End of Chapter Routine for Chapter 11
Chapter 2: Craft and Structure	☐ End of Section Routine for Science
☐ Complete lessons 2.1 – 2.3	☑ **Week 5: English and Language Usage**
☐ End of Chapter Routine for Chapter 2	Chapter 12: Conventions of Standard English
Chapter 3: Integration of Knowledge and Ideas	☐ Complete lessons 12.1 – 12.3
☐ Complete lessons 3.1 – 3.3	☐ End of Chapter Routine for Chapter 12
☐ End of Chapter Routine for Chapter 3	Chapter 13: Parts of Speech
☐ End of Section Routine for Reading	☐ Complete lessons 13.1 – 13.5
☑ **Week 2: Mathematics**	☐ End of Chapter Routine for Chapter 13
Chapter 4: Numbers and Basic Operations	Chapter 14: Knowledge of Language
☐ Complete lessons 4.1 – 4.6	☐ Complete lessons 14.1 – 14.4
☐ End of Chapter Routine for Chapter 4	☐ End of Chapter Routine for Chapter 14
Chapter 5: Algebra	Chapter 15: Vocabulary Acquisition
☐ Complete lessons 5.1 – 5.5	☐ Complete lessons 15.1 – 15.3
☐ End of Chapter Routine for Chapter 5	☐ End of Chapter Routine for Chapter 15
Chapter 6: Measurement and Data	☐ End of Section Routine for English and Language Usage
☐ Complete lessons 6.1 – 6.4	☑ **Week 6**
☐ End of Chapter Routine for Chapter 6	☐ Prepare to take the Full-Length Practice Exams by reviewing your notes and Practice Quizzes and Tests, including the answer explanations.
☐ End of Section Routine for Math	☐ Access and complete a Full-Length Practice Exam (from the book or online).
☑ **Week 3: Science – Anatomy & Physiology**	☐ Score the Practice Exam and analyze results.
Chapter 7: Human A&P: Organization of Systems	☐ Use the remaining Practice Exams as further preparation before your exam date. Remember: You can retake all the online tests as many times as you want.
☐ Complete lessons 7.1 – 7.6	Great job! You are ready to take your test!
☐ End of Chapter Routine for Chapter 7	
Chapter 8: Human A&P: Support and Movement	
☐ Complete lessons 8.1 – 8.3	
☐ End of Chapter Routine for Chapter 8	
Chapter 9: Human A&P: Integration and Control	
☐ Complete lessons 9.1 – 9.3	
☐ End of Chapter Routine for Chapter 9	

The Smart Edition Study Program

Study Strategies and Tips

MAKE STUDY SESSIONS A PRIORITY

Use a calendar to schedule your study sessions. Set aside a dedicated amount of time each day/week for studying. While it may seem challenging to manage, given your other responsibilities, remember that to reach your goals, it is crucial to dedicate the time now to prepare for this test. A satisfactory score on your exam is the key to unlocking a multitude of opportunities for your future success.

Do you work? Have children? Other obligations? Be sure to take these into account when creating your schedule. Work around them to ensure that your scheduled study sessions can be free of distractions.

> **TIPS FOR FINDING TIME TO STUDY.**
> Wake up 1–2 hours before your family for some quiet time.
> Study 1–2 hours before bedtime and after everything has quieted down.
> Utilize weekends for longer study periods.
> Hire a babysitter to watch children.

TAKE PRACTICE TESTS

Smart Edition Media offers practice tests, both online and in print. Take as many as you can to help be prepared. This will eliminate any surprises you may encounter during the exam.

KNOW YOUR LEARNING STYLE

- Identify your strengths and weaknesses as a student. All students are different, and everyone has a different learning style. Do not compare yourself to others.
- Howard Gardner, a developmental psychologist at Harvard University, has studied how people learn new information. He has identified seven distinct intelligences. According to his theory:

    "We are all able to know the world through language, logical-mathematical analysis, spatial representation, musical thinking, the use of the body to solve problems or to make things, an understanding of other individuals, and an understanding of ourselves. Where individuals differ is in the strength of these intelligences—the so-called profile of intelligences—and in the ways in which such intelligences are invoked and combined to carry out different tasks, solve diverse problems, and progress in various domains."

- Knowing your learning style can help you to tailor your studying efforts to suit your natural strengths.
- What ways help you learn best? Videos? Reading textbooks? Find the best way for you to study and learn/review the material.

> **WHAT IS YOUR LEARNING STYLE?**
>
> Visual-Spatial – Do you like to draw, do jigsaw puzzles, read maps, daydream? Creating drawings, graphic organizers, or watching videos might be useful for you.
>
> Bodily-Kinesthetic – Do you like movement, making things, physical activity? Do you communicate well through body language, or like to be taught through physical activity? Hands-on learning, acting out, role-playing are tools you might try.
>
> Musical – Do you show sensitivity to rhythm and sound? If you love music and are also sensitive to sounds in your environments, it might be beneficial to study with music in the background. You can turn lessons into lyrics or speak rhythmically to aid in content retention.
>
> Interpersonal – Do you have many friends, empathy for others, street smarts, and interact well with others? You might learn best in a group setting. Form a study group with other students who are preparing for the same exam. Technology makes it easy to connect. If you are unable to meet in person, teleconferencing or video chats are useful tools to aid interpersonal learners in connecting with others.
>
> Intrapersonal – Do you prefer to work alone rather than in a group? Are you in tune with your inner feelings, follow your intuition, and possess a strong will, confidence, and opinions? Independent study and introspection will be ideal for you. Reading books, using creative materials, keeping a diary of your progress will be helpful. Intrapersonal learners are the most independent of the learners.
>
> Linguistic – Do you use words effectively, have highly developed auditory skills, and often think in words? Do you like reading, playing word games, making up poetry or stories? Learning tools such as computers, games, and multimedia will be beneficial to your studies.
>
> Logical-Mathematical – Do you think conceptually, abstractly, and can see and explore patterns and relationships? Try exploring subject matter through logic games, experiments, and puzzles.

CREATE THE OPTIMAL STUDY ENVIRONMENT

Some people enjoy listening to soft background music when they study. (Instrumental music is a good choice.) Others need to have a silent space to concentrate. Which do you prefer? Either way, it is best to create an environment that is free of distractions for your study sessions.

Have study guide – Will travel! Leave your house: Daily routines and chores can be distractions. Check out your local library, a coffee shop, or other quiet space to remove yourself from distractions and daunting household tasks that will compete for your attention.

Create a Technology Free Zone. Silence the ringer on your cell phone and place it out of reach to prevent surfing the Web, social media interactions, and email/texting exchanges. Turn off the television, radio, or other devices while you study.

Are you comfy? Find a comfortable, but not too comfortable, place to study. Sit at a desk or table in a straight, upright chair. Avoid sitting on the couch, a bed, or in front of the TV. Wear clothing that is not binding and restricting.

Keep your area organized. Have all the materials you need available and ready: Smart Edition study guide, computer, notebook, pen, calculator, and pencil/eraser. Use a desk lamp or overhead light that provides ample lighting to prevent eye-strain and fatigue.

HEALTHY BODY, HEALTHY MIND

Consider these words of wisdom from Buddha, "To keep the body in good health is a duty—otherwise, we shall not be able to keep our mind strong and clear."

> **KEYS TO CREATING A HEALTHY BODY AND MIND:**
>
> Drink water – Stay hydrated! Limit drinks with excessive sugar or caffeine.
>
> Eat natural foods – Make smart food choices and avoid greasy, fatty, sugary foods.
>
> Think positively – You can do this! Do not doubt yourself and trust in the process.
>
> Exercise daily – If you have a workout routine, stick to it! If you are more sedentary, now is a great time to begin! Try yoga or a low-impact sport. Simply walking at a brisk pace will help to get your heart rate going.
>
> Sleep well – Getting a good night's sleep is essential, but too few of us make it a priority. Aim to get eight hours of uninterrupted sleep to maximize your mental focus, memory, learning, and physical wellbeing.

FINAL THOUGHTS

- Remember to relax and take breaks during study sessions.
- Review the testing material. Go over topics you already know for a refresher.
- Focus more time on less familiar subjects.

Exam Preparation

In addition to studying for your upcoming exam, it is vital to keep in mind that you need to prepare your mind and body as well. When preparing to take an exam as a whole, not just studying, taking practice exams, and reviewing math rules, it is critical to prepare your body to be mentally and physically ready. Often, your success rate will be much higher when you are fully prepared.

Here are some tips to keep in mind when preparing for your exam:

SEVERAL WEEKS/DAYS BEFORE THE EXAM

- Get a full night of sleep, approximately 8 hours.
- Turn off electronics before bed.
- Exercise regularly.
- Eat a healthy balanced diet, including fruits and vegetables.
- Drink water.

THE NIGHT BEFORE

- Eat a good dinner.
- Pack materials/bag, healthy snacks, and water.
- Gather materials needed for the test: your ID and receipt of the test. You do not want to be scrambling the morning of the exam. If you are unsure of what to bring with you, check with your testing center or test administrator.
- Map the location of the test center, identify how you will be getting there (driving, public transportation, uber, etc.), when you need to leave, and parking options.
- Lay your clothes out. Wear comfortable clothes and shoes, do not wear items that are too hot/cold.
- Allow a minimum of ~8 hours of sleep.
- Avoid coffee and alcohol.
- Do not take any medications or drugs to help you sleep.
- Set alarm.

THE DAY OF THE EXAM

- Wake up early, allow ample time to do all the things you need to do and for travel.
- Eat a healthy, well-rounded breakfast.
- Drink water.
- Leave early and arrive early, leave time for any traffic or any other unforeseeable circumstances.
- Arrive early and check in for the exam to give yourself enough time to relax, take off your coat, and become comfortable with your surroundings.

Take a deep breath, get ready, go! You got this!

SECTION I
READING

Reading: 45 questions, 55 minutes

Areas assessed: Key Ideas and Details, Craft and Structure, Integration of Knowledge and Ideas

READING TIPS

- If the question doesn't reference something in one of the answers, that answer is probably incorrect. Check to see what is/isn't referenced and choose the best answer from there.
- Do not assume facts about questions. Often, if information is not provided in the question, it will not be relevant. Stick to the facts that are provided.
- Some questions will focus on your ability to determine the difference between opinion and fact. Practice recognizing the difference between fact (the grass is green) and opinion (the grass smells nice).
- Read carefully and slowly. Questions may be confusing if you read too quickly.
- If you think that 2 answers could be correct, ask yourself, "What is it REALLY asking?"
- Study and know different types of writing styles (e.g., narrative, expository, entertaining, analytical, and persuasive). You may be asked to identify them.
- Know how to identify first person (I), second person (You), third person (Narration).
- Use only the information you are given. If it is not stated in the text, then don't assume it to be relevant.
- Use Process of Elimination. Eliminate answers you know are wrong and work your way to one, final answer.
- Know how to use an index, dictionary, almanac, encyclopedia, and glossary.
- Try to improve your reading speed and comprehension in advance. You want to ensure that you can finish the section before the time is up.
- Pay attention to the wording in questions. The wording in the question itself will usually provide helpful hints that can lead you toward the correct answer.

CHAPTER 1 KEY IDEAS AND DETAILS

LESSON 1.1 MAIN IDEAS, TOPIC SENTENCES, AND SUPPORTING DETAILS

To read effectively, you need to know how to identify the most important information in a text. You must also understand how ideas within a text relate to one other.

Main Ideas

The central or most important idea in a text is the **main idea**. As a reader, you need to avoid confusing the main idea with less important details that may be interesting but not central to the author's point.

The **topic** of a text is slightly different than the main idea. The topic is a word or phrase that describes roughly what a text is about. A main idea, in contrast, is a complete sentence that states the topic and explains what an author wants to say about it.

All types of texts can contain main ideas. Read the following informational paragraph and try to identify the main idea:

> The immune system is the body's defense mechanism. It fights off harmful bacteria, viruses, and substances that attack the body. To do this, it uses cells, tissues, and organs that work together to resist invasion.

The topic of this paragraph is the immune system. The main idea can be expressed in a sentence like this: "This paragraph defines and describes the immune system." Ideas about organisms and substances that invade the body are not the central focus. The topic and main idea must always be directly related to every sentence in the text, as the immune system is here.

Read the persuasive paragraph below and consider the topic and main idea:

> Football is not a healthy activity for kids. It causes head injuries that harm the ability to learn and achieve. It causes painful bodily injuries that can linger into adulthood. It teaches aggressive behavioral habits that make life harder for players after they have left the field.

The topic of this paragraph is youth football, and the main idea is that kids should not play the game. Note that if you are asked to state the main idea of a persuasive text, it is your job to be objective. This means you should describe the author's opinion, not make an argument of your own in response.

Both of the example paragraphs above state their main idea explicitly. Some texts have an implicit, or suggested, main idea. In this case, you need to figure out the main idea using the details as clues.

> **FOR EXAMPLE**
>
> The following fictional paragraph has an implicit main idea:
>
> Daisy parked her car and sat gripping the wheel, not getting out. A few steps to the door. A couple of knocks. She could give him the news in two words. She'd already decided what she was going to do, so it didn't matter what he said, not really. Still, she couldn't make her feet carry her to the door.
>
> The main idea here is that Daisy feels reluctant to speak to someone. This point is not stated outright, but it is clear from the details of Daisy's thoughts and actions.

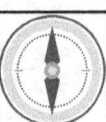

Topic Sentences

Many paragraphs identify the topic and main idea in a single sentence. This is called a **topic sentence,** and it often appears at the beginning of a paragraph. However, a writer may choose to place a topic sentence anywhere in the text.

Some paragraphs contain an introductory sentence to grab the reader's attention before clearly stating the topic. A paragraph may begin by asking a rhetorical question, presenting a striking idea, or showing why the topic is important. When authors use this strategy, the topic sentence usually comes second:

> Have you ever wondered how your body fights off a nasty cold? **It uses a complex defense mechanism called the immune system.** The immune system fights off harmful bacteria, viruses, and substances that attack the body. To do this, it uses cells, tissues, and organs that work together to resist invasion.

Here, the first sentence grabs the attention, and the second, **boldfaced** topic sentence states the main idea. The remaining sentences provide further information, explaining what the immune system does and identifying its basic components.

> **COMPARE!**
>
> The informational paragraph above contains a question that grabs the attention at the beginning. The writer could convey the same information with a little less flair by omitting this device. The version you read in Section 1 does exactly this. (The topic sentence below is **boldfaced.**)
>
> > **The immune system is the body's defense mechanism.** It fights off harmful bacteria, viruses, and substances that attack the body. To do this, it uses cells, tissues, and organs that work together to resist invasion.
>
> Look back at the football paragraph from Section 1. Which sentence is the topic sentence?

Sometimes writers wait until the end of a paragraph to reveal the main idea in a topic sentence. When you're reading a paragraph that is organized this way, you may feel like you're reading a bit of a puzzle. It's not fully clear what the piece is about until you get to the end:

Lesson 1.1 Main Ideas, Topic Sentences, and Supporting Details

It causes head injuries that harm the ability to learn and achieve. It causes painful bodily injuries that can linger through the passage of years. It teaches aggressive behavioral habits that make life harder for players after they have left the field. **Football is not a healthy activity for kids.**

Note that the topic—football—is not actually named until the final, **boldfaced** topic sentence. This is a strong hint that this final sentence is the topic sentence. Other paragraphs with this structure may contain several examples or related ideas and then tie them together with a summary statement near the end.

Supporting Details

The **supporting details** of a text develop the main idea, contribute further information, or provide examples.

All of the supporting details in a text must relate back to the main idea. In a text that sets out to define and describe the immune system, the supporting details could explain how the immune system works, define parts of the immune system, and so on.

Main Idea: The immune system is the body's defense mechanism.

Supporting Detail: It fights off harmful bacteria, viruses, and substances that attack the body.

Supporting Detail: To do this, it uses cells, tissues, and organs that work together to resist invasion.

The above text could go on to describe white blood cells, which are a vital part of the body's defense system against disease. However, the supporting details in such a text should *not* drift off into descriptions of parts of the body that make no contribution to immune response.

Supporting details may be facts or opinions. A single text can combine both facts and opinions to develop a single main idea.

Main Idea: Football is not a healthy activity for kids.

Supporting Detail: It teaches aggressive behavioral habits that make life harder for players after they have left the field.

Supporting Detail: In a study of teenage football players by Dr. Sophia Ortega at Harvard University, 28% reported involvement in fights or other violent incidents, compared with 19% of teenage boys who were not involved in sports.

The first supporting detail above states an opinion. The second is still related to the main idea, but it provides factual information to back up the opinion. Further development of this paragraph could contain other types of facts, including information about football injuries and anecdotes about real players who got hurt playing the game.

Let's Review!
- The main idea is the most important piece of information in a text.
- The main idea is often expressed in a topic sentence.
- Supporting details develop the main idea, contribute further information, or provide examples.

LESSON 1.2 Summarizing Text and Using Text Features

Effective readers need to know how to identify and restate the main idea of a text through summary. They must also follow complex instructions, figure out the sequence of events in a text that is not presented in order, and understand information presented in graphics.

Summary Basics

A **summary** is a text that restates the ideas from a different text in a new way. Every summary needs to include the main idea of the original. Some summaries may include information about the supporting details as well.

The content and level of detail in a summary vary depending on the purpose. For example, a journalist may summarize a recent scientific study in a newspaper profile of its authors. A graduate student might briefly summarize the same study in a paper questioning its conclusions. The journalist's version would likely use fairly simple language and restate only the main points. The student's version would likely use specialized scientific vocabulary and include certain supporting details, especially the ones most applicable to the argument the student intends to make later.

The language of a summary must be substantially different from the original. It should not retain the structure and word choice of the source text. Rather, it should provide a completely new way of stating the ideas.

Read the passage below and the short summary that follows:

> **Original:** There is no need for government regulations to maintain a minimum wage because free market forces naturally adjust wages on their own. Workers are in short supply in our thriving economy, and businesses must offer fair wages and working conditions to attract labor. Business owners pay employees well because common sense dictates that they cannot succeed any other way.
>
> **Effective Summary:** The author argues against minimum wage laws. He claims free market forces naturally keep wages high in a healthy economy with a limited labor supply.

The effective summary above restates the main ideas in a new but objective way. Objectivity is a key quality of an effective summary. A summary does not exaggerate, judge, or distort the author's original ideas.

> **Not a Summary:** The author makes a wild and unsupportable claim that minimum wage laws are unnecessary because market forces keep wages high without government intervention.

Although the above text might be appropriate in persuasive writing, it makes its own claims and judgments rather than simply restating the original author's ideas. It would not be an effective sentence in a summary.

> **KEY POINT!**
> Many ineffective summaries attempt to imitate the structure of the original text and change only individual words. This makes the writing process difficult, and it can lead to unintentional plagiarism.
>
> **Ineffective Summary (Plagiarism):** It is unnecessary for government regulations to create a minimum wage because capitalism adjusts wages without help. Good labor is rare in our excellent economy, and businesses need to offer fair wages and working conditions in order to attract workers.
>
> The above text is an example of structural plagiarism. Summary writing does not just involve rewriting the original words one by one. An effective summary restates the main ideas of the text in a wholly original way.

In some cases, particularly dealing with creative works like fiction and poetry, summaries may mention ideas that are clearly implied but not stated outright in the original text. For example, a mobster in a thriller novel might turn to another character and say menacingly, "I wouldn't want anything to happen to your sweet little kids." A summary of this passage could objectively say the mobster had threatened the other character. But everything in the summary needs to be clearly supportable in the text. The summary could not go on to say how the other character feels about the threat unless the author describes it.

Attending to Sequence and Instructions

Events happen in a sequence. However, many written texts present events out of order to create an effect on the reader. Nonfiction writers such as journalists and history writers may use this strategy to create surprise or bring particular ideas to the forefront. Fiction writers may interrupt the flow of a plot to interweave bits of a character's history or to provide flashes of insight into future events. Readers need to know how to untangle this presentation of events and figure out what actually happened first, second, and third. Consider the following passage:

> The man in dark glasses was looking for something. He checked his pockets. He checked his backpack. He walked back to his car, unlocked the doors, and inspected the area around the seats. Shaking his head, he re-locked the doors and rubbed his forehead in frustration. When his hand bumped his sunglasses, he finally realized where he had put them.

This passage does not mention putting the sunglasses on until the end, but it is clear from context that the man put them on first, before beginning his search. You can keep track of sequence by paying attention to time words like *when* and *before,* noticing grammatical constructions *he had* that indicate when events happened, and making common sense observations like the fact that the man is wearing his dark glasses in the first sentence.

Sequence is also an important aspect of reading technical and functional documents such as recipes and other instructions. If such documents present many steps in a large text block without illustrations or visual breaks, you may need to break them down and categorize them yourself. Always read all the steps first and think about how to follow them before jumping in. To see why, read the pancake recipe below:

> Combine flour, baking powder, sugar, and salt. Break the eggs into a separate bowl. Add milk and oil to the beaten eggs. Combine dry and liquid ingredients and stir. While you are doing the above, put a small amount of oil into a pan and heat it on medium heat. When it is hot, spoon batter onto the pan.

To follow directions like these effectively, a reader must break them down into categories, perhaps even rewriting them in a numbered list and noting when to start steps like heating the pan, which may be worth doing in a different order than it appears above.

Interpreting Graphics

Information is often presented in pictures, graphs, or diagrams. These **graphic elements** may provide information to back up an argument, illustrate factual information or instructions, or present key facts and statistics.

When you read charts and graphs, it is important to look carefully at all the information presented, including titles and labels, to be sure that you are interpreting the visuals correctly.

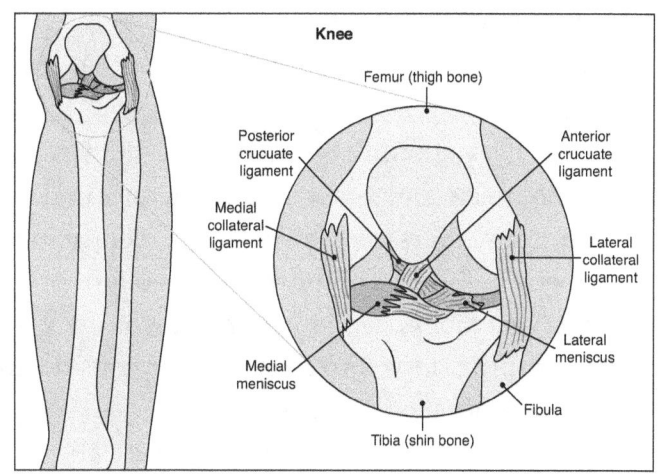

Diagram

A diagram presents a picture with labels that shows the parts of an object or functions of a mechanism. The diagram of a knee joint shows the parts of the knee. Like many diagrams, it is placed in relation to a larger object—in this case, a leg—to clarify how the labeled parts fit into a larger context.

Flowchart

A flowchart shows a sequence of actions or decisions involved in a complex process. A flowchart usually begins with an oval-shaped box that asks a yes-no question or gives an instruction. Readers follow arrows indicating possible responses. This helps readers figure out how to solve a problem, or it illustrates how a complex system works.

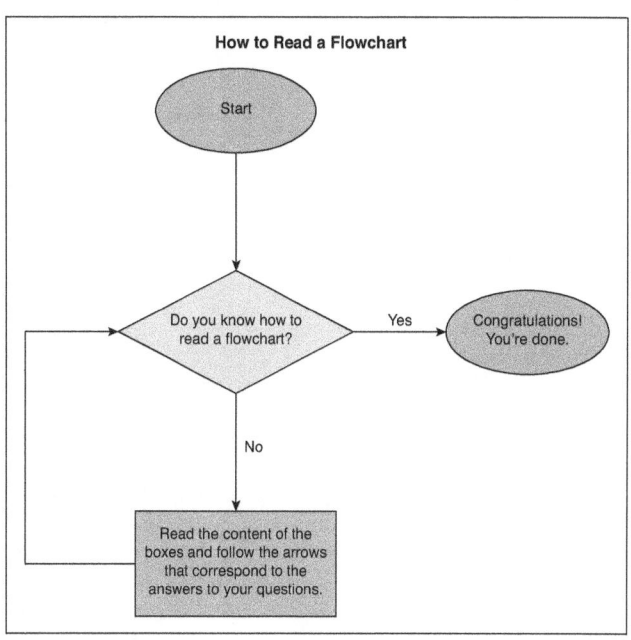

Bar Graph

A bar graph uses bars of different sizes to represent numbers. Larger bars show larger numbers to convey the magnitude of differences between two numeric values at a glance. In this case, each rectangle shows the number of candy bars of different types that a particular group of people ate.

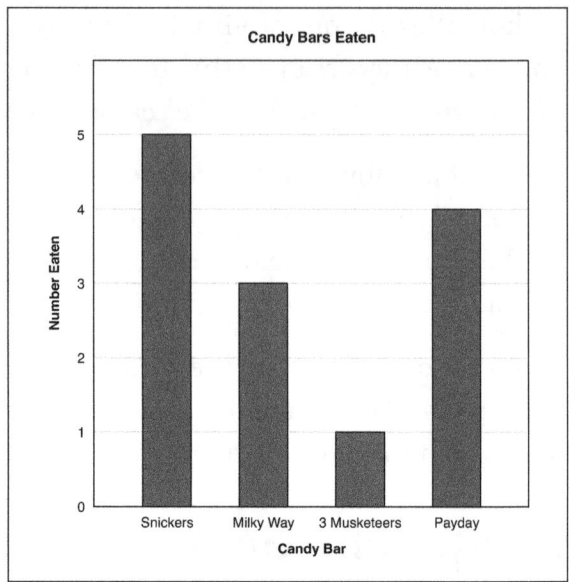

Pie Chart

A pie chart is useful for representing all of something—in this case, the whole group of people surveyed about their favorite kind of pie. Larger wedges mean larger percentages of people liked a particular kind of pie. Percentage values may be written directly on the chart or in a key to the side.

Let's Review!

- A summary restates the main ideas of a text in different words.
- A summary should objectively restate ideas in the present tense and give credit to the original author.
- Effective readers need to mentally reconstruct the basic sequence of events authors present out of order.
- Effective readers need to approach complex instructions by grouping steps into categories or considering how best to approach the steps.
- Information may be presented graphically in the form of diagrams, flowcharts, graphs, or charts.

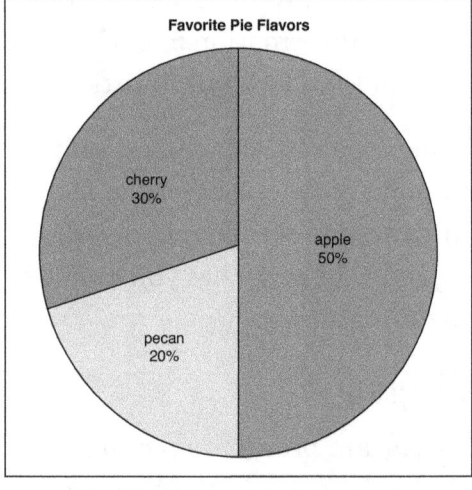

Chapter 1 Key Ideas and Details Practice Quiz

Read the following paragraph and answer questions 1-2.

Faith sighed as the old lady cooed at the baby and blabbed about her own children's early days. Four kids! They all walked and talked early! They were little geniuses! Blah blah blah! Faith spent twenty-four hours a day caring for a drooling, incontinent little person, and as a reward she had to hear constant stories about *other* drooling, incontinent little people. Maybe she should take a tip from the baby and erupt into a random fit of screaming.

1. **What is the topic sentence of the paragraph?**

    A. Maybe she should take a tip from the baby and erupt in a random fit of screaming.

    B. Faith spent twenty hours a day caring for a drooling, incontinent little person, and as a reward she had to hear four million stories about *other* drooling, incontinent little people.

    C. Faith sighed as the old lady cooed at the baby and blabbed about her own children's early days.

    D. None of the above; the main idea is implied.

2. **Which sentence best expresses the main idea of the paragraph?**

    A. Faith regrets that she ever became a mother and wishes she could give her baby up for adoption.

    B. Faith dislikes cleaning up drool and changing diapers, and she thinks the old lady is a liar or a fool.

    C. Faith feels frustrated when people bother her with nostalgic reminiscences about caring for small children.

    D. Faith is an unpleasant person with no empathy for lonely old ladies who desperately need to talk to someone.

Read the text below and answer question 3.

Before I came to America, I couldn't have known how difficult it would be. I knew I would miss my mother and my friends and my language, but I didn't know I would have to scrabble so desperately for so long to earn my place. Even when I had managed to make a living, I overworked myself with an animal terror. When I left home, I thought I was leaving poverty behind, but eventually I came to understand that I had escaped physical poverty by stepping into a poverty of the soul.

3. Which sequence accurately describes what happened first, second, and third in the passage?

    A. Arriving in America, overworking, escaping physical poverty.

    B. Coming to America, escaping physical poverty, stepping into a poverty of the soul.

    C. Knowing how difficult America would be, leaving home, stepping into a poverty of the soul.

    D. Expecting to miss friends, knowing how difficult America would be, arriving in America.

Read the text below and answer questions 4-5.

Carving a pumpkin is a fun activity that can create family memories to last a lifetime.

You Will Need

A pumpkin
A knife or kid-safe cutting tool
A bowl
A large spoon
A marker
Old newspapers or plastic sheeting (optional)
Your imagination!

What to Do

Before you start carving a pumpkin, choose your workspace carefully. Spread newspapers or plastic sheeting over the floor if desired.

First, hollow the pumpkin out. Do this by using your knife or kid-safe cutting tool to make a circular cut on the pumpkin around the stem. Carefully pull off the outer rind and reach into the pumpkin to scoop out the pulp and seeds. Scrape the bottom and inside edges of the pumpkin with the spoon to remove as much pulp as possible. A jack-o-lantern with a wet, pulpy interior is difficult to carve and rots quickly once it is on display.

Now it is time to create your jack-o-lantern's face. Clean the surface of the pumpkin if necessary and decide which side you'll use for the face. Errors cannot easily be fixed once you start to carve, so for best results, draw the design onto the pumpkin before making any cuts. Then use your knife or cutting tool to carefully carve your jack-o-lantern's features.

4. Which step comes just before the creation of the jack-o-lantern's face?

    A. Scooping out the pulp

    B. Cutting around the stem

    C. Rotting while on display

    D. Preparing the workspace

5. Why is it best to draw a design onto the pumpkin before cutting?

    A. It prevents injury.

    B. It prevents errors.

    C. It prevents rotting.

    D. It prevents messes.

Chapter 1 Key Ideas and Details Practice Quiz – Answer Key

1. D. This narrative paragraph about a fed-up young mother suggests its main idea rather than stating it outright. There is no topic sentence. **See Lesson: Main Ideas, Topic Sentences, and Supporting Details.**

2. C. The best statement of an implied main idea stays true to the words and ideas the author actually shares. In this case, the central idea is Faith's frustration with other people's reminiscences. **See Lesson: Main Ideas, Topic Sentences, and Supporting Details.**

3. B. This paragraph discusses the past and future in a way that shifts constantly between the two. Some events are vague and may overlap with others. However, coming to America is a clear event that happened before the escape from physical poverty and the entrance into the poverty of the soul. **See Lesson: Summarizing Text and Using Text Features.**

4. A. Although the text mentions that a jack-o-lantern can rot once it is on display, this is not a step to follow in the process. Scooping out the pulp is one of the steps. **See Lesson: Summarizing Text and Using Text Features.**

5. B. The text states that drawing a design on the pumpkin helps prevent cutting errors. **See Lesson: Summarizing Text and Using Text Features.**

CHAPTER 2 CRAFT AND STRUCTURE

LESSON 2.1 TONE, MOOD, AND TRANSITION WORDS

Authors use language to show their emotions and to make readers feel something too. They also use transition words to help guide the reader from one idea to the next.

Tone and Mood

The **tone** of a text is the author's or speaker's attitude toward the subject. The tone may reflect any feeling or attitude a person can express: happiness, excitement, anger, boredom, or arrogance.

Readers can identify tone primarily by analyzing word choice. The reader should be able to point to specific words and details that help to establish the tone.

Example: The train rolled past miles and miles of cornfields. The fields all looked the same. They swayed the same. They produced the same dull nausea in the pit of my stomach. I'd been sent out to see the world, and so I looked, obediently. What I saw was sameness.

Here, the author is expressing boredom and dissatisfaction. This is clear from the repetition of words like "same" and "sameness." There's also a sense of unpleasantness from phrases like "dull nausea" and passivity from words like "obediently."

Sometimes an author uses an ironic tone. Ironic texts often mean the opposite of what they actually say. To identify irony, you need to rely on your prior experience and common sense to help you identify texts with words and ideas that do not quite match.

Example: With that, the senator dismissed the petty little problem of mass shootings and returned to the really important issue: his approval ratings.

> **BE CAREFUL!**
> When you're asked to identify the tone of a text, be sure to keep track of *whose* tone you're supposed to identify, and which part of the text the question is referencing. The author's tone can be different from that of the characters in fiction or the people quoted in nonfiction.
>
> **Example:** The reporter walked quickly, panting to catch up to the senator's entourage. "Senator Biltong," she said. "Are you going to take action on mass shootings?"
>
> "Sure, sure. Soon," the senator said vaguely. Then he turned to greet a newcomer. "Ah ha! Here's the man who can fix my approval ratings!" And with that, he returned to the really important issue: his popularity.
> *
> In the example above, the author's tone is ironic and angry. But the tone of the senator's dialogue is different. The line beginning with the words "Sure, sure" has a distracted tone. The line beginning with "Ah ha!" has a pleased tone.

Here the author flips around the words most people would usually use to discuss mass murder and popularity. By calling a horrific issue "petty" and a trivial issue "important," the author highlights what she sees as a politician's backwards priorities. Except for the phrase "mass shootings," the words here are light and airy—but the tone is ironic and angry.

A concept related to tone is **mood**, or the feelings an author produces in the reader. To determine the mood of a text, a reader can consider setting and theme as well as word choice and tone. For example, a story set in a haunted house may produce an unsettled or frightened feeling in a reader.

Tone and mood are often confused. This is because they are sometimes the same. For instance, in an op-ed article that describes children starving while food aid lies rotting, the author may use an outraged tone and simultaneously arouse an outraged mood in the reader.

However, tone and mood can be different. When they are, it's useful to have different words to distinguish between the author's attitude and the reader's emotional reaction.

> **Example:** I had to fly out of town at 4 a.m. for my trip to the Bahamas, and my wife didn't even get out of bed to make me a cup of coffee. I told her to, but she refused just because she'd been up five times with our newborn. I'm only going on vacation for one week, and she's been off work for a month! She should show me a little consideration.

Here, the tone is indignant. The mood will vary depending on the reader, but it is likely to be unsympathetic.

Transitions

Authors use connecting words and phrases, or **transitions**, to link ideas and help readers follow the flow of their thoughts. The number of possible ways to transition between ideas is almost limitless.

Below are a few common transition words, categorized by the way they link ideas.

Transitions	Examples
Time and sequence transitions orient the reader within a text. They can also help show when events happened in time.	*First, second, next, now, then, at this point, after, afterward, before this, previously, formerly, thereafter, finally, in conclusion*
Addition or emphasis transitions let readers know the author is building on an established line of thought. Many place extra stress on an important idea.	*Moreover, also, likewise, furthermore, above all, indeed, in fact*
Example transitions introduce ideas that illustrate a point.	*For example, for instance, to illustrate, to demonstrate*
Causation transitions indicate a cause-and-effect relationship.	*As a result, consequently, thus*
Contrast transitions indicate a difference between ideas.	*Nevertheless, despite, in contrast, however*

Lesson 2.1 Tone, Mood, and Transition Words

Transitions may look different depending on their function within the text. Within a paragraph, writers often choose short words or expressions to provide transitions and smooth the flow. Between paragraphs or larger sections of text, transitions are usually longer. They may use some of the key words or ideas above, but the author often goes into detail restating larger concepts and explaining their relationships more thoroughly.

>**Between Sentences:** Students who cheat do not learn what they need to know. *As a result*, they get farther behind and face greater temptation to cheat in the future.

>**Between Paragraphs:** *As a result of the cheating behaviors described above,* students find themselves in a vicious cycle.

Longer transitions like the latter example may be useful for keeping the reader clued in to the author's focus in an extended text. But long transitions should have clear content and function. Some long transitions, such as the very wordy "due to the fact that" take up space without adding more meaning and are considered poor style.

Let's Review!

- Tone is the author's or speaker's attitude toward the subject.
- Mood is the feeling a text creates in the reader.
- Transitions are connecting words and phrases that help readers follow the flow of a writer's thoughts.

LESSON 2.2 THE AUTHOR'S PURPOSE AND POINT OF VIEW

In order to understand, analyze, and evaluate a text, readers must know how to identify the author's purpose and point of view. Readers also need to attend to an author's language and rhetorical strategies.

Author's Purpose

When writers put words on paper, they do it for a reason. This reason is the author's **purpose**. Most writing exists for one of three purposes: to inform, to persuade, or to entertain.

> **TEST TIP**
> You may have learned about a fourth purpose for writing: conveying an emotional experience. Many poems as well as some works of fiction, personal essays, and memoirs are written to give the reader a sense of how an event or moment might feel. This type of text is rarely included on placement tests, and if it is, it tends to be lumped in with literature meant to entertain.

If a text is designed to share knowledge, its purpose is to **inform**. Informational texts include technical documents, cookbooks, expository essays, journalistic newspaper articles, and many nonfiction books. Informational texts are based on facts and logic, and they usually attempt an objective tone. The style may otherwise vary; some informational texts are quite dry, whereas others have an engaging style.

If a text argues a point, its purpose is to **persuade**. A persuasive text attempts to convince a reader to believe a certain point of view or take a certain action. Persuasive texts include op-ed newspaper articles, book and movie reviews, project proposals, and argumentative essays. Key signs of persuasive texts include judgments, words like *should*, and other signs that the author is sharing opinions.

If a text is primarily for fun, its purpose is to **entertain**. Entertaining texts usually tell stories or present descriptions. Entertaining texts include novels, short stories, memoirs, and some poems. Virtually all stories are lumped into this category, even if they describe unpleasant experiences.

> **CONNECTIONS**
> You may have read elsewhere that readers can break writing down into the following basic categories. These categories are often linked to the author's purpose.
> **Narrative** writing tells a story and is usually meant to entertain.
> **Expository** writing explains an idea and is usually meant to inform.
> **Technical** writing explains a mechanism or process and is usually meant to inform.
> **Persuasive** writing argues a point and, as the label suggests, is meant to persuade.

A text can have more than one purpose. For example, many traditional children's stories come with morals or lessons. These are meant both to entertain children and persuade them to behave in ways society considers appropriate. Also, commercial nonfiction texts like popular science books are often written in an engaging or humorous style. The purpose of such a text is to inform while also entertaining the reader.

Point of View

Every author has a general outlook or set of opinions about the subject. These make up the author's **point of view**.

To determine point of view, a reader must recognize implicit clues in the text and use them to develop educated guesses about the author's worldview. In persuasive texts, the biggest clue is the author's explicit argument. From considering this argument, a reader can usually make some inferences about point of view. For instance, if an author argues that parents should offer kids opportunities to exercise throughout the day, it would be reasonable to infer that the author has an overall interest in children's health, and that he or she is troubled by the idea of kids pursuing sedentary behaviors like TV watching.

It is more challenging to determine point of view in a text meant to inform. Because the writer does not present an explicit argument, readers must examine assumptions and word choice to determine the writer's point of view.

> **Example:** Models suggest that at the current rate of global warming, hurricanes in 2100 will move 9 percent slower and drop 24 percent more rain. Longer storm durations and rainfall rates will likely translate to increased economic damage and human suffering.

It is reasonable to infer that the writer of this passage has a general trust for science and scientists. This writer assumes that global warming is happening, so it is clear he or she is not a global warming denier. Although the writer does not suggest a plan to prevent future storm damage, the emphasis on negative effects and the use of negative words like "damage" and "suffering" suggest that the author is worried about global warming.

Texts meant to entertain also contain clues about the author's point of view. That point of view is usually evident from the themes and deeper meanings. For instance, a memoirist who writes an upbeat story about a troubled but loving family is likely to believe strongly in the power of love. Note, however, that in this type of work, it is not possible to determine point of view merely from one character's words or actions. For instance, if a character says, "Your mother's love doesn't matter much if she can't take care of you," the reader should *not* automatically assume the writer agrees with that statement. Narrative writers often present a wide range of characters with varying outlooks on life. A reader can only determine the author's point of view by considering the work as a whole. The attitudes that are most emphasized and the ones that win out in the end are likely to reflect the author's point of view.

Rhetorical Strategies

Rhetorical strategies are the techniques an author uses to support an argument or develop a main idea. Effective readers need to study the language of a text and determine how the author is supporting his or her points.

One strategy is to appeal to the reader's reason. This is the foundation of effective writing, and it simply means that the writer relies on factual information and the logical conclusions that follow from it. Even persuasive writing uses this strategy by presenting facts and reasons to back up the author's opinions.

> **Ineffective:** Everyone knows *Sandra and the Lumps* is the best band of the new millennium.

> **Effective:** The three most recent albums by *Sandra and the Lumps* are the first, second, and third most popular records released since the turn of the millennium.

Another strategy is to establish trust. A writer can do this by choosing credible sources and by presenting ideas in a clear and professional way. In persuasive writing, writers may show they are trustworthy by openly acknowledging that some people hold contradicting opinions and by responding fairly to those positions. Writers should never attack or misrepresent their opponents' position.

> **Ineffective:** People who refuse to recycle are too lazy to protect their children's future.

> **Effective:** According to the annual Throw It Out Questionnaire, many people dislike the onerous task of sorting garbage, and some doubt that their effort brings any real gain.

A final strategy is to appeal to the reader's emotions. For instance, a journalist reporting on the opioid epidemic could include a personal story about an addict's attempts to overcome substance abuse. Emotional content can add a human dimension to a story that would be missing if the writer only included statistics and expert opinions. But emotions are easily manipulated, so writers who use this strategy need to be careful. Emotions should never be used to distort the truth or scare readers into agreeing with the writer.

> **Ineffective:** If you don't take action on gun control, you're basically killing children.

> **Effective:** Julie was puzzling over the Pythagorean Theorem when she heard the first gunshot.

Let's Review!
- Every text has a purpose.
- Most texts are meant to inform, persuade, or entertain.
- Texts contain clues that imply an author's outlook or set of opinions about the subject.
- Authors use rhetorical strategies to appeal to reason, establish trust, or invoke emotions.

LESSON 2.3 EVALUATING AND INTEGRATING DATA

Effective readers do more than absorb and analyze the content of sentences, paragraphs, and chapters. They recognize the importance of features that stand out in and around the text, and they understand and integrate knowledge from visual features like maps and charts.

Text Features

Elements that stand out from a text are called **text features**. Text features perform many vital functions.

- **Introducing the Topic and Organizing Information**

> **COMPARE!**
> The title on a fictional work does not always state the topic explicitly. While some titles do this, others are more concerned with hinting at a theme or setting up the tone.

  - *Titles* – The title of a nonfiction text typically introduces the topic. Titles are guiding features of organization because they give clues about what is and is not covered. The title of this section, "Text Features," covers exactly that—not, for example, implicit ideas.
  - *Headings and Subheadings* – Headings and subheadings provide subtopic information about supporting points and let readers scan to see how information is organized. The subheadings of this page organize text features according to the functions they perform.

- **Helping the Reader Find Information**

  - *Table of Contents* – The table of contents of a long work lists chapter titles and other large-scale information so readers can predict the content. This helps readers to determine whether or not a text will be useful to them and to find sections relevant to their research.
  - *Index* – In a book, the index is an alphabetical list of topics covered, complete with page numbers where the topics are discussed. Readers looking for information on one small subtopic can check the index to find out which pages to view.
  - *Footnotes and Endnotes* – When footnotes and endnotes list sources, they allow the reader to find and evaluate the information an author is citing.

- **Emphasizing Concepts**

  - *Formatting Features* – Authors may use formatting features such as *italics*, **boldfacing** or underlining to emphasize a word, phrase, or other important information in a text.
  - *Bulleting and numbering* – Bullet points and numbered lists set off information and allow readers to scan for bits of information they do not know. It also helps to break down a list of steps.

- **Presenting Information and Illustrating Ideas**
  - *Graphic Elements* – Charts, graphs, diagrams, and other graphic elements present data succinctly, illustrate complex ideas, or otherwise convey information that would be difficult to glean from text alone.

- **Providing Peripheral Information**
  - *Sidebars* – Sidebars are text boxes that contain information related to the topic but not essential to the overall point.
  - *Footnotes and Endnotes* – Some footnotes and endnotes contain information that is not essential to the development of the main point but may nevertheless interest readers and researchers.[1]

> **FUN FACT!**
> Online, a sidebar is sometimes called a *doobly doo*.
> P.S. This is an example of a sidebar.

Maps and Charts

To read maps and charts, you need to understand what the labels, symbols, and pictures mean. You also need to know how to make decisions using the information they contain.

Maps

Maps are stylized pictures of places as seen from above. A map may have a box labeled "Key" or "Legend" that provides information about the meanings of colors, lines, or symbols. On the map below, the key shows that a solid line is a road and a dotted line is a trail.

There may also be a line labeled "scale" that helps you figure out how far you need to travel to get from one point on the map to another. In the example below, an inch is only 100 feet, so a trip from one end to the other is not far.

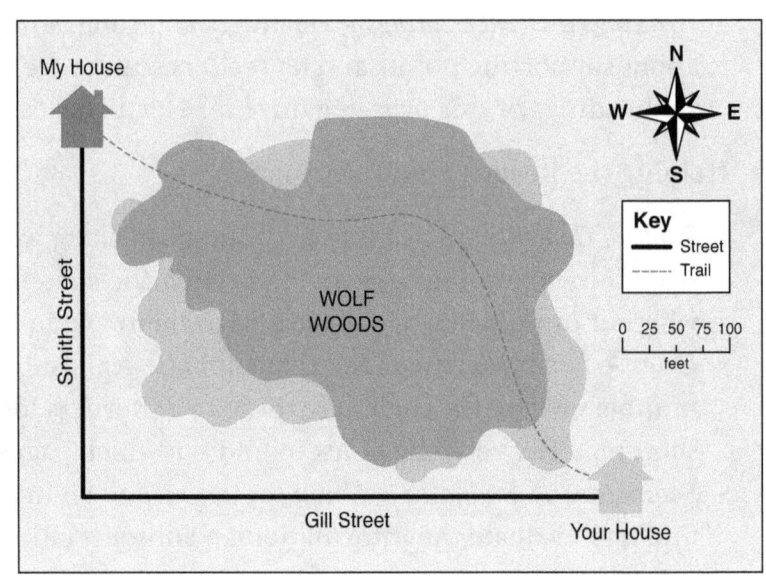

Some maps, including the example above, have compasses that show directions. If no compass is pictured, assume the top of the map is north.

---

[1] Anthony Grafton's book *The Footnote: A Curious History* is an in-depth history of the origins and development of the footnote. (Also, this is an example of a footnote.)

Charts

Nutrition Facts Labels

Nutrition facts labels are charts many people see daily, but not everyone knows how to read them. The top third of the label lists calorie counts, serving sizes, and amount of servings in a package. If a package contains more than one serving, a person who eats the entire contents of the package may be consuming many times the number of calories listed per serving.

The label below lists the content of nutrients such as fats and carbohydrates, and so on. According to the label, a person who eats one serving of the product in the package will ingest 30 mg of cholesterol, or 10% of the total cholesterol he or she should consume in a day.

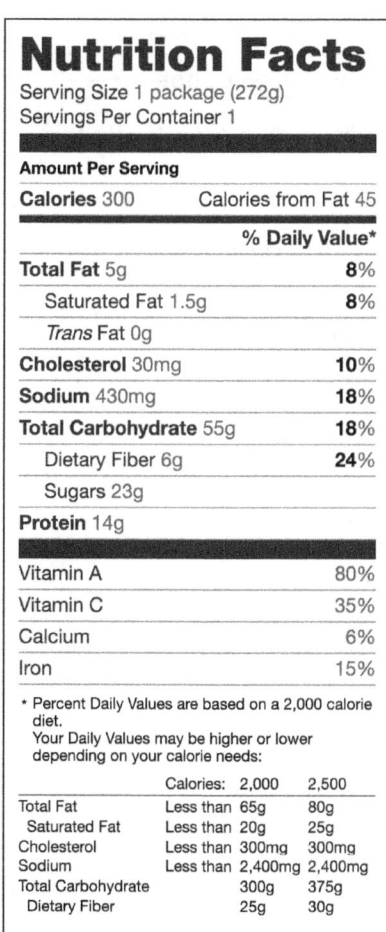

KEEP IN MIND . . .

The percentages on a Nutrition Facts label do not (and are not meant to) add up to 100. Instead, they show how much of a particular nutrient is contained in a serving of the product, as a proportion of a single person's Daily Value for that nutrient. The Daily Value is the total amount of a nutrient a person is supposed to eat in a day, based on a 2000-calorie diet.

In general, a percentage of 5% or less is considered low, whereas a percentage of 20% or more is considered high. A higher percentage can be good or bad, depending on whether or not a person should be trying to get more of a particular ingredient. People need to get plenty of vitamins, minerals, and fiber. In contrast, most people need to limit their intake of fat, cholesterol, and sodium.

Tables

Tables organize information into vertical columns and horizontal rows. Below is a table that shows how much water falls on areas of various sizes when it rains one inch. It shows, for instance, that a 40'x70' roof receives 1,743 gallons of rain during a one-inch rainfall event.

Area	Area (square miles)	Area (square kilometers)	Amount of water (gallons)	Amount of water (liters)
My roof 40x70 feet	.0001	.000257	1,743 gallons	6,601 liters
1 acre (1 square mile = 640 acres)	.00156	.004	27,154 gallons	102,789 liters
1 square mile	1	2.6	17.38 million gallons	65.78 million liters
Atlanta, Georgia	132.4	342.9	2.293 billion gallons	8.68 billion liters
United States	3,537,438	9,161,922	61,474 billion gallons	232,700 billion liters

Let's Review!

- Readers must understand how and why text features make certain information stand out from the text.
- Readers must understand and interpret the content of maps and charts.

Chapter 2 Craft and Structure Practice Quiz

1. Readers can determine tone primarily by examining:
   A. setting.
   B. word choice.
   C. their feelings.
   D. connecting words.

2. Which term refers to the feelings a text creates in the reader?
   A. Tone
   B. Irony
   C. Mood
   D. Theme

3. The tone of a text is:
   A. a word or phrase that links ideas.
   B. the reader's emotional response.
   C. a structural pattern in a series of words.
   D. the author's attitude toward the subject.

4. Which phrase describes the set of techniques an author uses to support an argument or develop a main idea?
   A. Points of view
   B. Logical fallacies
   C. Statistical analyses
   D. Rhetorical strategies

5. An author's point of view is a(n):
   A. lack of purpose.
   B. general outlook.
   C. rhetorical strategy.
   D. appeal to the emotions.

6. The author's _____ is the reason for writing.
   A. purpose
   B. rhetoric
   C. main idea
   D. point of view

7. Which of the following is not a formatting feature?
   A. Italics
   B. Charts
   C. Boldfacing
   D. Underlining

8. What is a text feature?
   A. A movie adaptation of a book
   B. An unwritten summary of a text
   C. A group of contiguous paragraphs
   D. An element that stands out from a text

9. What do footnotes do?
   A. Show the reader how ideas are organized
   B. Illustrate ideas that cannot clearly be stated in words
   C. Provide source information and peripheral information
   D. Provide nutrition facts about the contents of a package

CHAPTER 2 CRAFT AND STRUCTURE PRACTICE QUIZ – ANSWER KEY

1. **B.** Word choice, or diction, is the reader's most important tool in determining tone. **See Lesson: Tone, Mood, and Transition Words.**

2. **C.** Mood is the feeling a text creates in a reader; tone is the author's attitude toward the subject. **See Lesson: Tone, Mood, and Transition Words.**

3. **D.** Tone is the author's apparent attitude toward the subject of a text. It is distinguished from mood, which is the reader's emotional response. **See Lesson: Tone, Mood, and Transition Words.**

4. **D.** The techniques an author uses to support an argument or develop a main idea are called rhetorical strategies. **See Lesson: Understanding the Author's Purpose, Point of View, and Rhetorical Strategies.**

5. **B.** An author's point of view is a general outlook on the subject. **See Lesson: The Author's Purpose and Point of View.**

6. **A.** The main idea of a text is its key point, and the point of view is the author's outlook on the subject. The purpose is the reason for writing. **See Lesson: The Author's Purpose and Point of View.**

7. **B.** Formatting features make text stand out in a title or within a paragraph. Charts are graphic elements that present data or illustrate information. **See Lesson: Evaluating and Integrating Data.**

8. **D.** A text feature is any element that stands out from the text, such as a title, a boldfaced section, or a graphic element. **See Lesson: Evaluating and Integrating Data.**

9. **C.** Footnotes may provide information about source materials or give the reader interesting information that is not essential to the main point. **See Lesson: Evaluating and Integrating Data.**

Chapter 3 Integration of Knowledge and Ideas

Lesson 3.1 Facts, Opinions, and Evaluating an Argument

Nonfiction writing is based on facts and real events, but most nonfiction nevertheless expresses a point of view. Effective readers must evaluate the author's point of view and form their own conclusions about the points in the text.

Fact and Opinion

Many texts make an **argument**. In this context, the word *argument* has nothing to do with anger or fighting. It simply means the author is trying to convince readers of something.

Arguments are present in a wide variety of texts. Some relate to controversial issues, for instance by advocating support for a political candidate or change in laws. Others may defend a certain interpretation of facts or ideas. For example, a literature paper may argue that an author's story suggests a certain theme, or a science paper may argue for a certain interpretation of data. An argument may also present a plan of action such as a business strategy.

To evaluate an argument, readers must distinguish between **fact** and **opinion**. A fact is verifiably true. An opinion is someone's belief.

    Fact: Seattle gets an average of 37 inches of rain per year.

    Opinion: The dark, rainy, cloudy weather makes Seattle an unpleasant place to live in winter.

Meteorologists measure rainfall directly, so the above fact is verifiably true. The statement "it is unpleasant" clearly reflects a feeling, so the second sentence is an opinion.

The difference between fact and opinion is not always straightforward. For instance, a text may present a fact that contains an opinion within it:

    Fact: Nutritionist Fatima Antar questions the wisdom of extreme carbohydrate avoidance.

Assuming the writer can prove that this sentence genuinely reflects Fatima Antar's beliefs, it is a factual statement of her point of view. The reader may trust that Fatima Antar really holds this opinion, whether or not the reader is convinced by it.

If a text makes a judgment, it is not a fact:

> **Opinion:** The patient's seizure drug regimen caused horrendous side effects.

The above sentence uses language that different people would interpret in different ways. Because people have varying ideas about what they consider "horrendous," this sentence is an opinion as it is written, even though the actual side effects and the patient's opinion of them could both be verified.

> **COMPARE!**
>
> Small changes to the statement about seizure drugs could turn it into a factual statement:
>
> **Fact:** The patient's seizure drug regimen caused side effects such as migraines, confusion, and dangerously high blood pressure.
>
> The above statement can be verified because the patient and other witnesses could confirm the exact nature of her symptoms. This makes it a fact.
>
> **Fact:** The patient reported that her seizure drug regimen caused horrendous side effects.
>
> This statement can also be verified because the patient can verify that she considers the side effects horrendous. By framing the statement in this way, the writer leaves nothing up to interpretation and is clearly in the realm of fact.

The majority of all arguments contain both facts and opinions, and strong arguments may contain both fact and opinion elements. It is rare for an argument to be composed entirely of facts, but it can happen if the writer is attempting to convince readers to accept factual information that is little-known or widely questioned. Most arguments present an author's opinion and use facts, reasoning, and expert testimony to convince readers.

Evaluating an Argument

Effective readers must evaluate an argument and decide whether or not it is valid. To do this, readers must consider every claim the author presents, including both the main argument and any supporting statements. If an argument is based on poor reasoning or insufficient evidence, it is not valid—even if you agree with the main idea.

> **KEY POINT!**
>
> Most of us want to agree with arguments that reflect our own beliefs. But it is inadvisable to accept an argument that is not properly rooted in good reasoning. Consider the following statements about global climate change:
>
> **Poor Argument:** It just snowed fifteen inches! How can anyone say the world is getting warmer?
>
> **Poor Argument:** It's seventy degrees in the middle of February! How can anyone deny global warming?
>
> Both of these arguments are based on insufficient evidence. Each relies on *one* weather event in *one* location to support an argument that the entire world's climate is or is not changing. There is not nearly enough information here to support an argument on either side.

Lesson 3.1   Facts, Opinions, and Evaluating an Argument

Beware of any argument that presents opinion information as fact.

False Claim of Fact: I know vaccines cause autism because my niece began displaying autism symptoms after receiving her measles vaccine.

The statement above states a controversial idea as fact without adequate evidence to back it up. Specifically, it makes a false claim of cause and effect about an incident that has no clear causal relationship.

Any claim that is not supported by sufficient evidence is an example of **faulty reasoning**.

Type of Faulty Reasoning	Definition	Example	Explanation
Circular Reasoning	Restating the argument in different words instead of providing evidence	Baseball is the best game in the world because it is more fun than any other game.	Here, everything after the word *because* says approximately the same thing as everything before it. It looks like the author is providing a reason, but no evidence has actually been offered.
Either/Or Fallacy	Presenting an issue as if it involves only two choices when in fact it is not so simple	Women should focus on motherhood, not careers.	This statement assumes that women cannot do both. It also assumes that no woman needs a career in order to provide for her children.
Overgeneralizations	Making a broad claim based on too little evidence	All elderly people have negative stereotypes of teenagers.	This statement lumps a whole category of people into a group and claims the whole group shares the same belief—always an unlikely prospect.

Most texts about evaluating arguments focus on faulty reasoning and false statements of fact. But arguments that attempt to misrepresent facts as opinions are equally suspicious. A careful reader should be skeptical of any text that denies clear physical evidence or questions the truth of events that have been widely verified.

Assumptions and Biases

A well-reasoned argument should be supported by facts, logic, and clearly explained opinions. But most arguments are also based on **assumptions**, or unstated and unproven ideas about what is true. Consider the following argument:

Argument: To improve equality of opportunity for all children, schools in underprivileged areas should receive as much taxpayer funding as schools in wealthy districts.

This argument is based on several assumptions. First is the assumption that all children should have equal opportunities. Another is that taxpayer-funded public schools are the best way to provide these opportunities. Whether or not you disagree with either of these points, it is worth noting that the second idea in particular is not the only way to proceed. Readers who examine the assumptions behind an argument can sometimes find points of disagreement even if an author's claims and logic are otherwise sound.

Examining an author's assumptions can also reveal a writer's biases. A **bias** is a preconceived idea that makes a person more likely to show unfair favor for certain thoughts, people, or groups. Because every person has a different experience of the world, every person has a different set of biases. For example, a person who has traveled widely may feel differently about world political events than someone who has always lived in one place.

Virtually all writing is biased to some degree. However, effective writing attempts to avoid bias as much as possible. Writing that is highly biased may be based on poor assumptions that render the entire argument invalid.

Highly biased writing often includes overgeneralizations. Words like *all, always, never,* and so on may indicate that the writer is overstating a point. While these words can exist in true statements, unbiased writing is more likely to qualify ideas using words like *usually, often,* and *rarely.*

Another quality of biased writing is excessively emotional word choice. When writers insult people who disagree with them or engage the emotions in a way that feels manipulative, they are being biased.

> **Biased:** Power-hungry politicians don't care that their standardized testing requirements are producing a generation of overanxious, incurious, impractical kids.
>
> **Less biased:** Politicians need to recognize that current standardized testing requirements are causing severe anxiety and other negative effects in children.

Biased writing may also reflect stereotypical thinking. A **stereotype** is a particularly harmful type of bias that applies specifically to groups of people. Stereotypical thinking is behind racism, sexism, homophobia, and so on. Even people who do not consider themselves prejudiced can use language that reflects common stereotypes. For example, the negative use of the word *crazy* reflects a stereotype against people with mental illnesses.

Historically, writers in English have used male nouns and pronouns to indicate all people. Revising such language for more inclusivity is considered more effective in contemporary writing.

> **Biased:** The history of the human race proves that man is a violent creature.
>
> **Less biased:** The history of the human race proves that people are violent.

Let's Review!
- A text meant to convince someone of something is making an argument.
- Arguments may employ both facts and opinions.
- Effective arguments must use valid reasoning.
- Arguments are based on assumptions that may be reasonable or highly biased.
- Almost all writing is biased to some degree, but strong writing makes an effort to eliminate bias.

LESSON 3.2 — Understanding Primary Sources, Making Inferences, and Drawing Conclusions

Effective readers must understand the difference between types of sources and choose credible sources of information to support research. Readers must also consider the content of their reading materials and draw their own conclusions.

Primary Sources

When we read and research information, we must differentiate between different types of sources. Sources are often classified depending on how close they are to the original creation or discovery of the information they present.

Primary sources include firsthand witness accounts of events, research described by the people who conducted it, and any other original information. Contemporary researchers can often access mixed media versions of primary sources such as video and audio recordings, photographs of original work, and so on. Note that original content is still considered primary even if it is reproduced online or in a book.

> **Examples:** Diaries, scientific journal articles, witness testimony, academic conference presentations, business memos, speeches, letters, interviews, and original literature and artwork.

Secondary sources respond to, analyze, summarize, or comment on primary sources. They add value to a discussion of the topic by giving readers new ways to think about the content. However, they may also introduce errors or layers of bias. Secondary sources may be very good sources of information, but readers must evaluate them carefully.

> **Examples:** Biographies, books and articles that summarize research for wider audiences, analyses of original literature and artwork, histories, political commentary.

Tertiary sources compile information in a general, highly summarized, and sometimes simplified way. Their purpose is not to add anything to the information, but rather to present the information in an accessible manner, often for audiences who are only beginning to familiarize themselves with a topic.

> **Examples:** Encyclopedias, guidebooks, literature study guides.

Source Materials in Action

Primary sources are often considered most trustworthy because they are closest to the original material and least likely to contain errors. However, readers must take a common sense approach to evaluating trustworthiness. For example, a single letter written by one biased witness of a historical event may not provide as much insight into what really happened as a secondary account by a historian who has considered the points of view of a dozen firsthand witnesses.

Tertiary sources are useful for readers attempting to gain a quick overview of understanding about a subject. They are also a good starting point for readers looking for keywords and subtopics to use for further research of a subject. However, they are not sufficiently detailed or credible to support an article, academic paper, or other document intended to add valuable analysis and commentary on a subject.

Evaluating Credibility

Not everything you read is equally trustworthy. Many sources contain mistakes, faulty reasoning, or deliberate misinformation designed to manipulate you. Effective readers seek out information from **credible**, or trustworthy, sources.

There is no single formula for determining credibility. Readers must make judgment calls based on individual texts and their purpose.

> **FOR EXAMPLE**
>
> Most sources should attempt to be objective. But if you're reading an article that makes an argument, you do not need to demand perfect objectivity from the source. The purpose of a persuasive article is to defend a point of view. As long as the author does this openly and defends the point of view with facts, logic, and other good argumentative techniques, you may trust the source.
>
> Other sources may seem highly objective but not be credible. For example, some scientific studies meet all the criteria for credibility below except the one about trustworthy publishers. If a study is funded or conducted by a company that stands to profit from it, you should treat the results with skepticism no matter how good the information looks otherwise.

Sources and References

Credible texts are primary sources or secondary sources that refer to other trustworthy sources. If the author consults experts, they should be named, and their credentials should be explained. Authors should not attempt to hide where they got their information. Vague statements like "studies show" are not as trustworthy as statements that identify who completed a study.

Lesson 3.2 Understanding Primary Sources, Making Inferences, and Drawing Conclusions

Objectivity

Credible texts usually make an effort to be objective. They use clear, logical reasoning. They back arguments up with facts, expert opinions, or clear explanations. The assumptions behind the arguments do not contain obvious stereotypes.

Emotional arguments are acceptable in some argumentative writing, but they should not be manipulative. For example, photos of starving children may be acceptable for raising awareness of a famine, but they need to be respectful of both the victims and the audience—not just there for shock value.

Date of Publication

Information changes quickly in some fields, especially the sciences and technology. When researching a fast-changing topic, look for sources published in the last ten years.

Author Information

If an author and/or a respected organization take public credit for information, it is more likely to be reliable. Information published anonymously on the Internet may be suspicious because nobody is clearly responsible for mistakes. Authors with strong credentials such as university professors in a given field are more trustworthy than authors with no clear resume.

Publisher Information

Information published by the government, a university, a major national news organization, or another respected organization is often more credible. On the Internet, addresses ending in .edu or .gov may be more trustworthy than .com addresses. Publishers who stand to profit or otherwise benefit from the content of a text are always questionable.

> **BE CAREFUL!**
> Strong credentials only make a source more trustworthy if the credentials are related to the topic. A Columbia University Professor of Archeology is a credible source on ancient history. But if she writes a parenting article, it's not necessarily more credible than a parenting article by someone without a flashy university title.

Professionalism

Credible sources usually look professional and present information free of grammatical errors or major factual errors.

Making Inferences and Drawing Conclusions

In reading—and in life—people regularly make educated guesses based on limited information. When we use the information we have to figure out something nobody has told us directly, we are making an **inference**. People make inferences every day.

Example: You hear a loud thump. Then a pained voice says, "Honey, can you bring the first aid kit?"

From the information in this example, it is reasonable to infer that the speaker is hurt. The thumping noise, the pain in the speaker's voice, and the request for a first aid kit all suggest this conclusion.

When you make inferences from reading, you use clues presented in the text to help you draw logical conclusions about what the author means. Before you can make an inference, you must read the text carefully and understand the explicit, or overt, meaning. Next, you must look for clues to any implied, or suggested, meanings behind the text. Finally, consider the clues in light of your prior knowledge and the author's purpose, and draw a conclusion about the meaning.

> As soon as Raizel entered the party, someone handed her a plate. She stared down at the hot dog unhappily.
>
> "What?" asked an unfamiliar woman nearby with an edge to her voice. "You don't eat dead animal?"

From the passage above, it would be reasonable to infer that the unfamiliar woman has a poor opinion of vegetarians. Several pieces of information suggest this: her combative tone, the edge in her voice, and the mocking question at the end.

When you draw inferences from a text, make sure your conclusion is truly indicated by the clues provided.

> Author Glenda Davis had high hopes for her children's book *Basketball Days*. But when the novel was released with a picture of a girl on the cover, boys refused to pick it up. The author reported this to her publisher, and the paperback edition was released with a new cover—this time featuring a dog and a basketball hoop. After that, many boys read the book. And Davis never heard anyone complain that the main character was a girl.

BE CAREFUL!
Before you make a conclusion about a text, consider it in light of your prior knowledge and the clues presented.

After reading the paragraph above, you might suspect that Raizel is a vegetarian. But the text does not fully support that conclusion. There are many reasons why Raizel might not want to eat a hot dog.

Perhaps she is keeping kosher, or she has social anxiety that makes it difficult to eat at parties, or she simply isn't hungry. The above inference about the unfamiliar woman's dislike for vegetarians is strongly supported. But you'd need further evidence before you could safely conclude that Raizel is actually a vegetarian.

The text above implies that boys are reluctant to read books with a girl on the cover. A hasty reader might stop reading early and conclude that boys are reluctant to read about girls—but this inference is not suggested by the full text.

Let's Review!
- Effective readers must consider the credibility of their sources.
- Primary sources are usually considered the most trustworthy.
- Readers must often make inferences about ideas that are implied but not explicitly stated in a text.

LESSON 3.3 TYPES OF PASSAGES, TEXT STRUCTURES, GENRE AND THEME

To read effectively, you must understand what kind of text you are reading and how it is structured. You must also be able to look behind the text to find its deeper meanings.

Types of Passages

There are many ways of breaking texts down into categories. To do this, you need to consider the author's **purpose**, or what the text exists to do. Most texts exist to inform, persuade, or entertain. You also need to consider what the text does—whether it tells a story, describes facts, or develops a point of view.

Type of Passage	Examples
Narrative writing tells a story. The story can be fictional, or it can describe real events. The primary purpose of narrative writing is to entertain.	<ul><li>An autobiography</li><li>A memoir</li><li>A short story</li><li>A novel</li></ul>
Expository writing provides an explanation or a description. Many academic essays and informational nonfiction books are expository writing. Stylistically, expository writing is highly varied. Although the explanations can be dry and methodical, many writers use an artful or entertaining style. Expository writing is nonfiction. Its primary purpose is to inform.	<ul><li>A book about a historical event</li><li>An essay describing the social impacts of a new technology</li><li>A description of changing gender roles in marriages</li><li>A philosophical document exploring the nature of truth.</li><li>Recipes</li></ul>
Technical writing explains a complex process or mechanism. Whereas expository writing is often academic, technical writing is used in practical settings such as businesses. The style of a technical document is almost always straightforward and impersonal. Technical writing is nonfiction, and its purpose is to inform.	<ul><li>Instructions</li><li>User manuals</li><li>Process descriptions</li></ul>
Persuasive writing makes an argument. It asks readers to believe something or do something. Texts that make judgments, such as movie reviews, are persuasive because they are attempting to convince readers to accept a point of view. Texts that suggest a plan are also persuasive because they are trying to convince readers to take an action. As the name "persuasive writing" indicates, the author's primary purpose is to persuade.	<ul><li>Op-ed newspaper articles</li><li>Book reviews</li><li>Project proposals</li><li>Advertisements</li><li>Persuasive essays</li></ul>

> **BE CAREFUL!**
>
> Many texts have more than one purpose.
>
> A text that tells a story is usually meant to entertain, but it can also be meant to persuade. For example, there is a well-known story called "Never Cry Wolf" about a boy who habitually lies. At the end, when he needs help, nobody believes him. This story is meant to entertain, but it is also trying to convince readers not to tell lies.
>
> Similarly, many explanatory texts are meant to inform readers in an entertaining way. For example, a nonfiction author may describe a scientific topic using humor and wacky examples to make it fun for popular audiences to read.
>
> Also, expository writing can look similar to persuasive writing, especially when it touches on topics that are controversial or emotional. For example, if an essay says social media is changing society, many readers assume it means social media is changing society *in a negative way*. If the writing makes this kind of value judgment or uses words like *should*, it is persuasive writing. But if the author is merely describing changes, the text is expository.

Text Structures

Authors rarely present ideas within a text in a random order. Instead, they organize their thoughts carefully. To read effectively, you must be able to recognize the **structure** of a text. That is, you need to identify the strategies authors use to organize their ideas. The five most common text structures are listed below.

Text Structure	Examples
In a **sequence** text, an author explains what happened first, second, third, and so on. In other words, a sequence text is arranged in **chronological order**, or time order. This type of text may describe events that have already happened or events that may happen in the future.	• A story about a birthday party • A historical paper about World War II • A list of instructions for baking a cake • A series of proposed steps in a plan for business expansion
A **compare/contrast** text explains the similarities and differences between two or more subjects. Authors may compare and contrast people, places, ideas, events, cultures, and so on.	• An essay describing the similarities and differences between women's experiences in medieval Europe and Asia • A section in an op-ed newspaper article explaining the similarities and differences between two types of gun control
A **cause/effect** text describes an event or action and its results. The causes and effects discussed can be actual or theoretical. That is, the author can describe the results of a historical event or predict the results of a possible future event.	• An explanation of ocean acidification and the coral bleaching that results • A paper describing a proposed new law and its likely effects on the economy
A **problem-solution** text presents a problem and outlines a solution. Sometimes it also predicts or analyzes the results of the solution. The solution can be something that already happened or a plan the author is proposing. Note that a problem can sometimes be expressed in terms of a wish or desire that the solution fulfills.	• An explanation of the problems smallpox caused and the strategies scientists used to eradicate it • A business plan outlining a group of potential customers and the strategy a company should use to get their business

Lesson 3.3 Types of Passages, Text Structures, Genre and Theme

Text Structure	Examples
A **description** text creates a mental picture for the reader by presenting concrete details in a coherent order. Description texts are usually arranged spatially. For instance, authors may describe the subject from top to bottom, or they may describe the inside first and then the outside, etc.	• An explanation of the appearance of a character in a story • A paragraph in a field guide detailing the features of a bird • A section on an instruction sheet describing how the final product should look

> **KEEP IN MIND . . .**
> The text structures above do not always work in isolation. Authors often combine two or more structures within one text. For example, a business plan could be arranged in a problem-solution structure as the author describes what the business wants to achieve and how she proposes to achieve it. The "how" portion could also use a sequence structure as the author lists the steps to follow first, second, third, and so on.

> **CONNECTIONS**
> Different types of texts can use the same structures.
> 1. A story about a birthday party is a narrative, and its purpose is to entertain.
> 2. A historical paper about a war is an expository text meant to inform.
> 3. A list of instructions for baking a cake is a technical text meant to inform.
> 4. A series of proposed steps in a plan for business expansion is a persuasive text meant to persuade.
>
> If all of these texts list ideas in chronological order, explaining what happened (or what may happen in the future) first, second, third, and so on, they are all using a sequence structure.

Genre and Theme

Literature can be organized into categories called **genres**. The two major genres of literature are fiction and nonfiction.

Fiction is made up. It can be broken down into many sub-genres, or sub-categories. The following are some of the common ones:

- Short story – Short work of fiction.
- Novel – Book-length work of fiction.
- Science fiction – A story set in the future
- Romance – A love story
- Mystery – A story that answers a concrete question, often about who committed a crime
- Mythology – A traditional story that reflects cultural traditions and beliefs but does not usually teach an explicit lesson
- Legends – Traditional stories that are presented as histories, even though they often contain fantastical or magical elements
- Fables – Traditional stories meant to teach an explicit lesson

> **COMPARE!**
> The differences between myths and fables are sometimes hard to discern.
>
> Myths are often somewhat religious in nature. For instance, stories about Ancient Greek gods and goddesses are myths. These stories reflect cultural beliefs, for example by showing characters being punished for failing to please their gods. But the lesson is implicit. These stories do not usually end with a moral lesson that says to readers, "Do not displease the gods!"
>
> Fables are often for children, and they usually end with a sentence stating an explicit moral. For example, there's a story called "The Tortoise and the Hare," in which a tortoise and a hare agree to have a race. The hare, being a fast animal, gets cocky and takes a lot of breaks while the tortoise plods slowly toward the finish line without stopping. Because the tortoise keeps going, it eventually wins. The story usually ends with the moral, "Slow and steady win the race."

Nonfiction is true. Like fiction, it can be broken down into many sub-genres. The following are some of the common ones:

- Autobiography and memoir – The author's own life story
- Biography – Someone else's life story (not the author's)
- Histories – True stories about real events from the past
- Criticism and reviews – A response or judgment on another piece of writing or art
- Essay – A short piece describing the author's outlook or point of view.

> **CONNECTIONS**
> Everything under "Fiction" and several items under "Nonfiction" above are examples of narrative writing. We use labels like "narrative" and "persuasive" largely when we discuss writing tasks or the author's purpose. We could use these labels here too, but at the moment we're more concerned with the words that are most commonly used in discussions about literature's deeper meanings.

Literature reflects the human experience. Texts from different genres often share similar **themes**, or deeper meanings. Texts from different cultures do too. For example, a biography of a famous civil rights activist may highlight the same qualities of heroism and interconnectedness that appear in a work of mythology from Ancient India. Other common themes in literature may relate to war, love, survival, justice, suffering, growing up, and other experiences that are accessible to virtually all human beings.

Many students confuse the term *theme* with the term *moral*. A **moral** is an explicit message contained in the text, like "Don't lie" or "Crime doesn't pay." Morals are a common feature of fables and other traditional stories meant to teach lessons to children. Themes, in contrast, are implicit. Readers must consider the clues in the story and figure out themes for themselves. Because of this, themes are debatable. For testing purposes, questions focus on themes that are clearly and consistently indicated by clues within the text.

Lesson 3.3 Types of Passages, Text Structures, Genre and Theme

Let's Review!

- Written texts can be organized into the following categories: narrative, expository, technical, and persuasive.
- Texts of all categories may use the following organizational schemes or structures: sequence, compare/contrast, cause/effect, problem-solution, description.
- Literature can be organized into genres including fiction, nonfiction, and many sub-genres.
- Literature across genres and cultures often reflects the same deeper meanings, or themes.

Chapter 3 Integration of Knowledge and Ideas
Practice Quiz

1. An argument may be composed of:
   A. facts only.
   B. opinions only.
   C. both facts and opinions.
   D. neither facts nor opinions.

2. A statement that is probably true is a(n):
   A. fact.
   B. claim.
   C. opinion.
   D. argument.

3. What is the best definition of the word *argument* in the context of reading and writing?
   A. An eloquent summary
   B. An angry conversation
   C. A persuasive point in a text
   D. An object or direct object phrase

4. Which sources are usually considered most trustworthy?
   A. Primary sources
   B. Secondary sources
   C. Tertiary sources
   D. Quaternary sources

5. A source is not credible if:
   A. its publisher is government funded.
   B. any of its sources are primary sources.
   C. any of its sources are secondary sources.
   D. its publisher is profiting from the information.

6. A source is considered credible if readers can _____ it.
   A. trust
   B. publish
   C. analyze
   D. decipher

Chapter 3 Integration of Knowledge and Ideas
Practice Quiz – Answer Key

1. C. An argument may include both verifiably true statements, or facts, and statements based on belief, or opinions. **See Lesson: Facts, Opinions, and Evaluating an Argument.**

2. A. Unlike an opinion, a fact is verifiably true. An argument or claim may express a fact, an opinion, or a mixture of the two. **See Lesson: Facts, Opinions, and Evaluating an Argument.**

3. C. In the context of reading and writing, an argument is a statement meant to prove a point, not a heated disagreement. **See Lesson: Facts, Opinions, and Evaluating an Argument.**

4. A. The authors of primary sources witnessed the original creation or discovery of the information they present. For this reason, they are considered the most trustworthy. **See Lesson: Understanding Primary Sources, Making Inferences, and Drawing Conclusions.**

5. D. A text is highly unlikely to be credible if its publisher is an organization that stands to benefit if people believe the information it contains. **See Lesson: Understanding Primary Sources, Making Inferences, and Drawing Conclusions.**

6. A. The word *credible* means "trustworthy." **See Lesson: Understanding Primary Sources, Making Inferences, and Drawing Conclusions.**

SECTION II
MATHEMATICS

Math: 38 questions, 57 minutes

Areas assessed: Numbers and Algebra, Measurement, and Data Interpretation

MATH TIPS

- Read the questions thoroughly and slowly. Reread if necessary. The order/value they are expecting may be different that you are anticipating.
- Brush up on decimals, ratios, fractions, PEMDAS, percentages.
- Know addition, subtraction, multiplication, division problems.
- Be sure to know how to add, subtract, multiply, and divide fractions.
- Brush up on common math rules, i.e., when adding fractions, they must have a common denominator.
- You will be able to use a calculator. It will be provided by the testing center.

CHAPTER 4 NUMBERS AND BASIC OPERATIONS

LESSON 4.1 BASIC ADDITION AND SUBTRACTION

This lesson introduces the concept of numbers and their symbolic and graphical representations. It also describes how to add and subtract whole numbers.

Numbers

A **number** is a way to quantify a set of entities that share some characteristic. For example, a fruit basket might contain nine pieces of fruit. More specifically, it might contain three apples, two oranges, and four bananas. Note that a number is a quantity, but a **numeral** is the symbol that represents the number: 8 means the number eight, for instance.

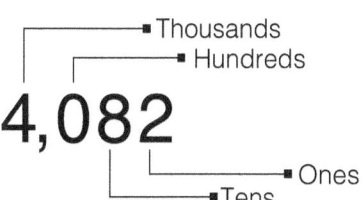

Although number representations vary, the most common is **base 10**. In base-10 format, each **digit** (or individual numeral) in a number is a quantity based on a multiple of 10. The base-10 system designates 0 through 9 as the numerals for zero through nine, respectively, and combines them to represent larger numbers. Thus, after counting from 1 to 9, the next number uses an additional digit: 10. That number means 1 group of 10 ones plus 0 additional ones. After 99, another digit is necessary, this time representing a hundred (10 sets of 10). This process of adding digits can go on indefinitely to express increasingly large numbers. For whole numbers, the rightmost digit is the ones place, the next digit to its left is the tens place, the next is the hundreds place, then the thousands place, and so on.

Classifying numbers can be convenient. The chart below lists a few common number sets.

Sets of Numbers	Members	Remarks
Natural numbers	1, 2, 3, 4, 5,…	The "counting" numbers
Whole numbers	0, 1, 2, 3, 4,…	The natural numbers plus 0
Integers	…, −3, −2, −1, 0, 1, 2, 3,…	The whole numbers plus all negative whole numbers
Real numbers	All numbers	The integers plus all fraction/decimal numbers in between
Rational numbers	All real numbers that can be expressed as p/q, where p and q are integers and q is nonzero	The natural numbers, whole numbers, and integers are all rational numbers
Irrational numbers	All real numbers that are not rational	The rational and irrational numbers together constitute the entire set of real numbers

Example

Jane has 4 pennies, 3 dimes, and 7 dollars. How many cents does she have?

  A. 347 B. 437 C. 734 D. 743

The correct answer is **C**. The correct solution is 734. A penny is 1 cent. A dime (10 pennies) is 10 cents, and a dollar (100 pennies) is 100 cents. Place the digits in base-10 format: 7 hundreds, 3 tens, 4 ones, or 734.

The Number Line

The **number line** is a model that illustrates the relationships among numbers. The complete number line is infinite and includes every real number—both positive and negative. A ruler, for example, is a portion of a number line that assigns a **unit** (such as inches or centimeters) to each number. Typically, number lines depict smaller numbers to the left and larger numbers to the right. For example, a portion of the number line centered on 0 might look like the following:

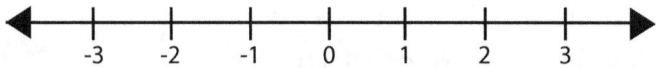

Because people learn about numbers in part through counting, they have a basic sense of how to order them. The number line builds on this sense by placing all the numbers (at least conceptually) from least to greatest. Whether a particular number is greater than or less than another is determined by comparing their relative positions. One number is greater than another if it is farther right on the number line. Likewise, a number is less than another if it is farther left on the number line. Symbolically, < means "is less than" and > means "is greater than." For example, 5 > 1 and 9 < 25.

Example

Place the following numbers in order from greatest to least: 5, –12, 0.

  A. 0, 5, –12   C. 5, 0, –12
  B. –12, 5, 0   D. –12, 0, 5

> **BE CAREFUL!**
> When ordering negative numbers, think of the number line. Although –10 > –2 may seem correct, it is incorrect. Because –10 is to the left of –2 on the number line, –10 < –2.

The correct answer is **C**. The correct solution is 5, 0, –12. Use the number line to order the numbers. Note that the question says *from greatest to least*.

Addition

Addition is the process of combining two or more numbers. For example, one set has 4 members and another set has 5 members. To combine the sets and find out how many members are in the new set, add 4 and 5 to get the **sum**. Symbolically, the expression is 4 + 5, where + is the **plus sign**. Pictorially, it might look like the following:

Lesson 4.1 Basic Addition and Subtraction

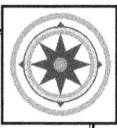

To get the sum, combine the two sets of circles and then count them. The result is 9.

> **KEY POINT**
> The order of the numbers is irrelevant when adding.

Another way to look at addition involves the number line. When adding 4 + 5, for example, start at 4 on the number line and take 5 steps to the right. The stopping point will be 9, which is the sum.

Counting little pictures or using the number line works for small numbers, but it becomes unwieldy for large ones—even numbers such as 24 and 37 would be difficult to add quickly and accurately. A simple algorithm enables much faster addition of large numbers. It works with two or more numbers.

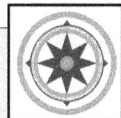

> **STEP BY STEP**
> **Step 1.** Stack the numbers, vertically aligning the digits for each place.
> **Step 2.** Draw a plus sign (+) to the left of the bottom number and draw a horizontal line below the last number.
> **Step 3.** Add the digits in the ones place.
> **Step 4.** If the sum from Step 3 is less than 10, write it in the same column below the horizontal line. Otherwise, write the first (ones) digit below the line, then **carry** the second (tens) digit to the top of the next column.
> **Step 5.** Going from right to left, repeat Steps 3–4 for the other places.
> **Step 6.** If applicable, write the remaining carry digit as the leftmost digit in the sum.

Example

Evaluate the expression 154 + 98.

A. 250   B. 252   C. 352   D. 15,498

The correct answer is **B**. The correct solution is 252. Carefully follow the addition algorithm (see below). The process involves carrying a digit twice.

$$\begin{array}{r}154\\+\ 98\\\hline\end{array} \rightarrow \begin{array}{r}{\scriptstyle 1}\\154\\+\ 98\\\hline 2\end{array} \rightarrow \begin{array}{r}{\scriptstyle 11}\\154\\+\ 98\\\hline 52\end{array} \rightarrow \begin{array}{r}{\scriptstyle 11}\\154\\+\ 98\\\hline 252\end{array}$$

Subtraction

Subtraction is the inverse (opposite) of addition. Instead of representing the sum of numbers, it represents the difference between them. For example, given a set containing 15 members, subtracting 3 of those members yields a **difference** of 12. Using the **minus sign,** the expression for this operation is 15 − 3 = 12. As with addition, two approaches are counting pictures and using the number line. The first case might involve drawing 15 circles and then crossing off 3 of them; the difference is the number of remaining circles (12). To use the number line, begin at 15 and move left 3 steps to reach 12.

Again, these approaches are unwieldy for large numbers, but the subtraction algorithm eases evaluation by hand. This algorithm is only practical for two numbers at a time.

STEP BY STEP

Step 1. Stack the numbers, vertically aligning the digits in each place. Put the number you are subtracting *from* on top.

Step 2. Draw a minus sign (−) to the left of the bottom number and draw a horizontal line below the stack of numbers.

Step 3. Start at the ones place. If the digit at the top is larger than the digit below it, write the difference under the line. Otherwise, **borrow** from the top digit in the next-higher place by crossing it off, subtracting 1 from it, and writing the difference above it. Then add 10 to the digit in the ones place and perform the subtraction as normal.

Step 4. Going from right to left, repeat Step 3 for the rest of the places. If borrowing was necessary, make sure to use the new digit in each place, not the original one.

When adding or subtracting with negative numbers, the following rules are helpful. Note that x and y are used as placeholders for any real number.

$x + (-y) = x - y$

$-x - y = -(x + y)$

$(-x) + (-y) = -(x + y)$

$x - y = -(y - x)$

BE CAREFUL!

When dealing with numbers that have units (such as weights, currencies, or volumes), addition and subtraction are only possible when the numbers have the same unit. If necessary, convert one or more of them to equivalent numbers with the same unit.

Lesson 4.1 Basic Addition and Subtraction

Example

Kevin has 120 minutes to complete an exam. If he has already used 43, how many minutes does he have left?

   A. 43   B. 77   C. 87   D. 163

The correct answer is **B**. The correct solution is 77. The first step is to convert this problem to a math expression. The goal is to find the difference between how many minutes Kevin has for the exam and how many he has left after 43 minutes have elapsed. The expression would be 120 − 43. Carefully follow the subtraction algorithm (see below). The process will involve borrowing a digit twice.

$$\begin{array}{r} 120 \\ -\ 43 \\ \hline \end{array} \rightarrow \begin{array}{r} \overset{1\,10}{12\!\!\!/0} \\ -\ 43 \\ \hline 7 \end{array} \rightarrow \begin{array}{r} \overset{0\ 11\,10}{\cancel{1}\cancel{2}\cancel{0}} \\ -\ 43 \\ \hline 77 \end{array}$$

Let's Review!

- Numbers are positive and negative quantities and often appear in base-10 format.
- The number line illustrates the ordering of numbers.
- Addition is the combination of numbers. It can be performed by counting objects or pictures, moving on the number line, or using the addition algorithm.
- Subtraction is finding the difference between numbers. Like addition, it can be performed by counting, moving on the number line, or using the subtraction algorithm

LESSON 4.2 BASIC MULTIPLICATION AND DIVISION

This lesson describes the process of multiplying and dividing numbers and introduces the order of operations, which governs how to evaluate expressions containing multiple arithmetic operations.

Multiplication

Addition can be tedious if it involves multiple instances of the same numbers. For example, evaluating 29 + 29 is easy, but evaluating 29 + 29 + 29 + 29 + 29 is laborious. Note that this example contains five instances—or multiples—of 29. **Multiplication** replaces the repeated addition of the same number with a single, more concise operation. Using the **multiplication (or times) symbol** (×), the expression is

29 + 29 + 29 + 29 + 29 = 5 × 29

The expression contains 5 multiples of 29. These numbers are the **factors** of multiplication. The result is called the **product.** In this case, addition shows that the product is 145. As with the other arithmetic operations, multiplication is easy for small numbers. Below is the multiplication table for whole numbers up to 12.

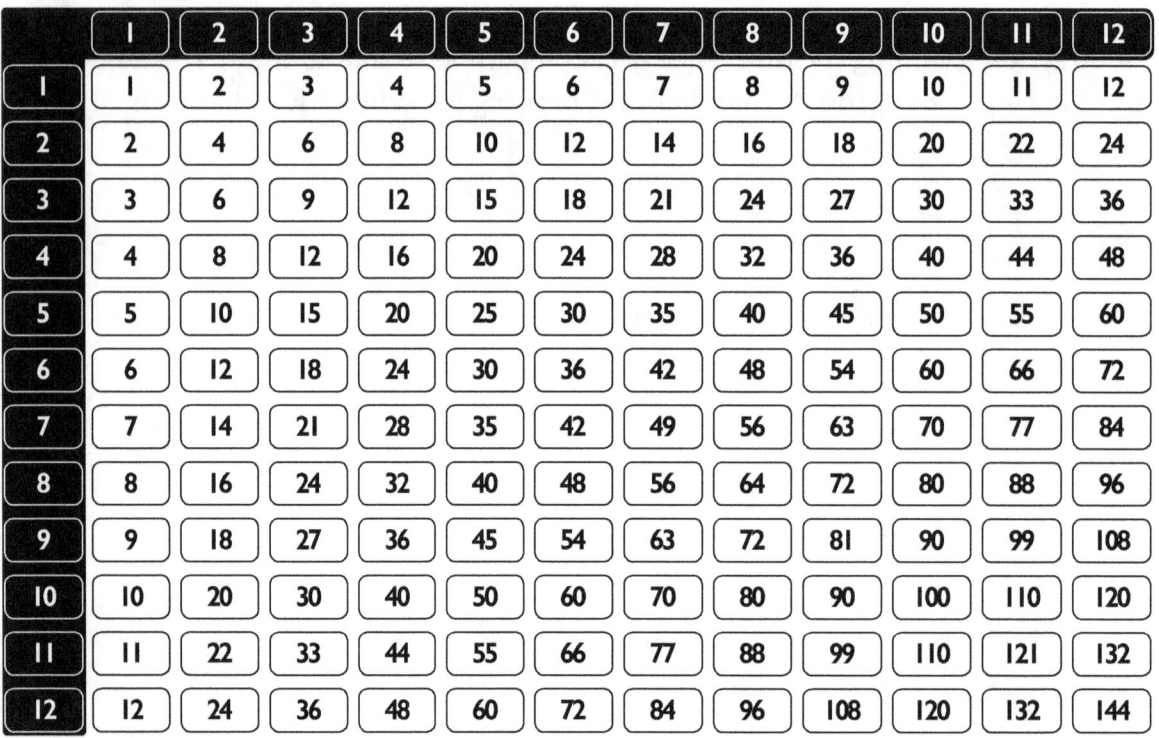

When dealing with large numbers, the multiplication algorithm is more practical than memorization. The ability to quickly recall the products in the multiplication table is nevertheless crucial to using this algorithm.

Lesson 4.2 Basic Multiplication and Division

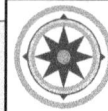

> **STEP BY STEP**
>
> **Step 1.** Stack the two factors, vertically aligning the digits in each place.
>
> **Step 2.** Draw a multiplication symbol (×) to the left of the bottom number and draw a horizontal line below the stack.
>
> **Step 3.** Begin with the ones digit in the lower factor. Multiply it with the ones digit from the top factor.
>
> **Step 4.** If the product from Step 3 is less than 10, write it in the same column below the horizontal line. Otherwise, write the first (ones) digit below the line and carry the second (tens) digit to the top of the next column.
>
> **Step 5.** Perform Step 4 for each digit in the top factor, adding any carry digit to the result. If an extra carry digit appears at the end, write it as the leftmost digit in the product.
>
> **Step 6.** Going right to left, repeat Steps 3–4 for the other places in the bottom factor, starting a new line in each case.
>
> **Step 7.** Add the numbers below the line to get the product.

Example

A certain type of screw comes in packs of 35. If a contractor orders 52 packs, how many screws does he receive?

A. 2   B. 57   C. 245   D. 1,820

The correct answer is **D**. The first step is to convert this problem to a math expression. The goal is to find how many screws the contractor receives if he orders 52 packs of 35 each. The expression would be 52×35 (or 35×52). Carefully follow the multiplication algorithm (see below).

$$
\begin{array}{r} 52 \\ \times\ 35 \\ \hline \end{array}
\rightarrow
\begin{array}{r} 1 \\ 52 \\ \times\ 35 \\ \hline 0 \end{array}
\rightarrow
\begin{array}{r} 1 \\ 52 \\ \times\ 35 \\ \hline 260 \end{array}
\rightarrow
\begin{array}{r} 1 \\ 52 \\ \times\ 35 \\ \hline 260 \\ 6 \end{array}
\rightarrow
\begin{array}{r} 11 \\ 52 \\ \times\ 35 \\ \hline 260 \\ 56 \end{array}
\rightarrow
\begin{array}{r} 11 \\ 52 \\ \times\ 35 \\ \hline 260 \\ 156 \end{array}
\rightarrow
\begin{array}{r} 11 \\ 52 \\ \times\ 35 \\ \hline 260 \\ +\ 156 \\ \hline 1{,}820 \end{array}
$$

> **KEY POINT**
>
> As with addition, the order of numbers in a multiplication expression is irrelevant to the product. For example, $6 \times 9 = 9 \times 6$.

Division

Division is the inverse of multiplication, like subtraction is the inverse of addition. Whereas multiplication asks how many individuals are in 8 groups of 9 (8 × 9 = 72), for example, division asks how many groups of 8 (or 9) are in 72. Division expressions use either the / or ÷ symbol. Therefore, 72 ÷ 9 means: How many groups of 9 are in 72, or how many times does 9 go into 72? Thinking about the meaning of multiplication shows that 72 ÷ 9 = 8 and 72 ÷ 8 = 9. In the expression 72 ÷ 8 = 9, 72 is the **dividend,** 8 is the **divisor,** and 9 is the **quotient.**

When the dividend is unevenly divisible by the divisor (e.g., 5 ÷ 2), calculating the quotient with a **remainder** can be convenient. The quotient in this case is the maximum number of times the divisor goes into the dividend plus how much of the dividend is left over. To express the remainder, use an R. For example, the quotient of 5 ÷ 2 is 2R1 because 2 goes into 5 twice with 1 left over.

Knowing the multiplication table allows quick evaluation of simple whole-number division. For larger numbers, the division algorithm enables evaluation by hand.

Unlike multiplication—but like subtraction—the order of the numbers in a division expression is important. Generally, changing the order changes the quotient.

> **STEP BY STEP**
>
> **Step 1.** Write the divisor and then the dividend on a single line.
>
> **Step 2.** Draw a vertical line between them, connecting to a horizontal line over the dividend.
>
> **Step 3.** If the divisor is smaller than the leftmost digit of the dividend, perform the remainder division and write the quotient (without the remainder) above that digit. If the divisor is larger than the leftmost digit, use the first two digits (or however many are necessary) until the number is greater than the divisor. Write the quotient over the rightmost digit in that number.
>
> **Step 4.** Multiply the quotient digit by the divisor and write it under the dividend, vertically aligning the ones digit of the product with the quotient digit.
>
> **Step 5.** Subtract the product from the digits above it.
>
> **Step 6.** Bring down the next digit from the dividend.
>
> **Step 7.** Perform Steps 3–6, using the most recent difference as the quotient.
>
> **Step 8.** Write the remainder next to the quotient.

Lesson 4.2 Basic Multiplication and Division

Example

Evaluate the expression 468 ÷ 26.

A. 18   B. 18R2   C. 494   D. 12,168

The correct answer is **A**. Carefully follow the division algorithm. In this case, the answer has no remainder.

> **KEY POINT**
> Division by 0 is undefined. If it appears in an expression, something is wrong.

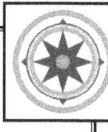

Signed Multiplication and Division

Multiplying and dividing signed numbers is simpler than adding and subtracting them because it only requires remembering two simple rules. First, if the two numbers have the same sign, their product or quotient is positive. Second, if they have different signs, their product or quotient is negative.

As a result, negative numbers can be multiplied or divided as if they are positive. Just keep track of the sign separately for the product or quotient. Note that negative numbers are sometimes written in parentheses to avoid the appearance of subtraction.

For Example:

$5 \times (-3) = -15$

$(-8) \times (-8) = 64$

$(-12) \div 3 = -4$

$(-100) \div (-25) = 4$

Example

Evaluate the expression (–7) × (–9).

A. −63   B. −16   C. 16   D. 63

The correct answer is **D**. Because both factors are negative, the product will be positive. Because the product of 7 and 9 is 63, the product of –7 and –9 is also 63.

Order of Operations

By default, math expressions work like most Western languages: they should be read and evaluated from left to right. However, some operations take precedence over others, which can change this default evaluation. Following this **order of operations** is critical. The mnemonic **PEMDAS (Please Excuse My Dear Aunt Sally)** helps in remembering how to evaluate an expression with multiple operations.

STEP BY STEP

- **P.** Evaluate operations in parentheses (or braces/brackets). If the expression has parentheses within parentheses, begin with the innermost ones.
- **E.** Evaluate exponential operations. (For expressions without exponents, ignore this step.)
- **MD.** Perform all multiplication and division operations, going through the expression from left to right.
- **AS.** Perform all addition and subtraction operations, going through the expression from left to right.

Because the order of numbers in multiplication and addition does not affect the result, the PEMDAS procedure only requires going from left to right when dividing or subtracting. At those points, going in the correct direction is critical to getting the right answer.

Calculators that can handle a series of numbers at once automatically evaluate an expression according to the order of operations. When available, calculators are a good way to check the results.

BE CAREFUL!
When evaluating an expression like $4 - 3 + 2 \times 5$, remember to go from left to right when adding and subtracting or when multiplying and dividing. The first step in this case (MD) yields $4 - 3 + 10$. Avoid the temptation to add first in the next step; instead, go from left to right. The result is $1 + 10 = 11$, *not* $4 - 13 = -9$.

Example

Evaluate the expression $8 \times (3 + 6) \div 3 - 2 + 5$.

A. 13   B. 17   C. 27   D. 77

The correct answer is **C**. Use the PEMDAS mnemonic. Start with parentheses. Then, do multiplication/division from left to right. Finally, do addition/subtraction from left to right.

$8 \times (3 + 6) \div 3 - 2 + 5$

$8 \times 9 \div 3 - 2 + 5$

$72 \div 3 - 2 + 5$

$24 - 2 + 5$

$22 + 5$

27

Working with Exponents

When following the order of operations, the second operation to evaluate within an expression are the exponents. Exponents imply an expression of repeated multiplication, otherwise known as a power. The exponent is a superscripted number for the number of times the base is multiplied. For example, 6^2 is the same as 6 times 6, or 36.

It is important to understand that any base to a power of 0 will equal 1. Otherwise written as a rule $n^0 = 1$. For example, $3^0 = 1$.

When exponents are written as negative values, these expressions are considered fractions or decimals. The value will be one portion of the base number and the exponent as a positive number. For example, $2^{-2} = \frac{1}{2^2} = \frac{1}{4}$.

Negative exponents are commonly used to represent small decimal numbers with a base of 10. For example, the expression 10^{-3} is equivalent to $\frac{1}{1000}$ or 0.001.

These rules are summarized in the chart below.

Property	Definition	Examples
Zero Exponent Rule	$a^0 = 1$	$64^0 = 1$ $y^0 = 1$
Negative Exponent Rule	$a^{-m} = \frac{1}{a^m}$	$3^{-3} = \frac{1}{3^3} = \frac{1}{27}$ $\frac{1}{x^{-3}} = x^3$

Let's Review!

- The multiplication table is important to memorize for both multiplying and dividing small whole numbers (up to about 12).
- Multiplication and division of large numbers by hand typically requires the multiplication and division algorithms.
- Multiplying and dividing signed numbers follows two simple rules: If the numbers have the same sign, the product or quotient is positive. If they have different signs, the product or quotient is negative.
- When evaluating expressions with several operations, carefully follow the order of operations; PEMDAS is a helpful mnemonic.

LESSON 4.3 DECIMALS AND FRACTIONS

This lesson introduces the basics of decimals and fractions. It also demonstrates changing decimals to fractions, changing fractions to decimals, and converting between fractions, decimals, and percentages.

Introduction to Fractions

A fraction represents part of a whole number. The top number of a fraction is the **numerator**, and the bottom number of a fraction is the **denominator**. The numerator is smaller than the denominator for a **proper fraction**. The numerator is larger than the denominator for an **improper fraction**.

Proper Fractions	Improper Fractions
$\frac{2}{5}$	$\frac{5}{2}$
$\frac{7}{12}$	$\frac{12}{7}$
$\frac{19}{20}$	$\frac{20}{19}$

An improper fraction can be changed to a **mixed number**. A mixed number is a whole number and a proper fraction. To write an improper fraction as a mixed number, divide the denominator into the numerator. The result is the whole number.

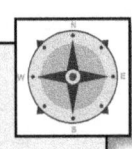

KEEP IN MIND

When comparing fractions, the denominators of the fractions must be the same.

The remainder is the numerator of the proper fraction, and the value of the denominator does not change. For example, $\frac{5}{2}$ is $2\frac{1}{2}$ because 2 goes into 5 twice with a remainder of 1. To write an mixed number as a improper fraction, multiply the whole number by the denominator and add the result to the numerator. The results become the new numerator. For example, $2\frac{1}{2}$ is $\frac{5}{2}$ because 2 times 2 plus 1 is 5 for the new numerator.

When comparing fractions, the denominators must be the same. Then, look at the numerator to determine which fraction is larger. If the fractions have different denominators, then a **least common denominator** must be found. This number is the smallest number that can be divided evenly into the denominators of all fractions being compared.

To determine the largest fraction from the group $\frac{1}{3}, \frac{3}{5}, \frac{2}{3}, \frac{2}{5}$ the first step is to find a common denominator. In this case, the least common denominator is 15 because 3 times 5 and 5 times 3 is 15. The second step is to convert the fractions to a denominator of 15.

The fractions with a denominator of 3 have the numerator and denominator multiplied by 5, and the fractions with a denominator of 5 have the numerator and denominator multiplied by 3, as shown below:

$\frac{1}{3} \times \frac{5}{5} = \frac{5}{15}, \frac{3}{5} \times \frac{3}{3} = \frac{9}{15}, \frac{2}{3} \times \frac{5}{5} = \frac{10}{15}, \frac{2}{5} \times \frac{3}{3} = \frac{6}{15}$

Lesson 4.3 Decimals and Fractions

Now, the numerators can be compared. The largest fraction is $\frac{2}{3}$ because it has a numerator of 10 after finding the common denominator.

Examples

1. **Which fraction is the least?**

   A. $\frac{3}{5}$ B. $\frac{3}{4}$ C. $\frac{1}{5}$ D. $\frac{1}{4}$

   The correct answer is **C**. The correct solution is $\frac{1}{5}$ because it has the smallest numerator compared to the other fractions with the same denominator. The fractions with a common denominator of 20 are $\frac{3}{5} = \frac{12}{20}, \frac{3}{4} = \frac{15}{20}, \frac{1}{5} = \frac{4}{20}, \frac{1}{4} = \frac{5}{20}$.

2. **Which fraction is the greatest?**

   A. $\frac{5}{6}$ B. $\frac{1}{2}$ C. $\frac{2}{3}$ D. $\frac{1}{6}$

   The correct answer is **A**. The correct solution is $\frac{5}{6}$ because it has the largest numerator compared to the other fractions with the same denominator. The fractions with a common denominator of 6 are $\frac{5}{6} = \frac{5}{6}, \frac{1}{2} = \frac{3}{6}, \frac{2}{3} = \frac{4}{6}, \frac{1}{6} = \frac{1}{6}$.

Introduction to Decimals

A **decimal** is a number that expresses part of a whole. Decimals show a portion of a number after a decimal point. Each number to the left and right of the decimal point has a specific place value. Identify the place values for 645.3207.

6 4 5.3 2 0 7

tens tenths thousandths

When comparing decimals, compare the numbers in the same place value. For example, determine the greatest decimal from the group 0.4, 0.41, 0.39, and 0.37. In these numbers, there is a value to the right of the decimal point. Comparing the tenths places, the numbers with 4 tenths (0.4 and 0.41) are greater than the numbers with three tenths (0.39 and 0.37).

0.4
↓
0.41
↓
0.39
↓
0.37

KEEP IN MIND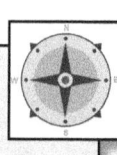

When comparing decimals, compare the place value where the numbers are different.

Then, compare the hundredths in the 4 tenths numbers. The value of 0.41 is greater because there is a 1 in the hundredths place versus a 0 in the hundredths place.

0.4
↓
0.41

ATI TEAS: Full Study Guide, Test Strategies and Secrets

Here is another example: determine the least decimal of the group 5.23, 5.32, 5.13, and 5.31. In this group, the ones value is 5 for all numbers. Then, comparing the tenths values, 5.13 is the smallest number because it is the only value with 1 tenth.

Examples

1. **Which decimal is the greatest?**

    A. 0.07   B. 0.007   C. 0.7   D. 0.0007

    The correct answer is **C**. The solution is 0.7 because it has the largest place value in the tenths.

2. **Which decimal is the least?**

    A. 0.0413   B. 0.0713   C. 0.0513   D. 0.0613

    The correct answer is **A**. The correct solution is 0.0413 because it has the smallest place value in the hundredths place.

> **HELPFUL TIPS**
>
> The multiplication and division algorithms can be used, even with decimal numbers. With the multiplication algorithm, count the total number of place values to the right the decimal must move in the multiplier numbers. Simply place the decimal the total number of place values to the *left* in the sum. For example, 0.5 × 0.5, the decimal must move one place value to the *right* for each number and a total of two place values. Place the decimal two place values to the *left* in the answer. After completing the algorithm, 25 becomes 0.25 from the decimal.
>
> For the division algorithm, move the decimal to the right as many place values as needed to make the divisor and dividend whole numbers. The place value should be moved the same amount of times in both numbers. For example, 180 ÷ 0.2, the divisor must have the place value moved one place value to the right to become 2. Move the decimal from 180 (180.0) the same amount, to complete long division with whole numbers: 1800 ÷ 2 = 900, which is equal to 180 ÷ 0.2 = 900.

Changing Decimals and Fractions

Three steps change a decimal to a fraction.

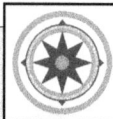

> **STEP BY STEP**
> **Step 1.** Write the decimal divided by 1 with the decimal as the numerator and 1 as the denominator.
> **Step 2.** Multiply the numerator and denominator by 10 for every number after the decimal point. (For example, if there is 1 decimal place, multiply by 10. If there are 2 decimal places, multiply by 100).
> **Step 3.** Reduce the fraction completely.

To change the decimal 0.37 to a fraction, start by writing the decimal as a fraction with a denominator of one, $\frac{0.37}{1}$. Because there are two decimal places, multiply the numerator and denominator by 100, $\frac{0.37 \times 100}{1 \times 100} = \frac{37}{100}$. The fraction does not reduce, so $\frac{37}{100}$ is 0.37 in fraction form.

Similarly, to change the decimal 2.4 to a fraction start by writing the decimal as a fraction with a denominator of one, $\frac{0.4}{1}$, and ignore the whole number. Because there is one decimal place, multiply the numerator and denominator by 10, $\frac{0.4 \times 10}{1 \times 10} = \frac{4}{10}$. The fraction does reduce: $2\frac{4}{10} = 2\frac{2}{5}$ is 2.4 in fraction form.

The decimal $0.\overline{3}$ as a fraction is $\frac{0.\overline{3}}{1}$. In the case of a repeating decimal, let $n = 0.\overline{3}$ and $10n = 3.\overline{3}$. Then, $10n - n = 3.\overline{3} - 0.\overline{3}$, resulting in $9n = 3$ and solution of $n = \frac{3}{9} = \frac{1}{3}$. The decimal $0.\overline{3}$ is $\frac{1}{3}$ as a fraction.

Examples

1. **Change 0.38 to a fraction. Simplify completely.**

   A. $\frac{3}{10}$ B. $\frac{9}{25}$ C. $\frac{19}{50}$ D. $\frac{2}{5}$

   The correct answer is **C**. The correct solution is $\frac{19}{50}$ because $\frac{0.38}{1} = \frac{38}{100} = \frac{19}{50}$.

2. **Change $1.\overline{1}$ to a fraction. Simplify completely.**

   A. $1\frac{1}{11}$ B. $1\frac{1}{9}$ C. $1\frac{1}{6}$ D. $1\frac{1}{3}$

   The correct answer is **B**. The correct solution is $1\frac{1}{9}$. Let $n = 1.\overline{1}$ and $10n = 11.\overline{1}$. Then, $10n - n = 11.\overline{1} - 1.\overline{1}$, resulting in $9n = 10$ and solution of $n = \frac{10}{9} = 1\frac{1}{9}$.

Two steps change a fraction to a decimal.

> **STEP BY STEP**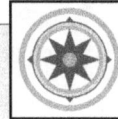
>
> **Step 1.** Divide the numerator by the denominator. Add zeros after the decimal point as needed.
>
> **Step 2.** Complete the process when there is no remainder or the decimal is repeating.

To convert $\frac{1}{5}$ to a decimal, rewrite $\frac{1}{5}$ as a long division problem and add zeros after the decimal point, $1.0 \div 5$. Complete the long division and $\frac{1}{5}$ as a decimal is 0.2. The division is complete because there is no remainder.

To convert $\frac{8}{9}$ to a decimal, rewrite $\frac{8}{9}$ as a long division problem and add zeros after the decimal point, $8.00 \div 9$. Complete the long division, and $\frac{8}{9}$ as a decimal is $0.\overline{8}$. The process is complete because the decimal is complete.

To rewrite the mixed number $2\frac{3}{4}$ as a decimal, the fraction needs to be changed to a decimal. Rewrite $\frac{3}{4}$ as a long division problem and add zeros after the decimal point, $3.00 \div 4$. The whole number is needed for the answer and is not included in the long division. Complete the long division, and $2\frac{3}{4}$ as a decimal is 2.75.

Examples

1. Change $\frac{9}{10}$ to a decimal. Simplify completely.

   A. 0.75   B. 0.8   C. 0.85   D. 0.9

   The correct answer is **D**. The correct answer is 0.9 because $\frac{9}{10} = 9.0 \div 10 = 0.9$.

2. Change $\frac{5}{6}$ to a decimal. Simplify completely.

   A. 0.73   B. $0.7\overline{6}$ C. $0.8\overline{3}$ D. 0.86

   The correct answer is **C**. The correct answer is $0.8\overline{3}$ because $\frac{5}{6} = 5.000 \div 6 = 0.8\overline{3}$.

Convert among Fractions, Decimals, and Percentages

Fractions, decimals, and percentages can change forms, but they are equivalent values.

There are two ways to change a decimal to a percent. One way is to multiply the decimal by 100 and add a percent sign. 0.24 as a percent is 24%.

Another way is to move the decimal point two places to the right. The decimal 0.635 is 63.5% as a percent when moving the decimal point two places to the right.

Any decimal, including repeating decimals, can change to a percent. $0.\overline{3}$ as a percent is $0.\overline{3} \times 100 = 33.\overline{3}\%$.

Lesson 4.3   Decimals and Fractions

Example

Write 0.345 as a percent.

   A.   3.45%   B.   34.5%   C.   345%   D.   3450%

   The correct answer is **B**. The correct answer is 34.5% because 0.345 as a percent is 34.5%.

There are two ways to change a percent to a decimal. One way is to remove the percent sign and divide the decimal by 100. For example, 73% as a decimal is 0.73.

Another way is to move the decimal point two places to the left. For example, 27.8% is 0.278 as a decimal when moving the decimal point two places to the left.

Any percent, including repeating percents, can change to a decimal. For example, $44.\overline{4}\%$ as a decimal is $44.\overline{4} \div 100 = 0.\overline{4}$.

Example

Write 131% as a decimal.

   A.   0.131   B.   1.31   C.   13.1   D.   131

   The correct answer is **B**. The correct answer is 1.31 because 131% as a decimal is $131 \div 100 = 1.31$.

Two steps change a fraction to a percent.

STEP BY STEP
Step 1.   Divide the numerator and denominator.
Step 2.   Multiply by 100 and add a percent sign.

To change the fraction $\frac{3}{5}$ to a decimal, perform long division to get 0.6. Then, multiply 0.6 by 100 and $\frac{3}{5}$ is the same as 60%.

To change the fraction $\frac{7}{8}$ to a decimal, perform long division to get 0.875. Then, multiply 0.875 by 100 and $\frac{7}{8}$ is the same as 87.5%.

Fractions that are repeating decimals can also be converted to a percent. To change the fraction $\frac{2}{3}$ to a decimal, perform long division to get $0.\overline{6}$. Then, multiply $0.\overline{6}$ by 100 and the percent is $66.\overline{6}\%$.

Example

Write $2\frac{1}{8}$ as a percent.

   A.   21.2%   B.   21.25%   C.   212%   D.   212.5%

   The correct answer is **D**. The correct answer is 212.5% because $2\frac{1}{8}$ as a percent is $2.125 \times 100 = 212.5\%$.

Two steps change a percent to a fraction.

> **STEP BY STEP**
> **Step 1.** Remove the percent sign and write the value as the numerator with a denominator of 100.
> **Step 2.** Simplify the fraction.

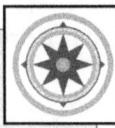

Remove the percent sign from 45% and write as a fraction with a denominator of 100, $\frac{45}{100}$. The fraction reduces to $\frac{9}{20}$.

Remove the percent sign from 22.8% and write as a fraction with a denominator of 100, $\frac{22.8}{100}$. The fraction reduces to $\frac{228}{1000} = \frac{57}{250}$.

Repeating percentages can change to a fraction. Remove the percent sign from $16.\overline{6}\%$ and write as a fraction with a denominator of 100, $\frac{16.\overline{6}}{100}$. The fraction simplifies to $\frac{0.1\overline{6}}{1} = \frac{1}{6}$.

Example

Write 72% as a fraction.

A. $\frac{27}{50}$ B. $\frac{7}{10}$ C. $\frac{18}{25}$ D. $\frac{3}{4}$

The correct answer is **C**. The correct answer is $\frac{18}{25}$ because 72% as a fraction is $\frac{72}{100} = \frac{18}{25}$.

It is useful to see how these numbers compare on a number line when working between fractions, decimals, and percentages. Use the table and number line below as a quick reference to draw comparisons.

0	$\frac{1}{8}$	$\frac{1}{5}$	$\frac{1}{4}$	$\frac{1}{3}$	$\frac{3}{8}$	$\frac{2}{5}$	$\frac{1}{2}$	$\frac{3}{5}$	$\frac{5}{8}$	$\frac{2}{3}$	$\frac{3}{4}$	$\frac{7}{8}$	$\frac{1}{1}$
0	0.125	0.2	0.25	0.333	0.375	0.4	0.5	0.6	0.625	0.666	0.75	0.875	1.00
0	12.5%	20%	25%	33.3%	37.5%	40%	50%	60%	62.5%	66.6%	75%	87.5%	100%

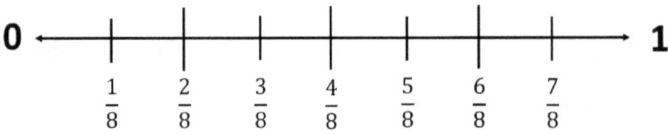

Let's Review!

- A fraction is a number with a numerator and a denominator. A fraction can be written as a proper fraction, an improper fraction, or a mixed number. Changing fractions to a common denominator enables you to determine the least or greatest fraction in a group of fractions.
- A decimal is a number that expresses part of a whole. By comparing the same place values, you can find the least or greatest decimal in a group of decimals.

LESSON 4.4 ADDITION AND SUBTRACTION OF FRACTIONS

This lesson introduces how to add and subtract fractions.

Adding a Fraction to a Fraction

Fractions with the same denominator are called **like fractions**. To add a fraction to a fraction with like denominators, simply add the numerators. For example, $\frac{2}{5} + \frac{1}{5} = \frac{3}{5}$.

Sometimes, the final solution reduces. For example, $\frac{3}{8} + \frac{3}{8} = \frac{6}{8} = \frac{3}{4}$. The fraction $\frac{6}{8}$ reduces to $\frac{3}{4}$.

A fraction added to another fraction may equal an answer greater than 1. For example, $\frac{4}{7} + \frac{4}{7} = \frac{8}{7}$. The answer may be written as an improper fraction or changed to a mixed number. In this example, $\frac{8}{7}$ may also be written as the mixed number $1\frac{1}{7}$.

> **KEEP IN MIND**
>
> The sum of two fractions may be greater than 1. The answer can be written as an improper fraction or a mixed number.

Examples

1. Add $\frac{2}{9} + \frac{5}{9}$.

   A. $\frac{7}{9}$ B. $\frac{4}{9}$ C. $\frac{5}{9}$ D. $\frac{8}{9}$

   The correct answer is **A**. The correct solution is $\frac{7}{9}$ because $\frac{2}{9} + \frac{5}{9} = 2 + \frac{5}{9} = \frac{7}{9}$.

2. Add $\frac{3}{10} + \frac{3}{10}$.

   A. $\frac{1}{5}$ B. $\frac{6}{20}$ C. $\frac{3}{20}$ D. $\frac{3}{5}$

   The correct answer is **D**. The correct solution is $\frac{3}{5}$ because $\frac{3}{10} + \frac{3}{10} = 3 + \frac{3}{10} = \frac{6}{10}$. The fraction $\frac{6}{10}$ reduces to $\frac{3}{5}$.

Subtracting a Fraction from a Fraction

The same basic steps apply when subtracting a fraction from a fraction. Information from the previous section is applicable.

When subtracting like fractions, subtract the numerators. For example, $\frac{8}{9} - \frac{2}{9} = \frac{6}{9} = \frac{2}{3}$. In this example, the answer was reduced to $\frac{2}{3}$.

Examples

1. Subtract $\frac{5}{7} - \frac{3}{7}$.

   A. $\frac{1}{7}$ B. $\frac{8}{7}$ C. $\frac{5}{14}$ D. $\frac{2}{7}$

   The correct answer is **D**. The correct solution is $\frac{2}{7}$ because $\frac{5}{7} - \frac{3}{7} = 5 - \frac{3}{7} = \frac{2}{7}$. See Lesson: **Multiplication and Division of Fractions**.

ATI TEAS: Full Study Guide, Test Strategies and Secrets

2. Subtract $\frac{9}{10} - \frac{7}{10}$.

   A. $1\frac{3}{5}$ B. $\frac{2}{5}$ C. $\frac{1}{5}$ D. $\frac{3}{10}$

   The correct answer is **C**. The correct solution is $\frac{1}{5}$ because $\frac{9}{10} - \frac{7}{10} = \frac{2}{10} = \frac{1}{5}$. See Lesson: **Multiplication and Division of Fractions**.

Adding Fractions Without Like Denominators

Fractions will not always have like denominators when adding them together. Rewrite the fractions to have a like denominator in order to add the fractions. To determine what the denominator should be, find the **lowest common multiple** between the numbers and convert the fractions to have the value as the denominator. This value is considered the **least common denominator**, or LCD.

Convert the fraction to have the LCD by multiplying the fraction by the necessary numerical value written as a fraction equal to 1.

For example, add $\frac{2}{5} + \frac{7}{15}$. The fractions must be converted to have like denominators in order to add them together. The number 15 is a multiple of 5 by multiplying it by the value 3. Multiply the numerator and denominator by $\frac{3}{3}$, a value equivalent to 1. Multiply $\frac{2}{5} \times \frac{3}{3} = 2 \times \frac{3}{5} \times 3 = \frac{6}{15}$. Now that the fraction is converted to have the LCD, the fractions can be added together by adding the numerators, $\frac{6}{15} + \frac{7}{15} = \frac{13}{15}$.

Sometimes both fractions will have to be converted to have the LCD. The fractions can be converted by different forms of the value 1. For example, add $\frac{1}{6} + \frac{4}{9}$. The LCD between the fractions is 18. The first fraction must be converted by multiplying it by $\frac{3}{3}$ because $\frac{1}{6} \times \frac{3}{3} = 1 \times \frac{3}{6} \times 3 = \frac{3}{18}$. The second fraction must be converted by multiplying it by $\frac{2}{2}$ because $\frac{4}{9} \times \frac{2}{2} = 4 \times \frac{2}{9} \times 2 = \frac{8}{18}$. The fractions can be added together with like denominators, $\frac{3}{18} + \frac{8}{18} = \frac{11}{18}$.

When adding a fraction to an improper fraction or mixed number, the process is similar.

For example, add $\frac{7}{11} + 2\frac{1}{2}$. Change the mixed number to an improper fraction, $\frac{7}{11} + \frac{5}{2}$. Convert each fraction to have the LCD, $\frac{7}{11} \times \frac{2}{2} = \frac{14}{22}$ and $\frac{5}{2} \times \frac{11}{11} = \frac{55}{22}$. Add the numerators together and reduce if necessary, $\frac{14}{22} + \frac{55}{22} = \frac{69}{22}$. The fraction $\frac{69}{22}$ cannot be reduced, but can be rewritten as a mixed number, $3\frac{3}{22}$.

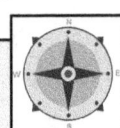

KEEP IN MIND
Change the fractions to have a common denominator in order to complete the operation.

Examples

1. Add $\frac{3}{8} + \frac{5}{6}$.

   A. $\frac{8}{14}$ B. $\frac{4}{7}$ C. $1\frac{1}{4}$ D. $1\frac{5}{24}$

   The correct answer is **D**. The correct solution is $1\frac{5}{24}$ because $\frac{3}{8} + \frac{5}{6} = \frac{9}{24} + \frac{20}{24} = \frac{29}{24} = 1\frac{5}{24}$.

Lesson 4.4 Addition and Subtraction of Fractions

2. Add $1\frac{1}{2} + \frac{2}{3}$.

   A. $\frac{5}{6}$ B. $2\frac{1}{6}$ C. $1\frac{5}{6}$ D. $1\frac{2}{5}$

   The correct answer is **B**. The correct solution is $2\frac{1}{6}$ because $1\frac{1}{2} + \frac{2}{3} = \frac{3}{2} + \frac{2}{3} = \frac{9}{6} + \frac{4}{6} = \frac{13}{6} = 2\frac{1}{6}$.

Subtracting Fractions Without Like Denominators

The same basic steps apply when subtracting fractions without like denominators. Similar steps can be used when subtracting a fraction from a mixed number or improper fraction, or subtracting a mixed number or improper fraction from a fraction.

STEP BY STEP

Step 1. Write any whole number as a fraction with a denominator of 1. Write any mixed numbers as improper fractions.

Step 2. Determine the least common multiple between denominators.

Step 3. Convert the fractions to have the least common multiple as the denominator.

Step 4. Subtract the numerators.

Step 5. Rewrite the fraction as a mixed number and reduce the fraction completely.

Subtract, $2\frac{1}{10} - \frac{6}{7}$. Rewrite the expression as $\frac{21}{10} - \frac{6}{7}$. Convert both fractions to have the lowest common denominator, $\frac{21}{10} \times \frac{7}{7} = \frac{147}{70}$ and $\frac{6}{7} \times \frac{10}{10} = \frac{60}{70}$. Subtract the numerators and reduce completely, $\frac{147}{70} - \frac{60}{70} = \frac{87}{70} = 1\frac{17}{70}$.

Subtract, $\frac{12}{5} - \frac{4}{9}$. Convert the fractions to have the lowest common denominator, $\frac{12}{5} \times \frac{9}{9} = \frac{108}{45}$ and $\frac{4}{9} \times \frac{5}{5} = \frac{20}{45}$. Subtract the numerators and reduce as necessary, $\frac{108}{45} - \frac{20}{45} = \frac{88}{45} = 1\frac{43}{45}$.

Examples

1. Subtract $\frac{15}{16} - \frac{3}{8}$.

   A. $\frac{3}{4}$ B. $\frac{9}{16}$ C. $\frac{7}{8}$ D. $\frac{1}{2}$

   The correct answer is **B**. The correct answer is $\frac{9}{16}$ because $\frac{15}{16} - \frac{3}{8} = \frac{15}{16} - \frac{6}{16} = \frac{9}{16}$.

2. Subtract $\frac{15}{10} - \frac{2}{3}$.

   A. $\frac{1}{2}$ B. $\frac{13}{7}$ C. $\frac{5}{6}$ D. $1\frac{3}{10}$

   The correct answer is **C**. The correct answer is $\frac{5}{6}$ because $\frac{15}{10} - \frac{2}{3} = \frac{45}{30} - \frac{20}{30} = \frac{25}{30} = \frac{5}{6}$.

Let's Review!

- The process of adding or subtracting like fractions requires the numerators to be added or subtracted. The answer may be reduced.
- Operations with fractions may produce an answer greater than the value of 1. The answer can be written as an improper fraction or a mixed number.
- The process to add or subtract fractions without like denominators requires the fractions to be converted in order to have the same denominator, also known as the least common denominator.

LESSON 4.5 — MULTIPLICATION AND DIVISION OF FRACTIONS

This lesson introduces how to multiply and divide fractions.

Multiplying a Fraction by a Fraction

The multiplication of fractions does not require changing any denominators like adding and subtracting fractions do. To multiply a fraction by a fraction, multiply the numerators together and multiply the denominators together. For example, $\frac{2}{3} \times \frac{4}{5}$ is $2 \times \frac{4}{3} \times 5$, which is $\frac{8}{15}$.

Sometimes, the final solution reduces. For example, $\frac{3}{5} \times \frac{1}{9} = 3 \times \frac{1}{5} \times 9 = \frac{3}{45}$. The fraction $\frac{3}{45}$ reduces to $\frac{1}{15}$.

Simplifying fractions can occur before completing the multiplication. In the previous problem, the numerator of 3 can be simplified with the denominator of 9: $\frac{3}{5} \times \frac{1}{9} = \frac{1}{15}$. This method of simplifying only occurs with the multiplication of fractions.

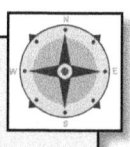

KEEP IN MIND
The product of multiplying a fraction by a fraction is always less than 1.

Examples

1. **Multiply $\frac{1}{2} \times \frac{3}{4}$.**

    A. $\frac{1}{4}$ B. $\frac{1}{2}$ C. $\frac{3}{8}$ D. $\frac{2}{3}$

    The correct answer is **C**. The correct solution is $\frac{3}{8}$ because $\frac{1}{2} \times \frac{3}{4} = \frac{3}{8}$.

2. **Multiply $\frac{2}{3} \times \frac{5}{6}$.**

    A. $\frac{1}{9}$ B. $\frac{5}{18}$ C. $\frac{5}{9}$ D. $\frac{7}{18}$

    The correct answer is **C**. The correct solution is $\frac{5}{9}$ because $\frac{2}{3} \times \frac{5}{6} = \frac{10}{18} = \frac{5}{9}$.

Multiply a Fraction by a Whole or Mixed Number

Multiplying a fraction by a whole or mixed number is similar to multiplying two fractions. When multiplying by a whole number, change the whole number to a fraction with a denominator of 1. Next, multiply the numerators together and the denominators together. Rewrite the final answer as a mixed number.

For example: $\frac{9}{10} \times 3 = \frac{9}{10} \times \frac{3}{1} = \frac{27}{10} = 2\frac{7}{10}$.

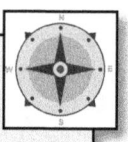

KEEP IN MIND
Always change a mixed number to an improper fraction when multiplying by a mixed number.

When multiplying a fraction by a mixed number or multiplying two mixed numbers, the process is similar.

For example, multiply $\frac{10}{11} \times 3\frac{1}{2}$. Change the mixed number to an improper fraction, $\frac{10}{11} \times \frac{7}{2}$. Multiply the numerators together and multiply the denominators together, $\frac{70}{22}$. Write the improper fraction as a mixed number, $3\frac{4}{22}$. Reduce if necessary, $3\frac{2}{11}$.

This process can also be used when multiplying a whole number by a mixed number or multiplying two mixed numbers.

Examples

1. **Multiply $4 \times \frac{5}{6}$.**

    A. $\frac{5}{24}$ B. $2\frac{3}{4}$ C. $3\frac{1}{3}$ D. $4\frac{5}{6}$

    The correct answer is **C**. The correct solution is $3\frac{1}{3}$ because $\frac{4}{1} \times \frac{5}{6} = \frac{20}{6} = 3\frac{2}{6} = 3\frac{1}{3}$.

2. **Multiply $1\frac{1}{2} \times 1\frac{1}{6}$.**

    A. $1\frac{1}{12}$ B. $1\frac{1}{4}$ C. $1\frac{3}{8}$ D. $1\frac{3}{4}$

    The correct answer is **D**. The correct solution is $1\frac{3}{4}$ because $\frac{3}{2} \times \frac{7}{6} = \frac{21}{12} = 1\frac{9}{12} = 1\frac{3}{4}$.

Dividing a Fraction by a Fraction

Some basic steps apply when dividing a fraction by a fraction. The information from the previous two sections is applicable to dividing fractions.

STEP BY STEP
Step 1. Leave the first fraction alone.
Step 2. Find the reciprocal of the second fraction.
Step 3. Multiply the first fraction by the reciprocal of the second fraction.
Step 4. Rewrite the fraction as a mixed number and reduce the fraction completely.

Divide, $\frac{3}{10} \div \frac{1}{2}$. Find the reciprocal of the second fraction, which is $\frac{2}{1}$.

Now, multiply the fractions, $\frac{3}{10} \times \frac{2}{1} = \frac{6}{10}$. Reduce $\frac{6}{10}$ to $\frac{3}{5}$.

Divide, $\frac{4}{5} \div \frac{3}{8}$. Find the reciprocal of the second fraction, which is $\frac{8}{3}$.

Now, multiply the fractions, $\frac{4}{5} \times \frac{8}{3} = \frac{32}{15}$. Rewrite the fraction as a mixed number, $\frac{32}{15} = 2\frac{2}{15}$.

Lesson 4.5 Multiplication and Division of Fractions

Examples

1. Divide $\frac{1}{2} \div \frac{5}{6}$.

   A. $\frac{5}{12}$ B. $\frac{3}{5}$ C. $\frac{5}{6}$ D. $1\frac{2}{3}$

   The correct answer is **B**. The correct solution is $\frac{3}{5}$ because $\frac{1}{2} \times \frac{6}{5} = \frac{6}{10} = \frac{3}{5}$.

2. Divide $\frac{2}{3} \div \frac{3}{5}$.

   A. $\frac{2}{15}$ B. $\frac{2}{5}$ C. $1\frac{1}{15}$ D. $1\frac{1}{9}$

   The correct answer is **D**. The correct solution is $1\frac{1}{9}$ because $\frac{2}{3} \times \frac{5}{3} = \frac{10}{9} = 1\frac{1}{9}$.

Dividing a Fraction and a Whole or Mixed Number

Some basic steps apply when dividing a fraction by a whole number or a mixed number.

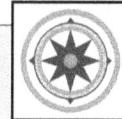

STEP BY STEP

Step 1. Write any whole number as a fraction with a denominator of 1. Write any mixed numbers as improper fractions.

Step 2. Leave the first fraction (improper fraction) alone.

Step 3. Find the reciprocal of the second fraction.

Step 4. Multiply the first fraction by the reciprocal of the second fraction.

Step 5. Rewrite the fraction as a mixed number and reduce the fraction completely.

Divide, $\frac{3}{10} \div 3$. Rewrite the expression as $\frac{3}{10} \div \frac{3}{1}$. Find the reciprocal of the second fraction, which is $\frac{1}{3}$. Multiply the fractions, $\frac{3}{10} \times \frac{1}{3} = \frac{3}{30} = \frac{1}{10}$. Reduce $\frac{3}{30}$ to $\frac{1}{10}$.

Divide, $2\frac{4}{5} \div 1\frac{3}{8}$. Rewrite the expression as $\frac{14}{5} \div \frac{11}{8}$. Find the reciprocal of the second fraction, which is $\frac{8}{11}$.

Multiply the fractions, $\frac{14}{5} \times \frac{8}{11} = \frac{112}{55} = 2\frac{2}{55}$. Reduce $\frac{112}{55}$ to $2\frac{2}{55}$.

Examples

1. Divide $\frac{2}{3} \div 4$.

   A. $\frac{1}{12}$ B. $\frac{1}{10}$ C. $\frac{1}{8}$ D. $\frac{1}{6}$

   The correct answer is **D**. The correct answer is $\frac{1}{6}$ because $\frac{2}{3} \times \frac{1}{4} = \frac{2}{12} = \frac{1}{6}$.

2. Divide $1\frac{5}{12} \div 1\frac{1}{2}$.

   A. $\frac{17}{18}$ B. $1\frac{5}{24}$ C. $1\frac{5}{6}$ D. $2\frac{1}{8}$

   The correct answer is **A**. The correct answer is $\frac{17}{18}$ because $\frac{17}{12} \div \frac{3}{2} = \frac{17}{12} \times \frac{2}{3} = \frac{34}{36} = \frac{17}{18}$.

Let's Review!

- The process to multiply fractions is to multiply the numerators together and multiply the denominators together. When there is a mixed number, change the mixed number to an improper fraction before multiplying.
- The process to divide fractions is to find the reciprocal of the second fraction and multiply the fractions. As with multiplying, change any mixed numbers to improper fractions before dividing.

LESSON 4.6 RATIOS, PROPORTIONS, AND PERCENTAGES

This lesson reviews percentages and ratios and their application to real-world problems. It also examines proportions and rates of change.

Percentages

A **percent** or **percentage** represents a fraction of some quantity. It is an integer or decimal number followed by the symbol %. The word *percent* means "per hundred." For example, 50% means 50 per 100. This is equivalent to half, or 1 out of 2.

Converting between numbers and percents is easy. Given a number, multiply by 100 and add the % symbol to get the equivalent percent. For instance, 0.67 is equal to $0.67 \times 100 = 67\%$, meaning 67 out of 100. Given a percent, eliminate the % symbol and divide by 100. For instance, 23.5% is equal to $23.5 \div 100 = 0.235$.

Although percentages between 0% and 100% are the most obvious, a percent can be any real number, including a negative number. For example, 1.35 = 135% and −0.872 = −87.2%. An example is a gasoline tank that is one-quarter full: one-quarter is $\frac{1}{4}$ or 0.25, so the tank is 25% full. Another example is a medical diagnostic test that has a certain maximum normal result. If a patient's test exceeds that value, its representation can be a percent greater than 100%. For instance, a reading that is 1.22 times the maximum normal value is 122% of the maximum normal value. Likewise, when measuring increases in a company's profits as a percent from one year to the next, a negative percent can represent a decline. That is, if the company's profits fell by one-tenth, the change was −10%.

Example

If 15 out of every 250 contest entries are winners, what percentage of entries are winners?

A. 0.06%   B. 6%   C. 15%   D. 17%

The correct answer is **B**. First, convert the fraction $\frac{15}{250}$ to a decimal: 0.06. To get the percent, multiply by 100% (that is, multiply by 100 and add the % symbol). Of all entries, 6% are winners.

Ratios

A **ratio** expresses the relationship between two numbers and is expressed using a colon or fraction notation. For instance, if 135 runners finish a marathon but 22 drop out, the ratio of finishers to non-finishers is 135:22 or $\frac{135}{22}$. These expressions are equal.

> **BE CAREFUL!**
> Avoid confusing standard ratios with odds (such as "3:1 odds"). Both may use a colon, but their meanings differ. In general, a ratio is the same as a fraction containing the same numbers.

Ratios also follow the rules of fractions. Performing arithmetic operations on ratios follows the same procedures as on fractions. Ratios should also generally appear in lowest terms. Therefore, the constituent numbers in a ratio represent the relative quantities of each side, not absolute quantities. For example, because the ratio 1:2 is equal to 2:4, 5:10, and 600:1,200, ratios are insufficient to determine the absolute number of entities in a problem.

Example

If the ratio of women to men in a certain industry is 5:4, how many people are in that industry?

A. 9   B. 20   C. 900   D. Not enough information

The correct answer is **D**. The ratio 5:4 is the industry's relative number of women to men. But the industry could have 10 women and 8 men, 100 women and 80 men, or any other breakdown whose ratio is 5:4. Therefore, the question provides too little information to answer. Had it provided the total number of people in the industry, it would have been possible to determine how many women and how many men are in the industry.

KEY POINT
Mathematically, ratios act just like fractions. For example, the ratio 8:13 is mathematically the same as the fraction $\frac{8}{13}$.

Proportions

A **proportion** is an equation of two ratios. An illustrative case is two equivalent fractions:

$$\frac{21}{28} = \frac{3}{4}$$

This example of a proportion should be familiar: going left to right, it is the conversion of one fraction to an equivalent fraction in lowest terms by dividing the numerator and denominator by the same number (7, in this case).

Equating fractions in this way is correct, but it provides little information. Proportions are more informative when one of the numbers is unknown. Using a question mark (?) to represent an unknown number, setting up a proportion can aid in solving problems involving different scales. For instance, if the ratio of maple saplings to oak saplings in an acre of young forest is 7:5 and that acre contains 65 oaks, the number of maples in that acre can be determined using a proportion: $\frac{7}{5} = \frac{?}{65}$

Note that to equate two ratios in this manner, the numerators must contain numbers that represent the same entity or type, and so must the denominators. In this example, the numerators represent maples and the denominators represent oaks.

$$\frac{7 \text{ maples}}{5 \text{ oaks}} = \frac{? \text{ maples}}{65 \text{ oaks}}$$

Lesson 4.6 Ratios, Proportions, and Percentages

Recall from the properties of fractions that if you multiply the numerator and denominator by the same number, the result is an equivalent fraction. Therefore, to find the unknown in this proportion, first divide the denominator on the right by the denominator on the left. Then, multiply the quotient by the numerator on the left.

$65 \div 5 = 13$

$7 \times \frac{13}{5} \times 13 = \frac{?}{65}$

The unknown (?) is $7 \times 13 = 91$. In the example, the acre of forest has 91 maple saplings.

> **DID YOU KNOW?**
> When taking the reciprocal of both sides of a proportion, the proportion still holds. When setting up a proportion, ensure that the numerators represent the same type and the denominators represent the same type.

Example

If a recipe calls for 3 parts flour to 2 parts sugar, how much sugar does a baker need if she uses 12 cups of flour?

A. 2 cups B. 3 cups C. 6 cups D. 8 cups

The correct answer is **D**. The baker needs 8 cups of sugar. First, note that "3 parts flour to 2 parts sugar" is the ratio 3:2. Set up the proportion using the given amount of flour (12 cups), putting the flour numbers in either the denominators or the numerators (either will yield the same answer): $\frac{3}{2} = \frac{12}{?}$.

Since $12 \div 3 = 4$, multiply 2×4 to get 8 cups of sugar.

Rates of Change

Numbers that describe current quantities can be informative, but how they change over time can provide even greater insight into a problem. The rate of change for some quantity is the ratio of the quantity's difference over a specific time period to the length of that period. For example, if an automobile increases its speed from 50 mph to 100 mph in 10 seconds, the rate of change of its speed (its acceleration) is

$$\frac{100 \text{ mph} - 50 \text{ mph}}{10 \text{ s}} = \frac{50 \text{ mph}}{10 \text{ s}} = 5 \text{ mph per second} = 5 \text{ mph/s}$$

The basic formula for the rate of change of some quantity is $\frac{x_f - x_i}{t_f - t_i}$ where t_f is the "final" (or ending) time and t_i is the "initial" (or starting) time. Also, x_f is the (final) quantity at (final) time t_f, and x_i is the (initial) quantity at (initial) time t_i. In this formula, the numerator is the difference between the two quantities and the denominator is the difference in time. In the example above, the final time is 10 seconds and the initial time is 0 seconds—hence the omission of the initial time from the calculation.

Consider that the final quantity occurs at the final time, and the initial quantity occurs at the initial time. As long as both quantities stay consistent in comparison, like with proportions, the order of the terms in the formula can be reversed.

$$\frac{x_f - x_i}{t_f - t_i} = \frac{x_i - x_f}{t_i - t_f}$$

This concept stays consistent with the rules of fractions, because multiplying the equation by -1 will result in the reversible formula.

The key to getting the correct rate of change is to ensure that the first number in the numerator and the first number in the denominator correspond to each other (that is, the quantity from the numerator corresponds to the time from the denominator). This must also be true for the second number.

Example

If the population of an endangered frog species fell from 2,250 individuals to 2,115 individuals in a year, what is that population's annual rate of increase?

A. −135%   B. −6%   C. 6%   D. 135%

The correct answer is **B**. The population's rate of increase was −6%. The solution in this case involves two steps. First, calculate the population's annual rate of change using the formula. It will yield the change in the number of individuals.

$$\frac{2{,}115 - 2{,}250}{1 \text{ year} - 0 \text{ year}} = -135 \text{ per year}$$

Second, divide the result by the initial population. Finally, convert to a percent.

$$\frac{-135 \text{ per year}}{2{,}250} = -0.06 \text{ per year}$$
$$(-0.06 \text{ per year}) \times 100\% = -6\% \text{ per year}$$

Since the question asks for the *annual* rate of increase, the "per year" can be dropped. Also, note that the answer must be negative to represent the decreasing population.

Let's Review!

- A percent—meaning "per hundred"—represents a relative quantity as a fraction or decimal. It is the absolute number multiplied by 100 and followed by the % symbol.
- A ratio is a relationship between two numbers expressed using fraction or colon notation (for example, $\frac{3}{2}$ or 3:2). Ratios behave mathematically just like fractions.
- An equation of two ratios is called a proportion. Proportions are used to solve problems involving scale
- Rates of change are the speeds at which quantities increase or decrease. The formula $\frac{x_f - x_i}{t_f - t_i}$ provides the rate of change of quantity x over the period between some initial (i) time and final (f) time.

Chapter 4 Numbers and Basic Operations Practice Quiz

1. Which mathematical statement is true?
   - A. 6 > 9
   - B. −3 > 2
   - C. 18 < −35
   - D. 20 > −21

2. Evaluate the expression 275 − 198.
   - A. −77
   - B. 77
   - C. 198
   - D. 473

3. Evaluate the expression 8 × 15.
   - A. 85
   - B. 105
   - C. 115
   - D. 120

4. Which statement about positive and negative numbers is true?
   - A. The product of two negative numbers is negative.
   - B. The product of two negative numbers is positive.
   - C. The product of two negative numbers is zero.
   - D. None of the above.

5. Which fraction is the least?
   - A. $\frac{5}{6}$
   - B. $\frac{3}{4}$
   - C. $\frac{17}{24}$
   - D. $\frac{2}{3}$

6. Which fraction is the greatest?
   - A. $\frac{3}{10}$
   - B. $\frac{2}{5}$
   - C. $\frac{1}{2}$
   - D. $\frac{1}{4}$

7. Subtract $1\frac{7}{9} - \frac{3}{4}$.
   - A. $1\frac{1}{36}$
   - B. $1\frac{4}{5}$
   - C. $\frac{3}{4}$
   - D. $\frac{11}{15}$

8. Subtract $2\frac{2}{3} - \frac{1}{6}$.
   - A. $2\frac{1}{3}$
   - B. $1\frac{2}{3}$
   - C. $2\frac{1}{2}$
   - D. $1\frac{1}{3}$

9. Multiply $\frac{6}{7} \times \frac{7}{10}$.
   - A. $\frac{1}{17}$
   - B. $\frac{1}{3}$
   - C. $\frac{3}{5}$
   - D. $\frac{13}{17}$

10. Divide $\frac{1}{3} \div \frac{1}{4}$.
    - A. $1\frac{1}{5}$
    - B. $1\frac{1}{4}$
    - C. $1\frac{1}{3}$
    - D. $1\frac{1}{2}$

11. Which expression is different from the others?
    - A. 2:5
    - B. $\frac{2}{5}$
    - C. 40%
    - D. 0.04

12. Which percent is closest to the ratio 7:3?
    - A. 23%
    - B. 43%
    - C. 73%
    - D. 233%

Chapter 4 Numbers and Basic Operations Practice Quiz – Answer Key

1. D. The correct solution is $20 > -21$. When in doubt, draw a number line and place the numbers on it, recalling that greater numbers are farther right than lesser numbers. Here, note that because a positive number is always greater than a negative number, $20 > -21$. **See Lesson: Basic Addition and Subtraction.**

2. B. The correct solution is 77. Use the subtraction algorithm. The process will involve borrowing from the tens place and then from the hundreds place. Alternatively, use a carefully drawn number line to estimate an answer or to check your results. **See Lesson: Basic Addition and Subtraction.**

3. D. Use the multiplication algorithm. It involves adding 40 and 80 to get the product of 120. **See Lesson: Basic Multiplication and Division.**

4. B. One of the two basic rules for multiplying signed numbers is that if the numbers have the same sign, their product is positive. **See Lesson: Basic Multiplication and Division.**

5. D. The correct solution is $\frac{2}{3}$ because $\frac{2}{3}$ has the smallest numerator when comparing to the other fractions with the same denominator. The fractions with a common denominator of 24 are $\frac{5}{6} = \frac{20}{24}, \frac{3}{4} = \frac{18}{24}, \frac{17}{24}, \frac{2}{3} = \frac{16}{24}$. **See Lesson: Decimals and Fractions.**

6. C. The correct solution is $\frac{1}{2}$ because $\frac{1}{2}$ has the largest numerator when comparing to the other fractions with the same denominator. The fractions with a common denominator of 20 are $\frac{3}{10} = \frac{6}{20}, \frac{2}{5} = \frac{8}{20}, \frac{1}{2} = \frac{10}{20}, \frac{1}{4} = \frac{5}{20}$. **See Lesson: Decimals and Fractions.**

7. A. The correct solution is $1\frac{1}{36}$ because $1\frac{7}{9} - \frac{3}{4} = \frac{16}{9} - \frac{3}{4} = \frac{64}{36} - \frac{27}{36} = \frac{37}{36} = 1\frac{1}{36}$. **See Lesson: Addition and Subtraction of Fractions.**

8. C. The correct solution is $2\frac{1}{2}$ because $2\frac{2}{3} - \frac{1}{6} = \frac{8}{3} - \frac{1}{6} = \frac{16}{6} - \frac{1}{6} = \frac{15}{6} = 2\frac{3}{6} = 2\frac{1}{2}$. **See Lesson: Addition and Subtraction of Fractions.**

9. C. The correct solution is $\frac{3}{5}$ because $\frac{6}{7} \times \frac{7}{10} = \frac{42}{70} = \frac{3}{5}$. **See Lesson: Multiplication and Division of Fractions.**

10. C. The correct solution is $1\frac{1}{3}$ because $\frac{1}{3} \times \frac{4}{1} = \frac{4}{3} = 1\frac{1}{3}$. **See Lesson: Multiplication and Division of Fractions.**

11. D. The expression 0.04 is different from the others. The expression in answer A is a fraction, and it is equal to the ratio in answer B. Dividing 2 by 5 yields 0.4, which is equal to 40%. The option left is 0.04, which is different from the others. **See Lesson: Ratios, Proportions, and Percentages.**

12. D. To convert a ratio to a percent, divide the numbers in the ratio (noting that its equivalent fraction is $\frac{7}{3}$) to get approximately 2.33. Then, multiply by 100%. **See Lesson: Ratios, Proportions, and Percentages.**

CHAPTER 5 ALGEBRA

LESSON 5.1 EQUATIONS WITH ONE VARIABLE

This lesson introduces how to solve linear equations and linear inequalities.

One-Step Linear Equations

A **linear equation** is an equation where two expressions are set equal to each other. The equation is in the form $ax + b = c$, where a is a non-zero constant and b and c are constants. The exponent on a linear equation is always 1, and there is no more than one solution to a linear equation.

There are four properties to help solve a linear equation.

Property	Definition	Example with Numbers	Example with Variables
Addition Property of Equality	Add the same number to both sides of the equation.	$x - 3 = 9$ $x - 3 + 3 = 9 + 3$ $x = 12$	$x - a = b$ $x - a + a = b + a$ $x = a + b$
Subtraction Property of Equality	Subtract the same number from both sides of the equation.	$x + 3 = 9$ $x + 3 - 3 = 9 - 3$ $x = 6$	$x + a = b$ $x + a - a = b - a$ $x = b - a$
Multiplication Property of Equality	Multiply both sides of the equation by the same number.	$\frac{x}{3} = 9$ $\frac{x}{3} \times 3 = 9 \times 3$ $x = 27$	$\frac{x}{a} = b$ $\frac{x}{a} \times a = b \times a$ $x = ab$
Division Property of Equality	Divide both sides of the equation by the same number.	$3x = 9$ $\frac{3x}{3} = \frac{9}{3}$ $x = 3$	$ax = b$ $\frac{ax}{a} = \frac{b}{a}$ $x = \frac{b}{a}$

Example

Solve the equation for the unknown, $\frac{w}{2} = -6$.

A. −12 B. −8 C. −4 D. −3

The correct answer is **A**. The correct solution is −12 because both sides of the equation are multiplied by 2.

Two-Step Linear Equations

A two-step linear equation is in the form $ax + b = c$, where a is a non-zero constant and b and c are constants. There are two basic steps in solving this equation.

STEP BY STEP

Step 1. Use addition and subtraction properties of an equation to move the variable to one side of the equation and all number terms to the other side of the equation.

Step 2. Use multiplication and division properties of an equation to remove the value in front of the variable.

EXAMPLES

1. Solve the equation for the unknown, $\frac{x}{-2} - 3 = 5$.

   A. −16   B. −8   C. 8   D. 16

   The correct answer is **A**. The correct solution is −16.

   $\frac{x}{-2} = 8$ Add 3 to both sides of the equation.
   $x = -16$ Multiply both sides of the equation by −2.

2. Solve the equation for the unknown, $4x + 3 = 8$.

   A. −2   B. $-\frac{5}{4}$ C. $\frac{5}{4}$ D. 2

   The correct answer is **C**. The correct solution is $\frac{5}{4}$.

   $4x = 5$ Subtract 3 from both sides of the equation.
   $x = \frac{5}{4}$ Divide both sides of the equation by 4.

3. Solve the equation for the unknown w, $P = 2l + 2w$.

   A. $2P - 2l = w$ B. $\frac{P - 2l}{2} = w$ C. $2P + 2l = w$ D. $\frac{P + 2l}{2} = w$

   The correct answer is **B**. The correct solution is $\frac{P - 2l}{2} = w$.

   $P - 2l = 2w$ Subtract $2l$ from both sides of the equation.
   $\frac{P - 2l}{2} = w$ Divide both sides of the equation by 2.

Multi-Step Linear Equations

In these basic examples of linear equations, the solution may be evident, but these properties demonstrate how to use an opposite operation to solve for a variable. Using these properties, there are three steps in solving a complex linear equation.

STEP BY STEP

Step 1. Simplify each side of the equation. This includes removing parentheses, removing fractions, and adding like terms.

Step 2. Use addition and subtraction properties of an equation to move the variable to one side of the equation and all number terms to the other side of the equation.

Step 3. Use multiplication and division properties of an equation to remove the value in front of the variable.

Lesson 5.1 Equations with One Variable

In Step 2, all of the variables may be placed on the left side or the right side of the equation. The examples in this lesson will place all of the variables on the left side of the equation.

When solving for a variable, apply the same steps as above. In this case, the equation is not being solved for a value, but for a specific variable.

Examples

1. Solve the equation for the unknown, $2(4x + 1) - 5 = 3 - (4x - 3)$.

    A. $\frac{1}{4}$ B. $\frac{3}{4}$ C. $\frac{4}{3}$ D. 4

    The correct answer is **B**. The correct solution is $\frac{3}{4}$.

$8x + 2 - 5 = 3 - 4x + 3$	Apply the distributive property.
$8x - 3 = -4x + 6$	Combine like terms on both sides of the equation.
$12x - 3 = 6$	Add $4x$ to both sides of the equation.
$12x = 9$	Add 3 to both sides of the equation.
$x = \frac{3}{4}$	Divide both sides of the equation by 12.

2. Solve the equation for the unknown, $\frac{2}{3}x + 2 = -\frac{1}{2}x + 2(x + 1)$.

    A. 0 B. 1 C. 2 D. 3

    The correct answer is **A**. The correct solution is 0.

$\frac{2}{3}x + 2 = -\frac{1}{2}x + 2x + 2$	Apply the distributive property.
$4x + 12 = -3x + 12x + 12$	Multiply all terms by the least common denominator of 6 to eliminate the fractions.
$4x + 12 = 9x + 12$	Combine like terms on the right side of the equation.
$-5x = 12$	Subtract $9x$ from both sides of the equation.
$-5x = 0$	Subtract 12 from both sides of the equation.
$x = 0$	Divide both sides of the equation by -5.

3. Solve the equation for the unknown for x, $y - y_1 = m(x - x_1)$.

    A. $y - y_1 + mx_1$ B. $my - my_1 + mx_1$ C. $\frac{y - y_1 + x_1}{m}$ D. $\frac{y - y_1 + mx_1}{m}$

    The correct answer is **D**. The correct solution is $\frac{y - y_1 + mx_1}{m}$.

$y - y_1 = mx - mx_1$	Apply the distributive property.
$y - y_1 + mx_1 = mx$	Add mx_1 to both sides of the equation.
$\frac{y - y_1 + mx_1}{m} = x$	Divide both sides of the equation by m.

Solving Linear Inequalities

A **linear inequality** is similar to a linear equation, but it contains an inequality sign ($<, >, \leq, \geq$). Many of the steps for solving linear inequalities are the same as for solving linear equations.

The major difference is that the solution is an infinite number of values. There are four properties to help solve a linear inequality.

Property	Definition	Example
Addition Property of Inequality	Add the same number to both sides of the inequality.	$x - 3 < 9$ $x - 3 + 3 < 9 + 3$ $x < 12$
Subtraction Property of Inequality	Subtract the same number from both sides of the inequality.	$x + 3 > 9$ $x + 3 - 3 > 9 - 3$ $x > 6$
Multiplication Property of Inequality (when multiplying by a positive number)	Multiply both sides of the inequality by the same number.	$\frac{x}{3} \geq 9$ $\frac{x}{3} \times 3 \geq 9 \times 3$ $x \geq 27$
Division Property of Inequality (when multiplying by a positive number)	Divide both sides of the inequality by the same number.	$3x \leq 9$ $\frac{3x}{3} \leq \frac{9}{3}$ $x \leq 3$
Multiplication Property of Inequality (when multiplying by a negative number)	Multiply both sides of the inequality by the same number.	$\frac{x}{-3} \geq 9$ $\frac{x}{-3} \times -3 \geq 9 \times -3$ $x \leq -27$
Division Property of Inequality (when multiplying by a negative number)	Divide both sides of the inequality by the same number.	$-3x \leq 9$ $\frac{-3x}{-3} \leq \frac{9}{-3}$ $x \geq -3$

Multiplying or dividing both sides of the inequality by a negative number reverses the sign of the inequality.

In these basic examples, the solution may be evident, but these properties demonstrate how to use an opposite operation to solve for a variable. Using these properties, there are three steps in solving a complex linear inequality.

Lesson 5.1 Equations with One Variable

STEP BY STEP

Step 1. Simplify each side of the inequality. This includes removing parentheses, removing fractions, and adding like terms.

Step 2. Use addition and subtraction properties of an inequality to move the variable to one side of the equation and all number terms to the other side of the equation.

Step 3. Use multiplication and division properties of an inequality to remove the value in front of the variable. Reverse the inequality sign if multiplying or dividing by a negative number.

In Step 2, all of the variables may be placed on the left side or the right side of the inequality. The examples in this lesson will place all of the variables on the left side of the inequality.

Examples

1. **Solve the inequality for the unknown, $3(2 + x) < 2(3x - 1)$.**

    A. $x < -\frac{8}{3}$ B. $x > -\frac{8}{3}$ C. $x < \frac{8}{3}$ D. $x > \frac{8}{3}$

    The correct answer is **D**. The correct solution is $x > \frac{8}{3}$.

$6 + 3x < 6x - 2$	Apply the distributive property.
$6 - 3x < -2$	Subtract $6x$ from both sides of the inequality.
$-3x < -8$	Subtract 6 from both sides of the inequality.
$x > \frac{8}{3}$	Divide both sides of the inequality by -3.

2. **Solve the inequality for the unknown, $\frac{1}{2}(2x - 3) \geq \frac{1}{4}(2x + 1) - 2$.**

    A. $x > -7$ B. $x > -3$ C. $x \geq -\frac{3}{2}$ D. $x \geq -\frac{1}{2}$

    The correct answer is **D**. The correct solution is $x \geq -\frac{1}{2}$.

$2(2x - 3) \geq 2x + 1 - 8$	Multiply all terms by the least common denominator of 4 to eliminate the fractions.
$4x - 6 \geq 2x + 1 - 8$	Apply the distributive property.
$4x - 6 \geq 2x - 7$	Combine like terms on the right side of the inequality.
$2x - 6 \geq -7$	Subtract $2x$ from both sides of the inequality.
$2x \geq -1$	Add 6 to both sides of the inequality.
$x \geq -\frac{1}{2}$	Divide both sides of the inequality by 2.

Let's Review!

- A linear equation is an equation with one solution. Using opposite operations solves a linear equation.
- The process to solve a linear equation or inequality is to eliminate fractions and parentheses and combine like terms on the same side of the sign. Then, solve the equation or inequality by using inverse operations.

LESSON 5.2 SOLVING REAL-WORLD MATHEMATICAL PROBLEMS

This lesson introduces solving real-world mathematical problems by using estimation and mental computation. This lesson also includes real-world applications involving integers, fractions, and decimals.

Estimating

Estimations are rough calculations of a solution to a problem. The most common use for estimation is completing calculations without a calculator or other tool. There are many estimation techniques, but this lesson focuses on integers, decimals, and fractions.

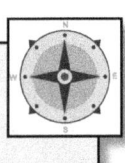

KEEP IN MIND

An estimation is an educated guess at the solution to a problem.

To round a whole number, round the value to the nearest ten or hundred. The number 142 rounds to 140 for the nearest ten and to 100 for the nearest hundred. The context of the problem determines the place value to which to round.

In most problems with fractions and decimals, the context of the problem requires rounding to the nearest whole number. Rounding these values makes calculation easier and provides an accurate estimation to the solution of the problem.

Other estimation strategies include the following:

- Using friendly or compatible numbers
- Using numbers that are easy to compute
- Adjusting numbers after rounding

Example

There are 168 hours in a week. Carson does the following:

- Sleeps 7.5 hours each day of the week
- Goes to school 6.75 hours five days a week
- Practices martial arts and basketball 1.5 hours each three times a week
- Reads and studies 1.75 hours every day
- Eats 1.5 hours every day

Estimate the remaining number of hours.

A. 20   B. 30   C. 40   D. 50

The correct answer is **C**. The correct solution is 40. He sleeps about 56 hours, goes to school for 35 hours, practices for 12 hours, read and studies for about 14 hours, and eats about 14 hours. This is 131 hours. Therefore, Carson has about 40 hours remaining.

Lesson 5.2   Solving Real-World Mathematical Problems

Real-World Integer Problems

The following five steps can make solving word problems easier:

1. Read the problem for understanding.
2. Visualize the problem by drawing a picture or diagram.
3. Make a plan by writing an expression to represent the problem.
4. Solve the problem by applying mathematical techniques.
5. Check the answer to make sure it answers the question asked.

BE CAREFUL!
Make sure that you read the problem fully before visualizing and making a plan.

In basic problems, the solution may be evident, but make sure to demonstrate knowledge of writing the expression. In multi-step problems, first make a plan with the correct expression. Then, apply the correct calculation.

Examples

1. The temperature on Monday was –9°F, and on Tuesday it was 8°F. What is the difference in temperature, in °F?

    A. –17°   B. –1°   C. 1°   D. 17°

    The correct answer is **D**. The correct solution is 17° because 8–(–9) = 17°F.

2. A golfer's last 12 rounds were –2, +4, –3, –1, +5, +3, –4, –5, –2, –6, –1, and 0. What is the average of these rounds?

    A. –12   B. –1   C. 1   D. 12

    The correct answer is **B**. The correct solution is –1. The total of the scores is –12. The average is –12 divided by 12, which is –1.

Real-World Fraction and Decimal Problems

The five steps in the previous section are applicable to solving real-world fraction and decimal problems. The expressions with one step require only one calculation: addition, subtraction, multiplication, or division. The problems with multiple steps require writing out the expressions and performing the correct calculations.

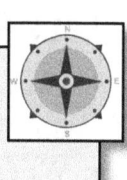

KEEP IN MIND
Estimating the solution first can help determine if a calculation is completed correctly.

83

Examples

1. The length of a room is $7\frac{2}{3}$ feet. When the length of the room is doubled, what is the new length in feet?

   A. $14\frac{2}{3}$ B. $15\frac{1}{3}$ C. $15\frac{2}{3}$ D. $16\frac{1}{3}$

   The correct answer is **B**. The correct solution is $15\frac{1}{3}$. The length is multiplied by 2, $7\frac{2}{3} \times 2 = \frac{23}{3} \times \frac{2}{1} = \frac{46}{3} = 15\frac{1}{3}$ feet.

2. A fruit salad is a mixture of $1\frac{3}{4}$ pounds of apples, $2\frac{1}{4}$ pounds of grapes, and $1\frac{1}{4}$ pounds of bananas. After the fruit is mixed, $1\frac{1}{2}$ pounds are set aside, and the rest is divided into three containers. What is the weight in pounds of one container?

   A. $1\frac{1}{5}$ B. $1\frac{1}{4}$ C. $1\frac{1}{3}$ D. $1\frac{1}{2}$

   The correct answer is **B**. The correct solution is $1\frac{1}{4}$. The amount available for the containers is $1\frac{3}{4} + 2\frac{1}{4} + 1\frac{1}{4} - 1\frac{1}{2} = 5\frac{1}{4} - 1\frac{1}{2} = 5\frac{1}{4} - 1\frac{2}{4} = 4\frac{5}{4} - 1\frac{2}{4} = 3\frac{3}{4}$. This amount is divided into three containers, $3\frac{3}{4} \div 3 = \frac{15}{4} \times \frac{1}{3} = \frac{15}{12} = 1\frac{3}{12} = 1\frac{1}{4}$ pounds.

3. In 2016, a town had 17.4 inches of snowfall. In 2017, it had 45.2 inches of snowfall. What is the difference in inches?

   A. 27.2 B. 27.8 C. 28.2 D. 28.8

   The correct answer is **B**. The correct solution is 27.8 because 45.2–17.4 = 27.8 inches.

4. Mike bought items that cost $4.78, $3.49, $6.79, $9.78, and $14.05. He had a coupon worth $5.00. If he paid with a $50.00 bill, then how much change does he receive?

   A. $16.11 B. $18.11 C. $21.11 D. $23.11

   The correct answer is **A**. The correct solution is $16.11. The total bill is $38.89, less the coupon is $33.89. The amount of change is $50.00 – $33.89 = $16.11.

Let's Review!

- Using estimation is beneficial to determine an approximate solution to the problem when the numbers are complex.
- When solving a word problem with integers, fractions, or decimals, first read and visualize the problem. Then, make a plan, solve, and check the answer.

LESSON 5.3 POWERS & EXPONENTS, ROOTS & RADICALS, WITH POLYNOMIALS

This lesson examines exponents and how they relate to square roots and cube roots. It also discusses powers of 10 and polynomials.

Powers

We have explained in previous lessons that exponents imply an expression of repeated multiplication, otherwise known as a power. There are many rules associated with exponents. Recall that any number to a power of 0 will equal 1, or $n^0 = 1$. Additionally, the negative exponent rule reveals that numbers with a negative power are equal to a fraction.

Powers can express repeated multiplication, and radicals operate to undo that multiplication. The **square** of a number is the number raised to the power of 2. The **square root** of a number, when the number is squared, gives that number. $10^2 = 100$, so the square of 100 is 10, or $\sqrt{100} = 10$. **Perfect squares** are numbers with whole number square roots, such as 1, 4, 9, 16, and 25.

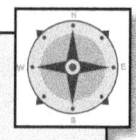

KEEP IN MIND

Most square roots and cube roots are not perfect roots.

Squaring a number and taking a square root are opposite operations, meaning that the operations undo each other. This means that $\sqrt{x^2} = x$ and $(\sqrt{x})^2 = x$. When solving the equation $x^2 = p$, the solutions are $x = \pm\sqrt{p}$ because a negative value squared is a positive solution.

The **cube** of a number is the number raised to the power of 3. The **cube root** of a number, when the number is cubed, gives that number. $10^3 = 1000$, so the cube of 1,000 is 100, or $\sqrt[3]{1000} = 10$. **Perfect cubes** are numbers with whole number cube roots, such as 1, 8, 27, 64, and 125.

Cubing a number and taking a cube root are opposite operations, meaning that the operations undo each other. This means that $\sqrt[3]{x^3} = x$ and $(\sqrt[3]{x})^3 = x$. When solving the equation $x^3 = p$, the solution is $x = \sqrt[3]{p}$.

If a number is not a perfect square root or cube root, the solution is an approximation. When this occurs, the solution is an irrational number. For example, $\sqrt{2}$ is the irrational solution to $x^2 = 2$.

ATI TEAS: Full Study Guide, Test Strategies and Secrets

Below is a table of commonly known perfect squares and cubes.

$1^2 = 1$	$\sqrt{1} = 1$	$7^2 = 49$	$\sqrt{49} = 7$	$1^3 = 1$	$\sqrt[3]{1} = 1$	$7^3 = 343$	$\sqrt[3]{343} = 7$
$2^2 = 4$	$\sqrt{4} = 2$	$8^2 = 64$	$\sqrt{64} = 8$	$2^3 = 8$	$\sqrt[3]{8} = 2$	$8^3 = 512$	$\sqrt[3]{512} = 8$
$3^2 = 9$	$\sqrt{9} = 3$	$9^2 = 81$	$\sqrt{81} = 9$	$3^3 = 27$	$\sqrt[3]{27} = 3$	$9^3 = 729$	$\sqrt[3]{729} = 9$
$4^2 = 16$	$\sqrt{16} = 4$	$10^2 = 100$	$\sqrt{100} = 10$	$4^3 = 64$	$\sqrt[3]{64} = 4$	$10^3 = 1000$	$\sqrt[3]{1000} = 10$
$5^2 = 25$	$\sqrt{25} = 5$	$11^2 = 121$	$\sqrt{121} = 11$	$5^3 = 125$	$\sqrt[3]{125} = 5$		
$6^2 = 36$	$\sqrt{36} = 6$	$12^2 = 144$	$\sqrt{144} = 12$	$6^3 = 216$	$\sqrt[3]{216} = 6$		

Examples

1. **Solve $x^2 = 121$.**

   A. –10, 10 B. –11, 11 C. –12, 12 D. –13, 13

   The correct answer is **B**. The correct solution is –11, 11 because the square root of 121 is 11. The values of –11 and 11 make the equation true.

2. **Solve $x^3 = 125$.**

   A. 1 B. 5 C. 10 D. 25

   The correct answer is **B**. The correct solution is 5 because the cube root of 125 is 5.

Understanding Exponents

Negative exponents are commonly used to represent small decimal numbers, but positive exponents can also be used to represent larger values. **Scientific notation** is a large or small number written in two parts. The first part is a number between 1 and 10. In these problems, the first digit will be a single digit. The number is followed by a multiple to a power of 10. A positive integer exponent means the number is greater than 1, while a negative integer exponent means the number is smaller than 1.

The number 3×10^4 is the same as $3 \times 10,000 = 30,000$.

The number 3×10^{-4} is the same as $3 \times 0.0001 = 0.0003$.

KEEP IN MIND

A positive exponent in scientific notation represents a large number, while a negative exponent represents a small number.

For example, the population of the United States is about 3×10^8, and the population of the world is about 7×10^9. The population of the United States is 300,000,000, and the population of the world is 7,000,000,000. The world population is about 20 times larger than the population of the United States.

Polynomials

A **polynomial** is an expression that contains exponents, as well as variables, constants, and operations. The exponents of the variables are only whole numbers, and there is no division by a variable. The operations are addition, subtraction, multiplication, and division. Constants are terms without a variable. A polynomial of one term is a **monomial**; a polynomial of two terms is a **binomial**; and a polynomial of three terms is a **trinomial**.

To add polynomials, combine like terms and write the solution from the term with the highest exponent to the term with the lowest exponent. To simplify, first rearrange and group like terms. Next, combine like terms.

$(3x^2 + 5x - 6) + (4x^3 - 3x + 4)$
$= 4x^3 + 3x^2 + (5x - 3x) + (-6 + 4)$
$= 4x^3 + 3x^2 + 2x - 2$

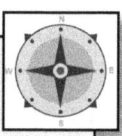

KEEP IN MIND

The solution is an expression, and a value is not calculated for the variable.

To subtract polynomials, rewrite the second polynomial using an additive inverse. Change the minus sign to a plus sign, and change the sign of every term inside the parentheses. Then, add the polynomials.

$(3x^2 + 5x - 6) - (4x^3 - 3x + 4)$
$= (3x^2 + 5x - 6) + (-4x^3 + 3x - 4)$
$= -4x^3 + 3x^2 + (5x + 3x) + (-6 - 4)$
$= -4x^3 + 3x^2 + 8x - 10$

Examples

1. **Perform the operation, $(2y^2 - 5y + 1) + (-3y^2 + 6y + 2)$.**

   A. $y^2 + y + 3$ B. $-y^2 - y + 3$ C. $y^2 - y + 3$ D. $-y^2 + y + 3$

   The correct answer is **D**. The correct solution is $-y^2 + y + 3$.

   $(2y^2 - 5y + 1) + (-3y^2 + 6y + 2)$
   $= (2y^2 - 3y^2) + (-5y + 6y) + (1 + 2)$
   $= -y^2 + y + 3$

2. **Perform the operation, $(3x^2y + 4xy - 5xy^2) - (x^2y - 3xy - 2xy^2)$.**

   A. $2x^2y - 7xy + 3xy^2$ B. $2x^2y + 7xy + 3xy^2$ C. $2x^2y + 7xy - 3xy^2$ D. $2x^2y - 7xy - 3xy^2$

   The correct answer is **C**. The correct solution is $2x^2y + 7xy - 3xy^2$.

   $(3x^2y + 4xy - 5xy^2) - (x^2y - 3xy - 2xy^2)$
   $= (3x^2y + 4xy - 5xy^2) + (-x^2y + 3xy + 2xy^2)$
   $= (3x^2y - x^2y) + (4xy + 3xy) + (-5xy^2 + 2xy^2)$
   $= 2x^2y + 7xy - 3xy^2$

There are many polynomial identities that show relationships between expressions Addition and subtraction expressions can be squared, and the square of a **binomial** expression can be written in two different forms:

- $(a + b)^2 = a^2 + 2ab + b^2$
- $(a - b)^2 = a^2 - 2ab + b^2$

A simple way for solving a binomial is to remember to **FOIL** the expression. The square implies to repeat the multiplication of the operation. To solve the expression would require multiplying the First, Outside, Inside, and then Last variables which results in the relationship of the expressions.

Familiarizing yourself with perfect squares is useful for dealing with exponents, and familiarizing yourself with the square of a binomial can similarly help in identifying binomials.

BE CAREFUL!

Pay attention to the details of each variable and operation.

Example

Apply the polynomial identity to rewrite $x^2 + 6x + 9$.

   A. $x^2 + 9$ B. $(x^2 + 3)^2$ C. $(x + 3)^2$ D. $(3x)^2$

The correct answer is **C**. The correct solution is $(x + 3)^2$. The expression $x^2 + 6x + 9$ is rewritten as $(x + 3)^2$ because the value of a is x and the value of b is 3.

Let's Review!

- Powers represent repeated multiplication and radicals are the inverse operation of exponents.
- Numbers expressed in scientific notation are useful to compare large or small numbers.
- Polynomials are expressions that include exponents, as well as variables, constants, and operations.
- Polynomials can be added, subtracted, and even squared.
- Squared polynomials are binomial expressions that can be written in different forms.

Chapter 5 Algebra Practice Quiz

1. Solve the equation for the unknown, $x - 20 = -10$.

   A. -30
   B. 10
   C. 2
   D. 200

2. Solve the inequality for the unknown, $3(4x - 1) > 5(2x + 3)$.

   A. $x > 2$
   B. $x > 9$
   C. $x > 10$
   D. $x > 18$

3. Solve for the value of y when $x = 6$.
   $y = (x^2 - 4) \div 8$

   A. 3
   B. 1
   C. 4
   D. 2

4. If $2 + x \geq 7$, then

   A. $x \leq 5$
   B. $x \geq 5$
   C. $x \leq 9$
   D. $x \geq 9$

5. Perform the operation,
   $(4y^3 + 5y^2 - 6y) + (7y^2 + 2y - 5)$.

   A. $4y^3 + 12y^2 + 4y - 5$
   B. $4y^3 + 10y^2 - 4y - 5$
   C. $4y^3 + 12y^2 - 4y - 5$
   D. $4y^3 + 10y^2 + 4y - 5$

6. Perform the operation.
   $(3y^2 + 4y) - (5y^3 - 2y^2 + 3)$

   A. $-5y^3 + y^2 + 4y - 3$
   B. $-5y^3 + 5y^2 + 4y + 3$
   C. $-5y^3 + y^2 + 4y + 3$
   D. $-5y^3 + 5y^2 + 4y - 3$

7. Solve $x^2 = 225$.

   A. $-5, 5$
   B. $-10, 10$
   C. $-15, 15$
   D. $-20, 20$

8. A historical society has 8 tours daily 5 days a week, with 32 people on each tour. Estimate the number of people who can be on the tour in 50 weeks.

   A. 25,000
   B. 50,000
   C. 75,000
   D. 100,000

9. Ron is training for a marathon. If he trains by running 57.5 miles every 5 days, then about how many miles will he run in 43 days?

   A. 120
   B. 300
   C. 480
   D. 60

Chapter 5 Algebra
Practice Quiz – Answer Key

1. **B.** The correct solution is 10 because 20 is added to both sides of the equation. **See Lesson: Equations with One Variable.**

2. **B.** The correct solution is $x > 9$.

$12x - 3 > 10x + 15$	Apply the distributive property.
$2x - 3 > 15$	Subtract $10x$ from both sides of the inequality.
$2x > 18$	Add 3 to both sides of the inequality.
$x > 9$	Divide both sides of the inequality by 2.

   See Lesson: Equations with One Variable.

3. **C.** The correct solution is 4 because $6^2 = 36 - 4 = 32 \div 8 = 4$. **See Lesson: Equations with One Variable.**

4. **B.** The correct solution is $x \geq 5$ because subtracting 2 from each side of the inequality reveals that $x \geq 5$. No sign flip is required because negative numbers are not being used in the equation. **See Lesson: Equations with One Variable.**

5. **C.** The correct solution is $4y^3 + 12y^2 - 4y - 5$.

   $(4y^3 + 5y^2 - 6y) + (7y^2 + 2y - 5) = 4y^3 + (5y^2 + 7y^2) + (-6y + 2y) - 5 = 4y^3 + 12y^2 - 4y - 5$

   See Lesson: Powers & Exponents, Roots & Radicals, with Polynomials.

6. **D.** The correct solution is $-5y^3 + 5y^2 + 4y - 3$.

   $(3y^2 + 4y) - (5y^3 - 2y^2 + 3) = (3y^2 + 4y) + (-5y^3 + 2y^2 - 3)$

   $= -5y^3 + (3y^2 + 2y^2) + 4y - 3 = -5y^3 + 5y^2 + 4y - 3$

   See Lesson: Powers & Exponents, Roots & Radicals, with Polynomials.

7. **C.** The correct solution is –15, 15 because the square root of 225 is 15. The values of –15 and 15 make the equation true. **See Lesson: Powers & Exponents, Roots & Radicals, with Polynomials.**

8. **C.** The correct solution is 75,000 because by estimation $10(5)(30)(50) = 75,000$ people can be on the tour in 50 weeks. **See Lesson: Solving Real World Mathematical Problems.**

9. **C.** The correct solution is 480 because by estimation Ron runs about $60(8) = 480$ miles. **See Lesson: Solving Real-World Mathematical Problems.**

CHAPTER 6 MEASUREMENT AND DATA

LESSON 6.1 STANDARDS OF MEASURE

This lesson discusses the conversion within and between the standard system and the metric system and between 12-hour clock time and military time.

Length Conversions

The basic units of measure of length in the standard measurement system are inches, feet, yards, and miles. There are 12 inches (in.) in 1 foot (ft.), 3 feet (ft.) in 1 yard (yd.), and 5,280 feet (ft.) in 1 mile (mi.).

The basic unit of measure of metric length is meters. There are 1,000 millimeters (mm), 100 centimeters (cm), and 10 decimeters (dm) in 1 meter (m). There are 10 meters (m) in 1 dekameter (dam), 100 meters (m) in 1 hectometer (hm), and 1,000 meters (m) in 1 kilometer (km).

BE CAREFUL!
There are some cases where multiple conversions must be performed to determine the correct units.

To convert from one unit to the other, multiply by the appropriate factor.

Examples

1. **Convert 27 inches to feet.**

    A. 2 feet
    B. 2.25 feet
    C. 3 feet
    D. 3.25 feet

    The correct answer is **B**. The correct solution is 2.25 feet. $27 \text{ in} \times \frac{1 \text{ ft}}{12 \text{ in}} = \frac{27}{12} = 2.25$ ft.

2. **Convert 67 millimeters to centimeters.**

    A. 0.0067 centimeters
    B. 0.067 centimeters
    C. 0.67 centimeters
    D. 6.7 centimeters

    The correct answer is **D**. The correct solution is 6.7 centimeters. $67 \text{ mm} \times \frac{1 \text{ cm}}{10 \text{ mm}} = \frac{67}{10} = 6.7$ cm.

Volume and Weight Conversions

There are volume conversion factors for standard and metric volumes.

The volume conversions for standard volume are shown in the table.

Measurement	Conversion
Pints (pt.) and fluid ounces (fl. oz.)	1 pint equals 16 fluid ounces
Quarts (qt.) and pints (pt.)	1 quart equals 2 pints
Quarts (qt.) and gallons (gal.)	1 gallon equals 4 quarts

ATI TEAS: Full Study Guide, Test Strategies and Secrets

The basic unit of volume for the metric system is liters. There are 1,000 milliliters (mL) in 1 liter (L) and 1,000 liters (L) in 1 kiloliter (kL).

There are weight conversion factors for standard and metric weights.

The basic unit of weight for the standard measurement system is pounds. There are

16 ounces (oz.) in 1 pound (lb.) and

2,000 pounds (lb.) in 1 ton (T).

The basic unit of weight for the metric system is grams.

KEEP IN MIND
The conversions within the metric system are multiples of 10.

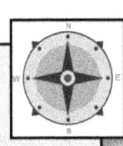

Measurement	Conversion
Milligrams (mg) and grams (g)	1,000 milligrams equals 1 gram
Centigrams (cg) and grams (g)	100 centigrams equals 1 gram
Kilograms (kg) and grams (g)	1 kilogram equals 1,000 grams
Metric tons (t) and kilograms (kg)	1 metric ton equals 1,000 kilograms

Examples

1. **Convert 8 gallons to pints.**

   A. 1 pint   B. 4 pints   C. 16 pints   D. 64 pints

   The correct answer is **D**. The correct solution is 64 pints. $8 \text{ gal} \times \frac{4 \text{ qt}}{1 \text{ gal}} \times \frac{2 \text{ pt}}{1 \text{ qt}} = 64 \text{ pt}$.

2. **Convert 7.5 liters to milliliters.**

   A. 75 mL   B. 750 mL   C. 7,500 m   D. 75,000 ml

   The correct answer is **C**. The correct solution is 7,500 milliliters. $7.5 \text{ L} \times \frac{1,000 \text{ mL}}{1 \text{ L}} = 7,500 \text{ mL}$.

3. **Convert 12.5 pounds to ounces.**

   A. 142 ounces   B. 150 ounces   C. 192 ounces   D. 200 ounces

   The correct answer is **D**. The correct solution is 200 ounces. $12.5 \text{ lb} \times \frac{16 \text{ oz}}{1 \text{ lb}} = 200 \text{ oz}$.

4. **Convert 84 grams to centigrams.**

   A. 0.84 cg   B. 8.4 cg   C. 840 cg   D. 8,400 cg

   The correct answer is **D**. The correct solution is 8,400 centigrams. $84 \text{ g} \times \frac{100 \text{ cg}}{1 \text{ g}} = 8,400 \text{ cg}$.

Lesson 6.1 Standards of Measure

Conversions between Standard and Metric Systems

The table shows the common conversions of length, volume, and weight between the standard and metric systems.

Measurement	Conversion
Centimeters (cm) and inches (in.)	2.54 centimeters equals 1 inch
Meters (m) and feet (ft.)	1 meter equals 3.28 feet
Kilometers (km) and miles (mi.)	1.61 kilometers equals 1 mile
Quarts (qt.) and liters (L)	1.06 quarts equals 1 liter
Liters (L) and gallons (gal.)	3.79 liters equals 1 gallon
Grams (g) and ounces (oz.)	28.3 grams equals 1 ounce
Kilograms (kg) and pounds (lb.)	1 kilogram equals 2.2 pounds

There are many additional conversion factors, but this lesson uses only the common ones. Most factors have been rounded to the nearest hundredth for accuracy.

STEP BY STEP

Step 1. Choose the appropriate conversion factor within each system, if necessary.

Step 2. Choose the appropriate conversion factor from the standard and metric conversion.

Step 3. Multiply and simplify to the nearest hundredth.

Examples

1. **Convert 12 inches to centimeters.**

   A. 4.72 centimeters
   B. 14.54 centimeters
   C. 28.36 centimeters
   D. 30.48 centimeters

   The correct answer is **D**. The correct solution is 30.48 centimeters. $12 \text{ in} \times \frac{2.54 \text{ cm}}{1 \text{ in}} = 30.48 \text{ cm}$.

2. **Convert 8 kilometers to feet.**

   A. 13,118.01 feet
   B. 26,236.02 feet
   C. 34,003.20 feet
   D. 68,006.40 feet

   The correct answer is **B**. The correct solution is 26,236.02 feet. $8 \text{ km} \times \frac{1 \text{ mi}}{1.61 \text{ km}} \times \frac{5,280 \text{ ft}}{1 \text{ mi}} = \frac{42,240}{1.61} = 26,236.02 \text{ ft}$.

3. **Convert 2 gallons to milliliters.**

   A. 527 milliliters
   B. 758 milliliters
   C. 5,270 milliliters
   D. 7,580 milliliters

   The correct answer is **D**. The correct solution is 7,580 milliliters. $2 \text{ gal} \times \frac{3.79 \text{ L}}{1 \text{ gal}} \times \frac{1,000 \text{ mL}}{1 \text{ L}} = 7,580 \text{ mL}$.

4. **Convert 16 kilograms to pounds.**

    A. 7.27 pounds   B. 18.2 pounds   C. 19.27 pounds   D. 35.2 pounds

    The correct answer is **D**. The correct solution is 35.2 pounds. $16 \text{ kg} \times \frac{2.2 \text{ lb}}{1 \text{ kg}} = 35.2 \text{ lb}$.

Time Conversions

Two ways to keep time are 12-hour clock time using a.m. and p.m. and military time based on a 24-hour clock. Keep these three key points in mind:

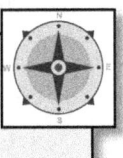

KEEP IN MIND
Midnight (12:00 a.m.) is 2400 or 0000 in military time.

- The hours from 1:00 a.m. to 12:59 p.m. are the same in both methods. For example, 9:15 a.m. in 12-hour clock time is 0915 in military time.
- From 1:00 p.m. to 11:59 p.m., add 12 hours to obtain military time. For example, 4:07 p.m. in 12-hour clock time is 1607 in military time.
- From 12:01 a.m. to 12:59 a.m. in 12-hour clock time, military time is from 0001 to 0059.

Example

Identify 9:27 p.m. in military time.

   A. 0927   B. 1927   C. 2127   D. 2427

   The correct answer is **C**. The correct solution is 2127. Add 1200 to the time, 1200 + 927 = 2127.

Temperature Conversions

Temperatures can be written using the Fahrenheit English system or the Celsius metric system. The Fahrenheit temperature scale is part of the English system which bases the freezing point of water off of 32°F and the boiling point of water as 212°F. Water freezes at 0°C and 100°C in the metric system.

While these topics are covered in further depth within the sciences, it is important to know that formulas help convert between the two systems. The following formulas are used to convert temperatures:

$°C = \frac{5}{9}(°F - 32)$	$°F = \frac{9}{5}°C + 32$

It is helpful to recall the order of operations in order to convert temperatures. Consider the following examples:

Examples

1. **Convert 100°F to Celsius.**

    A. 38°C   B. 100°C   C. 74°C   D. 122°C

    The correct solution is **A**.

$100°F = \frac{9}{5}°C + 32$	Subtract 32 from each side.
$68 = \frac{9}{5}°C$	Multiply each side of the equation by 5.
$340 = 9C$	Divide each side of the equation by 9.
$37.7°C$	100°F is equivalent to approximately 38°C.

2. **Convert 50°C to Fahrenheit.**

   A. 60°F B. 90°F C. 122°F D. 58°F

   The correct solution is **C**.

$50°C = \frac{5}{9}(°F - 32)$	Multiply each side of the equation by 9.
$450 = 5(°F - 32)$	Divide each side of the equation by 5.
$90 = °F - 32$	Add 32 to each side of the equation.
$122°F$	50°C is equivalent to 122°F.

Let's Review!

- To convert from one unit to another, choose the appropriate conversion factors.
- In many cases, it is necessary to use multiple conversion factors.

Metric	English
Volume	
1 cubic centimeter = 1 milliliter	30 milliliters = 1 ounce
1,000 milliliters = 1 liter	8 ounces = 1 cup
	2 cups = 1 pint
	2 pints = 1 quart
	4 quarts = 1 gallon
Weight	
1,000 milligrams = 1 gram	16 ounces = 1 pound
100 centigrams = 1 gram	2.2 pounds = 1 kilogram
1,000 grams = 1 kilogram	2,000 pounds = 1 ton
1,000 kilograms = 1 ton	
Distance	
10 millimeters = 1 centimeter	12 inches = 1 foot
2.54 centimeters = 1 inch	3 feet = 1 yard
100 centimeters = 1 meter	5,280 feet = 1,760 yards = 1 mile
1,000 meters = 1 kilometer	

LESSON 6.2 INTERPRETING GRAPHICS

This lesson discusses how to create a bar, line, and circle graph and how to interpret data from these graphs. It also explores how to calculate and interpret the measures of central tendency.

Creating a Line, Bar, and Circle Graph

A line graph is a graph with points connected by segments that examines changes over time. The horizontal axis contains the independent variable (the input value), which is usually time. The vertical axis contains the dependent variable (the output value), which is an item that measures a quantity. A line graph will have a title and an appropriate scale to display the data. The graph can include more than one line.

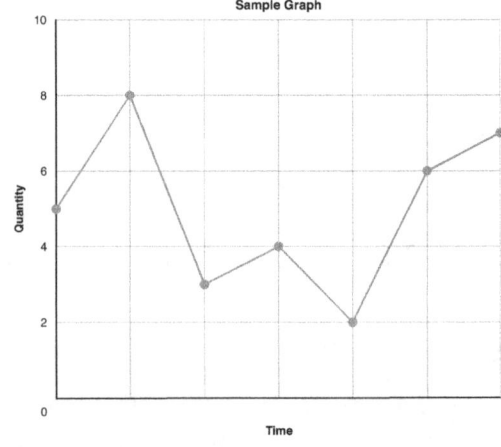

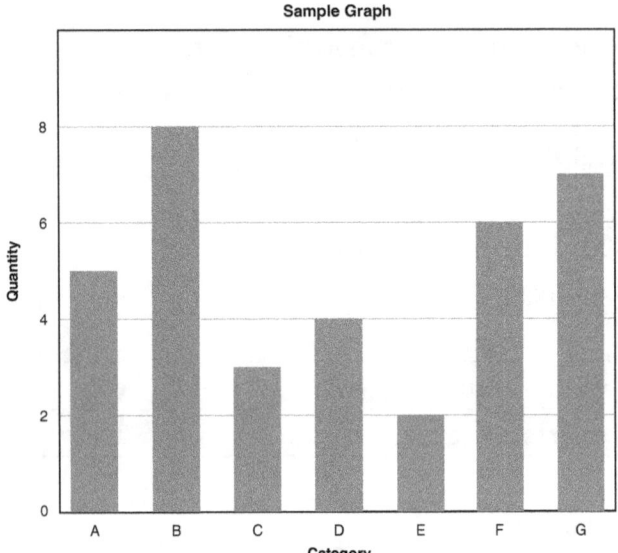

A bar graph uses rectangular horizontal or vertical bars to display information. A bar graph has categories on the horizontal axis and the quantity on the vertical axis. Bar graphs need a title and an appropriate scale for the frequency. The graph can include more than one bar.

BE CAREFUL
Make sure to use the appropriate scale for each type of graph.

Lesson 6.2 Interpreting Graphics

A circle graph is a circular chart that is divided into parts, and each part shows the relative size of the value. To create a circle graph, find the total number and divide each part by the total to find the percentage. Then, to find the part of the circle, multiply each percent by 360°. Draw each part of the circle and create a title.

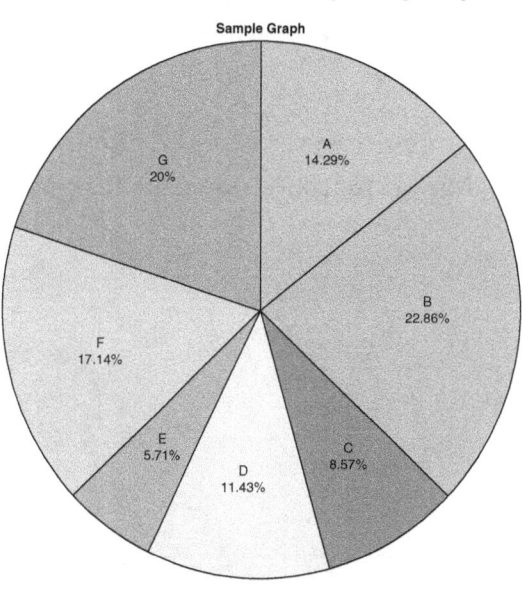

Examples

1. The table shows the amount of rainfall in inches. Select the line graph that represents this data.

Day	1	2	3	4	5	6	7	8	9	10	11	12
Rainfall Amount	0.5	0.2	0.4	1.1	1.6	0.9	0.7	1.3	1.5	0.8	0.5	0.1

A.
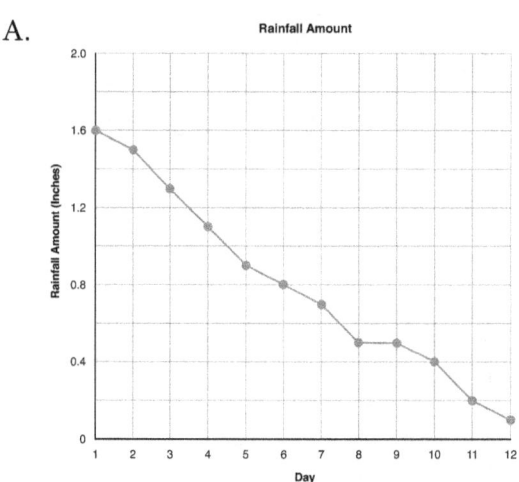

C.
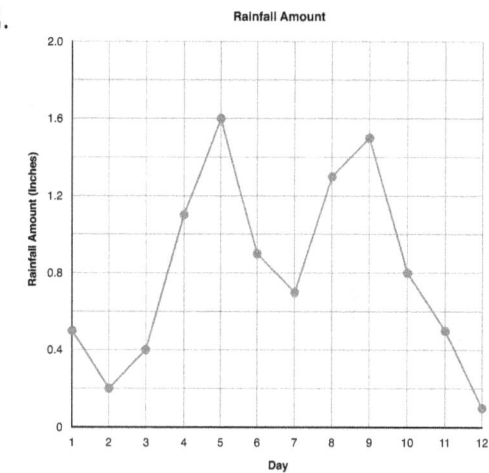

B.
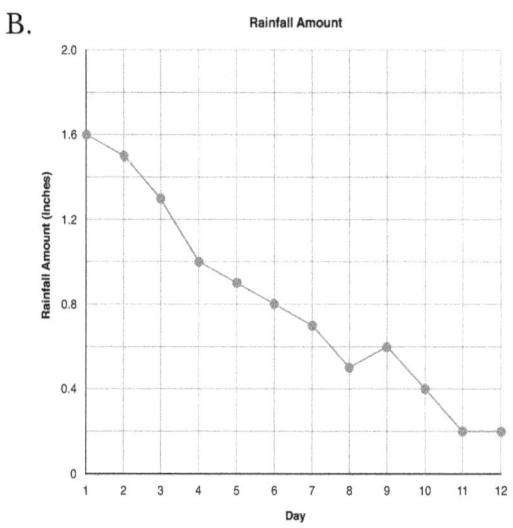

D.
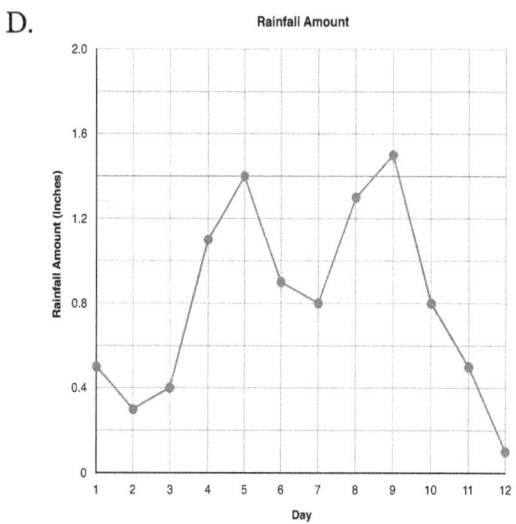

97

The correct answer is **C**. The graph is displayed correctly for the days with the appropriate labels.

2. Students were surveyed about their favorite pet, and the table shows the results. Select the bar graph that represents this data.

Pet	Quantity
Dog	14
Cat	16
Fish	4
Bird	8
Gerbil	7
Pig	3

A.
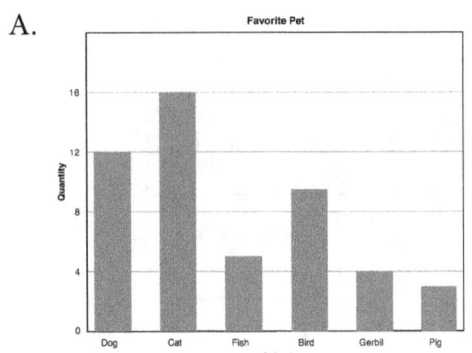

C.
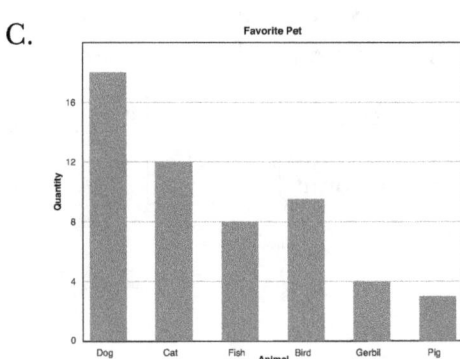

B.
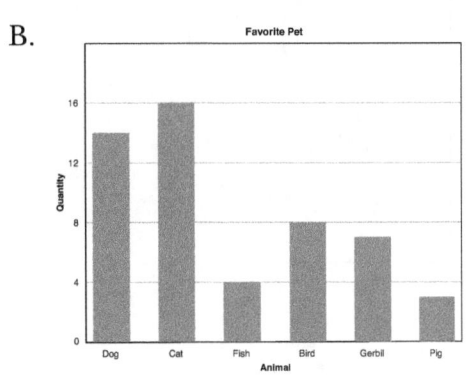

D.
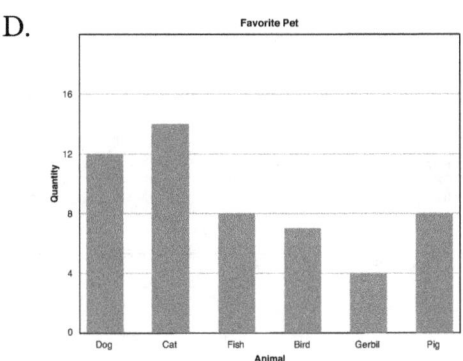

The correct answer is **B**. The bar graph represents each pet correctly and is labeled correctly.

Lesson 6.2 Interpreting Graphics

3. The table shows the amount a family spends each month. Select the circle graph that represents the data.

Item	Food/Household Items	Bills	Mortgage	Savings	Miscellaneous
Amount	$700	$600	$400	$200	$100

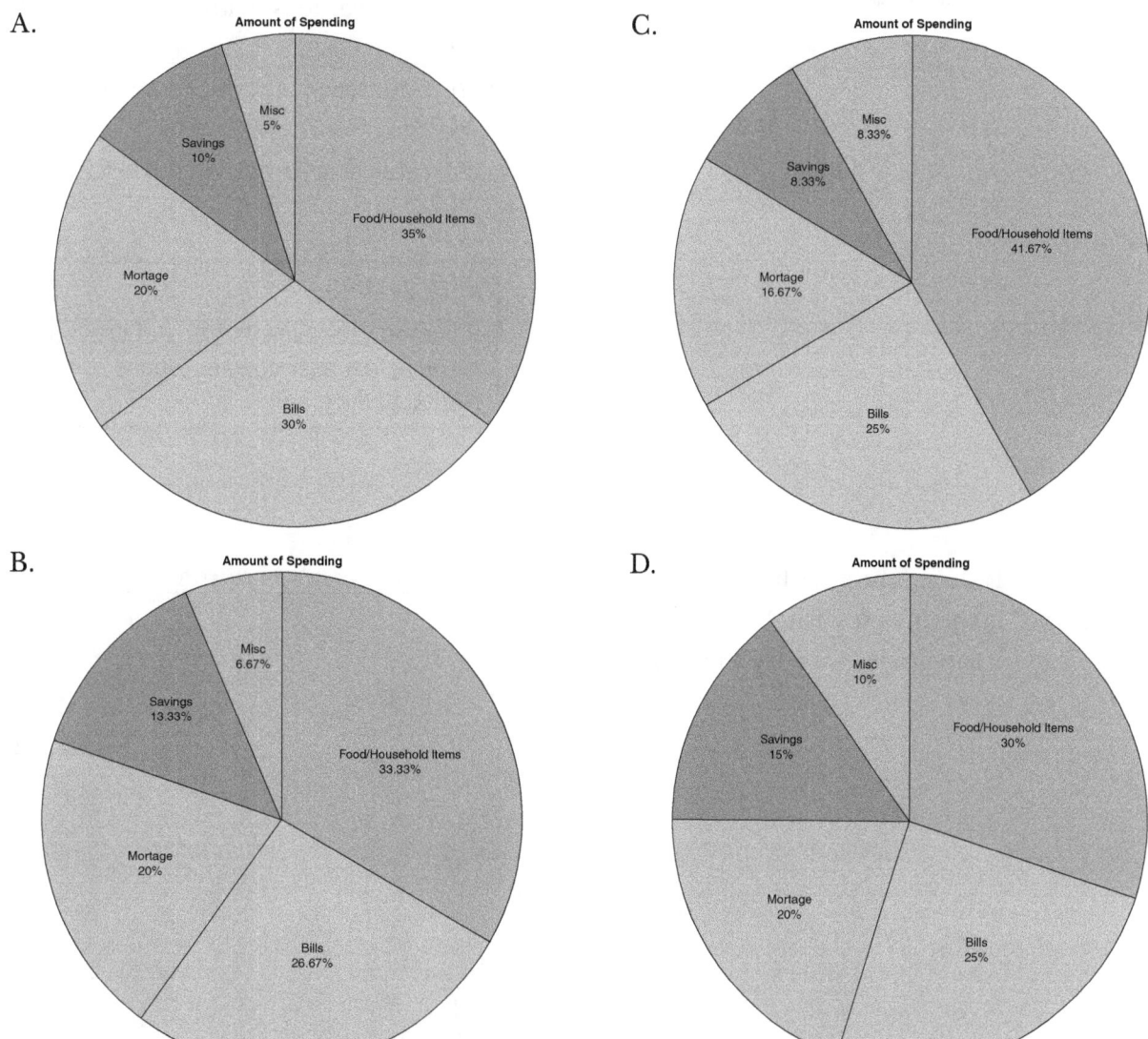

The correct answer is **A**. The total amount spent each month is $2,000. The section of the circle for food and household items is $\frac{700}{2,000} = 0.35 = 35\%$. The section of the circle for bills is $\frac{600}{2,000} = 0.30 = 30\%$. The section of the circle for mortgage is $\frac{400}{2,000} = 0.20 = 20\%$. The section of the circle for savings is $\frac{200}{2,000} = 0.10 = 10\%$. The section of the circle for miscellaneous is $\frac{100}{2,000} = 0.05 = 5\%$.

ATI TEAS: Full Study Guide, Test Strategies and Secrets

Interpreting and Evaluating Line, Bar, and Circle Graphs

Graph and charts are used to create visual examples of information, and it is important to be able to interpret them. The examples from Section 1 can show a variety of conclusions.

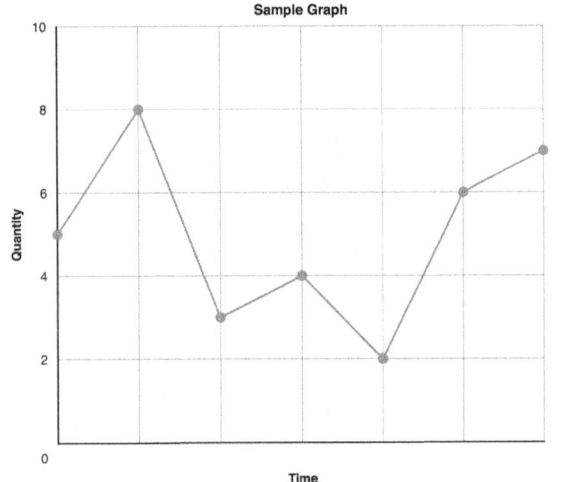

- The minimum value is 2, and the maximum value is 8.
- The largest decrease is between the second and third points.
- The largest increase is between the fifth and sixth points.

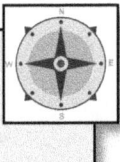

KEEP IN MIND

Read and determine the parts of the graph before answering questions related to the graph.

- Category B is the highest with 8.
- Category E is the lowest with 2.
- There are no categories that are the same.

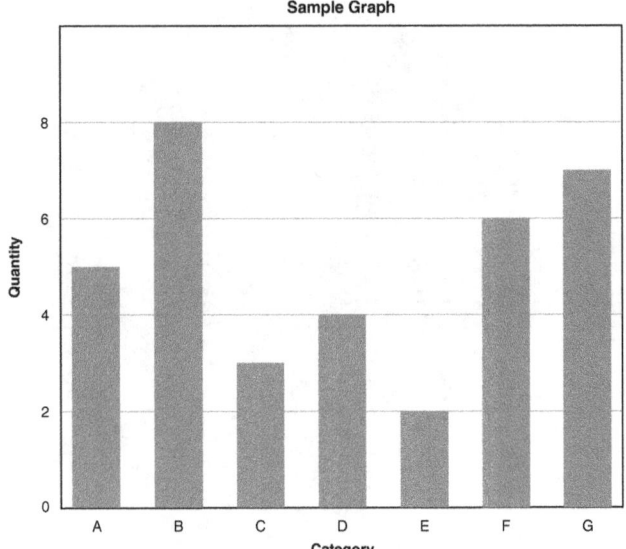

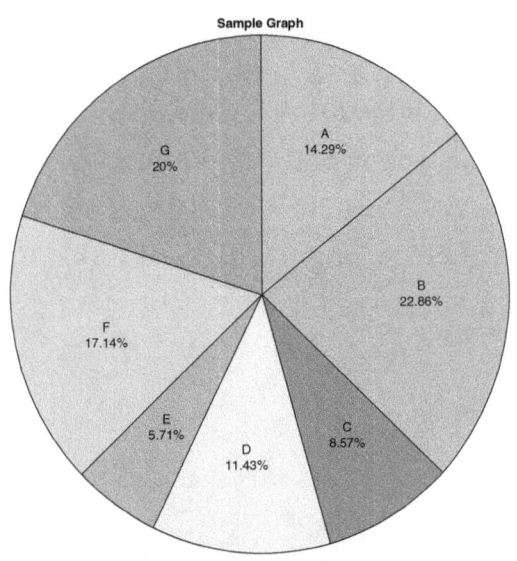

- Category B is the largest with 22.86%.
- Category E is the smallest with 5.71%.
- All of the categories are less than one-fourth of the graph.

Examples

1. The line chart shows the number of minutes a commuter drove to work during a month. Which statement is true for the line chart?

   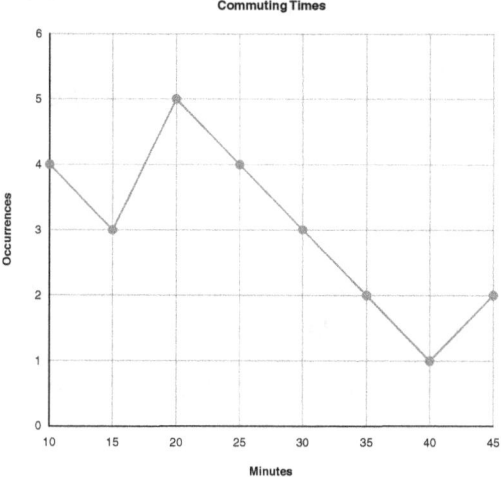

   A. The commuter drove 25 minutes to work the most times
   B. The commuter drove 25 minutes to work the fewest times.
   C. The commuter took 10 minutes and 25 minutes twice during the month.
   D. The commuter took 35 minutes and 45 minutes twice during the month.

   The correct answer is **D**. The commuter took 35 minutes and 45 minutes twice during the month.

2. The bar chart shows the distance different families traveled for summer vacation. Which statement is true for the bar chart?

   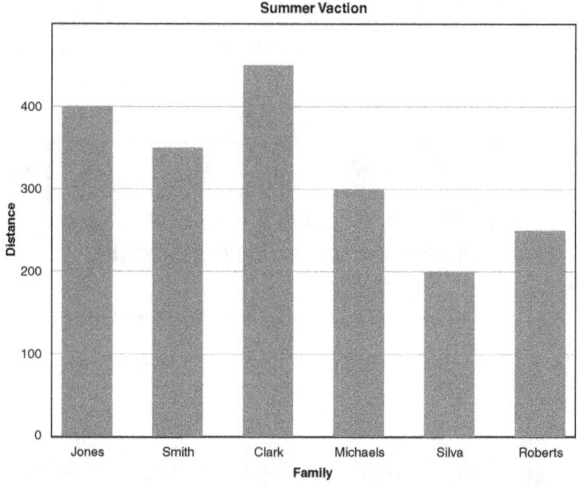

   A. All families drove more than 200 miles.
   B. The Clark family traveled 250 miles more than the Silva family.
   C. The Roberts family traveled more miles than the Michaels family.
   D. The Jones family is the only family that traveled 400 miles or more.

The correct answer is **B**. The correct solution is the Clark family traveled 250 miles more than the Silva family. The Clark family traveled 450 miles, and the Silva family traveled 200 miles, making the difference 250 miles.

3. Students were interviewed about their favorite subject in school. The circle graph shows the results. Which statement is true for the circle graph?

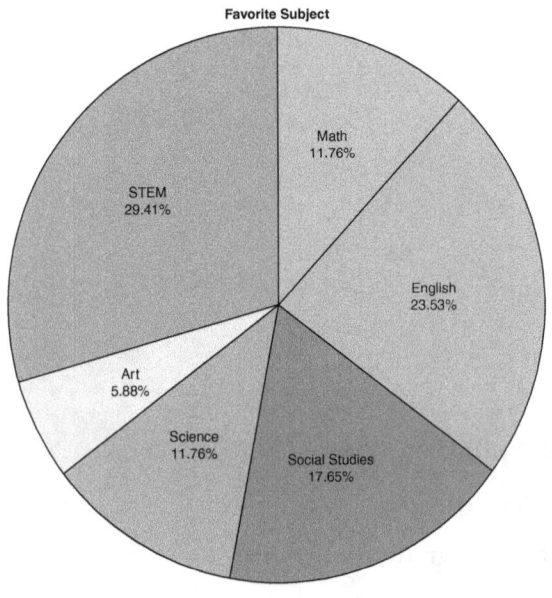

A. Math is the smallest percent for favorite subject.

B. The same number of students favor science and social studies.

C. English and STEM together are more than half of the respondents.

D. English and social students together are more than half of the respondents.

The correct answer is **C**. The correct solution is English and STEM together are more than half of the respondents because these values are more than 50% combined.

Mean, Median, Mode, and Range

The mean, median, mode, and range are common values related to data sets. These values can be calculated using the data set 2, 4, 7, 6, 8, 5, 6, and 3.

The mean is the sum of all numbers in a data set divided by the number of elements in the set. The sum of items in the data set is 41. Divide the value of 41 by the 8 items in the set. The mean is 5.125.

The median is the middle number of a data set when written in order. If there are an odd number of items, the median is the middle number. If there are an even number of items, the median is the mean of the middle two numbers. The

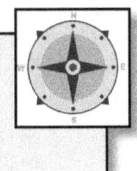

KEEP IN MIND

The mean, median, mode, and range can have the same values, depending on the data set.

numbers in order are 2, 3, 4, 5, 6, 6, 7, 8. The middle two numbers are 5 and 6. The mean of the two middle numbers is 5.5, which is the median.

The mode is the number or numbers that occur most often. There can be no modes, one mode, or many modes. In the data set, the number 6 appears twice, making 6 the mode.

The range is the difference between the highest and lowest values in a data set. The highest value is 8 and the lowest value is 2, for a range of 6.

Lesson 6.2 Interpreting Graphics

Examples

1. **Find the mean and the median for the data set 10, 20, 40, 20, 30, 50, 40, 60, 30, 10, 40, 20, 50, 70, and 80.**

   A. The mean is 40, and the median is 38.
   B. The mean is 38, and the median is 40.
   C. The mean is 36, and the median is 50.
   D. The mean is 50, and the median is 36.

   The correct answer is **B**. The correct solution is the mean is 38 and the median is 40. The sum of all items is 570 divided by 15, which is 38. The data set in order is 10, 10, 20, 20, 20, 30, 30, 40, 40, 40, 50, 50, 60, 70, 80. The median number is 40.

2. **Find the mode and the range for the data set 10, 20, 40, 20, 30, 50, 40, 60, 30, 10, 40, 20, 50, 70, and 80.**

   A. The mode is 20, and the range is 70.
   B. The mode is 40, and the range is 70.
   C. The modes are 20 and 40, and the range is 70.
   D. The modes are 20, 40, and 70, and the range is 70.

   The correct answer is **C**. The correct solution is the modes are 20 and 40 and the range is 70. The modes are 20 and 40 because each of these numbers appears three times. The range is the difference between 80 and 10, which is 70.

Let's Review!

- A bar graph, line graph, and circle graph are different ways to summarize and represent data.
- The mean, median, mode, and range are values that can be used to interpret the meaning of a set of numbers.

LESSON 6.3 SIMILARITY, RIGHT TRIANGLES, AND TRIGONOMETRY

This lesson defines and applies terminology associated with coordinate planes. It also demonstrates how to find the area of two-dimensional shapes and the surface area and volume of three-dimensional cubes and right prisms.

Coordinate Plane

The **coordinate plane** is a two-dimensional number line with the horizontal axis called the **x-axis** and the vertical axis called the **y-axis**. Each **ordered pair** or **coordinate** is listed as (x, y). The center point is the origin and has an ordered pair of (0, 0). A coordinate plane has four quadrants.

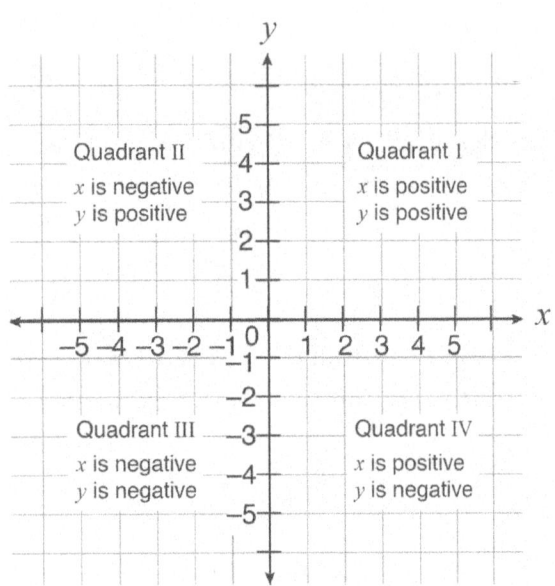

> **KEEP IN MIND**
> The x-coordinates are positive to the right of the y-axis. The y-coordinates are positive above the x-axis.

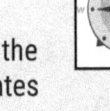

To graph a point in the coordinate plane, start with the x-coordinate. This point states the number of steps to the left (negative) or to the right (positive) from the origin. Then, the y-coordinate states the number of steps up (positive) or down (negative) from the x-coordinate.

Given a set of ordered pairs, points can be drawn in the coordinate plane to create polygons. The length of a segment can be found if the segment has the same first coordinate or the same second coordinate.

> **PRO TEST TIP**
> While your test may not directly test you on graphing, understanding the coordinate plane is an essential skill in reading graphs and extending your knowledge to area and dimension for geometric figures. Graphs can be helpful for visualizing area, but the geometry section is largely meant to test for the ability to use equations properly.

Lesson 6.3 Similarity, Right Triangles, and Trigonometry

Examples

1. Draw a triangle with the coordinates (–2, –1), (–3, 5), (–4, 2).

   A.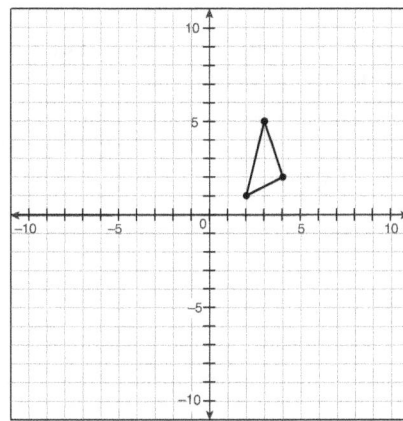

   C.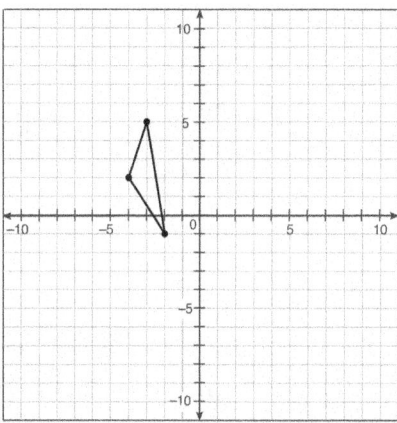

   B.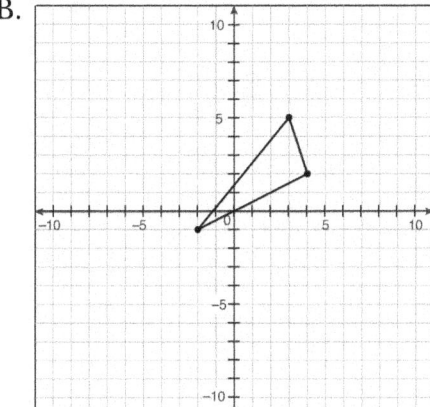

   D.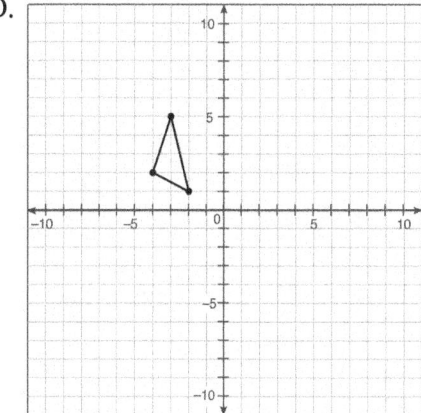

   The correct answer is **C**. The first point is in the third quadrant because x is negative and y is negative, and the last two points are in the second quadrant because x is negative and y is positive.

2. Given the coordinates for a rectangle (4, 8), (4, –2), (–1, –2), (–1, 8), find the length of each side of the rectangle.

   A. 3 units and 6 units

   B. 3 units and 10 units

   C. 5 units and 6 units

   D. 5 units and 10 units

   The correct answer is **D**. The correct solution is 5 units and 10 units. The difference between the x-coordinates is 4 – (–1) = 5 units, and the difference between the y-coordinates is 8 – (–2) = 10 units.

3. The dimensions for a soccer field are 45 meters by 90 meters. One corner of a soccer field on the coordinate plane is (–45, –30). What could a second coordinate be?

   A. (–45, 30)   B. (–45, 45)   C. (–45, 60)   D. (–45, 75)

   The correct answer is **C**. The correct solution is (–45, 60) because 90 can be added to the y-coordinate, –30 + 90 = 60.

Area of Two-Dimensional Objects

The **area** is the number of unit squares that fit inside a two-dimensional object. A unit square is one unit long by one unit wide, which includes 1 foot by 1 foot and 1 meter by 1 meter. The unit of measurement for area is units squared (or feet squared, meters squared, and so on). The following are formulas for calculating the area of various shapes.

BE CAREFUL!
Make sure that you apply the correct formula for area of each two-dimensional object.

- Rectangle: The product of the length and the width, $A = lw$.
- Parallelogram: The product of the base and the height, $A = bh$.
- Square: The side length squared, $A = s^2$.
- Triangle: The product of one-half the base and the height, $A = \frac{1}{2}bh$.
- Trapezoid: The product of one-half the height and the sum of the bases, $A = \frac{1}{2}h(b_1 + b_2)$.
- Regular polygon: The product of one-half the **apothem** (a line from the center of the regular polygon that is perpendicular to a side) and the sum of the perimeter, $A = \frac{1}{2}ap$.

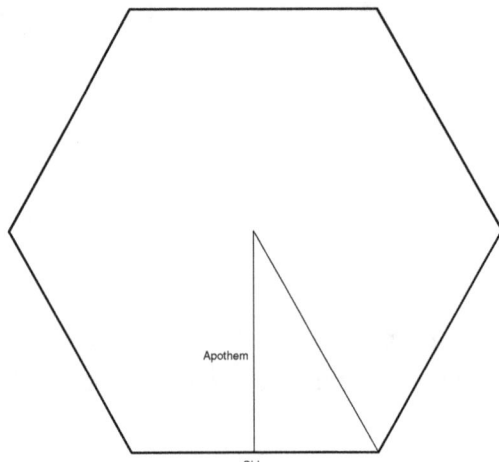

Examples

1. A trapezoid has a height of 3 centimeters and bases of 8 centimeters and 10 centimeters. Find the area in square centimeters.

   A. 18   B. 27   C. 52   D. 55

   The correct answer is **B**. The correct solution is 27. Substitute the values into the formula and simplify using the order of operations, $A = \frac{1}{2}h(b_1 + b_2) = \frac{1}{2}(3)(8 + 10) = \frac{1}{2}(3)(18) = 27$ square centimeters.

2. A regular decagon has a side length of 12 inches and an apothem of 6 inches. Find the area in square inches.

   A. 120   B. 360   C. 720   D. 960

   The correct answer is **B**. The correct solution is 360. Simplify using the order of operations, $A = \frac{1}{2}ap = \frac{1}{2}(6)(12(10)) = 360$ square inches.

Lesson 6.3 Similarity, Right Triangles, and Trigonometry

3. Two rectangular rooms need to be carpeted. The dimensions of the first room are 18 feet by 19 feet, and the dimensions of the second room are 12 feet by 10 feet. What is the total area to be carpeted in square feet?

   A. 118   B. 236   C. 342   D. 462

   The correct answer is **D**. The correct solution is 462. Substitute the values into the formula and simplify using the order of operations, $A = lw + lw = 18(19) + 12(10) = 342 + 120 = 462$ square feet.

4. A picture frame is in the shape of a right triangle with legs 9 centimeters and 12 centimeters and hypotenuse of 15 centimeters. What is the area in square centimeters?

   A. 54   B. 90   C. 108   D. 180

   The correct answer is **A**. The correct solution is 54. Substitute the values into the formula and simplify using the order of operations, $A = \frac{1}{2}bh = \frac{1}{2}(9)12 = 54$ square centimeters.

Surface Area and Volume of Cubes and Right Prisms

A three-dimensional object has length, width, and height. **Cubes** are made up of six congruent square faces. A **right prism** is made of three sets of congruent faces, with at least two sets of congruent rectangles.

BE CAREFUL!
Surface area is a two-dimensional calculation, and volume is a three-dimensional calculation.

The **surface area** of any three-dimensional object is the sum of the area of all faces. The formula for the surface area of a cube is $SA = 6s^2$ because there are six congruent faces. For a right rectangular prism, the surface area formula is $SA = 2lw + 2lh + 2hw$ because there are three sets of congruent rectangles. For a triangular prism, the surface area formula is twice the area of the base plus the area of the other three rectangles that make up the prism.

The **volume** of any three-dimensional object is the amount of space inside the object. The volume formula for a cube is $V = s^3$. The volume formula for a rectangular prism is the area of the base times the height, or $V = Bh$.

Examples

1. A cube has a side length of 5 centimeters. What is the surface area in square centimeters?

   A. 20   B. 25   C. 125   D. 150

   The correct answer is **D**. The correct solution is 150. Substitute the values into the formula and simplify using the order of operations, $SA = 6s^2 = 6(5^2) = 6(25) = 150$ square centimeters.

2. A cube has a side length of 5 centimeters. What is the volume in cubic centimeters?

   A. 20   B. 25   C. 125   D. 180

   The correct answer is **C**. The correct solution is 125. Substitute the values into the formula and simplify using the order of operations, $V = s^3 = 5^3 = 125$ cubic centimeters.

3. A right rectangular prism has dimensions of 4 inches by 5 inches by 6 inches. What is the surface area in square inches?

   A. 60 B. 74 C. 120 D. 148

   The correct answer is **D**. The correct solution is 148. Substitute the values into the formula and simplify using the order of operations, $SA = 2lw + 2lh + 2hw = 2(4)(5) + 2(4)(6) + 2(6)(5) = 40 + 48 + 60 = 148$ square inches.

4. A right rectangular prism has dimensions of 4 inches by 5 inches by 6 inches. What is the volume in cubic inches?

   A. 60 B. 62 C. 120 D. 124

   The correct answer is **C**. The correct solution is 120. Substitute the values into the formula and simplify using the order of operations, $V = lwh = 4(5)(6) = 120$ cubic inches.

Let's Review!

- The coordinate plane is a two-dimensional number line that is used to display ordered pairs. Two-dimensional shapes can be drawn on the plane, and the length of the objects can be determined based on the given coordinates.
- The area of a two-dimensional object is the amount of space inside the shape. There are area formulas to use to calculate the area of various shapes.
- For a three-dimensional object, the surface area is the sum of the area of the faces and the volume is the amount of space inside the object. Cubes and right rectangular prisms are common three-dimensional solids.

LESSON 6.4 CIRCLES

This lesson introduces concepts of circles, including finding the circumference and the area of the circle.

Circle Terminology

A **circle** is a figure composed of points that are equidistant from a given point. The **center** is the point from which all points are equidistant. A **chord** is a segment whose endpoints are on the circle, and the **diameter** is a chord that goes through the center of the circle. The **radius** is a segment with one endpoint at the center of the circle and one endpoint on the circle. **Arcs** have two endpoints on the circle and all points on a circle between those endpoints.

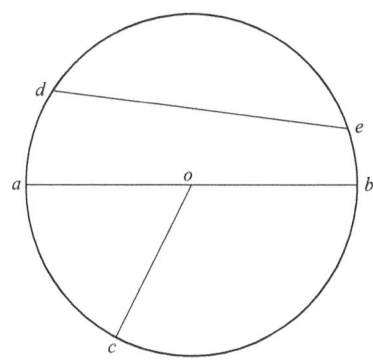

In the circle at the right, O is the center, $\overline{OC}$ is the radius, $\overline{AB}$ is the diameter, $\overline{DE}$ is a chord, and $\overset{\frown}{AD}$ is an arc.

Example

Identify a diameter of the circle.

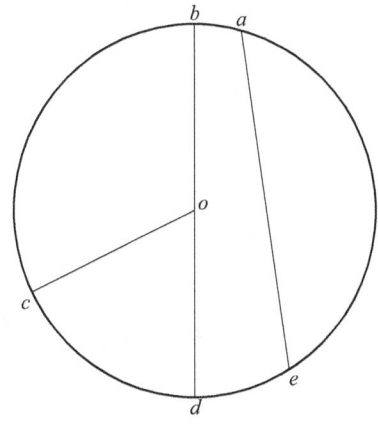

KEEP IN MIND

The radius is one-half the length of the diameter of the circle.

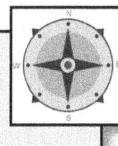

A. $\overline{BD}$ B. $\overline{OC}$ C. $\overline{DO}$ D. $\overline{AE}$

The correct answer is **A**. The correct solution is $\overline{BD}$ because points B and D are on the circle and the segment goes through the center O.

Circumference and Area of a Circle

The **circumference** of a circle is the perimeter, or the distance, around the circle. There are two ways to find the circumference. The formulas are the product of the diameter and pi or the product of twice the radius and pi. In symbol form, the formulas are $C = \pi d$ or $C = 2\pi r$.

BE CAREFUL!
Make sure that you apply the correct formula for circumference and area of a circle.

The **area** of a circle is the amount of space inside a circle. The formula is the product of pi and the radius squared. In symbol form, the formula is $A = \pi r^2$. The area is always expressed in square units.

Given the circumference or the area of a circle, the radius and the diameter can be determined. The given measurement is substituted into the appropriate formula. Then, the equation is solved for the radius or the diameter.

Examples

1. Find the circumference in centimeters of a circle with a diameter of 8 centimeters. Use 3.14 for π.

    A. 12.56 B. 25.12 C. 50.24 D. 100.48

    The correct answer is **B**. The correct solution is 25.12 because $C = \pi d \approx 3.14(8) \approx 25.12$ centimeters.

2. Find the area in square inches of a circle with a radius of 15 inches. Use 3.14 for π.

    A. 94.2 B. 176.63 C. 706.5 D. 828.96

    The correct answer is **C**. The correct solution is 706.5 because $A = \pi r^2 \approx 3.14 (15) 2 \approx 3.14(225) \approx 706.5$ square inches.

3. A circle has a circumference of 70 centimeters. Find the diameter to the nearest tenth of a centimeter. Use 3.14 for π.

    A. 11.1 B. 22.3 C. 33.5 D. 44.7

    The correct answer is **B**. The correct solution is 22.3 because $C = \pi d; 70 = 3.14d; d \approx 22.3$ centimeters.

4. A circle has an area of 95 square centimeters. Find the radius to the nearest tenth of a centimeter. Use 3.14 for π.

    A. 2.7 B. 5.5 C. 8.2 D. 10.9

    The correct answer is **B**. The correct solution is 5.5 because $A = \pi r\ 2; 95 = 3.14r^2; 30.25 = r^2; r \approx 5.5$ centimeters.

Lesson 6.4 Circles

Finding Circumference or Area Given the Other Value

Given the circumference of a circle, the area of the circle can be found. First, substitute the circumference into the formula and find the radius. Substitute the radius into the area formula and simplify.

Reverse the process to find the circumference given the area. First, substitute the area into the area formula and find the radius. Substitute the radius into the circumference formula and simplify.

BE CAREFUL!
Pay attention to the details with each formula and apply them in the correct order.

Examples

1. The circumference of a circle is 45 inches. Find the area of the circle in square inches. Round to the nearest tenth. Use 3.14 for π.

   A. 51.8   B. 65.1   C. 162.8   D. 204.5

   The correct answer is **C**. The correct solution is 162.8.

   $C = 2\pi r$; $45 = 2(3.14)r$; $45 = 6.28r$; $r \approx 7.2$ inches. $A = \pi r^2 \approx 3.14(7.2)^2 \approx 3.14(51.84) \approx 162.8$ square inches.

2. The area of a circle is 60 square centimeters. Find the circumference of the circle in centimeters. Round to the nearest tenth. Use 3.14 for π.

   A. 4.4   B. 13.8   C. 19.1   D. 27.6

   The correct answer is **D**. The correct solution is 27.6.

   $A = \pi r^2$; $60 = 3.14r^2$; $19.11 = r^2$; $r \approx 4.4$ centimeters. $C = 2\pi r$; $C = 2(3.14)4.4 \approx 27.6$ centimeters.

Let's Review!

- Key terms related to circles are *radius, diameter, chord,* and *arc*. Note that the diameter is twice the radius.
- The circumference or the perimeter of a circle is the product of pi and the diameter or twice the radius and pi.
- The area of the circle is the product of pi and the radius squared.

Chapter 6 Measurement and Data Practice Quiz

1. Identify a radius of the circle.

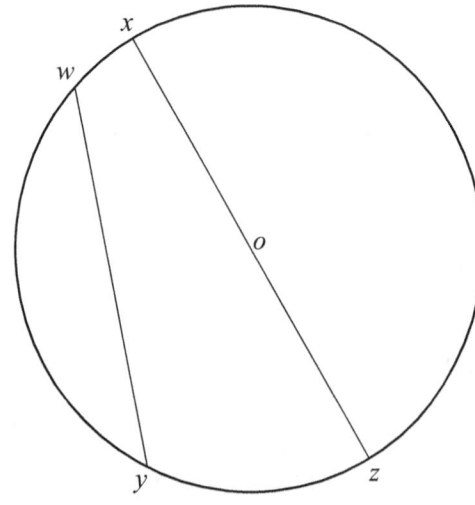

   A. $\overline{WY}$ B. $\overline{XZ}$ C. $\overline{XO}$ D. $\overline{YZ}$

2. Find the circumference, in inches, of a circle with a diameter of 6 inches. Use 3.14 for π.

   A. 9.42
   B. 18.84
   C. 25.12
   D. 37.68

3. The table shows the speed in miles per hour of different roller coasters at an amusement park. Select the correct line graph for this data.

Amusement Park Roller Coasters	1	2	3	4	5	6	7	8
Speed (miles per hour)	120	105	75	100	60	85	110	90

A.
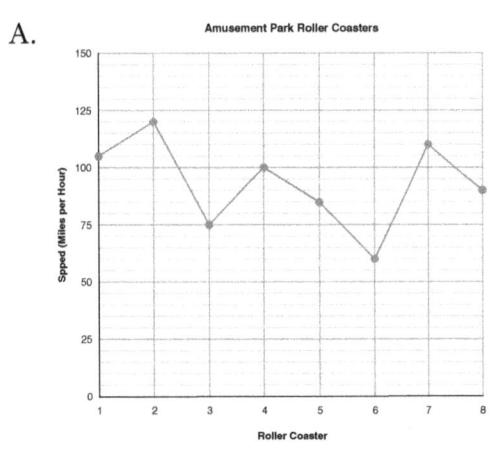

B.
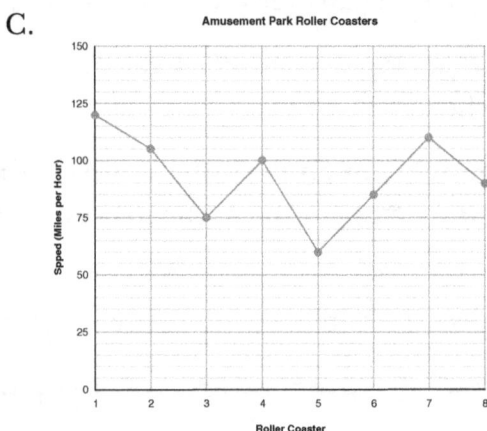

C.

D.
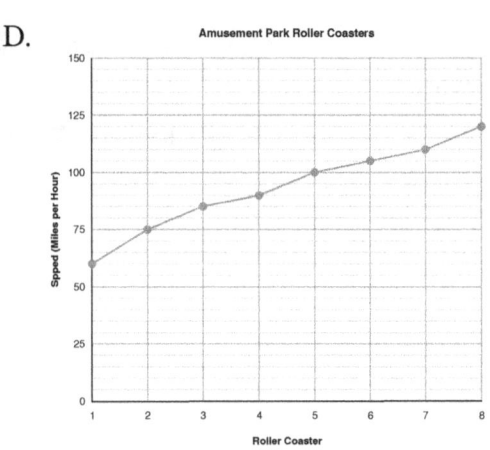

4. A college class had one group use a traditional textbook and another group use an online textbook. The attendance for the class was compared. Determine the independent variable.

   A. Class attendance
   B. Type of textbook
   C. Grade for the class
   D. Online version of the textbook

5. Draw a square with the coordinates (–3, 4), (–3, –2), (3, –2), (3, 4).

   A.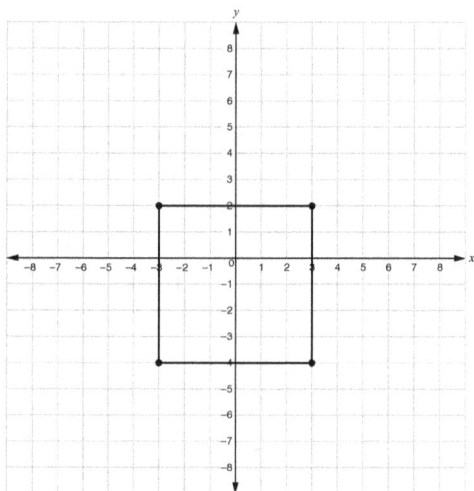

   B.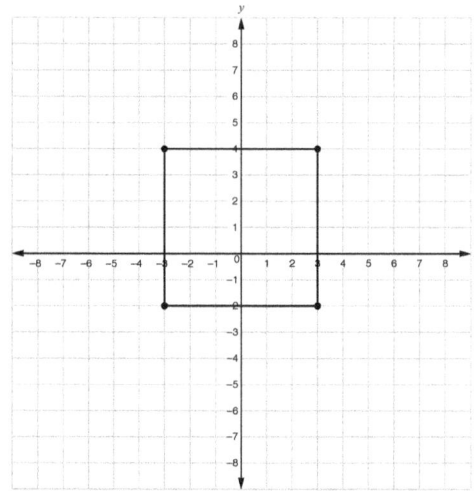

   C.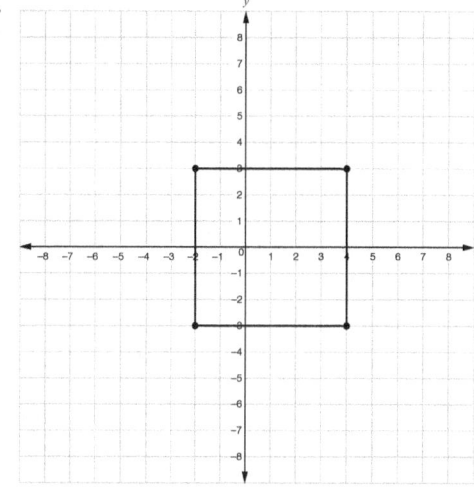

   D.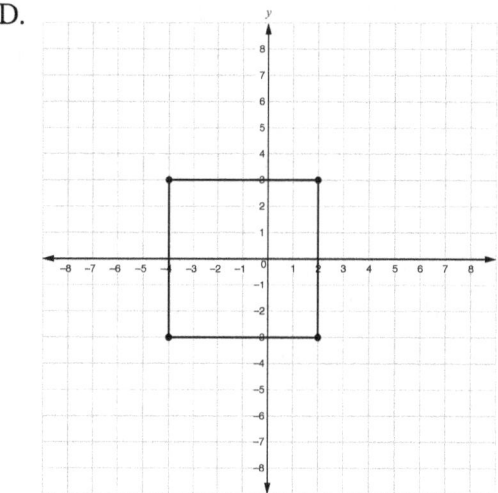

6. Given the coordinates for a square (–6, 6), (6, 6), (6, –6), (–6, –6), find the length of each side of the square.

   A. 0 units   C. 12 units
   B. 6 units   D. 18 units

7. Identify 3:00 p.m. in military time.

   A. 0300   C. 1200
   B. 0600   D. 1500

8. Convert 14 feet to yards.

   A. $4\frac{2}{3}$ yards   C. $40\frac{2}{3}$ yards
   B. 5 yards   D. 42 yards

Chapter 6 Measurement and Data Practice Quiz – Answer Key

1. **C.** The correct solution is $\overline{XO}$ because X is on the circle and O is the center of the circle. **See Lesson: Circles.**

2. **B.** The correct solution is 18.84 because $C = \pi d \approx 3.14(6) \approx 18.84$ inches. **See Lesson: Circles.**

3. **C.** The line graph has the correct values for each roller coaster. **See Lesson: Interpreting Graphics.**

4. **B.** The correct solution is the type of textbook because the other variables do not change the type of textbook. **See Lesson: Interpreting Graphics.**

5. **B.** The first point is in the second quadrant, the second point is in the third quadrant, the third point is in the fourth quadrant, and the last point is in the first quadrant. **See Lesson: Similarity, Right Triangles, and Trigonometry.**

6. **C.** The correct solution 12 units. The difference between the x-coordinates is $6 - (-6) = 12$ units and the difference between the y-coordinates is $6 - (-6) = 12$ units. **See Lesson: Similarity, Right Triangles, and Trigonometry.**

7. **D.** The correct solution is 1500. Add 1200 to the time, $1200 + 300 = 1500$. **See Lesson: Standards of Measure.**

8. **A.** The correct solution is $4\frac{2}{3}$ yards. $14 \text{ ft} \times \frac{1 \text{ yd}}{3 \text{ ft}} = \frac{14}{3} = 4\frac{2}{3}$ yd. **See Lesson: Standards of Measure.**

SECTION III
SCIENCE

Science: 50 questions, 60 minutes, Human A&P, Life and physical sciences, scientific reasoning

Areas assessed: Human Anatomy and Physiology, Life and Physical Sciences, Scientific Reasoning

SCIENCE TIPS

- Know your anatomy, physiology, and microbiology.
- Review the periodic table.
- Know basics of the 11 systems of the body, organelles, and basic biology.
- Know how to balance an equation in chemistry (atomic mass, protons, neutrons, etc.).
- Know quick facts about population growth and decline, and birth and fertility rates.

CHAPTER 7 HUMAN ANATOMY AND PHYSIOLOGY: ORGANIZATION OF SYSTEMS

LESSON 7.1 ORGANIZATION OF THE HUMAN BODY

Human anatomy and physiology is the study of the structures and functions of the human body.

Levels of Organization and Body Cavities

The body can be studied at seven structural levels: **chemical**, **organelle**, **cell**, **tissue**, **organ**, **organ system**, and **organism**.

- **Chemical:** The chemical level involves interactions among atoms and their combination into molecules.
- **Organelle:** An organelle is a small structure contained within a cell that performs one or more specific functions.
- **Cell:** Cells are the basic functional units of life. All cells share many characteristics, but they differ in structure and function.
- **Tissue:** A tissue is a group of cells with similar structures and functions.
- **Organ:** An organ is composed of two or more tissue types that together perform one or more common function.
- **Organ system:** An organ system is a group of organs classified as a unit because of a common function or set of functions.
- **Organism:** An organism is any living thing considered as a whole. Organisms can have anywhere from a single cell to trillions of cells.

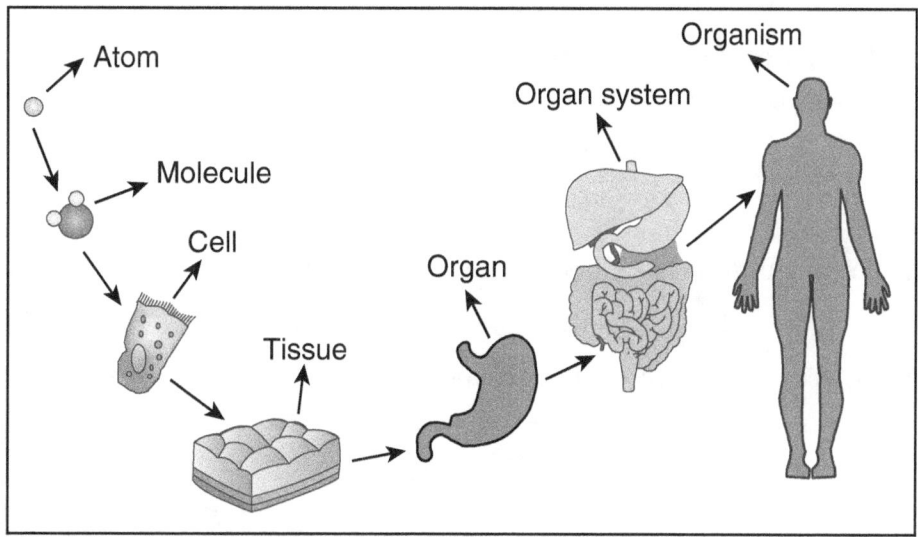

Body Cavities

The human body has many cavities, some of which open to the exterior. A **cavity** is a fluid-filled space in the body that holds and protects internal organs. The **ventral cavity** (front of the body) contains three major cavities:

- The **thoracic cavity** is surrounded by the rib cage and separated from the abdominal cavity by the diaphragm. It is divided into right and left halves by a structure called the mediastinum. It contains the esophagus, trachea, thymus gland, heart, and both lungs, along with other structures.
- The **abdominal cavity** is bounded by the abdominal muscles below the thoracic cavity and contains the stomach, intestines, liver, spleen, pancreas, and kidneys.
- The **pelvic cavity** is enclosed by the bones of the pelvis and contains the urinary bladder, part of the intestines, and the internal reproductive organs. The abdominal and pelvic cavities are sometimes referred to as the abdominopelvic cavity.

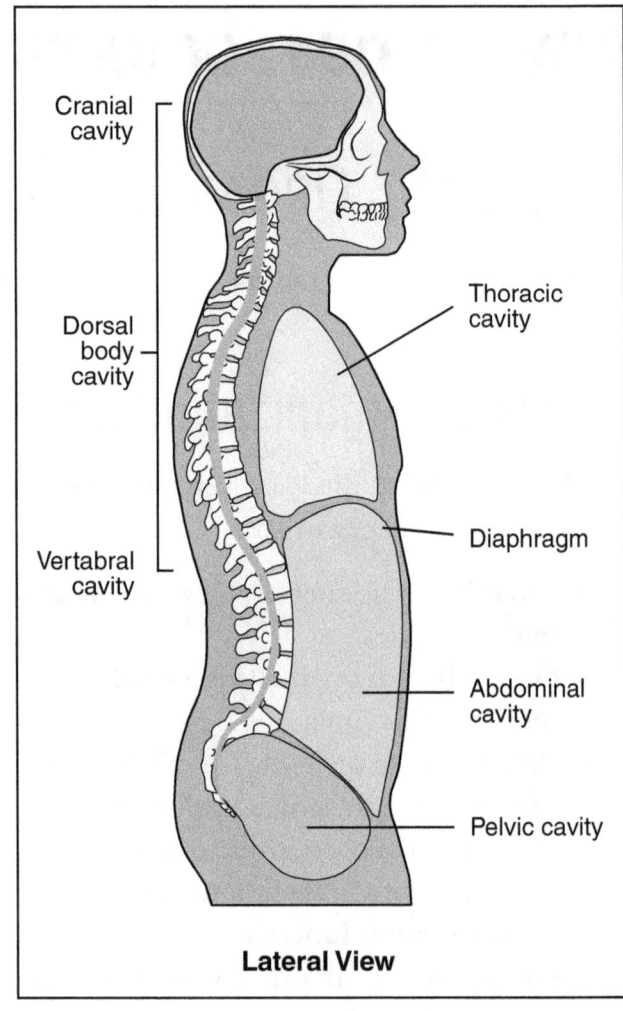

Lateral View

The **dorsal cavity** is the back of the human body, and it is subdivided into two cavities: cranial and spinal.

- The **cranial cavity** contains the brain.
- The **spinal cavity** contains the spinal cord.

Example

Which of the following organs is located in the pelvic cavity?

A. Heart   B. Intestines   C. Liver   D. Pancreas

The correct answer is **B**. The intestines are located in both the abdominal and pelvic cavities.

Lesson 7.1 Organization of the Human Body

Terminology and the Body Planes and Regions

Directional terms refer to the body in the **anatomical position**, regardless of its actual position. The term *anatomical position* refers to a person standing erect with the feet forward, arms hanging to the sides, and the palms of the hands facing forward.

Terminology

Term	Definition
Inferior	A structure below another
Superior	A structure above another
Anterior	Toward the front of the body
Posterior	Toward the back of the body
Dorsal	Toward the back
Ventral	Toward the front
Proximal	Closer to the point of attachment to the body than another structure
Distal	Farther from the point of attachment to the body
Lateral	Away from the midline of the body
Medial	Toward the middle or midline of the body
Superficial	Toward or on the surface
Deep	Away from the surface
Anterosuperior	In front or above
Midline	A median line
Supine position	Lying flat with face and torso facing upward
Prone position	Lying face down

Body Planes

Sectioning the body is a way to look inside and observe the body's structures. The following are the major planes of the body:

- The **sagittal plane** runs vertically through the body and separates the body into right and left parts.
- The **midsagittal plane** divides the body into two equal halves.
- The **transverse plane** runs parallel to the surface of the ground and divides the body into superior and inferior planes.
- The **coronal plane**, sometimes called the frontal plane, runs vertically from left to right and divides the body into anterior and posterior parts.

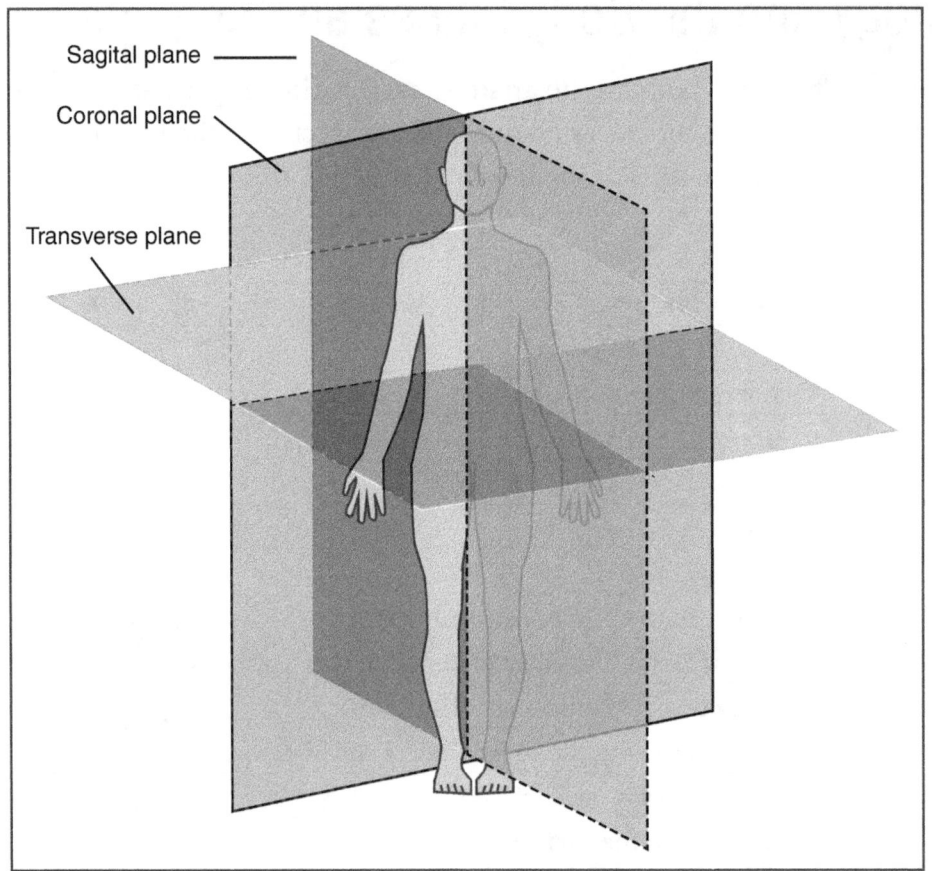

Body Regions

The body is divided into the following four regions:

- **Upper limb:** The upper limb includes the arm, forearm, wrist, and hand.
- **Lower limb:** The lower limb is divided into the thigh, leg, ankle, and foot.
- **Central region:** The central region includes the neck and trunk.
- **Head region:** The head region includes the entire head.

Example

The wrist is _____ to the shoulder.

    A. distal   B. lateral   C. median   D. superior

The correct answer is **A**. The wrist is farther from the point of attachment than the shoulder is, so it is distal to the shoulder.

Human Tissues

A **tissue** is a group of cells with similar structure and function and similar extracellular substances located between the cells. The table below describes the four primary tissues found in the human body.

Lesson 7.1 Organization of the Human Body

Tissue	Structure	Function	Example
Connective	characterized by extracellular material that separate cells from one another	enclosing and separating connecting tissues to one another supportive and moving storing cushioning and insulating transporting protecting	cells of the immune system and blood
Epithelial	classified according to the number of cell layers and shapes	protecting underlying structures acting as barriers permitting the passage of substances secreting substances	skin, linings of internal organs
Muscle	cells of muscles resemble long threads and are called *fibers*	providing movement	heart, organs of digestive system
Neural	cells are composed of dendrites, cell bodies, and axons	coordinating and controlling many body activities	brain, spinal cord

Four Types of Tissue

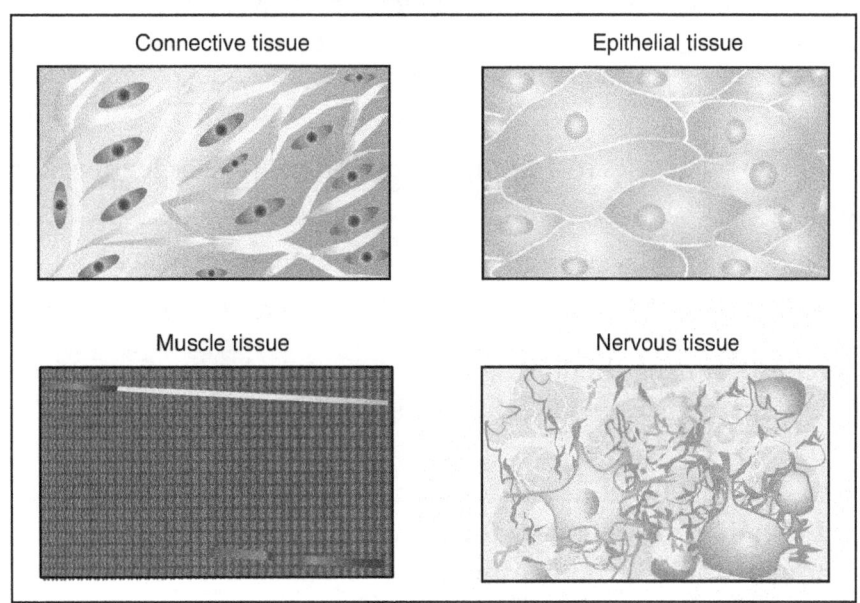

Example

Which type of tissue controls when the heart beats?

A. Connective   B. Epithelial   C. Muscle   D. Nervous

The correct answer is **D**. Although the muscle tissue is responsible for the actual movement of the heart, the neural tissue "tells" the heart when to beat.

Homeostasis and Feedback Mechanisms

Homeostasis is the existence and maintenance of a relatively constant environment within the body. Each cell of the body is surrounded by a small amount of fluid, and the normal functions of each cell depend on the maintenance of its fluid environment within a narrow range of conditions, including temperature, volume, and chemical content. These conditions are known as **variables**. For example, body temperature is a variable that can increase in a hot environment or decrease in a cold environment.

There are two types of feedback mechanisms in the human body: negative and positive.

Negative Feedback

Most systems of the body are regulated by **negative feedback mechanisms**, which maintain homeostasis. *Negative* means that any deviation from the set point is made smaller or is resisted. The maintenance of normal blood pressure is a negative-feedback mechanism. Normal blood pressure is important because it is responsible for moving blood from the heart to tissues.

Positive Feedback

Positive-feedback mechanisms are not homeostatic and are rare in healthy individuals. *Positive* means that when a deviation from a normal value occurs, the response of the system is to make the deviation even greater. Positive feedback therefore usually creates a cycle leading away from homeostasis and, in some cases, results in death. Inadequate delivery of blood to cardiac muscle is an example of positive feedback.

Example

Childbirth is a response to hormones in a woman's body. What type of feedback mechanism is at work during childbirth?

- A. Neutral feedback
- B. Positive feedback
- C. Negative feedback
- D. Need more information

The correct answer is **B**. During childbirth, the frequency and strength of the contractions increases until the contractions are powerful enough to deliver the baby.

Let's Review!

- The body can be studied at seven structural levels.
- The human body has multiple body cavities.
- Directional terms refer to the body in the anatomical position.
- Sectioning the body is a way to look inside and observe the body's structures.
- The four primary tissues found in the human body are connective, epithelial, muscular and nervous.
- Homeostasis is the existence and maintenance of a relatively constant environment within the body.
- The two types of feedback mechanisms in the human body are negative and positive feedback mechanisms.

LESSON 7.2   THE CARDIOVASCULAR SYSTEM

This lesson introduces the anatomy of blood and its connection to the cardiovascular system. Explore the parts that make up the cardiovascular system and how this system functions.

Anatomy of Blood

Blood is a type of fluid connective tissue that circulates throughout the body, carrying substances to and away from bodily tissues. It has a pH of about 7.4 and is more viscous than water. Blood consists of three types of formed elements, an extracellular matrix called **plasma,** molecules, cell fragments, and debris. The formed elements consist of red blood cells, white blood cells, and platelets. They are also referred to as **erythrocytes**, **leukocytes**, and **thrombocytes**, respectively. The following table details key characteristics of these elements.

Characteristic	Red Blood Cells	White Blood Cells	Platelets
Scientific Name	Erythrocytes	Leukocytes	Thrombocytes
Size (Diameter)	0.008 mm	0.02 mm	0.003 mm
Function	Participate in gas exchange, primarily with oxygen and carbon dioxide	Protect the body from foreign substances by eliciting an immune response	Aid in blood clotting and wound healing

Plasma is different from other types of connective tissue because it is a fluid. Consisting of about 92% water, formed elements remain suspended in the matrix where they are circulated throughout the body.

> **DID YOU KNOW?**
> The average volume of blood in the human body, for a 70-kilogram person, is 5 liters. Blood accounts for roughly 8% of a person's body weight.

Consider the following image, which illustrates the composition of blood in a person's blood sample. When a blood sample is spun in a centrifuge, less-dense plasma floats on top of a reddish mass that consists of red blood cells. There is also a thin white layer called the **buffy coat** that consists of white blood cells and platelets. This layer is found between the reddish mass and plasma layers.

> **KEEP IN MIND**
> Blood viscosity is indirectly proportional to blood flow throughout the body. If the viscosity of blood is high, blood flow decreases. When blood viscosity is low, or blood is thin, blood flow increases.

Example

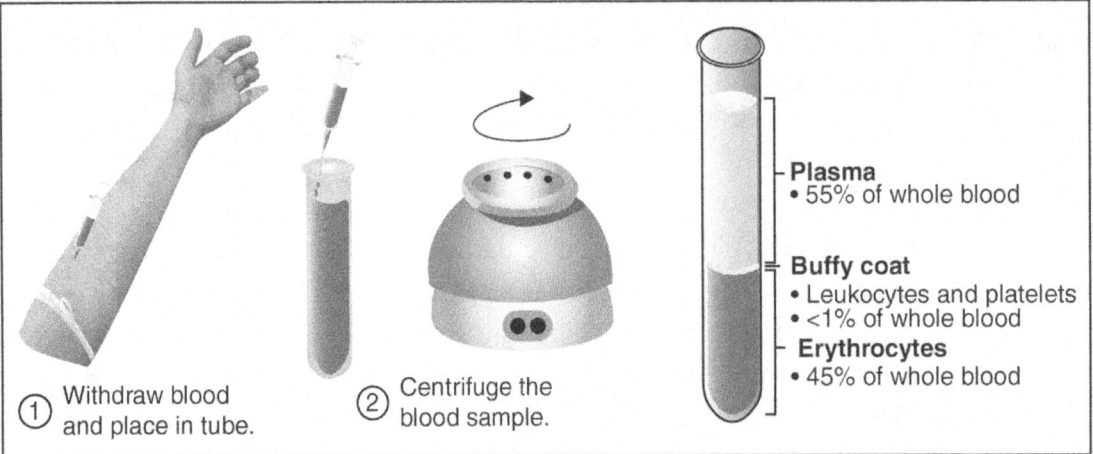

A laboratory technician needs to determine the leukocyte count in a patient. From which part of a blood sample are these cells extracted?

A. Water   B. Buffy coat   C. Liquid plasma   D. Reddish mass

The correct answer is **B**. Buffy coat contains white blood cells (or leukocytes) and platelets in blood.

Functions of Blood

Transportation, regulation, and protection are three primary functions of blood. Blood transports the following substances throughout the body:

- Gases: Blood delivers oxygen from the lungs to all cells in the body. It also transports carbon dioxide to the lungs for elimination from the body.
- Nutrients: Blood transports nutrients from the digestive tract and storage sites in the body to various places in the body.
- Wastes: Blood transports waste products to the liver, where they are excreted as bile. Waste products also travel by blood to the kidneys when they need to be excreted as urine.
- Hormones: Blood transports hormones from the glands where they are produced to their target organs.

KEEP IN MIND

Albumin is the main protein in blood, accounting for roughly 60% of the plasma proteins in blood. It plays a role in water balance and functions as a carrier protein, shuttling certain molecules throughout the body.

Although blood's primary function is to distribute substances throughout the body, it also has regulatory functions. These functions include the regulation of body temperature, chemical balance, and water balance. Blood ensures the right body temperature is maintained with help from plasma and the speed of blood flow. Plasma is able to absorb or give off heat. As shown in the following image, when blood vessels expand, or **vasodilate**, blood flows slowly, causing heat loss. This occurs when the temperature of the external environment is high. If external environmental temperatures are low, blood vessels contract, or **vasoconstrict**, causing less heat to be released.

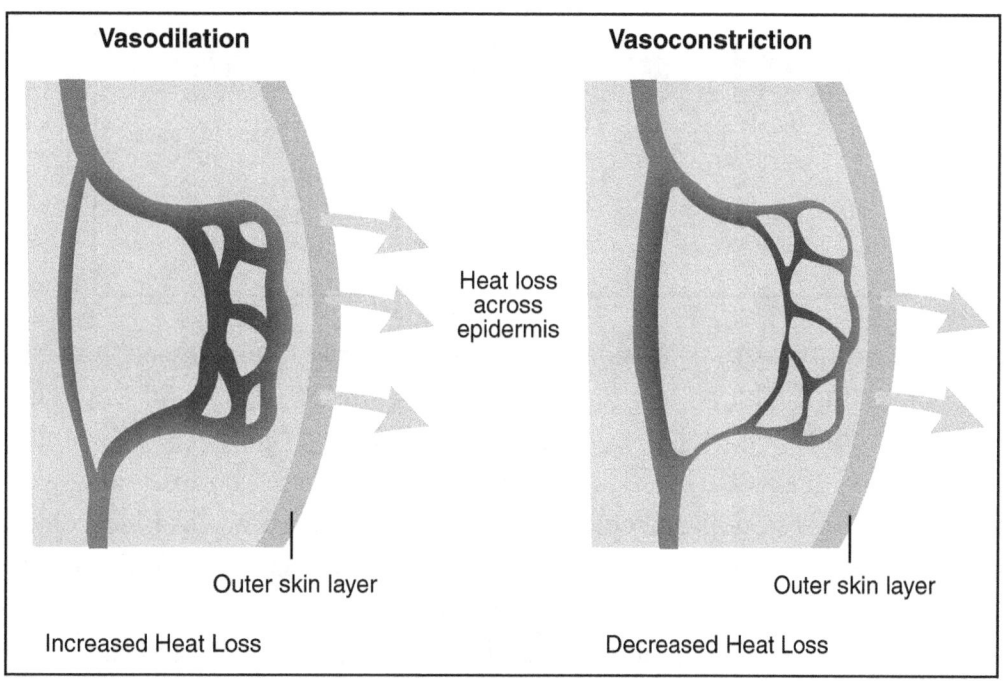

Blood also functions as a form of protection, defending the body against foreign invaders or **pathogens** that harm the body. As blood circulates through the body, it carries white blood cells and **antibodies** that destroy any pathogens they encounter. With the help of platelets and plasma proteins, blood also protects the body from extensive blood loss if a blood vessel is damaged.

Example

Platelets are important because they

- A. give blood its natural color.
- B. repair broken blood vessels.
- C. transport nutrients to the cells.
- D. protect the body against infection.

The correct answer is **B**. At the site of injury or damage to a blood vessel, platelets help repair the damaged area.

Hemostasis

Recall that a function of platelets and plasma proteins is to repair damaged blood vessels. When blood vessels are damaged, a physiological process called hemostasis is activated. **Hemostasis** helps maintain blood in its fluid state and stops blood from leaking out of a damaged blood vessel through clot formation. As shown in the image below, there are three steps of hemostasis.

Steps of Hemostasis

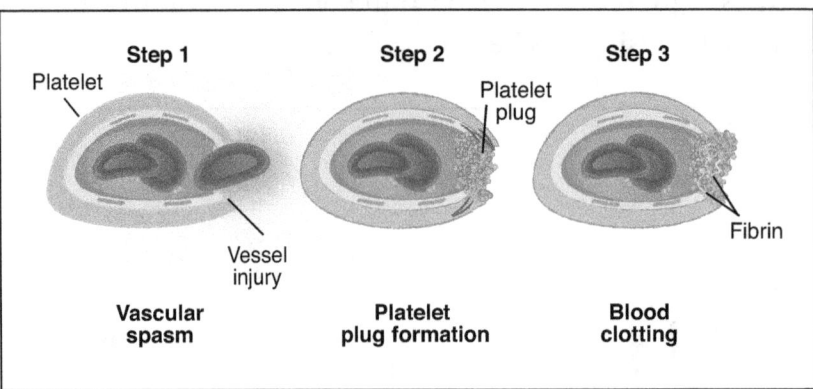

The first step is **vascular spasm**, or vasoconstriction, where the blood vessels constrict to reduce blood loss. Reducing blood loss for several hours, this process works best with small blood vessels. The second step is platelet plug formation. Platelets adhere to the epithelial wall of the blood vessel and aggregate by sticking together. This creates a temporary seal over the damaged site. In the third step, **blood coagulation** occurs. Also known as **blood clotting**, this process is a series of events that strengthen the platelet plug by using fibrin threads to form a mesh around the plug. The protein mesh functions as a molecular glue, securing the plug to the damaged site. Red blood cells and platelets remain trapped at the damaged site, forming a clot that facilitates wound healing.

Example

What happens after platelets aggregate at a damaged blood vessel site?

   A. The site of the wound is healed.

   B. The damaged blood vessel constricts.

   C. The platelets stick together and form a plug.

   D. Red blood cells are recruited to the injured site.

The correct answer is **C**. After the platelets aggregate at the damaged site, they stick together to form a plug. Next, blood coagulation occurs when a fibrin mesh forms around the platelet aggregate.

Blood Grouping and Agglutination

There are several different types or groups of blood, and the major groups are A, B, AB, and O. Blood group is a way to classify blood according to inherited differences of red blood cell **antigens** found on the surface of a red blood cell. The type of antibody in blood also identifies a particular blood group. **Antibodies** are proteins found in the plasma. They function as part of the body's natural defense to recognize foreign substances and alert the immune system.

Depending on which antigen is inherited, parental offspring will have one of the four major blood groups. Collectively, the following major blood groups comprise the ABO system:

- Blood group A: Displays type A antigens on the surface of a red blood cell and contains B antibodies in the plasma.
- Blood group B: Displays type B antigens on the red blood cell's surface and contains A antibodies in the plasma.
- Blood group O: Does not display A or B antigens on the surface of a red blood cell. Both A and B antibodies are in the plasma.
- Blood group AB: Displays type A and B antigens on the red blood cell's surface, but neither A nor B antibodies are in the plasma.

KEEP IN MIND

A person can be a universal blood donor or acceptor. A universal blood donor has type O blood, while a universal blood acceptor has type AB blood.

In addition to antigens, the **Rh factor** protein may exist on a red blood cell's surface. Because this protein can be either present (+) or absent (-), it increases the number of major blood groups from four to eight: A+, A-, B+, B-, O+, O-, AB+, and AB-. The following table summarizes what blood types a person can receive or donate.

Blood Group	Can accept blood from	Can donate blood to
A	A, O	A, AB
B	B, O	B, AB
AB	AB, A, B, O	AB
O	O	AB, A, B, O

When determining an individual's blood type, a sample of blood is mixed with an antiserum. If **agglutination**, or clumping, occurs during this process, the antibody has found an antigen with which to interact. This means there are antigens on the surface of the red blood cell to which the antibodies can bind. Evidence of agglutination is used to interpret the final blood type result from a sample.

Example

People with type O blood can accept blood from people with _____ blood.

A. type O B. type B C. type AB D. type A

The correct answer is **A**. People with type O blood are universal donors but can accept blood only from people with type O blood.

Cardiovascular Anatomy

The **cardiovascular system** circulates substances throughout the body using blood as a transporting mechanism. The organs of the cardiovascular system work together to supply cells and tissues with oxygen and nutrients and remove cellular wastes such as carbon dioxide. Blood, heart, and blood vessels form this system.

Because blood circulation is a closed loop system, blood is contained within the heart or blood vessels at all times. There are three types of blood vessels: arteries, veins, and capillaries. **Arteries** carry blood away from the heart, toward organs and tissues. **Veins** carry blood toward the heart, away from organs and tissues. Arteries branch into smaller blood vessels called **arterioles**, which further divide into capillaries. As shown in the following image, **capillaries** are tiny vessels that form a network around tissues. Veins branch into venules before further dividing into capillaries.

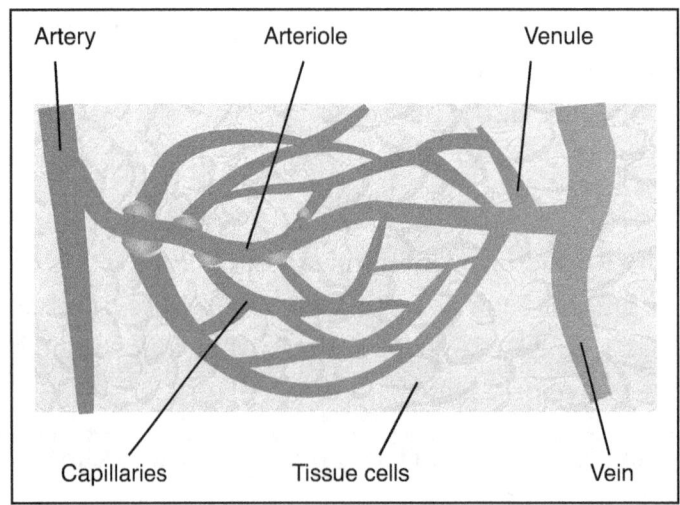

The heart is found between the lungs in the middle of the chest. It rests behind and slightly to the left of the sternum, or breastbone. The human heart is a muscular organ composed primarily of cardiac muscle. It consists of four chambers: two upper chambers called the **atria** and two lower chambers called the **ventricles**. The atria are separated from the ventricles by a muscular structure called the **septum**. Three layers make up the heart wall. These are the **pericardium** or outer layer, the **myocardium** or middle layer, and the **endocardium** or innermost layer. Most cardiac muscle tissue is found in the myocardium.

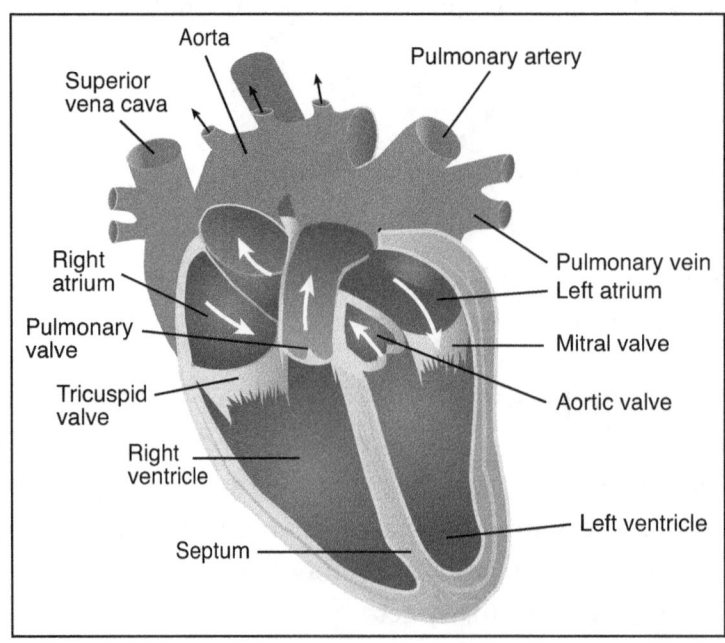

> **DID YOU KNOW?**
> Capillaries have thin walls and a very large surface area. Because of the capillaries' thin walls, blood flow slows to facilitate exchanges between blood and the body's tissues.

In addition to the four chambers, the heart has four valves that regulate blood flow into and out of the heart:

- **Tricuspid valve** regulates blood flow between the right atrium and right ventricle.
- **Pulmonary valve** regulates blood flow from the right ventricle into the pulmonary artery.
- **Mitral valve** regulates blood flow from the left atrium into the left ventricle.
- **Aortic valve** regulates blood flow from the left ventricle to the **aorta**. The aorta is the largest artery in the body.

Example

Which heart layer is composed primarily of cardiac muscle?

A. Myocardium B. Pericardium C. Septum D. Sternum

The correct answer is **A**. The heart is composed of three layers, the middle of which is the myocardium. The myocardium contains cardiac muscle tissue.

Circulation and the Cardiac Cycle

Blood continually flows in one direction, beginning in the heart and proceeding to the arteries, arterioles, and capillaries. When blood reaches the capillaries, exchanges occur between blood and tissues. After this exchange happens, blood is collected into venules, which feed into veins and eventually flow back to the heart's atrium. The heart must relax between two heartbeats for blood circulation to begin. Two types of circulatory processes occur in the body:

Systemic circulation
1. The pulmonary vein pushes oxygenated blood into the left atrium.
2. As the atrium relaxes, oxygenated blood drains into the left ventricle through the mitral valve.
3. The left ventricle pumps oxygenated blood to the aorta.
4. Blood travels through the arteries and arterioles before reaching the capillaries that surround the tissues.

Pulmonary circulation
1. Two major veins, the Superior Vena Cava and the Inferior Vena Cava, brings deoxygenated blood from the upper and lower half of the body.
2. Deoxygenated blood is pooled into the right atrium and then sent into the right ventricle through the tricuspid valve, which prevents blood from flowing backward.

3. The right ventricle contracts, causing the blood to be pushed through the pulmonary valve into the pulmonary artery.
4. Deoxygenated blood becomes oxygenated in the lungs.
5. Oxygenated blood returns from the lungs to the left atrium through the pulmonary veins.

The following image shows the heart's role in systemic and pulmonary circulation.

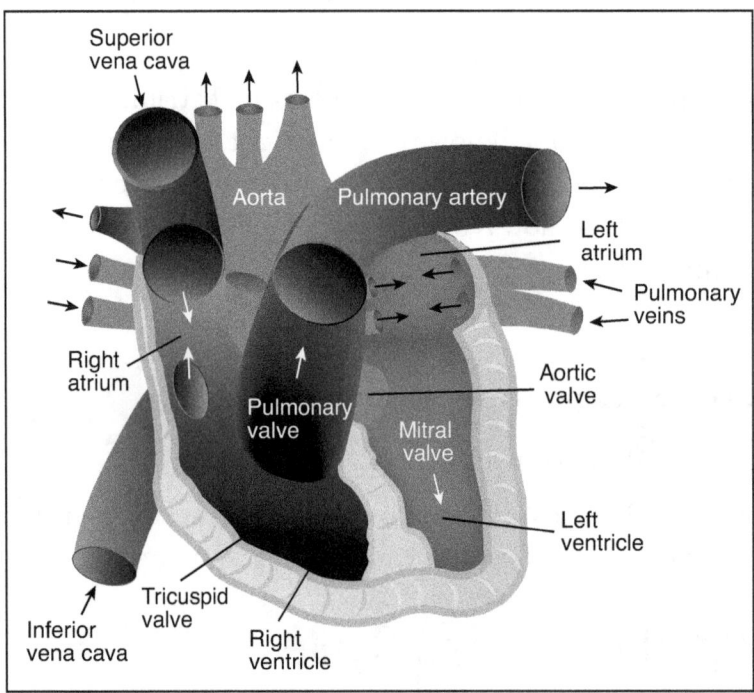

The complete cycle beginning with atrial contraction and ending with ventricular contraction is called the **cardiac cycle**. When the heart contracts and pumps blood into systemic circulation, this is called **systole**. **Diastole** refers to the period of relaxation when the heart chambers fill with blood.

KEEP IN MIND

Blood flow is regulated by many mechanisms in the body. This regulated variable is also directly proportional to blood pressure. If blood volume increases, blood pressure increases. The opposite occurs if blood pressure decreases.

Because the heart is a muscle, it transmits electrical impulses that cause the heart to contract. This electrical activity can be recorded using an **electrocardiogram**, or EKG. An EKG is a graph that shows the heart's rate and rhythm over a period of time. As shown in the following image of an EKG, waves in the graph have different meanings.

The first wave on an EKG is the P wave. This indicates atrial contraction or systole. The QRS complex represents the combination of Q, R, and S waves. This indicates ventricular systole or contraction. The T wave indicates ventricular diastole. The flat line between the S and T wave is the ST segment.

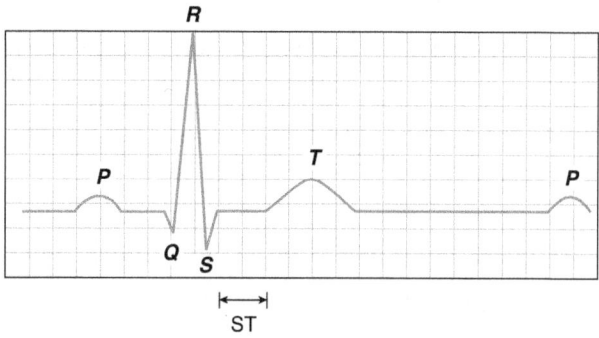

Example

What segment of the electrocardiogram is associated with atrial systole?

A. P wave   B. S wave   C. ST segment   D. QRS complex

The correct answer is **A**. Atrial systole occurs when the atrium contracts. On an EKG, atrial systole is indicated by a P wave.

Let's Review!

- Blood is a type of connective tissue composed of formed elements, plasma, and other substances.
- Erythrocytes, leukocytes, and thrombocytes are the formed elements that make up blood.
- Blood transports substances throughout the body, regulates physiological processes, and protects the body.
- There are four common blood groups that are determined by inherited differences in antigens on red blood cells.
- Agglutination, or clumping, can be used to help interpret the blood type of a blood sample.
- The cardiovascular system circulates blood throughout the body in a closed loop structure.
- The heart is a muscular organ with four chambers: two atria and two ventricles.
- Deoxygenated blood flows through pulmonary circulation, and oxygenated blood flows through systemic circulation.
- The cardiac cycle refers to the contraction and relaxation states of the atria and ventricles.
- An electrocardiogram, or EKG, is used to record heart beat and rhythm.

LESSON 7.3 THE RESPIRATORY SYSTEM

This lesson introduces the anatomy of the respiratory system and how each organ within this system functions. It also discusses the mechanics of breathing and respiration.

Anatomy of the Respiratory System

Every living thing requires oxygen for survival. Humans can live for days without water and for weeks without food. But they can only survive a few minutes without air. The respiratory system's primary function is to bring oxygen into the body, in exchange for carbon dioxide. As shown in the following image, organs of the respiratory system include the nose, nasal cavity, mouth, larynx, pharynx, lungs, and diaphragm.

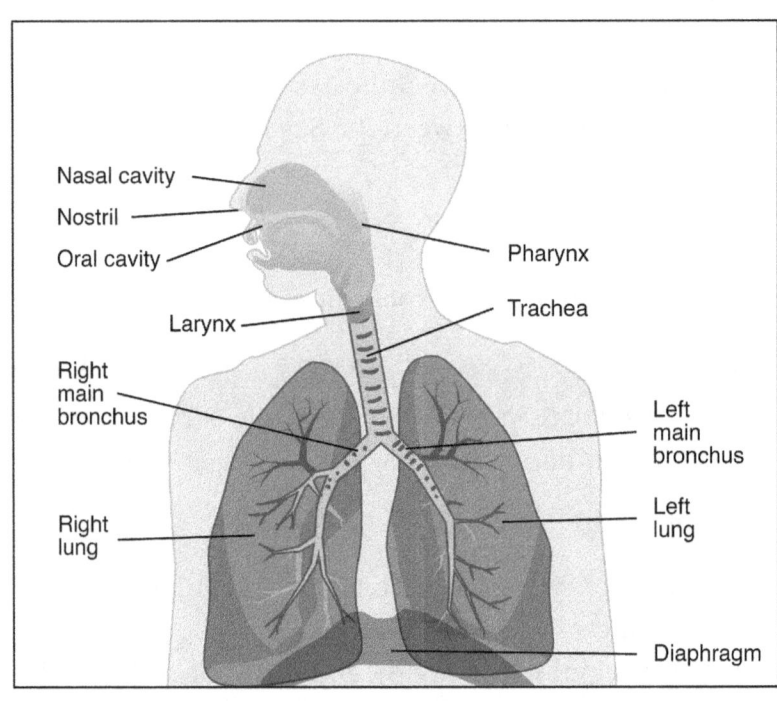

The respiratory organs can be divided into the upper and lower respiratory tract. The **upper respiratory tract** includes the nasal cavity, pharynx, and larynx. The trachea, bronchus, and lungs belong to the **lower respiratory tract**. The **nasal cavity** opens to the nose. The nose and nasal cavity warm and moisten air as a person breathes. As a defensive mechanism, tiny nose hairs and mucus produced by the epithelial mucosa cells in the nose help prevent particles in the air from entering the lungs.

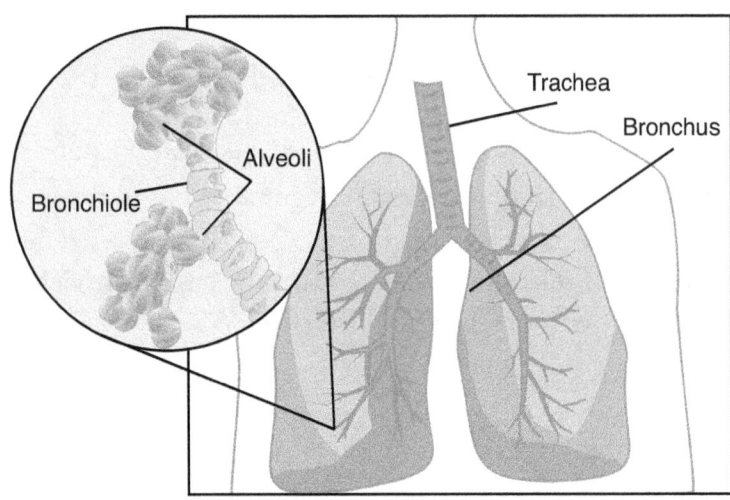

Behind the nasal cavity is the **pharynx**. Both food and air pass through this long tube. Just below the pharynx is the **larynx**, or voice box. It channels air to the trachea and pushes food past the **epiglottis**, which covers the trachea during swallowing to prevent food from entering the lungs. Once food passes the epiglottis, it moves toward the esophagus. When air reaches the **trachea**, or windpipe, it travels down a long tube that branches into **bronchi**. The bronchi enter the lungs. As shown in the image, the bronchi branch into **bronchioles** before reaching tiny air sacs in the lung called **alveoli**. Gas exchange occurs in the alveolar region.

The **diaphragm** is a muscle that plays a large role in breathing. It is found at the base of the lungs and spreads across the bottom of the rib cage, forming the chest cavity. The human body has two lungs that vary in size and weight. The right lung, which is larger and heavier, has three lobes. The left lung has two lobes.

> **DID YOU KNOW?**
> The total surface area of the alveoli in the lungs is roughly the size of a tennis court. Such a large surface area is needed to facilitate gas exchange and ensure the body is oxygenated at all times.

Pulmonary **surfactant** consists of chemical compounds that lines the alveolar surfaces of the lungs. They are lipopolysaccharides which have both a hydrophobic and hydrophilic layer to help keep the lungs inflated or prevent them from collapsing. On the outside of the lungs are serous membranes that cover each lung, called **pleura**. They form a two-layered membrane that cushions the lungs while reducing friction between the lungs and chest cavity or rib cage.

Example

Which organ uses hairs to filter out particles that try to enter the lungs?

A. Alveoli   B. Bronchus   C. Larynx   D. Nose

The correct answer is **D**. The nose is part of the upper respiratory tract. Because it is the site where air enters the body, nose hairs help prevent airborne particles from entering the lungs.

Respiratory Functions and Breathing Mechanics

Recall that the primary function of the respiratory system is to provide oxygen to and remove carbon dioxide from the body. In addition to gas exchange, the respiratory system enables a person to breathe. Breathing, or inhalation, is essential to life. It is the mechanism that provides oxygen to the body. Without oxygen, cells are unable to perform their functions necessary to keep the body alive.

The primary muscle of **inspiration** is the diaphragm. Known as the chest cavity, this dome-shaped structure flattens when it contracts. The rib cage moves outward, allowing outside air to be drawn into the lungs. During relaxation, the diaphragm returns to its dome shape and the rib cage moves back to its natural position. This causes the chest cavity to push air out of the lungs.

The respiratory system can be functionally divided into two parts:

- **Air-conducting portion:** Air is delivered to the lungs. This region consists of the upper and lower respiratory tract—specifically, the larynx, trachea, bronchi, and bronchioles.
- **Gas exchange portion:** Gas exchange takes place between the air and the blood. This portion includes the lungs, alveoli, and capillaries.

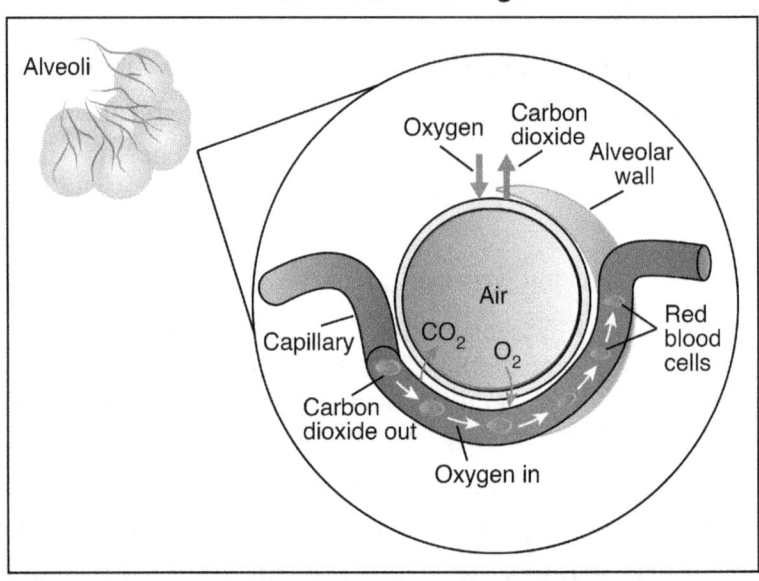

Oxygen from the air enters the body through the respiratory system. But the cardiovascular system circulates oxygen throughout the body via the blood. As shown in the image, alveoli are surrounded by a capillary bed in the lung.

This anatomical structure allows blood to absorb oxygen and transport it through a network of blood vessels to cells in various tissues throughout the body. During the process of gas exchange, the blood system absorbs carbon dioxide from cells and carries it to the respiratory system, where it is exhaled from the body.

The respiratory system works closely with both the cardiovascular and nervous systems to maintain blood gas and pH **homeostasis**. The body must regulate blood pH levels. When there is too much carbon dioxide in the blood, it is acidic (that is, its pH value is too low). If there is not enough carbon dioxide in the blood, it will be too alkaline (its pH value will be too high).

BE CAREFUL!
When regulating blood gas and pH homeostasis levels, carbon dioxide, not oxygen, must be closely monitored.

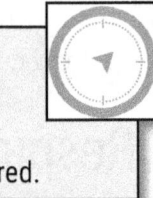

Example

What structure is directly involved in gas exchange?

A. Alveolus   B. Bronchiole   C. Pharynx   D. Trachea

The correct answer is **A**. The alveolus is a tiny air sac found in the lung. Its primary function is to help the respiratory system perform gas exchange.

The Mechanics of Respiration

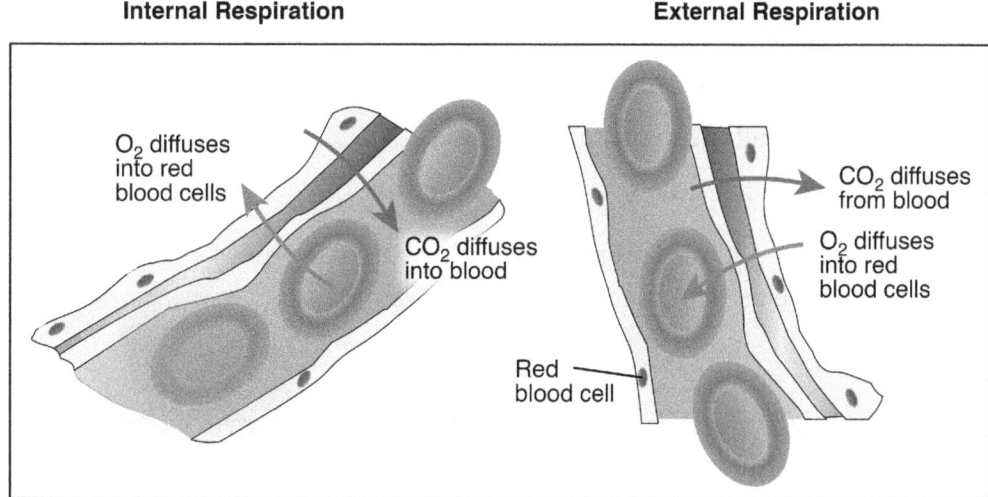

As shown in the image, the process of gas exchange between the outside air and the body is called **respiration**. It occurs on two levels: internal and external.

- **External respiration** occurs between the lungs and blood. When a person inhales, alveoli fill with oxygen through **diffusion**. Oxygen content is much higher than carbon dioxide levels. While in the alveoli region, blood becomes oxygen-rich. Once oxygenated, the blood leaves the lungs and travels through the left side of the heart, where it is pumped into circulation.

> **STEP-BY-STEP**
> The following four steps summarize respiration:
>
> **Step 1.** Air moves in and out of the lungs, which is called pulmonary ventilation.
>
> **Step 2.** Gases are exchanged between air and blood in the lungs by diffusion.
>
> **Step 3.** Gases are transported by circulation of the blood, with help from the heart.
>
> **Step 4.** Gases are exchanged by diffusion between blood and tissues throughout the body.

- **Internal respiration** occurs between the blood and tissues. Once blood enters circulation, it reaches the capillaries. Oxygen diffuses through the capillaries into the cells. Carbon dioxide diffuses from the cells into the capillaries. Because carbon dioxide content is higher than oxygen content in blood at this point, it is called oxygen-poor blood. This oxygen-poor blood travels to the right side of the heart. It moves through the pulmonary circuit, where external respiration begins.

Example

What happens during internal respiration?

    A. Air is inhaled into the body.

    B. Oxygen-rich blood travels to the heart.

    C. Air moves into and out of the pulmonary circuit.

    D. Oxygen is exchanged for carbon dioxide in circulation.

The correct answer is **D**. During internal respiration, oxygen-poor blood is created as oxygen diffuses into the cells in exchange for carbon dioxide.

Let's Review!

- The respiratory system supplies oxygen to the body and removes carbon dioxide.
- Blood pH levels are regulated by the respiratory, cardiovascular, and nervous systems.
- Respiratory organs are anatomically divided into the upper and lower tract.
- Breathing is a mechanical process that provides oxygen, which is essential to all living things.
- Internal respiration involves gas exchange between blood and body tissues.
- External respiration is a gas exchange that happens between blood and the lungs.

LESSON 7.4 THE GASTROINTESTINAL SYSTEM

This lesson introduces the structures and functions of the digestive system.

Anatomy of the Digestive System

The following are the functions of the digestive system:

1. Take in food.
2. Break down food.
3. Absorb digested molecules.
4. Provide nutrients.
5. Eliminate wastes.

The digestive system consists of the **digestive tract**, which is a tube extending from the mouth to the anus, and the associated organs, which secrete fluids into the digestive tract. The term **gastrointestinal tract** technically refers to only the stomach and intestines.

The Path of Food

Food takes the path outlined below as it moves through the body.

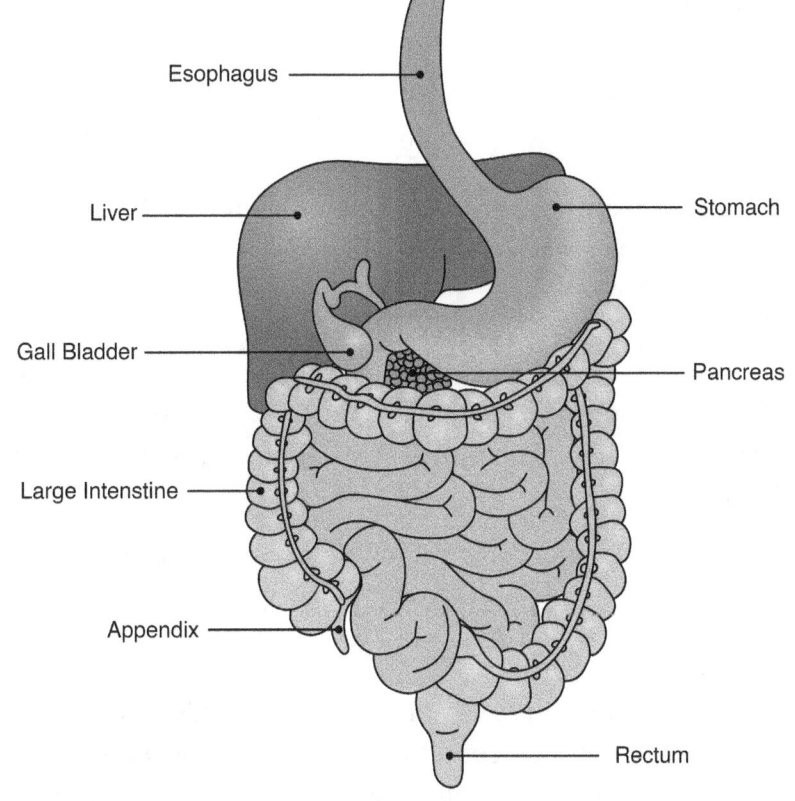

- The **oral cavity**, or the mouth, is the first part of the digestive system. It is bounded by the lips and cheeks and contains the teeth and tongue. Its primary function is to masticate, or chew, and moisten the food.
- The **pharynx**, or throat, connects the mouth to the esophagus.
- The **esophagus** is a muscular tube about 25 centimeters long. Food travels down it to the cardiac sphincter of the stomach.
- The **stomach** is an enlarged segment of the digestive tract.
- The opening of the stomach is the **cardiac sphincter**.
- The muscular layer of the stomach is different from other regions because it has folds called **rugae** that increase the surface area.

- The exit of the stomach is the **pyloric sphincter**.
- The **small intestine** is about 6 meters long and consists of three parts: duodenum, jejunum, and ileum.
  - The duodenum has more **villi** (finger-like projections), has a larger diameter, and is thicker than the other two parts.
  - This increases the surface area in the duodenum, which allows for more absorption of nutrients.
  - The small intestine is the primary site for diffusion of nutrients into the blood.
- The **large intestine** consists of the cecum, colon, rectum, and anal canal. The cecum is located where the small and large intestine meet.
  - The colon is about 1.5 to 1.8 meters long and consists of four parts: the ascending, transverse, descending, and sigmoid colon.
  - The primary function of the large intestine is to compress the waste and collect any excess water that can be recycled.

Example

Digestive organs include structures such as villi and rugae. Which of the following is a purpose they serve?

   A. Increase surface area
   B. Increase blood supply
   C. Increase mucus secretion
   D. Increase bacterial content

The correct answer is **A**. Structures such as the rugae and villi increase surface area. This allows for greater absorption.

Accessory Organs

Accessory organs contribute to the process of digestion. Food does not pass through these organs, but they play critical roles in the digestion of food. The accessory organs are listed below.

The **liver** weighs about 1.36 kilograms and is located in the upper-right quadrant of the abdomen. It is divided into two major lobes: the right lobe and left lobe. The liver has multiple functions:

- **Digestion:** Bile salts emulsify and help break down fats into fatty acids and glycerol.
- **Excretion:** Bile contains excretory products from the hemoglobin breakdown.
- **Nutrient storage:** The liver removes sugar from the blood and stores fats, vitamins, copper, and iron
- **Nutrient conversion:** The liver converts some nutrients into others. For example, it coverts amino acids to lipids or glucose

- **Detoxification of harmful chemicals:** The liver removes ammonia from the blood and converts it to urea.
- **Synthesis of new molecules:** The liver synthesizes new blood proteins such as albumins and fibrinogens.

The **pancreas** is a complex organ composed of both endocrine and exocrine tissues that perform several functions:

- It secretes bicarbonate ions, which neutralize acids.
- It secretes digestive enzymes that are important to all classes of foods.
- It produces insulin and glucagon, which regulate blood sugar levels.

The **gallbladder**, nestled under the liver, stores concentrated bile.

The **tongue** is a large, muscular organ that occupies most of the oral cavity. It moves food in the mouth and, in cooperation with the lips and cheeks, holds the food in place during mastication.

Saliva keeps the oral cavity moist and begins the process of chemical digestion with the enzyme amylase. There are three pairs of **salivary glands**:

- **Parotid** (largest, located in front of the ears)
- **Submandibular** (located below the mandible)
- **Sublingual** (smallest, located in the bottom of oral cavity)

These glands produce saliva, which is a mixture of serous (watery) and mucus fluids that contain digestive enzymes.

Example

Which of the following organs maintains a healthy pH level when a person eats an orange?

A. Gallbladder   B. Liver   C. Pancreas   D. Tongue

The correct answer is **C**. One of the functions of the pancreas is to release bicarbonate ions, which neutralize acids.

Digestion

Digestion is the breakdown of food into molecules that are small enough to be absorbed into the bloodstream. There are two types of digestion: mechanical and chemical. **Mechanical digestion** breaks down large food particles into smaller ones and is evident as a person's teeth grind food into smaller pieces. During **chemical digestion**, digestive enzymes break covalent chemical bonds into organic molecules.

Carbohydrates are broken down into monosaccharides, **proteins** are broken down into amino acids, and **fats or lipids** are broken down into fatty acids and glycerol. Monosaccharides, amino acids, fatty acids, and glycerol molecules are small enough to diffuse across the membranes of the digestive system and enter the bloodstream, to be taken where they are needed.

Absorption begins in the stomach, where small, lipid-soluble molecules, such as alcohol and aspirin, can pass through the stomach epithelium into circulation. Most absorption occurs in the duodenum and jejunum, although some occurs in the ileum. Some molecules can diffuse through the intestinal wall. Others must be transported across the intestinal wall. Transport requires a carrier molecule. If the transport is active, energy is required to move the transported molecule across the intestinal wall.

Enzymes:

Most enzymes are recognizable by the *-ase* ending. Here are some of the most common enzymes:

- **Amylase** is produced in the mouth and breaks down carbohydrates.
- **Pepsin** is produced in the stomach and breaks down proteins.
- **Lipase** is produced in the pancreas and secreted into the small intestine to break down lipids.
- **Peptidase** is produced in the pancreas and secreted into the small intestine to break down peptides into amino acids.
- **Sucrase** is produced in the small intestine and breaks down sucrose into glucose.
- **Lactase** is produced in the small intestine and breaks down lactose into glucose.

Example

What are the building blocks of carbohydrates?

A. Glycerols

B. Fatty acids

C. Amino acids

D. Monosaccharides

The correct answer is **D**. Monosaccharides are the foundational units of carbohydrates.

Disorders of the Digestive System

The following are disorders of the digestive system.

Stomach:

- **Vomiting** results primarily from irritation of the stomach and small intestine. After the vomiting center has been stimulated, a sequence of events occurs that result in vomiting.
- **Ulcers** occur from a specific bacterium, *Helicobacter pylori*. Ulcers were previously thought to be caused by stress, but they can be treated successfully with antibiotics.
- **Peptic ulcer** is a condition in which the stomach acids digest the mucus lining of the duodenum. These ulcers are sometimes called **duodenal ulcers**. People who experience a great deal of stress tend to secrete as much as 15 percent more HCl than normal, which causes the **chyme**, semifluid food mass, to be highly acidic. There are not enough sodium bicarbonate ions to neutralize the acidic chyme, and it eats away at the mucus lining, causing ulcers.

Liver:

- **Cirrhosis** is a disease characterized by damage or death of liver cells, which are replaced by connective tissue. This causes abnormal blood flow in the liver and interferes with normal liver functions.
- **Hepatitis** is an inflammation of the liver. Liver cells can die and be replaced with scar tissue.

Intestine:

- **Irritable bowel disease** is the general term for Crohn's disease or ulcerative colitis.
  - **Crohn's disease** includes a localized inflammatory degeneration that causes the wall of the small intestine to thicken. This disease causes diarrhea, abdominal pain, and weight loss.
  - **Ulcerative colitis** is limited to the mucosa of the large intestine. The involved mucosa exhibits inflammation, including edema, vascular congestion, and hemorrhaging.
- **Irritable bowel syndrome (IBS)** is a disorder of unknown cause in which intestinal mobility is abnormal. Patients exhibit pain in the left lower quadrant, especially after eating, and have alternating bouts of diarrhea and constipation.
- **Malabsorption syndrome** is a spectrum of disorders of the small intestine that result in abnormal nutrient absorption.
- **Appendicitis** is an inflammation of the appendix that usually occurs because of an obstruction.

Example

How is a duodenal ulcer different from an ulcer?

   A. Antibiotics are ineffective with ulcers.

   B. A duodenal ulcer is only found in adults.

   C. An ulcer can occur from a variety of bacteria.

   D. An increase in stomach acids can produce a duodenal ulcer.

The correct answer is **D**. Duodenal ulcers can occur as a result of an increase in the acidic levels in the duodenum. Regular ulcers are caused by bacteria.

Let's Review!

- The digestive system consists of the digestive tract, which is a tube extending from the mouth to the anus, and accessory organs.
- Accessory organs contribute to the process of digestion.
- Food does not pass through the accessory organs.
- Digestion is the breakdown of food into molecules that are small enough to be absorbed into the bloodstream.
- The two types of digestion are mechanical and chemical.

LESSON 7.5 THE REPRODUCTIVE SYSTEM

This lesson covers the human reproductive system. Through sexual intercourse, this system enables internal fertilization and delivery of an infant.

The Male Reproductive System

Like all biological systems, the male reproductive system is comprised of several organs. These organs are located outside or within the pelvis.

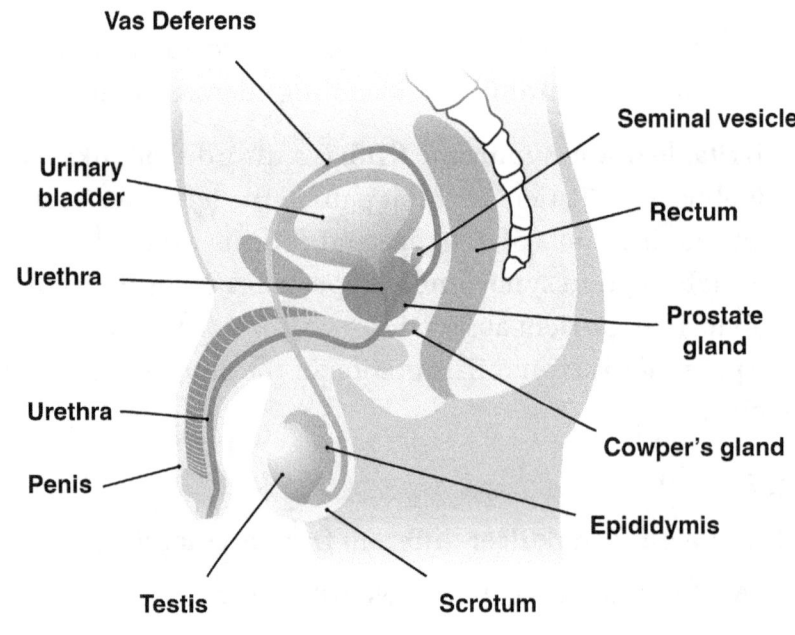

Male Reproductive System

The main male reproductive organs are the **penis** and the **testicles**, which are located external to the body. The penis is composed of a long shaft and a bulbous end called the glans penis. The glans penis is usually surrounded by an extension of skin called the foreskin (though this often is removed in a cosmetic procedure called **circumcision**). The penis has three internal compartments (the corpus cavernosum) that contain erectile tissue. When a male is sexually aroused, this tissue becomes suffused with blood, increasing pressure, and the penis becomes larger and erect.

The **testes** (analogous to the female ovaries), or testicles, are retained in a pouch of skin called the **scrotum**, which descends from the base of the penis. The scrotum contains nerves and blood vessels needed to support the testicles' functions. The scrotum also regulates the temperature of the testicles by contracting (drawing the testicles closer to the warmer body) or relaxing (allowing the testicles to move away from the warmer body).

Each testicle (or testis) produces **sperm** (analogous to the female ova), which are passed into a series of coiled tubules called the **epididymis**. The epididymis stores and nurtures sperm until they are passed into the **vas deferens**, a tubule that is about 30 centimeters long, extending from the testicle into the pelvis and ending at the ejaculatory duct. The epididymis and vas deferens are supported by several accessory glands (the seminal vesicles, the prostate gland, and the Cowper glands) that produce fluid components of **semen** and support the sperm cells. During male orgasm, semen passes through the ejaculatory duct into the urethra and is ejaculated from the penis through the urethral opening.

Example

Where is the male reproductive system located?

A. The male reproductive system is located entirely within the pelvis.

B. The male reproductive system is located entirely outside the pelvis.

C. The male reproductive system is located primarily within the pelvis, though some components are outside the pelvis.

D. The male reproductive system is located primarily outside the pelvis, though some components are located within the pelvis.

The correct answer is **D**. Most of the components of the male reproductive system (penis, scrotum, testes, and epididymis) are external of the body, though some components (vas deferens and accessory glands) are located within the pelvis. The corpus cavernosum extends from within the pelvis into the penis.

The Female Reproductive System

Like all biological systems, the female reproductive system is comprised of several organs. These organs are located within the pelvis or external to the body.

The main female reproductive organs are the **uterus** (the "womb") and the **ovaries**, which are located in the pelvis. The ovaries (analogous to the male testes) produce several important hormones and the **ova** (analogous to the male sperm). After ovulation, the ovum is transported from the ovary to the uterus though the **Fallopian tube**. If sperm are present in the Fallopian tube, **fertilization** may occur. A fertilized **zygote** embeds in the endometrium of the uterus for gestation; an unfertilized ovum passes out of the body during subsequent menstruation.

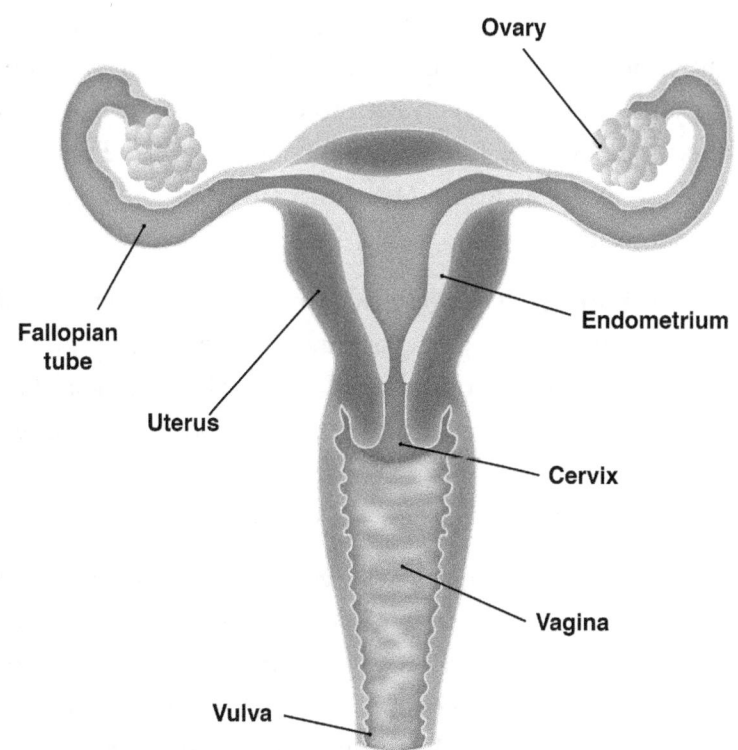

Female Reproductive System

The uterus has a lower opening called the **cervix**, which connects the uterus to the vagina. The female reproductive system has several organs that are external to the body, collectively known as genitals or, specifically, the vulva, including the labia (majora and minora), clitoris, and vaginal opening. When a female is sexually aroused, these external organs become suffused with blood, becoming larger and more erect, and the vagina becomes lubricated.

The uterus performs numerous critical functions during reproduction. It provides mechanical protection, nutritional support, and waste removal for the developing embryo (though a complex interfacing with the embryo's placenta). In addition, it is a powerful, muscular organ that is capable of contractions that push the fetus through the vagina at the time of birth.

Example

An embryo develops into a fetus in the _____.

  A. Fallopian tube   B. ovary   C. uterus   D. vagina

The correct answer is **C**. The zygote implants into the endometrium (uterine wall) and develops into an embryo; the embryo then develops into a fetus within the uterus.

Reproduction

Human reproduce sexually, with a male partner (the "father") providing sperm and a female partner (the "mother") providing an ovum and all subsequent protection and nourishment until the fetus is delivered.

Post-natal feeding is provided by the female's breasts. Human intercourse consists of the male introducing sperm into the female's reproductive system. Sperm may then pass through the female's reproductive system to the Fallopian tubes where one sperm fertilizes an ovum, creating a zygote. The zygote passes out of the Fallopian tube and implants into the uterine wall to begin gestation. Over nine months, the zygote develops and grows into an **embryo** and then a **fetus**.

At the abdomen, the fetus is connected to the **umbilical cord**, which connects to the **placenta**. The umbilical cord and placenta are formed from fetal tissue. The placenta shares a complex interface with the endometrial lining of the uterus. The endometrium and uterus are maternal tissue. Hormones, food, and fetal waste all pass through the placental/uterine interface and along the umbilical cord. As the fetus grows, the placenta also grows. The fetus is encapsulated in a tough container of fetal tissue, filled with fluid, called the **amniotic sac**.

During the early stages of delivery, the amniotic sac ruptures and the fluid passes through the mother's vagina (this is colloquially known as "water breaking"). Also, the cervix softens and dilates to accommodate the fetus. Powerful muscular contractions of the uterus force the fetus through the cervix and out the vagina, normally with the head emerging first. After the fetus is delivered, hormonal signals in the mother's body cause the endometrial lining to quickly disconnect from the placenta, and the placenta is delivered through the vagina (the "afterbirth").

In some cases, surgical removal of the fetus may be desirable or necessary. This process delivers a live baby and colloquially is known as Caesarean section (or C-section).

Example

An expectant mother's water "breaks" immediately before _____.

    A. childbirth   B. fertilization   C. menstruation   D. puberty

The correct answer is **A**. The amniotic sac ruptures, releasing the amniotic fluid, in the early stages of childbirth. This rupturing releases a large amount of fluid and is colloquially known as "water breaking."

Development

Human newborn infants are unable to care for themselves and survive only with a large amount of parental care extending over at least the first several years of life. At birth, humans have all of the basic structures of the adult reproductive system, though some are undeveloped. At about 10–11 years old in females and about 11–12 years old in males, a child enters **puberty**, during which hormonal changes cause the reproductive system to develop fully. Puberty lasts for about 5–7 years.

Menstruation is a cyclical process occurring in the female body, especially the reproductive system, from about the end of puberty until menopause. During each period of menstruation, fluctuating hormone levels cause the uterus to change in anticipation of receiving a zygote. At the midpoint of the menstrual cycle, an ovum is released from an ovary and travels down the Fallopian tube. If the ovum is not fertilized, it passes out of the body along with the endometrium (lining of the uterus), causing menstrual bleeding. If the ovum is fertilized, the zygote implants in the endometrium and pregnancy follows.

There are significant differences between male and female bodies. The primary differences can be noted in the reproductive organs, but numerous other differences are the result of secondary sex characteristics. Male secondary sex characteristics include facial hair and a generally larger body. Female secondary sex characteristics include enlargement of the breasts and widening of the hips.

Example

Which statement best characterizes the changes that occur during puberty?

A. Puberty is a recurring cycle involving fluctuating levels of hormones.

B. During puberty, the male's penis or the female's vulva develops basic structures.

C. During puberty, males and females reach sexual maturity and develop secondary sex characteristics.

D. Puberty occurs during the first trimester of pregnancy and results in the zygote developing into an embryo.

The correct answer is **C**. Puberty occurs during the early teenage years and results in sexual maturity. It is marked by the development of secondary sex characteristics.

Let's Review!

- The reproductive system enables sexual reproduction in humans.
- Components of the reproductive system are often known by multiple names, some of which are common or "slang" terms; the correct biological or medical terms are always preferred.
- The male reproductive system provides the sperm, the carrier of the genetic contribution from the father.
- The female reproductive system provides the ovum, or egg cell, which contains the genetic contribution from the mother. Additionally, the female reproductive system supports fertilization; provides the mechanical protection and nurturing environment needed for embryogenesis and gestation; and performs the actions necessary for the birth of the infant.
- The male testicles are analogous to the female ovaries. There are other similarities in the male and female reproductive systems.
- Sexual maturity occurs during puberty. Humans are capable of reproduction for several decades

LESSON 7.6 THE URINARY SYSTEM

This lesson introduces the anatomy of the urinary system and how it functions. This lesson also explores the role of other body systems, particularly the circulatory and endocrine systems, in aiding with urinary excretion, absorption, and filtration.

Anatomy of the Urinary System

Inside the body, the kidney, ureters, bladder, and urethra make up the **urinary system**, which is also called the renal system. The ureters, bladder, and urethra comprise the **urinary tract**. This system has many functions, some of which are outlined below:

- **Waste elimination:** Urea, creatinine, uric acid, and ammonium are the primary types of nitrogenous wastes excreted from the body. The urinary system also detects and excretes excess water from the blood and out of the body.
- **Osmoregulation of blood and water:** There must be a continual balance of water and salt in the blood. The urinary system, specifically the kidneys, help maintain this balance. It also balances levels of metabolites or electrolytes such as sodium, potassium, and calcium.
- **Hormone secretion:** The kidneys secrete several hormones to regulate processes that range from blood pressure and red blood cell production to calcium uptake via vitamin D.

Several of these functions are performed with help from other body systems, specifically the cardiovascular and respiratory systems.

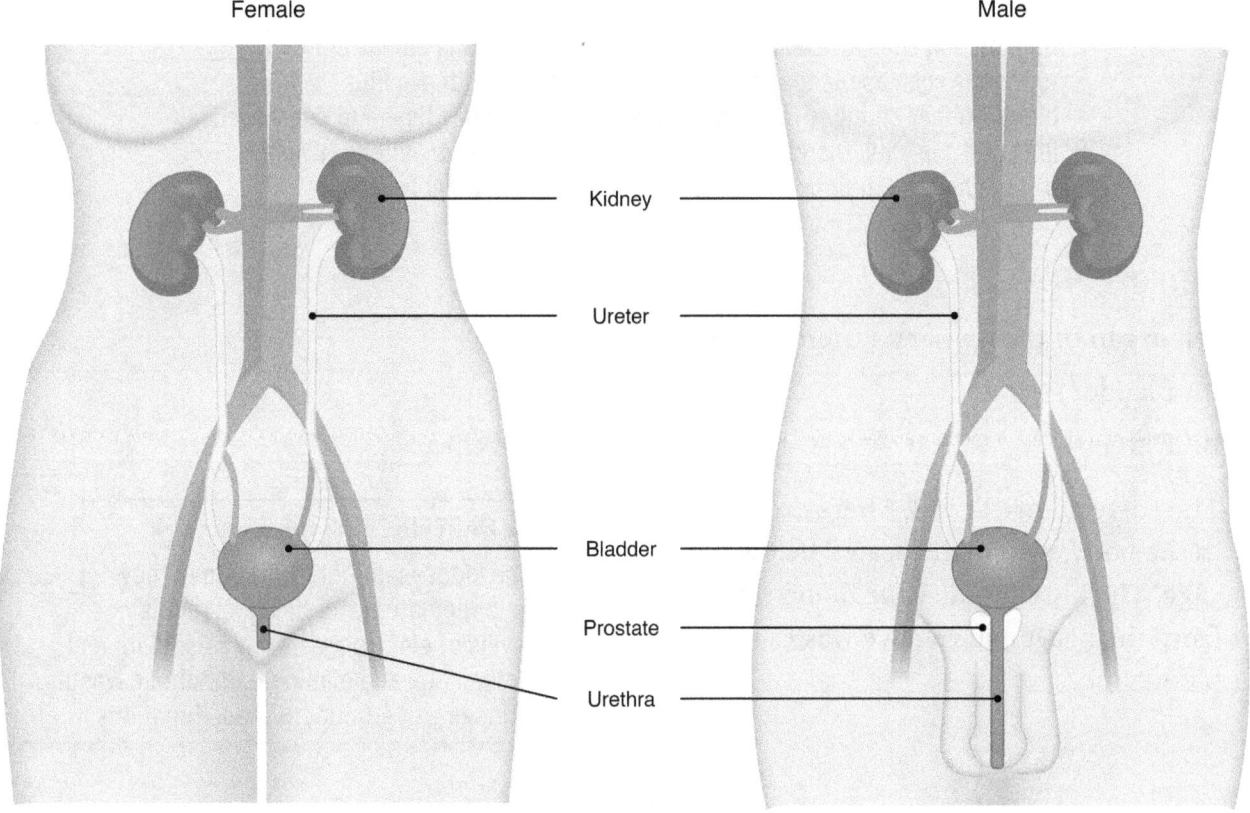

The following table outlines key characteristics of each organ that is labeled in the image above.

Organ	Shape	Characteristics
Kidney	Resembles beans, reddish-brown in color	The body has two kidneys, which excrete wastes in the urine out of the body.
Ureters	Tubular	Send urine from the kidney to the bladder.
Bladder	Pear (when emptied)	Stores urine until the body expels the fluid from the body. Has three openings: two for the ureters and one for the urethra.
Urethra	Tubular	Site where urine from the urinary bladder travels to an external opening. Removes urine from the body.

The primary organ of the urinary system is the kidney. Blood from the heart flows through the kidneys via the **renal artery**. As blood drains from the kidney, it exits through a series of veins, the most prominent of which is the **renal vein**. When urine is produced, it does not drain through the tubes through which blood flows. Rather, urine flows through two ureters before emptying into the urinary bladder. The following steps outline how the urinary system works:

1. Kidney filters and excretes wastes from blood, producing urine.
2. Urine flows down the ureters.
3. Urine empties into the bladder and is temporarily stored.
4. Bladder, when filled, empties urine out of the body via the urethra.

> **DID YOU KNOW?**
> As a person ages, the kidneys and bladder change. This can affect functions such as bladder control and how well the kidneys filter blood. Kidney changes range from a decrease in kidney tissue to decreased filtration capacity. Bladder changes include decreased elasticity (which affects how much urine is stored) and weakened bladder muscles.

Example

Which organ of the urinary system filters blood?

A. Bladder

B. Kidney

C. Ureter

D. Urethra

The correct answer is **B**. There are two kidneys in the body, which are located below the rib cage. The kidneys filter the blood that comes from the heart and remove wastes from the blood.

> **BE CAREFUL!**
> The kidneys do not make urine. They help regulate water balance, regulate levels of electrolytes such as sodium and potassium, and eliminate metabolic wastes. Urine is a byproduct of these functions.

Nephrons and Urine Formation

The functional and structural unit of a kidney is a **nephron**. One kidney contains more than one million nephrons. An illustration of these functional units is shown below:

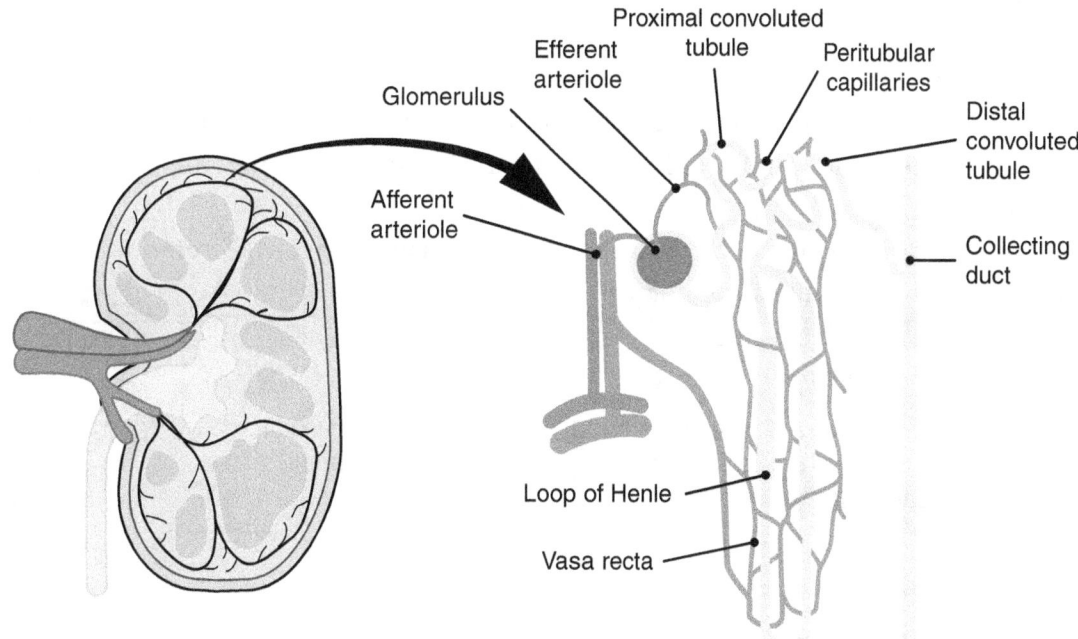

The nephron consists of two parts: the **renal corpuscle** and the **renal tubule**. The renal corpuscle can be divided into the **glomerulus** and **glomerular capsule** (or Bowman's capsule). The glomerulus is a type of capillary bed that functions as a filtration system, filtering solutes as blood enters the kidneys from the renal artery. Surrounding the glomerulus is Bowman's capsule. The renal tubule is a duct that connects to the glomerulus and terminates at the tip of the medullary pyramid. This tubule is divided into the following four regions: (1) **proximal convoluted tubule**, (2) **loop of Henle**, (3) **distal convoluted tubule**, and (4) **collecting duct**.

> **KEEP IN MIND**
>
> It is helpful to think of each nephron as a tiny filtering structure. Each nephron filters blood and forms urine. With more than one million nephrons in a single kidney, it is no wonder the kidneys are so efficient at filtering and excreting wastes from blood!

The components that make up the nephron filter blood and form urine. The following steps outline the pathway for urine formation. The steps are divided into three processes:

1. Glomerular filtration:
   a. Blood enters the kidney through the renal artery.
   b. This artery branches off into capillaries, allowing blood to flow into the glomerulus of the nephron.
   c. Blood pressure forces water and solutes (smaller than proteins) to diffuse from blood across the capillary walls and through pores of Bowman's capsule into the tubule.

2. Tubular reabsorption:
   a. The filtered fluid flows toward the proximal tubule. This is the major site of reabsorption of water and solutes such as glucose, amino acids, and certain ions.
   b. The fluid travels to the loop of Henle, which is another site of reabsorption.
   c. Next, the fluid reaches the distal convoluted tubule. Reabsorption and secretion take place in this segment.
3. Tubular secretion:
   a. In the final segment, the collecting duct, fluid that remains in the duct is called urine. Reabsorption of some water and its return to the bloodstream may happen at this segment.
   b. At this site, creatinine and other nitrogenous wastes are actively secreted into the urine so they can be excreted out of the body.

> **DID YOU KNOW?**
> About 180 liters of blood pass through the nephrons of the kidney each day. This explains why much of this fluid and its contents must be reabsorbed.

Example

Where does urine form?

A. Loop of Henle

B. Collecting duct

C. Distal convoluted tubule

D. Proximal convoluted tubule

The correct answer is **B**. The nephron is the functional unit of the kidney. This structure consists of four major components: proximal and distal convoluted tubules, loop of Henle, and collecting duct. As blood travels through each of these segments, it is filtered to create urine in the collecting duct.

Urine Excretion and ADH

After blood is filtered through the nephron and the byproduct of urine is produced, urine accumulates in the collecting ducts of the nephron. Eventually, urine enters the ureters, which are muscular tubes. With help from muscle contractions, the ureters contract to move urine into the bladder. Urine is stored until the bladder is about half full.

Upon reaching this level, a neural impulse is transmitted telling a **sphincter** in the bladder to relax and allow urine to exit the bladder. Contraction of this sphincter, which is a muscular tube, is under involuntary control. Urine flows from the bladder into the urethra, which expels

> **BE CAREFUL!**
> The urethra in males and females are different sizes due to the reproductive anatomy. The male urethra is about 20 centimeters long. It passes through the length of the penis and terminates at the end of the penis, where urine is removed from the body. The female urethra is about four centimeters long.

Lesson 7.6 The Urinary System

urine out of the body. A second sphincter enables urine to leave the body. This process is known as urination.

Recall that the urinary system works closely with the cardiovascular system to filter blood and return important substances back to the bloodstream during tubular reabsorption. To help maintain water and solute concentration either excreted from or reabsorbed by the body, the urinary system works with hormones that are part of the endocrine system to regulate this process. One of these hormones is the **antidiuretic hormone**, also known as ADH. This hormone is secreted from the posterior pituitary gland, which is found at the base of the brain.

One of the most important functions of ADH is to regulate urine concentration and volume by controlling how much water is reabsorbed in the tubules of the nephrons. The following image shows how ADH controls urine formation.

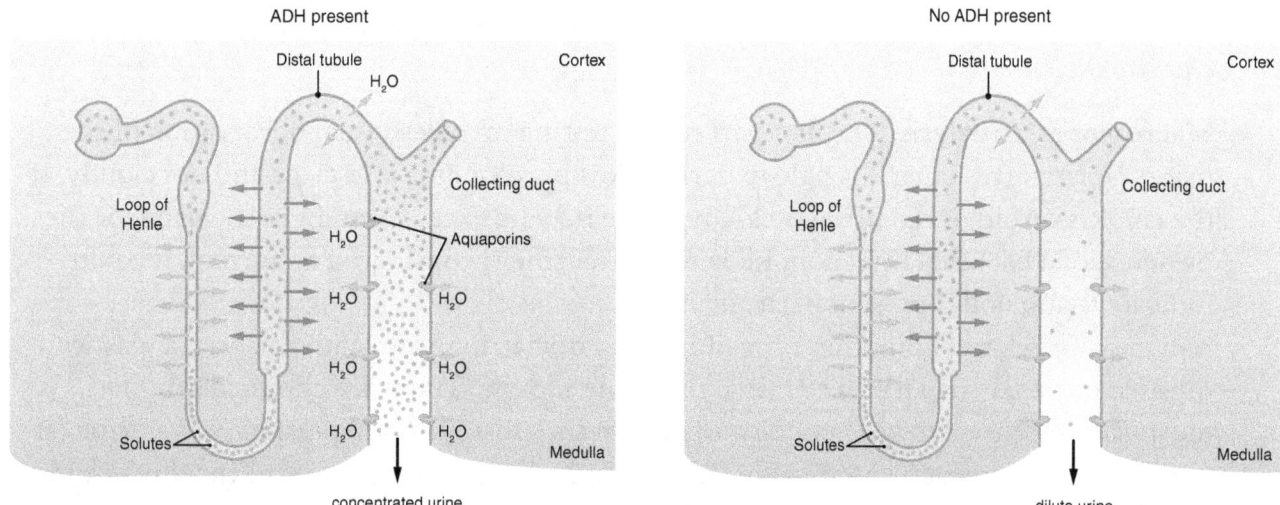

As shown in the image, when ADH is present, there is an increased permeability of water at the distal convoluted tubule and collecting duct. This causes more water to be reabsorbed and retained. It also decreases the volume of urine produced and concentrates the urine. The opposite occurs when ADH is not actively communicating with the kidneys and regulating urine formation.

> **DID YOU KNOW?**
> ADH control of urine formation is intimately connected to diabetes insipdus. When people have this disease, ADH does not communicate properly with the kidneys. As a result, symptoms include excessive thirst and frequent urination.

Example

The antidiuretic hormone primarily controls tubular reabsorption of which substance?

   A. Calcium   B. Creatinine   C. Urea   D. Water

The correct answer is **D**. Regulating how much water the body excretes or reabsorbs is a key function of the urinary system. To perform this function, kidneys must communicate with the hormone ADH, which is released from the posterior pituitary gland in the brain.

Urinalysis

Medical professionals can determine diseases that affect the urinary system by conducting a **urinalysis**. This type of test can reveal disease that does not necessarily present observable symptoms. Diseases confirmed through urinalysis include diabetes mellitus, different types of glomerulonephritis, and urinary tract infections. Both macroscopic and microscopic urinalysis can be performed.

- **Macroscopic urinalysis:** The first part of this testing involves visual observation of the urine. Normal fresh urine is pale to dark yellow in color. It is also clear and not cloudy. If the color is turbid or the urine is cloudy, there may be excess protein in the urine or the presence of a bacterial infection. Red or brown urine is considered abnormal. It could indicate that blood is present in the urine.
- A urine dipstick test is another type of macroscopic urinalysis. With this test, a plastic dipstick or paper strip is inserted into the urine sample. There are chemicals on the dipstick that cause it to change color when certain substances are present in the urine (at a specific concentration). Medical professionals can compare the color of the dipstick to a standard chart to analyze a urine sample.
- When the liquid is removed, this sediment is mounted to a microscope slide and analyzed using a microscope. Typically, this test is performed to look at blood cells in the urinary tract, bacteria, parasites, or even tumor cells. This test also helps confirm the diagnosis of various urinary problems like kidney disease, cancer, microbial infections, and liver disease.
- **Microscopic urinalysis:** This type of urinalysis requires the use of a light microscope. Typically, a urine sample is spun down, or centrifuged, in a test tube. This causes a sediment consisting of red blood cells, fat cells, and other large particles to aggregate and separate from the liquid portion of the urine.

Example

What is most likely analyzed during microscopic urinalysis?

A. Volume of water in urine

B. Amount of urea excreted

C. Sodium levels in the urine

D. Presence of white blood cells

The correct answer is **D**. During microscopic urinalysis, large substances like blood cells and bacteria are separated from the liquid portion of urine. These substances are placed on a microscopic slide and analyzed to make or confirm a diagnosis.

Let's Review!

- The urinary system eliminates wastes from the body, regulates blood and water levels, and secretes hormones that directly influence various physiological processes in the body.
- The circulatory and endocrine systems work with the urinary system to perform various functions.
- Nephrons are functional units and structures of the kidneys that play a large role in filtration, reabsorption, and secretion.
- After blood enters the kidneys through the renal artery, it is filtered in the glomerulus. Then, it travels through the proximal tubule, the loop of Henle, and the distal convoluted tubule before accumulating as urine in the collecting duct.
- The kidneys form urine as a byproduct, which travels through the ureter before being stored in the bladder and eventually excreted from the body via the urethra.
- Urinalysis is a method used to evaluate the quality of urine and help diagnose various urinary health problems.

Chapter 7 Human Anatomy and Physiology: Organization of Systems Practice Quiz

1. What are the subdivisions of the dorsal cavity, located in the back of the human body?
   A. Cranial and spinal
   B. Dorsal and ventral
   C. Lateral and proximal
   D. Inferior and superior

2. Which of the following cavities contains the urinary bladder, part of the intestines, and the internal reproductive organs?
   A. Abdominal
   B. Dorsal
   C. Pelvic
   D. Thoracic

3. Which blood group is a universal acceptor?
   A. A
   B. B
   C. AB
   D. O

4. Which organ is responsible for producing oxygenated blood?
   A. Heart
   B. Kidney
   C. Lung
   D. Stomach

5. What structure channels food to the esophagus and air to the trachea?
   A. Bronchiole
   B. Capillary
   C. Larynx
   D. Lung

6. Which forms a network around the alveoli to facilitate gas exchange?
   A. Rib cage
   B. Capillaries
   C. Bronchioles
   D. Epithelial cells

7. What is the most common cause of appendicitis?
   A. Spicy foods
   B. Poor nutrition
   C. An obstruction
   D. Inherited factor

8. What organ of the digestive system has villi?
   A. Pancreas
   B. Gallbladder
   C. Large intestine
   D. Small intestine

9. The ova are produced in the _____.
   A. vagina
   B. ovaries
   C. uterine wall
   D. Fallopian tube

10. Which statement about puberty is true?
    A. Puberty results from an unfertilized ovum.
    B. Males begin puberty at a younger age than females.
    C. Females begin puberty at a younger age than males.
    D. Puberty is a cyclical process occurring in the female body.

11. The antidiuretic hormone ADH is known to alter _____ concentration that is excreted from the urinary system.
    A. ammonia
    B. creatinine
    C. sodium
    D. urine

12. Where does fluid flow directly after leaving through the pores of Bowman's capsule?
    A. Bladder
    B. Glomerulus
    C. Loop of Henle
    D. Proximal convoluted tubule

Chapter 7 Human Anatomy and Physiology: Organization of Systems Practice Quiz – Answer Key

1. A. The dorsal cavity has two subdivisions: the cranial cavity and the spinal cavity. **See Lesson: Organization of the Human Body.**

2. C. The pelvic cavity is a small space enclosed by the bones of the pelvis that contains the urinary bladder, part of the intestines, and the internal reproductive organs. **See Lesson: Organization of the Human Body.**

3. C. Type AB blood is a universal acceptor, while type O blood is a universal donor. **See Lesson: Cardiovascular System.**

4. C. The lungs contain oxygen that diffuses into the bloodstream, allowing deoxygenated blood to be converted to oxygenated blood. **See Lesson: Cardiovascular System.**

5. C. The larynx contains the voice box. It funnels air to the trachea and food past the epiglottis and down the esophagus. **See Lesson: The Respiratory System.**

6. B. Capillaries are blood vessels that form a network around the alveolar sacs to facilitate gas exchange between blood and the lungs. **See Lesson: The Respiratory System.**

7. C. The most common cause of appendicitis is an obstruction. **See Lesson: Gastrointestinal System.**

8. D. The small intestine has finger-like projections called villi covering the internal surface. **See Lesson: Gastrointestinal System.**

9. B. The ova are produced in the ovaries. **See Lesson: Reproductive System.**

10. C. Females generally begin puberty at 10–11 years old; males generally begin puberty about a year later, at 11–12 years old. **See Lesson: Reproductive System.**

11. D. The posterior pituitary gland at the base of the brain secretes the hormone ADH. This hormone alters how much water is excreted from urine by the kidneys. Thus, it controls the concentration and volume of urine in the body. **See Lesson: The Urinary System.**

12. D. After filtered fluid leaves Bowman's capsule, which encloses the glomerulus, it travels to the proximal convoluted tubule before ending up in the loop of Henle. **See Lesson: The Urinary System.**

CHAPTER 8 HUMAN ANATOMY AND PHYSIOLOGY: SUPPORT AND MOVEMENT

LESSON 8.1 THE SKELETAL SYSTEM

This lesson introduces the anatomy and functions of the skeletal system. This lesson also explores how bone forms, remodels, and constantly changes as a person grows.

Skeletal System Overview

A human is born with roughly 270 bones. As a person grows, this number decreases to approximately 206. This is because many of the bones fuse.

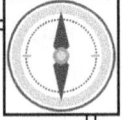

FOR EXAMPLE
Half of the pelvic bone has three separate bones at birth: the ilium, ischium, and pubis. By adulthood, these bones fuse into one bone called the hipbone.

Anatomically, the skeletal system is divided into two major divisions: axial skeleton and appendicular skeleton. The **axial skeleton** consists of the bones of the skull, sternum, vertebral column, and ribcage. The **appendicular skeleton** comprises the bones of the upper and lower extremities and the associated girdles that connect the extremities to the vertebral column. The following table summarizes the number of bones found in each skeletal division.

Axial	80 bones
Inner ear ossicles	6
Skull and hyoid	23
Sternum and ribs	25
Vertebral column	26
Appendicular	126
Pectoral girdle	4
Upper extremities	60
Pelvic girdle	2
Lower extremities	60

Twenty-four of the bones in the vertebral column are called the pre-sacral vertebrae. These consist of 7 cervical, 12 thoracic, and 5 lumbar vertebrae. The last two bones of the vertebral column are the sacrum and coccyx.

Lesson 8.1 The Skeletal System

The skeletal system consists of **bones**, **cartilage**, and **ligaments** that are tightly bound together to form a strong, yet flexible, framework. Bone is an active form of **connective tissue**. This tissue plays a role in many of the functions of the skeletal system:

- **Support:** Bones and cartilage support body posture because both structures are rigid. They also allow a person to remain upright and provide a framework to which soft tissues like muscles and organs can attach.
- **Movement:** Bones of the skeletal system interact with the muscular system to help the body move. Bones themselves cannot move. But when connected to each other by ligaments, along with the action of muscles, a human body can move.
- **Protection:** The skeletal system protects vital organs from external damage. The skull protects the brain, the vertebral column protects the spinal cord, and the sternum and ribcage protect the lungs.
- **Mineral storage:** Bone functions as a storage site for important minerals like calcium and phosphorus. These minerals are used for a variety of physiological functions in the body.
- **Hematopoiesis:** This is the process bones use to produce red blood cells and stem cells, which differentiate to a variety of different cell types in the body.

The following image illustrates the anatomy of the skeletal system.

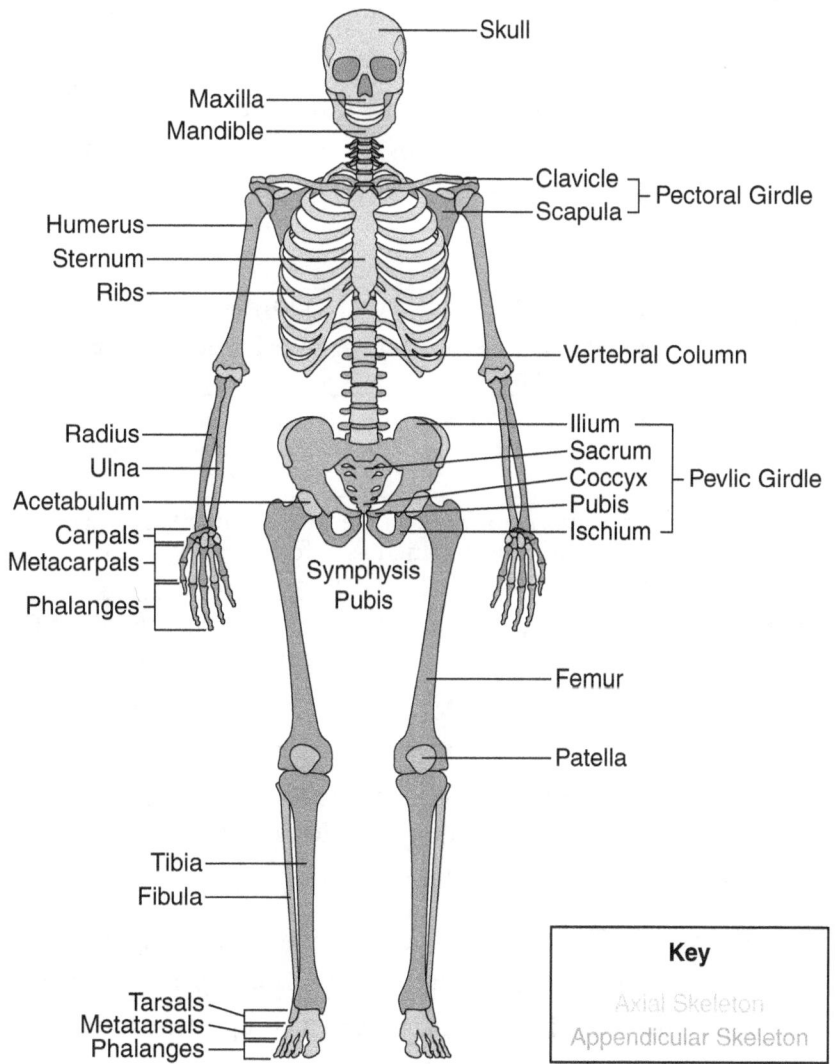

157

Example

Which of the following is part of the axial skeleton?

A. Carpals   B. Femur   C. Patella   D. Skull

The correct answer is **D**. The axial skeleton consists of bones that do not belong to the upper and lower extremities: the skull, vertebral column, sternum, and ribcage.

Bone Shape and Structure

The overall structure of bone consists of an outer shell called **compact bone**. It encloses another type of bone tissue that is loosely organized called **spongy** or **cancellous bone**. Compact bone is made of units called **osteons**. These structures look like cylinders. They contain a mineral matrix and living bone cells. Each osteon also contains a **Haversian canal** that houses the bone's blood vessels and nerve fibers.

Surrounding the compact bone is a fibrous membrane called the **periosteum**. This consists of blood vessels, nerves, and lymphatic vessels that nourish the compact bone.

KEEP IN MIND

As the name implies, spongy bone is lighter and less dense than compact bone. It is spongy because it consists of open sections called pores. Viewed under a microscope, these sections look like a kitchen sponge.

There are five types of bones in the human body: long, short, flat, irregular, and sesamoid. The following table details the characteristics of each and where they are found.

Bone type	Appearance	Function	Example
Long	Elongated bones; longer than they are wide	Mechanical strength	Femur, tibia, clavicle, humerus, and metacarpals
Flat	Broad bones that are thin	Site of muscle attachment; provide protection	Scapula, hip bone (os coxa), sternum, nasal bone, and occipital/ parietal/ frontal bones of the skull
Irregular	Have a non-uniform shape that cannot be classified as any other bone type	Mechanical support for the body	Vertebrae
Sesamoid	Small bones	Mechanical support; provide protection	Patella (kneecap)
Short	About same width as length	Provide support; little movement	Carpal and tarsal bones of the wrist and feet

To visualize the anatomy of all bone types, it is helpful to view the anatomy of long bone. As shown in the following image, the long bone consists of three major sections: proximal epiphysis, diaphysis, and distal epiphysis.

- **Epiphysis:** This is found at each end of the long bone. It consists primarily of spongy bone with a thin layer of compact bone. Bone growth occurs at the epiphysis.
- **Articular cartilage:** This covers the epiphysis. It decreases frictions at the joints.

Lesson 8.1 The Skeletal System

- **Diaphysis:** This is the longest part of the long bone. It consists primarily of compact bone.
- **Medullary cavity:** This is found inside the long bone. It is composed of red and yellow bone marrow. Red marrow is where hematopoiesis occurs. Yellow marrow consists primarily of fat cells.

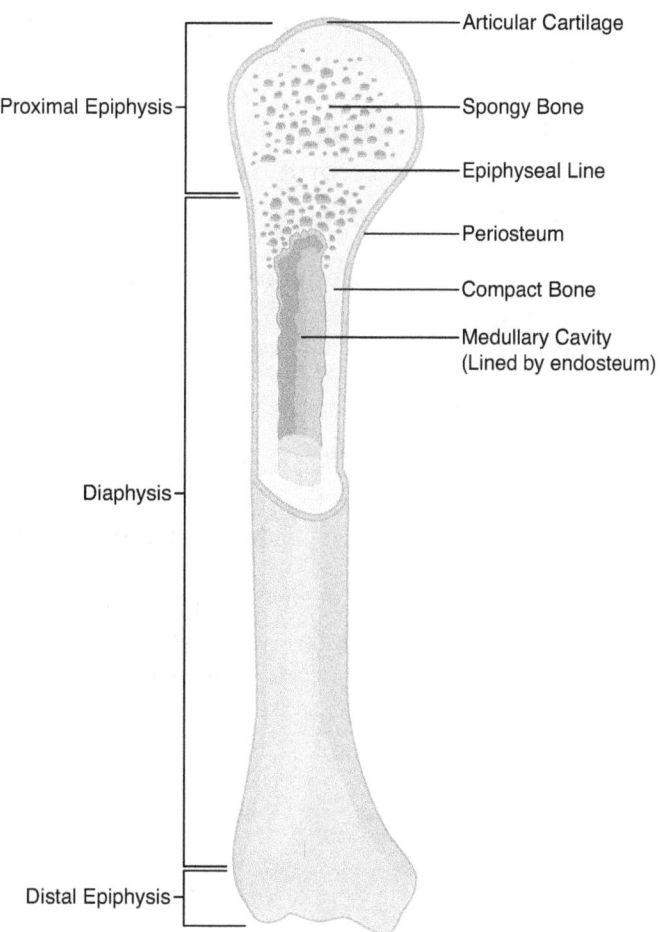

Example

A histologist cracks open a tibia. While viewing the inside, what does he see?

A. Diaphysis   B. Soft tissue   C. Spongy bone   D. Proximal epiphysis

The correct answer is **C**. When looking inside a long bone, such as the tibia, the histologist sees the spongy bone. This is found at the proximal and distal ends of the epiphysis.

Ossification and Bone Remodeling

Although bone is a hard structure, it can grow. This is especially important in childhood. **Ossification** is the process of bone formation that occurs first during embryonic development. This process transforms soft, flexible cartilage to hard bone. It does so by replacing the cartilage with mineral deposits, specifically calcium and phosphorus. Ossification begins in the center of bones and spreads toward the end of the bones.

When a baby is born, a lot of cartilage is still found in the skeleton, particularly in the long bones. But there are **growth plates** at the end of long bones. This region is also made of cartilage. As the child grows, this area of cartilage at the growth plate experiences ossification to elongate the bone, enabling a person to grow taller.

Ossification also plays a role in **bone remodeling**. Mature bone tissue is constantly being broken down through a process called **bone resorption**. Through ossification, new bone tissue replaces this old bone. There are three types of bone cells:

- **Osteocytes:** These are bone cells. They produce collagen and other substances that create the extracellular matrix of bone.
- **Osteoblasts:** These are called bone-forming cells. They are found on the surface of bone and can be stimulated to differentiate into other type of bone cells called osteocytes.
- **Osteoclasts:** These are called bone-resorbing cells. They are found on the surface of bone. They dissolve the bone.

KEEP IN MIND

Bone resorption frees calcium and other minerals from bone for use in the body and clears out older pieces of bone. In doing so, this process promotes the deposition of new bone.

Recall that osteons are found in compact bone. As shown in the following image, the extracellular matrix of bone and osteocytes are found within the osteon. Osteoblasts and osteoclasts are found on the bone surface.

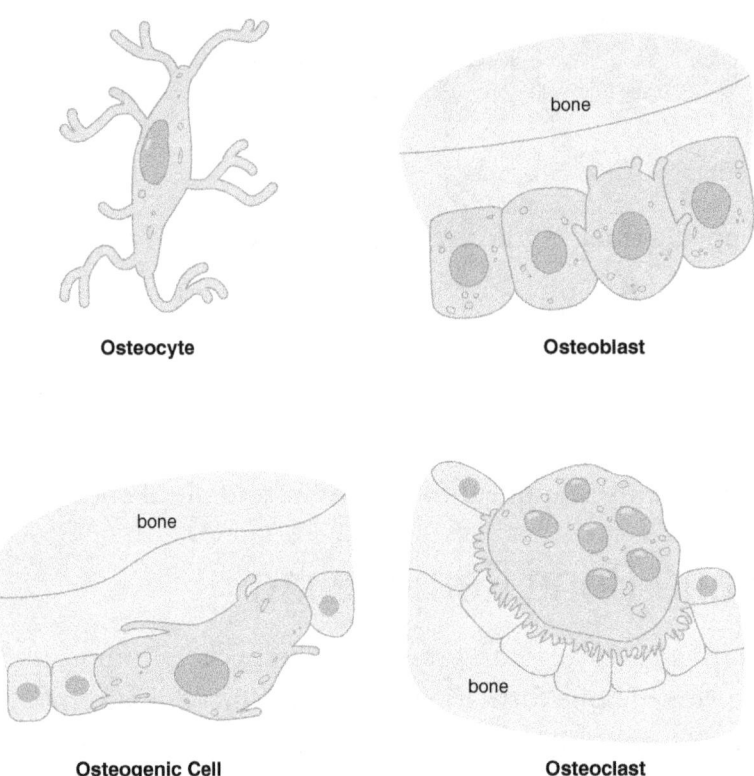

Example

What bone cell is a bone-forming cell?

A. Osteoblast B. Osteoclast C. Osteocyte D. Osteon

The correct answer is **A**. Osteoblasts are bone-forming cells found on the bone's surface. They help form new bone as older bone is broken down through resorption.

Let's Review!

- The skeletal system provides structural support and protection, aids in movement, serves as a mineral reservoir, and helps produce cells.
- The appendicular skeleton consists of the upper and lower extremities.
- The axial skeleton consists of the skull, sternum, ribcage, and vertebral column.
- The five bone types in the human body are: long, short, flat, irregular, and sesamoid.
- Ossification is a bone-forming process typically performed in childhood.
- Bone remodeling is a process that involves replacing old, mature bone tissue with new bone.
- Osteons are bone cells found in compact bone that contain the Haversian canal, which is the site for blood vessels and nerve fibers.
- Osteoblasts are bone-forming cells, and osteoclasts are bone-dissolving or resorbing cells.
- Osteocytes are bone cells found deep within bone that produce substances like cartilage.

LESSON 8.2 THE MUSCULAR SYSTEM

This lesson introduces the anatomy of the muscular system, including the three different muscle tissues. This lesson also describes the role of the muscular system in movement and the physiology of muscle contraction.

Anatomy of the Muscle

The **muscular system** is responsible for all types of body movement. Additional functions of this system include providing support, stabilizing joints, and generating heat for the body. All muscles consist of specialized cells known as **muscle fibers**, which contract to facilitate body movement. For the body to move, muscles must be attached to bones. Muscles are also attached to internal organs and blood vessels. Thus, most of the body's movements occur because of muscle contraction from muscle fibers.

> **DID YOU KNOW?**
> There are over 600 muscles in the body. Muscles are grouped according to characteristics such as size, shape, and location.

The body is comprised of three types of muscles: cardiac, smooth, and skeletal. As shown in the image below, these muscles look different. They also perform different functions.

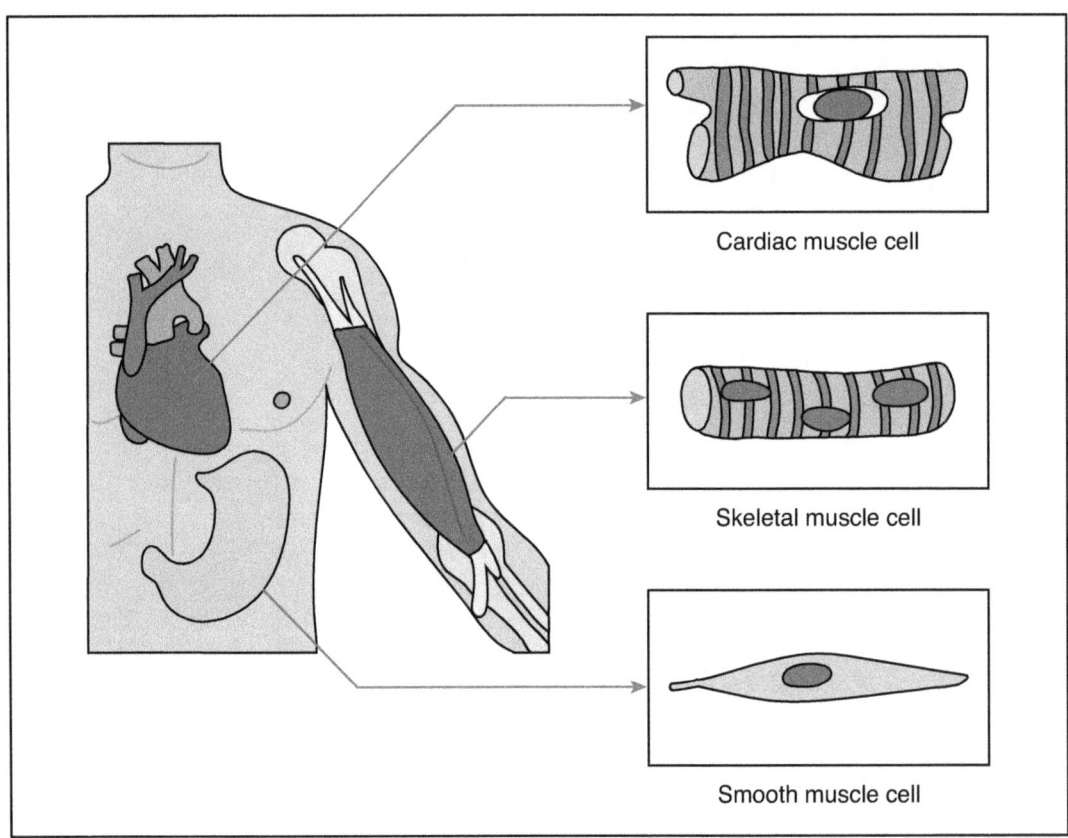

- **Cardiac muscle:** This muscle consists of muscle cells that are striated, short, and branched. These cells contain one nucleus, are branched, and are rectangular. Cardiac muscle contraction is an involuntary process, which is why it is under the control of the autonomic nervous system. This muscle is found in the walls of the heart.
- **Skeletal muscle:** This muscle cell is striated, long, and cylindrical. There are many nuclei in a skeletal muscle cell. Attached to bones in the body, skeletal muscle contracts voluntarily, meaning that it is under conscious control.

> **BE CAREFUL!**
> Skeletal muscles are excited by the nervous system. Cardiac and smooth muscles are stimulated by the nervous system and by circulating hormones.

- **Smooth muscle:** This muscle consists of non-striated muscle cells that are spindle-shaped. Like cardiac muscle cells, smooth muscle cells contain one nucleus. This muscle type is found in the walls of internal organs like the bladder and stomach. Smooth muscle contraction is involuntary and controlled by the autonomic nervous system.

Despite the differences among cardiac, smooth, and skeletal muscles, they share four properties: excitability, contractility (muscle shortening), extensibility (muscle stretching), and elasticity.

Example

What is a purpose of the muscular system?

A. Connects one bone to another

B. Helps the bones of the body move

C. Protects the body from external injury

D. Determines how blood circulates in the body

The correct answer is **B**. One of the primary functions of the muscular system is to aid in movement. Muscles help the bones of the skeletal system move. Muscles contract and relax to facilitate movement.

Skeletal Muscle Anatomy

Bones move with the help of skeletal muscles, through contraction and extension. Skeletal muscles must be attached to the bones to pull on the bones and cause them to move. This movement is performed when the skeletal muscle shortens, or contracts.

As shown in the following image, connective tissue attaches skeletal muscle to bone or other tissues. Skeletal muscle consists of three types of connective tissue. The **endomysium** encases individual skeletal muscle fibers. These muscle fibers are bundled together by a connective tissue called the **perimysium**. Bundles of skeletal muscle fibers are called **fasciculi**. Each fascicle is bundled together by a strong connective tissue called the **epimysium**.

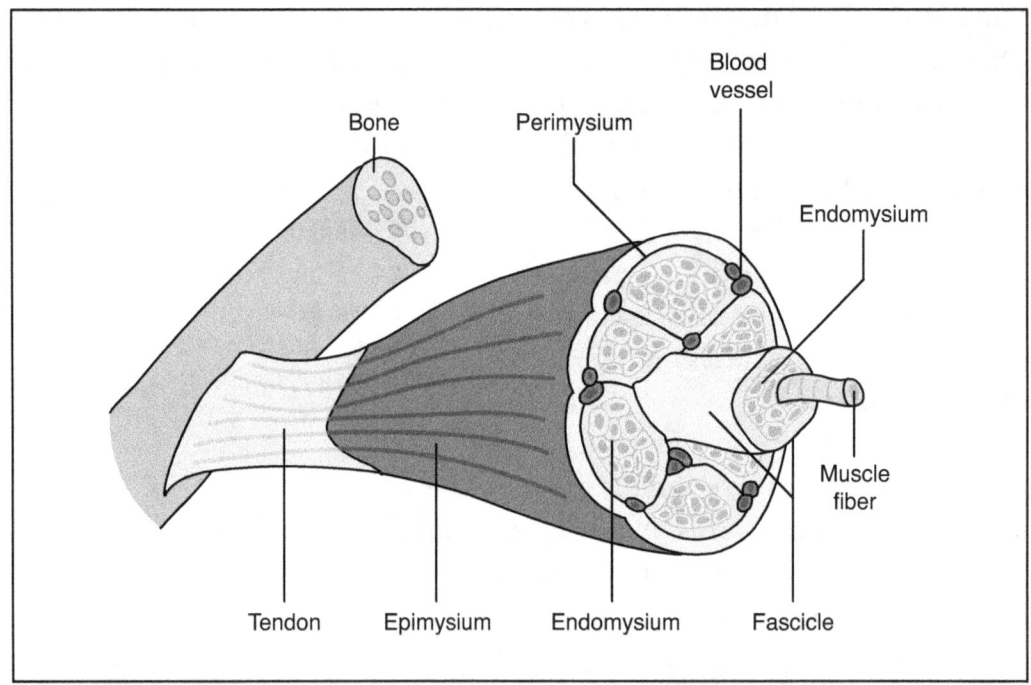

> **KEEP IN MIND**
> The connective tissue supports and protects muscle fibers. This tissue also provides a way for nerve and blood vessels to innervate the skeletal muscle.

The cell membrane that surrounds a skeletal muscle fiber is called a **sarcolemma**. The cytoplasm of the skeletal muscle fiber is the **sarcoplasm**. One muscle fiber is filled with several long, cylindrical proteins called **myofibrils**, which are the contractile units of the fiber. The smallest contractile unit in a myofibril is a **sarcomere**. Several protein **myofilaments** make up a myofibril. There are two types of myofilaments: thick bands and thin bands. Thick bands, or myofilaments, are made of several protein molecules called **myosin**. Several protein molecules, called **actin**, link together to form the thin bands. These thin actin bands are attached to a **Z-disk** (or Z-line).

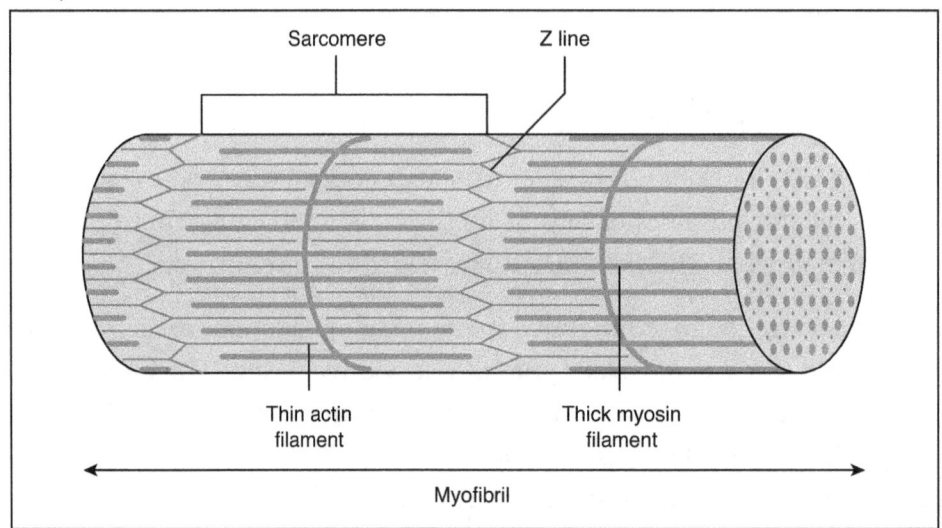

Lesson 8.2 The Muscular System

Example

What is the smallest contractile unit of skeletal muscle?

A. Actin B. Epimysium C. Myofibril D. Sarcomere

The correct answer is **D**. Several contractile units called myofibrils are found within a single muscle fiber. Smaller contractile units called sarcomeres make up a myofibril.

Muscle Contraction

Keep in mind that the dark, striped Z-disc marks where one sarcomere ends and another begins. As shown in the image below, there are light-colored bands called **I-bands** and dark-colored bands called **A-bands**. The Z-line is found in the middle of the I-bands, while the **H zone** is found in the middle of the A-bands. In the middle of the H-zone is the **M line**, which is the center of the sarcomere.

TEST TIP

The following guide can be used to remember the components of the various lines in a skeletal muscle:

A-band	Thick and thin filaments
I-band	Thin filaments only
Z-line	Actin filament attachment site
H-band	Thick filaments only

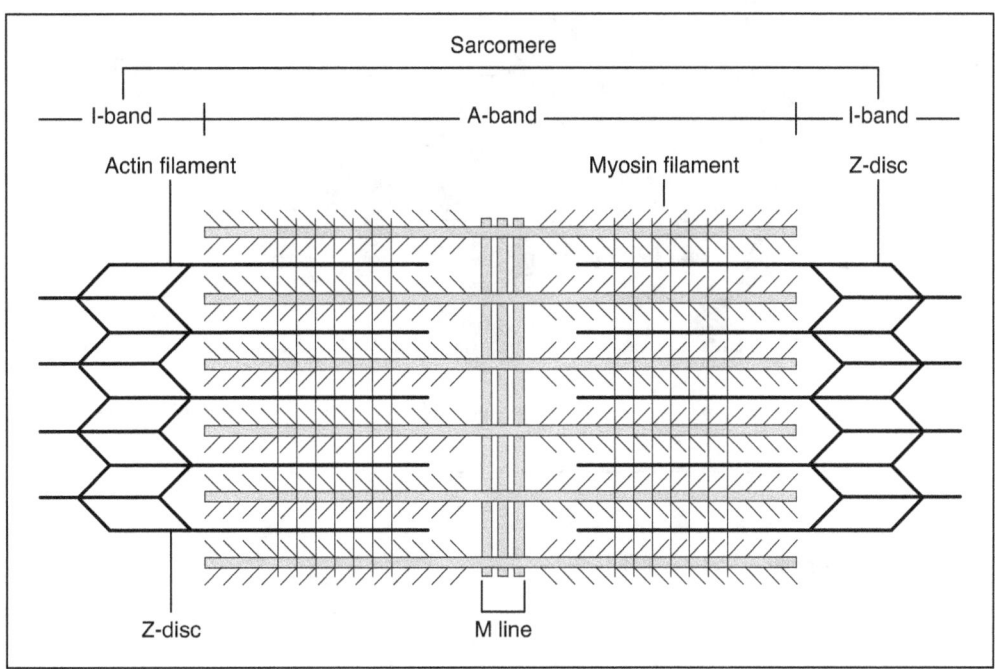

Slide filament theory explains muscle contraction. According to this theory, actin filaments slide past myosin filaments, pulling the actin filaments closer to the center of the sarcomere, or M line. As shown in the image below, this sliding action happens because of interactions between the heads of actin and myosin. The heads of myosin form attachments with the actin myofilaments. These attachments are known as **crossbridges**.

> **KEEP IN MIND**
> The head of actin is a round protein shaped like a ball. Several of these round proteins link together to form a long chain, or thin myofilament. Myosin is a thick protein with a head that resembles a golf club. When several myosin proteins join together, they create a myosin filament, where the heads point outward.

With the help of energy in the form of ATP, the myosin heads are energized to attach to binding sites in actin and form a crossbridge. After energy in the myosin head is released, the myosin pulls actin myofilaments closer to the M line. This head can only form another crossbridge when another molecule of ATP attaches to the head, reenergizing it. Calcium also plays an important role in determining when contraction happens. This ion is found in the **sarcoplasmic reticulum**, which surrounds myofibrils.

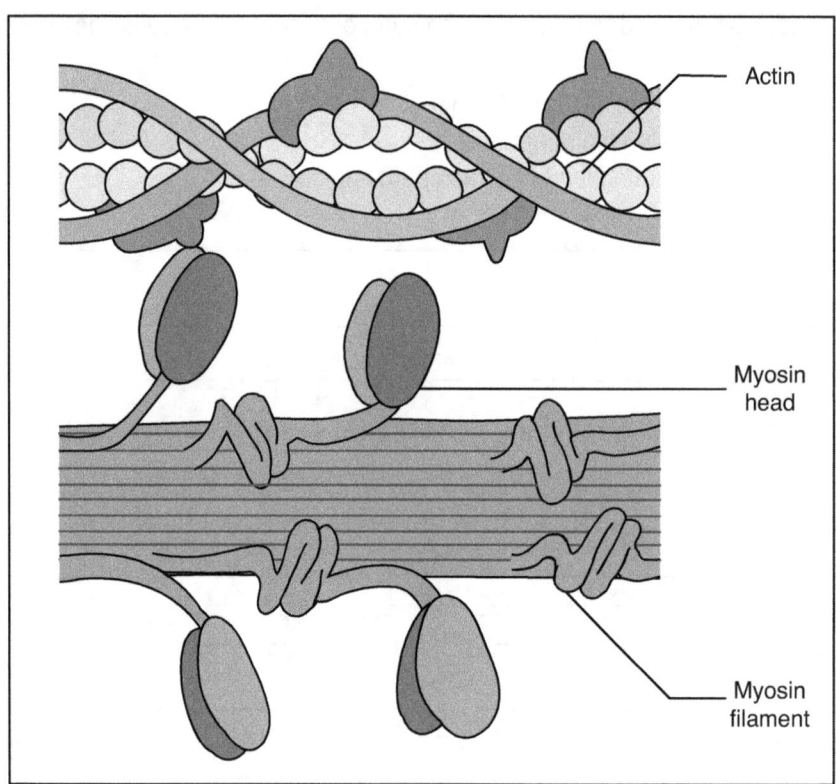

Example

What structure is reenergized with ATP?

  A. Actin B. Myosin C. Myofibril D. Sarcomere

The correct answer is **B**. Myosin heads attach to thin actin filaments to form crossbridges. These attachments can only form when the myosin head is energized with ATP.

Lesson 8.2 The Muscular System

Coordinating Movement

Ligaments attach bones to bones. Where ligaments connect bones, they form a **joint**. Thus, joints are the site where individual bones meet. There are three types of joints:

- **Immovable:** Also known as fibrous joints, these consist of bones held together by connective tissues. The bones are in very close contact. An example of an immovable joint is the intersection of cranial bones in the skull.
- **Partly movable:** Also known as cartilaginous joints, these consist of bones held together by cartilage. These joints allow some degree of movement. Partly movable joints include the vertebral discs in the spine.
- **Synovial:** These allow the largest freedom of movement because the bones are separated by a joint cavity. Examples of synovial joints are the hip and shoulder.

The muscular system works with the skeletal system to move the body. Thus, the muscles must be attached to bone. **Tendons** attach muscle to bone. Tendons consist of tough connective tissue that is found on either side of the joint where two bones are connected. Tendons work with skeletal muscles to move bones. When muscles contract, they shorten. This pulls on the bones, with the help of the tendon, to allow the body to move.

> **FOR EXAMPLE**
> Biceps and triceps muscles in the arm work together to bend and lengthen the elbow. As a biceps muscle contracts, the triceps muscle remains elongated, or relaxed. Thus, the biceps is the flexor and the triceps is the extensor of the elbow joint.

Muscles must work in pairs to move bones at the joint. The muscle that causes a joint to bend is called a **flexor muscle**. The muscle that contracts and causes a joint to straighten is called an **extension muscle**. If one muscle in the pair contracts, the other remains elongated.

Example

How many muscles must work together during contraction and extension?

A. 2   B. 10   C. 206   D. 600

The correct answer is **A**. Muscles work in pairs during contraction and extension. When one muscle contracts, the other extends, or relaxes.

Let's Review!

- A muscle is a fibrous tissue that aids in body movement, provides support, and generates heat energy for the body.
- Cardiac, smooth, and skeletal muscles are the three muscle types found in the body.
- Cardiac and smooth muscle are under involuntary control, while skeletal muscle is under voluntary control.
- Cardiac and skeletal muscles are striated, while smooth muscle is non-striated.

- Three types of muscle tissues comprise a skeletal muscle: epimysium, endomysium, and perimysium.
- A single skeletal muscle fiber consists of several contractile units called myofibrils, which consist of actin and myosin myofilaments.
- According to the slide filament theory, actin and myosin myofilaments form crossbridges to shorten a sarcomere, which shortens a skeletal muscle.
- Tendons attach muscle to bone and help bones move.
- Joints are the regions between bones that influence the degree of flexibility with body movement.
- Skeletal muscles move bones by working in muscle pairs to contract and elongate.

LESSON 8.3 THE INTEGUMENTARY SYSTEM

This lesson introduces the anatomy of the integumentary system, including the system's function. This lesson also describes the effects of aging and cancer on the integumentary system.

The Skin's Many Layers

The **integumentary system** is a body system comprised of the skin and accessory structures, including the hair, sebaceous and sweat glands, and nails. This system protects the body, maintains homeostasis, and provides sensory information about the external environment.

The largest organ in the integumentary system is the skin. Often not thought of as an organ, the skin is made of four different tissues that work together to perform a variety of functions such as preventing toxic substances from entering the body and regulating body temperature.

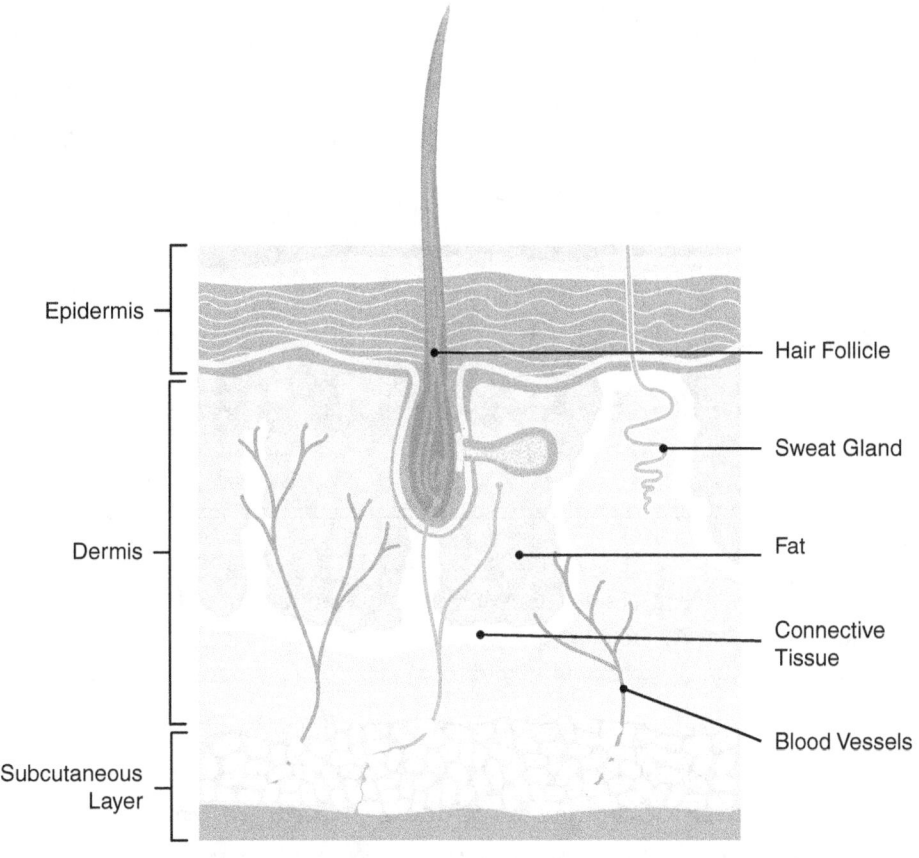

As shown in the image, the skin consists of several layers. These layers are divided into three regions: epidermis, dermis, and subcutaneous tissue. The **epidermis** is the outermost layer composed of **keratin** and stratified squamous epithelium tissue. Keratin is made of keratinocytes, which toughen and waterproof skin. Other cell types that make up the epidermis are melanocytes, which give skin its color, merkel cells, and Langerhans cells. The epidermis can have either four or five layers depending on where it is located on the body. As shown in the following image, these layers consist of the stratum basale (innermost layer), stratum spinosum, stratum granulosum, stratum lucidum, and stratum corneum.

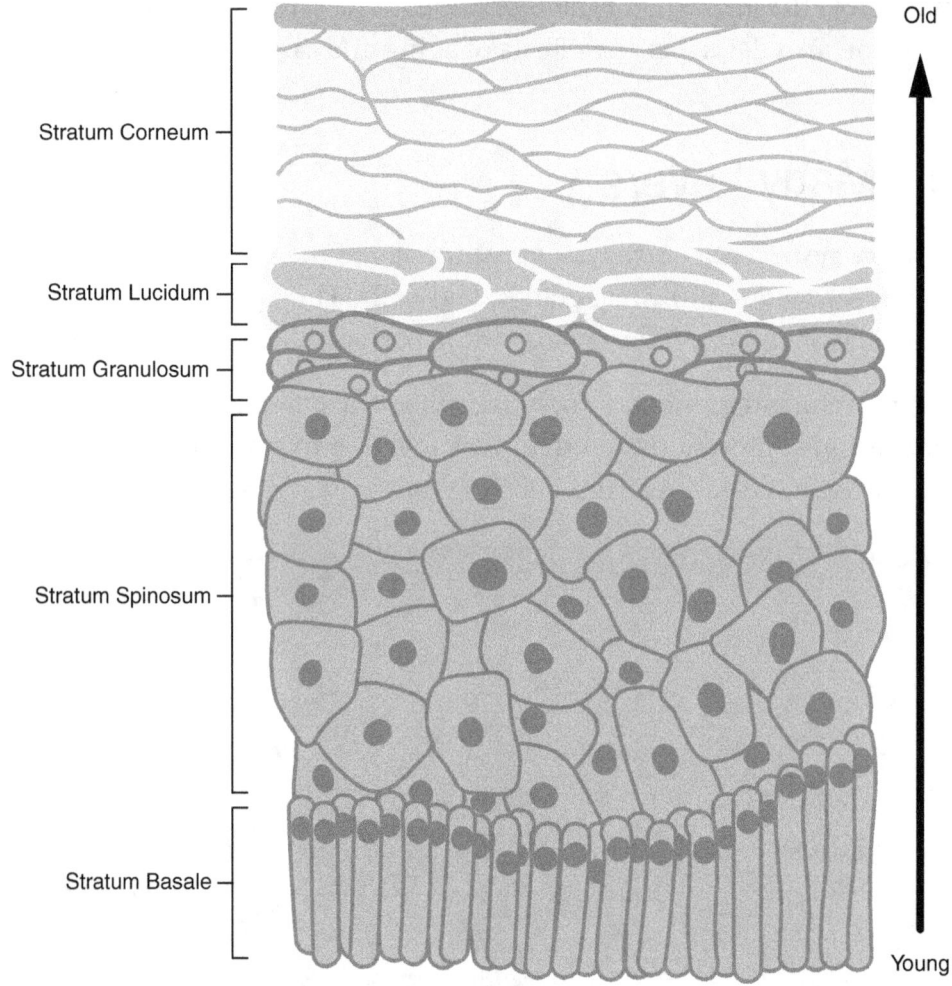

FOR EXAMPLE
The soles of the feet have five layers because they are exposed to a lot of friction as a person walks. The epidermis on the leg consists of only four layers.

Nerve endings and blood vessels are not found in the epidermis. Epidermal cells are found deep in the stratum basale and constantly undergo mitosis to make new cells. As new cells are made, they travel to the outer skin surface, producing the protein keratin. Epidermal cells fill with keratin and die upon reaching the skin's surface. When this happens, the leftover keratin from the dead cells help form the stratum corneum, which is the waterproof layer. These dead epidermal cells are gradually shed from the skin and replaced with new cells.

Example

How many epidermal layers make up the face?

A. 3   B. 4   C. 5   D. 6

The correct answer is **B**. The epidermis consists of either four or five layers. This depends on the part of the body where the epidermis is located. The soles of the feet and palms of the hand have five layers, and all other parts of the body, including the face, have four layers.

The Dermis Layer, Hypodermis, and Glands

The **dermis**, or dermal layer, is found directly under the epidermis. This deep, thick layer is made of tough connective tissue. It is connected to the epidermis by collagen fibers. Unlike the epidermis, nerve endings and blood vessels flow through the dermis. This means the dermal layer is responsible for a person feeling the sensations associated with touch, pain, heat, and cold. There are two major regions of the dermis: papillary region and reticular region. Both these regions provide elasticity to the skin, enabling it to stretch. This is helpful during physiological events like pregnancy, during which the abdominal area must stretch.

> **DID YOU KNOW?**
> The dermis layer of a young person is more elastic than that of an elderly person. This is because the dermis of elderly people has fewer elastic fibers. As the body ages, there is a reduction in physiological processes such as cell division, blood circulation, and muscle strength. These changes lead to a less elastic and thinner dermis.

Hair follicles and glands are also part of the dermis. Hair follicles are the sites where hair strands originate before protruding from the epidermal layer and onto the skin's surface. The two types of glands found in the dermis are detailed below:

- **Sweat glands:** These glands produce a fluid that contains water, salts, and other waste products. They are made of ducts that extend through the epidermis and look like pores on the skin's surface. There are two types of sweat glands:

  - **Apocrine:** These glands are found primarily in the armpits and groin area, where hair follicles are abundant. These glands are attached to hair follicles and create a watery fluid that contains proteins and fats. Apocrine glands are typically inactive until a person reaches puberty. They produce sweat when the body is anxious or experiencing stress.
  - **Eccrine:** These glands are found all over the body, primarily on the forehead, neck, palms, and soles of feet. They are not connected to hair follicles. They regulate body temperature with sweating if the body becomes too hot.

- **Sebaceous glands:** These oil-producing glands are typically attached to hair follicles. They release **sebum**, which is a fatty, oily substance. It waterproofs the hair and skin, preventing both structures from drying out. Sebum also has antimicrobial properties, which help the skin fight off infections.

> **DID YOU KNOW?**
> Sebaceous glands are found all over the body, but they are not found on the palms of the hands or soles of feet. The face and head contain the most sebum.

Right beneath the dermis is a third region of the integumentary system that contains subcutaneous tissue. This region is known as the **hypodermis**. It contains fat, or adipose tissue, that supplies energy for cells and provides insulation to regulate body temperature.

Example

Which structure produces sebum?

A. Hair follicles B. Eccrine glands C. Langerhans cells D. Sebaceous glands

The correct answer is **D**. The dermis is made of sebaceous glands and sweat glands. Eccrine and apocrine glands are two types of sweat glands, neither of which produce sebum. Sebaceous glands produce sebum, which is a fluid that flows through a hair follicle.

Hair and Nails

Nails and hair are accessory organs of the integumentary system. Fingernails and toenails are made of keratin, which is also found in the hair and skin. In addition to mechanical functions such as grasping things and picking up objects, nails prevent injuries to the ends of fingers. As shown in the image below, the nail is made of several parts.

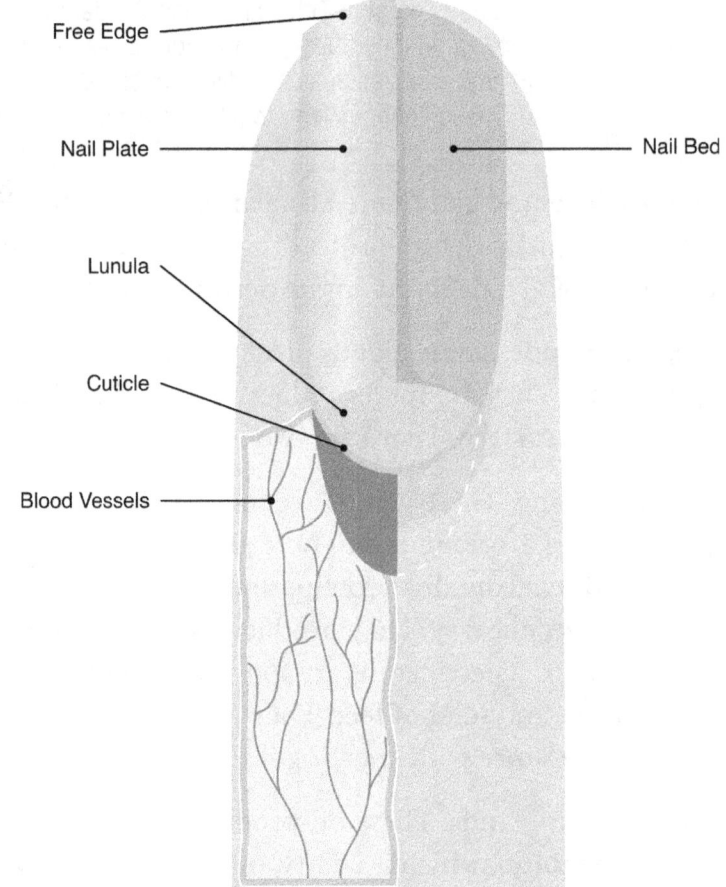

The nail plate is the hard outer part of the nail. Adjoining the nail plate is the free edge, which overhangs the fingertip. This is the part of the nail that is commonly groomed and cut down. The nail bed is a layer of skin found under the nail plate. This layer of skin is comprised of epidermal cells. The white space between the nail bed and **cuticle** is called the **lunula**. The cuticle is a layer of dead skin cells that accumulate and form a thick overhang layer at the base of the nail and around the nail edge. During nail care, cuticles are removed. Beneath the cuticle is the **matrix**, which is a layer of tissue that contains blood vessels and nerves.

> **FOR EXAMPLE**
> Consider eyelashes and eyebrows. These structures protect the eyes from irritants like dirt and water. In the nose, there are tiny hairs that trap dust particles and microorganisms to keep the air entering the lungs clean.

Hair

Hair consists of dead keratinized cells and grows from the dermis out of the epidermis and onto the surface of the body. This accessory organ provides insulation for the body, especially for the head.

Recall that within the dermis is the hair follicle. This is where hair strands in the epidermis originate. The **hair shaft** is not attached to the follicle. It consists of the hair that is exposed on the surface of the body. The **hair root** is attached to

> **KEEP IN MIND**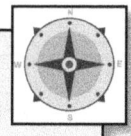
> Aging affects the accessory organs. It causes hair and nails to thin over time.

the follicles and found beneath the skin's surface. Extending beyond the root, deep beneath the skin is the **hair bulb**, which contains actively dividing basal cells.

Example

What is the outer layer of the nail called?

A. Bed   B. Matrix   C. Plate   D. Shaft

The correct answer is **C**. The nail plate is the outer part of the nail that protects the edges of the finger. This structure is hard and connected to the free edge of the nail.

Skin Cancer

Skin cancer is the most common type of cancer that affects the integumentary system. There are many causes of skin cancer, including as genetics, but the strongest risk factor is exposure to ultraviolet (UV) radiation. Sources of UV radiation include sunlight and tanning beds.

Overexposure to UV radiation damages DNA in the body's cells. Exposure to UV radiation causes distinct mutations in skin cells. If the body does not repair the damage to these cells, the mutations accumulate. As a result, the cells can transform into cancerous cells and grow uncontrollably. The uncontrolled cell growth can lead to cancerous tumor formations. Most tumors are harmless, but some produce cells that can move away from the original site of DNA damage and establish new tumors in other organs. This process is called **metastasis**.

> **DID YOU KNOW?**
> There are different types of UV rays. UVA rays penetrate the dermis and can cause skin cancer. UVB rays penetrate the epidermis and cause damage to epidermal cells. UVB rays are responsible for sunburn and most skin cancers.

There are three types of skin cancer:

1. **Basal cell carcinoma:** This is the most common type of skin cancer that occurs in the basal cells of the epidermis. These cells are found in the stratum basale layer and divide to create keratinocytes. Basal cell carcinoma rarely spreads or undergoes metastasis.
2. **Squamous cell carcinoma:** This type of skin cancer occurs in the squamous cells of the epidermis. It affects the keratinocytes in the stratum spinosum. This is the second-most-common type of skin cancer. Because this type of skin cancer is more aggressive than basal cell carcinoma, if this carcinoma is not removed it can metastasize.
3. **Malignant melanoma:** This type of skin cancer occurs when there is an uncontrolled growth of melanocytes in the epidermis. Because melanocytes contribute to the pigmentation of the skin, melanoma is often associated with a dark patch on the body. It is the most dangerous and fatal type of skin cancer.

Example

What is a source of UV radiation?

A. Tanning bed

B. Indoor lighting

C. Topical products

D. Outdoor irritants

The correct answer is **A**. Tanning beds and overexposure to the sun are common sources of UV radiation. UVA and UVB rays are known to cause skin cancer in people.

Let's Review!

- The integumentary system is a body system composed of the skin, hair and nails.
- Skin is the largest organ of the body that primarily functions to protect the body and maintain homeostasis.
- The epidermis, dermis, and subcutaneous layer are the three layers of skin.
- The epidermis has four or five layers: the stratum basale, stratum granulosum, stratum lucidum, stratum spinosum, and stratum corneum.
- Two types of glands, sebaceous glands and sweat glands, are found in the dermis.
- Eccrine glands are found all over the body. Apocrine glands are found mainly in the armpits.
- Hair, nails, and skin all contain keratin, which hardens and toughens each structure.
- Exposure to UV radiation can cause three types of skin cancer.
- Aging affects the integrity and structure of the skin, hair, and nails.

Chapter 8 Human Anatomy and Physiology: Support and Movement Practice Quiz

1. Which bone is classified as an irregular bone?
   - A. Coccyx
   - B. Knee cap
   - C. Humerus
   - D. Nasal bone

2. How many bones are in the adult human body?
   - A. 200
   - B. 206
   - C. 250
   - D. 270

3. Which muscle or region surrounded by a muscle is under voluntary control?
   - A. Bicep
   - B. Heart
   - C. Lung
   - D. Stomach

4. Which muscle causes a joint to bend?
   - A. Cardiac
   - B. Extension
   - C. Flexor
   - D. Smooth

5. The hypodermis is primarily composed of _____ tissue.
   - A. adipose
   - B. connective
   - C. epithelial
   - D. muscle

6. Most common types of skin cancer directly affect the _____ of the skin.
   - A. dermis
   - B. epidermis
   - C. sebaceous glands
   - D. subcutaneous layer

Chapter 8 Human Anatomy and Physiology: Support and Movement Practice Quiz – Answer Key

1. A. The coccyx is part of the vertebral column. This bone region is classified as an irregular bone. **See Lesson: Skeletal System.**

2. B. At birth, a human has roughly 270 bones. As some of these bones fuse, this number deceases to 206, the number of bones in the adult human body. **See Lesson: Skeletal System.**

3. A. A bicep is a muscle found in the upper arm. It is a skeletal muscle that helps move bones in the arm. A bicep is under voluntary control. **See Lesson: Muscular System.**

4. C. Flexor muscles are one part of a skeletal muscle pair that helps bones in the body move. They do so by causing a joint to bend. **See Lesson: Muscular System.**

5. A. The hypodermis is the subcutaneous layer beneath the dermis. It consists of fat, or adipose tissue, which serves as a layer of insulation deep inside the skin. This region also functions as an energy reservoir, supplying energy to cells. **See Lesson: Integumentary System.**

6. B. Basal cell carcinoma affects basal cells in the epidermis, while squamous cell carcinoma affects keratinocytes in the epidermis. Malignant melanoma affects melanocytes in the epidermis. **See Lesson: Integumentary System.**

CHAPTER 9 HUMAN ANATOMY AND PHYSIOLOGY: INTEGRATION AND CONTROL

LESSON 9.1 THE NERVOUS SYSTEM

This lesson introduces the anatomy of the nervous system, including its functions and divisions. It also explores the parts of neuron, neural conduction, and synaptic transmission.

What Is the Nervous System?

From perceptions to daily experiences, the **nervous system** controls many aspects of the human body. This system coordinates several activities in the body. It governs people's consciousness, their personalities, how they learn, and their ability to memorize. Working with the endocrine system, the nervous system regulates and maintains homeostasis.

The nervous system is anatomically divided into two parts:

1. **Central nervous system** (CNS): The central nervous system is comprised of the brain and spinal cord. It is where information processing and control occurs.
2. **Peripheral nervous system** (PNS): The peripheral nervous system is comprised of the nerves associated with the CNS. It connects all nerves of the body to the CNS. There are two types of fibers in the PNS: (a) **afferent fibers** that transmit impulses from organs and tissues of the body to the CNS; and (b) **efferent fibers** that transmit impulses from the CNS to the organs and tissues of the body.

The PNS is further divided into the somatic and autonomic nervous systems. The **somatic nervous system** primarily controls voluntary activities such as walking and riding a bicycle. Thus, this system sends information to the CNS and motor nerve fibers that are attached to skeletal muscle. The **autonomic nervous system** is responsible for activities that are non-voluntary and under unconscious control. Because this system controls glands and the smooth muscles of internal organs, it governs activities ranging from heart rate to breathing and digestion. The autonomic nervous system is further divided into the following:

- **Sympathetic nervous system:** The sympathetic nervous system focuses on emergency situations by preparing the body for fight or flight.
- **Parasympathetic nervous system:** The parasympathetic nervous system controls involuntarily processes unrelated to emergencies. This system deals with "rest or digest" activities.

> **TEST TIP**
> The first letter in the parasympathetic and sympathetic nervous system can be used to tell them apart:
> **S**ympathetic = **s**tress   **P**arasympathetic = **p**eace

Based on the activities of the nervous system, this system can be functionally divided into three parts:

1. **Sensory:** Information is gathered (both internally and externally) and carried to the CNS. The senses gather the information that the sensory nervous system transmits.
2. **Integrative:** The integrative nervous system is where the CNS process and interprets information received from the sensory nerves.
3. **Motor:** Motor nerves convey information that is processed by the CNS to muscles and glands.

The following flow chart summarizes the divisions of the nervous system:

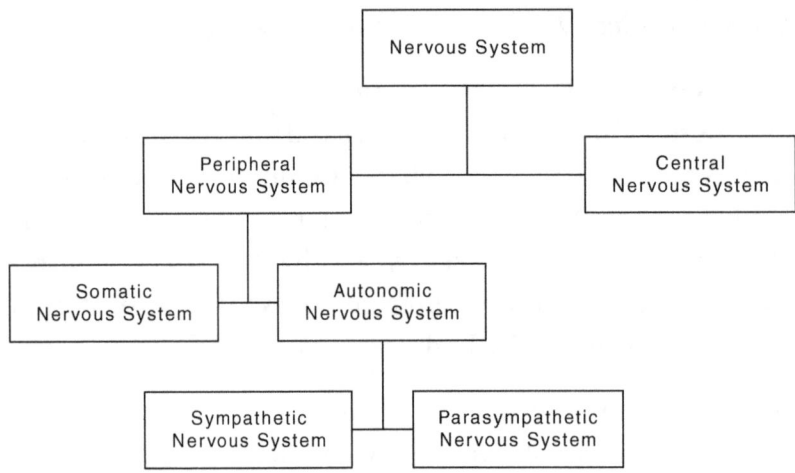

Examples

1. Which organ is part of the central nervous system?

   A. Brain   B. Heart   C. Lung   D. Stomach

   The correct answer is **A**. The nervous system is anatomically divided into two parts, the central and peripheral nervous systems. The central nervous system consists of the brain and spinal cord.

2. What part of the nervous system controls blood vessel contraction?

   A. Autonomic   B. Central   C. Somatic   D. Sympathetic

   The correct answer is **A**. The peripheral nervous system is divided into the somatic and autonomic nervous systems. The autonomic nervous system transmits neural signals to the smooth muscle found in the walls of internal organs and structures like blood vessels.

Lesson 9.1 The Nervous System

Anatomy of the Brain

The brain is a mass of tissue that is made of billions of nerve cells called neurons. This complex organ controls a wide range of processes and integrates information received from the five senses. Protected by the skull, the brain consists of four cavities called **ventricles**. These cavities are filled with **cerebrospinal fluid (CSF)**, which surrounds the CNS. This fluid serves many purposes such as protecting the brain from physical shocks and removing wastes from the neural tissue in the brain.

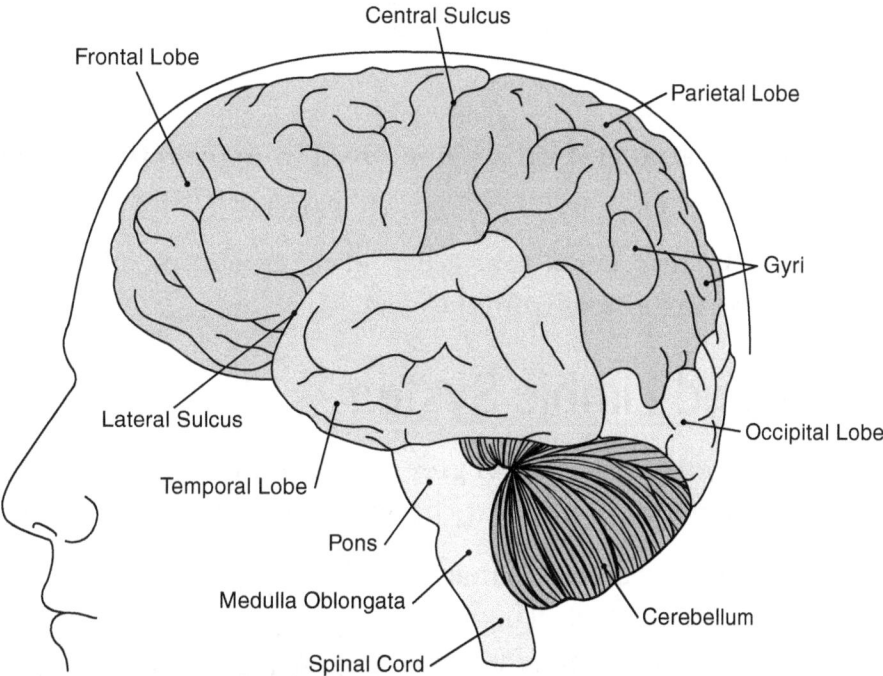

As shown in the above image, the brain is divided into the following three regions:

- **Cerebellum:** This is found beneath the cerebrum and behind the brainstem. It helps coordinate body movements, posture, and balance.
- **Brainstem:** This is found between the thalamus and the spinal cord. It is the lowest part of the brain that connects the brain with the spinal cord. Unconscious functions like breathing, heart rate, and blood pressure are controlled by the brainstem.
- **Cerebrum:** This part of the brain is the largest and part of the **forebrain**. The cerebrum controls higher-order functions such as interpreting touch, speech and language, reasoning, emotions, and fine motor control.

The **cerebral cortex** is **grey (or gray) matter** that surrounds the entire cerebrum. It is divided into a left and right hemisphere. The ridges of the cerebral cortex are called **gyri**, and the grooves are called **sulci**. The very large grooves are called **fissures**. The cerebral cortex is divided into four lobes: the frontal, parietal, temporal, and occipital

KEEP IN MIND

The lobes are named after the bones of the skull that protect each lobe. For example, the frontal bone protects the frontal lobe.

lobe. The cerebral cortex is the most complex part of the brain, and each lobe has specific functions that are outlined in the following table.

Lobe	Function
Frontal	Processes high-level cognitive skills, reasoning, concentration, motor skills, language, and functions as a control center for emotions.
Parietal	Integration site for visual perception and sensory information such as touch, pain, and pressure.
Temporal	Organizes sounds and processes language that is heard. Helps form memories, speech perception, and language skills.
Occipital	Interprets visual stimuli and information.

Example

What lobe helps a person interpret information received from the retinas of eyes?

   A. Frontal   B. Occipital   C. Parietal   D. Temporal

The correct answer is **B**. The occipital lobe is part of the cerebrum. It interprets visual stimuli and information that comes from the eyes.

The Thalamus and Limbic System

Recall that the cerebral cortex is composed of grey matter. This matter is a type of neural tissue that contains three types of **neurons**, which are nerve cells that make up the nervous system:

- **Sensory neurons:** Afferent nerve cells that send information toward the CNS. This information is what is sensed, using the five senses, from the external environment.
- **Motor neurons:** Efferent nerve cells that carry impulses away from the CNS to the effectors, which are typically tissues and muscles of the body.
- **Interneurons:** Nerve cells that act as a bridge between motor and sensory neurons in the CNS. These neurons help form neural circuits, which helps neurons communicate with each other.

> **BE CAREFUL!**
> Grey matter is different from **white matter.** White matter is found in the spinal cord and surrounds the grey matter. It contains bundles of interneurons.

Another part of the forebrain incudes the **limbic system**, which controls emotions and memory. As shown in the image, this system is found right beneath the cerebral cortex and sits above the brainstem.

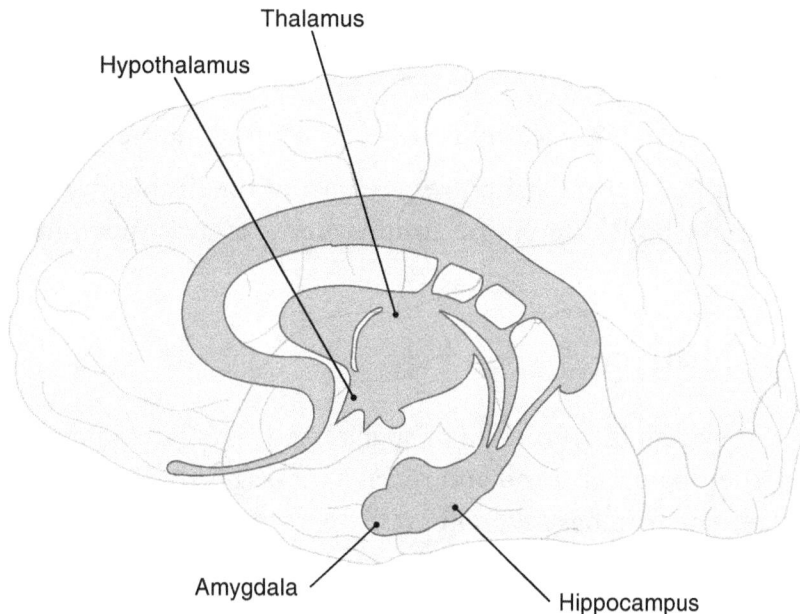

Four major structures of the brain comprise the limbic system:

- **Hypothalamus:** Found below the thalamus, this structure plays a role in regulating the autonomic nervous system. It is primarily concerned with homeostasis and regulates various activities such as hunger, anger, and the response to pain. The hypothalamus works with the pituitary gland from the endocrine system. This gland uses hormones, or chemical messengers, to generate responses in the body.
- **Amygdala:** Recognized as the aggression center, areas of this region produces feelings such as anger, violence, fear, and anxiety.
- **Thalamus:** Different sensory inputs come through the nerves and end at the thalamus, which directs this information to various parts of the cerebral cortex. The sense of smell is the only sense that bypasses the thalamus. Information related to movement is also processed by the thalamus.
- **Hippocampus:** Helps convert short-term memory to long-term memory. If the hippocampus is destroyed, new memories cannot be formed but old memories are retained.

> **DID YOU KNOW?**
> Kluver-Bucy syndrome is a condition that includes destruction of the amygdala. This means a person will present with erratic emotional behavior symptoms like hypersexuality, compulsive eating, and putting objects in the mouth.

Example

Which structure controls memory?

A. Amygdala B. Hippocampus C. Hypothalamus D. Thalamus

The correct answer is **B**. All these structures are part of the limbic system and perform specific functions in the body. The hippocampus converts short-term memory into long-term memory.

Anatomy of a Neuron

Recall that the nervous system is comprised of specialized cells called neurons. A large network of neurons work together to quickly send and receive messages throughout the body. As shown in the following image, a neuron has several parts.

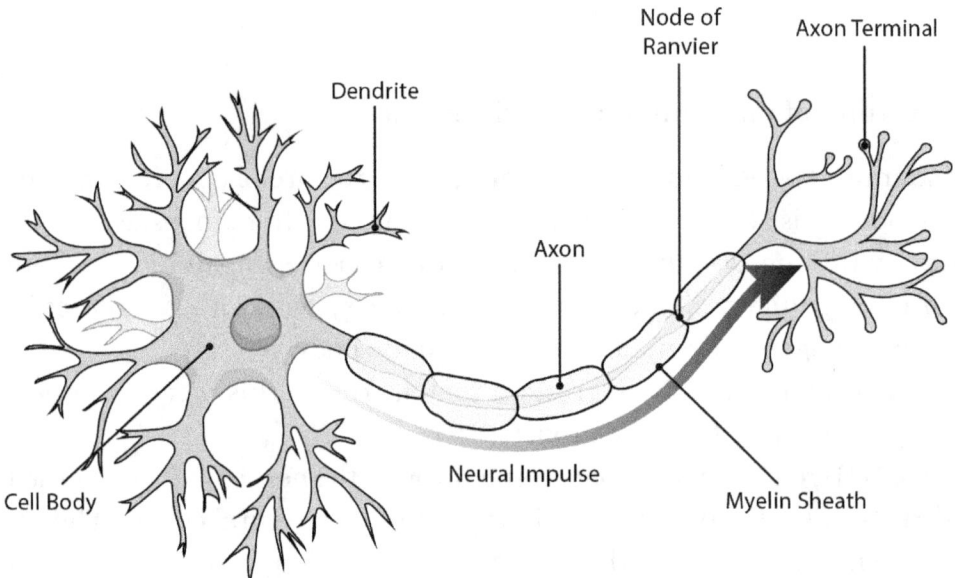

A neuron's structure is designed to transmit electric signals before they are transmitted as chemical signals to a target cell. The following three basic parts make up a single nerve cell:

- **Cell body:** This is the main part of the neuron that contains the nucleus of the nerve cell. Also called the soma, other organelles are also found in the cell body.
- **Dendrites:** These are appendages attached to the cell body that receive signals from other neurons.
- **Axon:** This is the long structure attached to the cell body. It conducts and transmits information to other cells. Branches at the end of the axon form **axon terminals**. These branches facilitate communication between neurons and target cells.

Lesson 9.1 The Nervous System

> **BE CAREFUL!**
> Do not confuse a neuron with a **neuroglial cell**. Neuroglial cells do not conduct nerve impulses like neurons. Rather, they provide support and protect neurons. Astrocytes, oligodendrocytes, microglial cell, and ependymal cells are the four major types of neuroglial cells in the CNS. Schwann and satellite cells are in the PNS.

Also shown in the image is a **myelin sheath** and **node of Ranvier**. The myelin sheath is a protein and lipid structure produced by a type of glial cell called a **Schwann cell**. This sheath functions like a blanket that provides a layer of insulation around the axon of a neuron, increasing the speed of electrical signal transmission. Regularly spaced gaps called nodes of Ranvier are found between the myleinated sheaths. Electric signals jump from one node to the next, thereby increasing the speed of signal transmission.

> **DID YOU KNOW?**
> Several diseases cause degeneration of the myelin sheath, or **demyelination**. One example is multiple sclerosis. When demyelination occurs, it can lead to severe neurological problems like motor and cognitive function. Demyelination reduces the speed at which neural impulses are transmitted along the axon.

Examples

1. What structure receives information from another neuron?

   A. Axon   B. Dendrite   C. Myelin   D. Soma

   The correct answer is **B**. Dendrites are appendages attached to the cell body, or soma, of a neuron. They receive information from other neurons and transmit this information to the cell body.

2. How many types of neuroglia are found in the CNS?

   A. 2   B. 4   C. 11   D. 17

   The correct answer is **B**. Neuroglia are cells that support neurons in the body. More neuroglia are present in the body than neurons. Four types are found in the CNS, and two types are found in the PNS.

Synaptic Transmission and Nerve Impulses

The electric signals neurons transmit are called **neural impulses**. Neurons must be excited to create a nerve impulse. A stimulus triggers excitation. At the resting state, the inside of the neuron is more negatively charged, while the outside of the neuron is more positively charged. This difference in electrical charge because of potassium and sodium ions establishes the **resting potential**.

> **DID YOU KNOW?**
>
> As a person ages, the rate of **neuroplasticity**, or ability for the brain to form neural connections through synapses, decreases. Neuroplasticity is important because it helps the brain adapt to new stimulation, damage, or changes in the environment.

During **action potential**, a reverse in electrical charge occurs across the membrane of a neuron in its resting state. As shown in the following image, this happens when a neuron receives a neural impulse by way of a stimulus or a chemical signal from another neuron. The inside of the neuron becomes more positively charged, while the outside of the neuron becomes more negatively charged. This reverse in charge travels down the axon as an electric current.

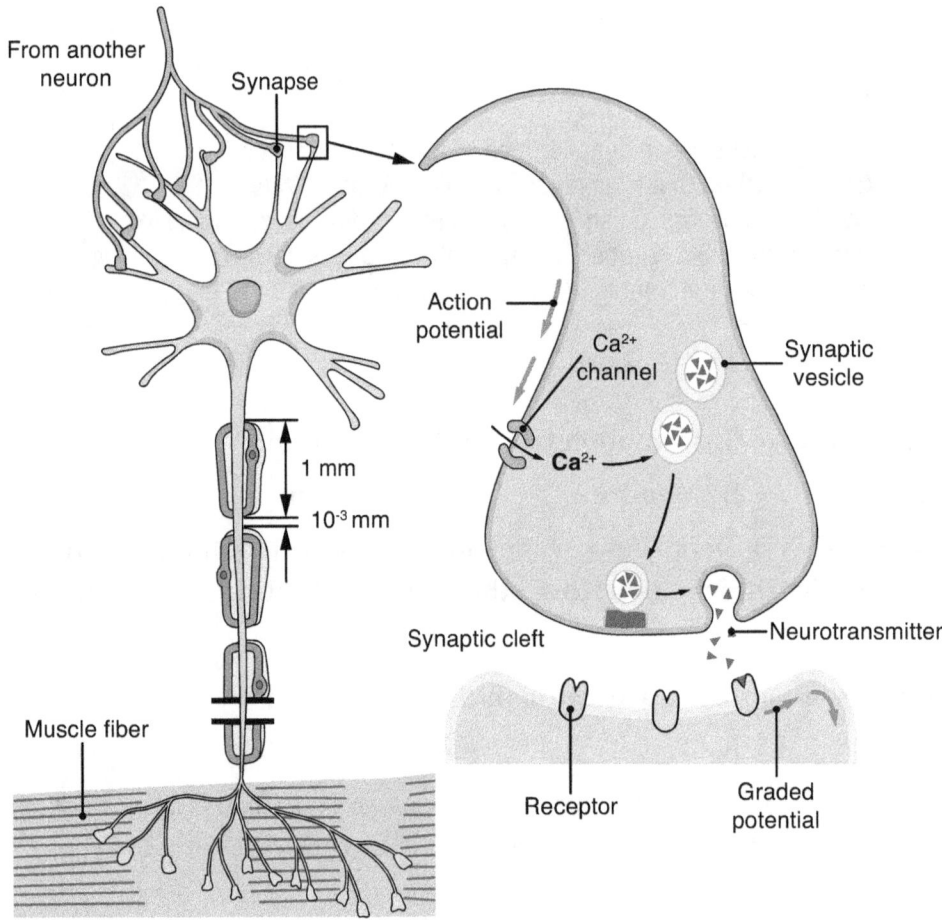

1. Once the action potential reaches the terminal bulbs of the axon terminal, the synaptic transmission process begins. The sequential numbers in the image outline the steps of synaptic transmission. The details of each numbered step are outlined below:An action potential travels down the axon and reaches the terminal branches of the axon. Voltage gated sodium gates open, causing sodium to enter the axon terminal bulb.
2. Voltage gated Ca2+ channels open at the same time.
3. Calcium ions move into the axon terminal bulb of the presynaptic neuron.

4. Calcium ions bind with proteins on synaptic vesicles that carry chemical messages called **neurotransmitters**.
5. This binding causes the vesicles to contract and move to the presynaptic membrane.
6. Neurotransmitters are released from the vesicles via exocytosis and diffuse across the **synaptic cleft**.
7. Neurotransmitters bind with receptors on the postsynaptic membrane of a neuron, gland, or muscle.
8. Depending on what the postsynaptic target cell is, the following responses will happen:

- Axon to dendrite: Action potential travels to next neuron.
- Axon and muscle cell: Muscle contraction.
- Axon and gland: Hormones released from gland.

Example

Which ion helps establish an action potential along an axon?

   A. Barium   B. Calcium   C. Magnesium   D. Potassium

The correct answer is **D**. Electrical impulses travel along the axon of a neuron when the inside of a cell is positively charged and the outside of a cell is negatively charged. This difference in charge is due an exchange in the flow of sodium and potassium ions in and out the cell.

Let's Review!

- The nervous system is divided into the central nervous system (CNS) and peripheral nervous system (PNS).
- The somatic nervous system controls voluntary activities, while the autonomic nervous system is responsible for involuntary activities under unconscious control.
- The nervous system performs sensory, integrative, and motor functions.
- The three major regions of the brain are the cerebrum, brainstem, and cerebellum.
- Four lobes comprise the cerebral cortex, which is grey matter that surrounds the cerebrum.
- The limbic system consists of the hypothalamus, thalamus, hippocampus, and amygdala, each of which has different purposes.
- Neurons are made of dendrites, a cell body, an axon, and an axon terminal.
- Myelin sheaths insulate the axon of neuron, increasing the spread of electric signal transmission.
- A neuron must be excited from a stimulus to create a nerve impulse.
- Resting potentials are established when the outside of a nerve cell is more positively charged than the inside of a nerve cell.
- Action potentials are established when the reverse of a resting potential occurs.
- Synaptic transmission occurs in several steps and only occurs following an action potential.
- Neurotransmitters are chemical messengers released during an electrically stimulated synaptic transmission process.

LESSON 9.2 THE ENDOCRINE SYSTEM

This lesson introduces the endocrine system and the role it plays in the maintenance of homeostasis.

Functions of the Endocrine System

The endocrine system works with the nervous system to regulate the activities critical to the maintenance of homeostasis. The following are the main functions of the endocrine system:

- Water balance
- Uterine contractions and milk release
- Growth, metabolism, and tissue maturation
- Ion regulation
- Heart rate and blood pressure regulation
- Blood glucose control
- Immune system regulation
- Reproductive functions control

Chemical Signals

Chemical signals, or **ligands**, are molecules released from one location that move to another location to produce a response. **Intracellular chemical signals** are produced in one part of a cell, such as the cell membrane, and travel to another part *of the same cell* and bind to receptors, either in the cytoplasm or in the nucleus. **Intercellular chemical signals** are released from one cell, are carried in the intercellular fluid, and bind to receptors that are found in *other* cells, but usually not in all cells of the body.

Intercellular chemical signals can be placed into functional categories on the basis of the tissues from which they are secreted and the tissues they regulate.

Autocrine chemical signals: These chemical signals are released by cells and have a local effect on the same cell type. Example: prostaglandin-like chemicals that are secreted in response to inflammation.

Paracrine chemical signals: These chemical signals are released by cells and have effects on other cell types. Example: somatostatin, secreted by the pancreas, inhibits the release of insulin by other cells in the pancreas.

Neuromodulators and neurotransmitters: These chemical signals are secreted by nerve cells and aid the nervous system. Example: acetylcholine produced during stressful encounters.

Pheromones: These chemical signals are secreted into the environment and modify the behavior and physiology of other individuals. Example: those produced by women can influence the length of the menstrual cycle of other women.

Example

Which chemical signal would respond to the redness caused by an infected wound?

A. Autocrines

B. Neuromodulators

C. Paracrines

D. Pheromones

The correct answer is **A**. Autocrine chemical signals include prostaglandin-like chemicals that are secreted in response to inflammation, which can indicate an infection.

Receptors

Chemical signals bind to proteins or glycoproteins called **receptor molecules** to produce a response. The shape and chemical characteristics of each receptor site allow only certain chemical signals to bind to it. This tendency is called **specificity**.

There are two major types of receptor molecules that respond to an intercellular chemical signal:

Intracellular receptors: These receptors are located in either the cytoplasm or the nucleus of the cell. Signals diffuse across the cell membrane and bind to the receptor sites on intracellular receptors.

Membrane-bound receptors: These receptors extend across the cell membrane, with their receptor sites on the outer surface of the cell membrane. They respond to intercellular chemical signals that are large, water-soluble molecules that do not diffuse across the cell membrane.

When an intercellular signal binds to a membrane-bound receptor, three general types of responses are possible:

Receptors that directly alter membrane permeability: For example, acetylcholine (adrenaline) from nerve fiber endings binds to receptors that are part of the membrane channels for sodium ions.

Receptors and G proteins: A G proteins (guanine nucleotide-binding proteins) are found on the inner surface of the plasma membrane and function as receptors of hormones. For example, chemical signals include cyclic adenosine monophosphate glycerol and inositol triphosphate that bind to receptor molecules in the cell and alter their activity to produce a response.

Receptors that alter the activity of enzymes: For example, increasing the activity of an enzyme responsible for the breakdown of glycogen into glucose makes glucose available as an energy source for muscle contractions.

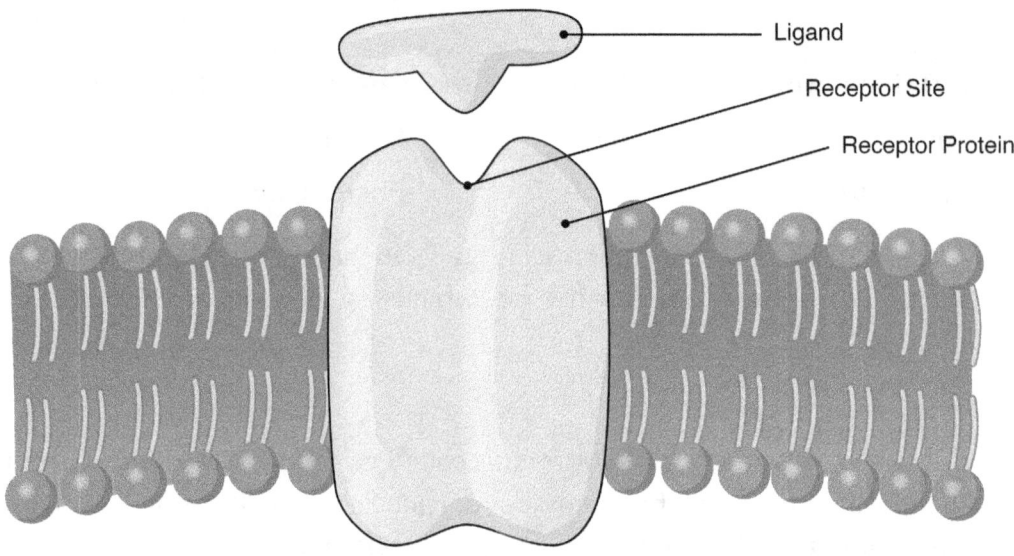

Some intercellular chemical signals diffuse across cell membranes and bind to intracellular receptors. Because these intracellular chemical signals are relatively small and soluble in lipids, they can diffuse through the cell membrane. The chemical signal and the receptor bind to DNA in the nucleus and increase specific messenger RNA synthesis in the nucleus of the cell. The messenger RNA then moves to the ribosomes, then to the cytoplasm, where new proteins are produced.

In contrast, intercellular chemical signals that bind to membrane-bound receptors produce rapid responses. For example, a few intercellular chemical signals can bind to their membrane-bound receptors, and each activated receptor can produce many intracellular chemical signal molecules that rapidly activate many specific enzymes inside the cell. This pattern of response is called the **cascade effect**.

Example

A friend is changing the tire on her car, and the jack breaks. Her hand is caught under the car. A passerby notices, runs over, and lifts the car off her hand. Which type of intercellular signal has responded?

A. Receptors and G proteins

B. Receptors that alter the activity of enzymes

C. Receptors that directly alter membrane permeability

D. Receptors that indirectly alter membrane permeability

The correct answer is **C**. Nerve fiber endings bind to receptors that are part of the membrane channels for sodium ions to enable adrenaline to respond.

Hormones

The term **endocrine** implies that intercellular chemical signals are produced within and secreted from endocrine glands, but the chemical signals have effects at locations that are away from, or separate from, the endocrine glands that secrete them. The intercellular chemical signals, or hormones, are transported in the blood to tissues some distance from the glands. **Hormones** are produced in minute amounts by a collection of cells to influence the activity of those tissues in a specific way. For example, **neurohormones** are hormones secreted from cells of the nervous system.

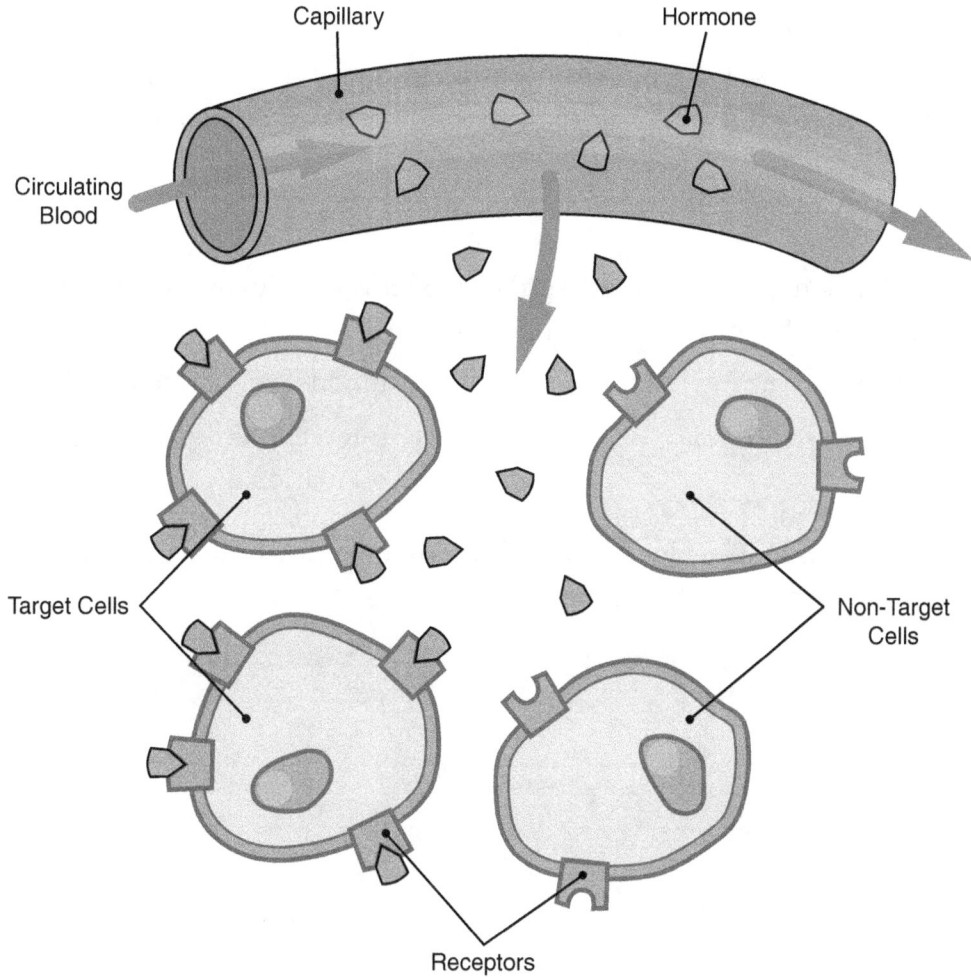

Hormones are distributed in the blood to all parts of the body, but only certain tissues, called **target tissues**, respond to each type of hormone. Target tissue is made up of cells that have receptor molecules for a specific hormone. Each hormone can only bind to its receptor molecules and cannot influence the function of cells that do not have receptor molecules for the hormone.

Regulation of Hormone Secretion

The secretion of hormones is controlled by negative-feedback mechanisms. Negative-feedback mechanisms keep the body functioning within a narrow range of values consistent with life. Hormone secretion is regulated in three ways:

1. **Blood levels of chemicals:** The secretion of some hormones is directly controlled by the blood levels of certain chemicals. For example, blood glucose levels control insulin secretion.
2. **Hormones:** The secretion of some hormones is controlled by other hormones. For example, hormones from the pituitary gland act on the ovaries and the testes, causing those organs to secrete sex hormones.
3. **Nervous system:** These hormones are controlled by the nervous system. For example, epinephrine is released from the adrenal medulla as a result of nervous system stimulation.

Example

The negative-feedback mechanism that regulates the level of glucose in a person's blood is an example of what type of hormone secretion regulation?

A. Hormone regulation

B. Nervous system regulation

C. Blood levels of chemicals regulation

D. Intercellular ion concentration regulation

The correct answer is **C**. The blood levels of certain chemicals, such as insulin, directly control the secretion of some hormones.

Endocrine Glands and Their Secretions

The endocrine system consists of ductless glands that secrete hormones directly into the blood. An extensive network of blood vessels supplies the endocrine glands. The following is a table of hormones secreted by the anterior pituitary gland.

Anterior Pituitary Gland		
Hormone	Target	Response
Growth hormone	Most tissues	Increases protein synthesis
Thyroid-stimulating hormone	Thyroid gland	Increases thyroid hormone secretion
Adrenocorticotropic	Adrenal cortex	Increases secretion of cortisol
Melanocyte-stimulating hormone	Melanocytes in skin	Increases melanin production to make skin darker
Luteinizing hormone	Females: ovaries Males: testes	Females: promotes ovulation Males: promotes sperm cell production
Follicle-stimulating hormone	Females: ovarian follicles Males: seminiferous tubules	Females: promotes follicle maturation Males: promotes sperm cell production
Prolactin	Ovary and mammary glands	Prolongs progesterone secretion

Additional common hormones are listed in the chart below.

Gland	Hormone	Target Tissue	Response	Under- or Overproduction of Hormone
Thyroid gland	Thyroid hormone	Most cells of the body	Increases metabolic rate	Hypothyroidism Hyperthyroidism
Adrenal medulla	Epinephrine	Heart, blood vessels, liver, adipose cells	Increases cardiac output and blood flow	Addison's disease
Pancreas	Insulin and glucagon	Liver, skeletal muscles, and adipose tissue	Insulin: increases uptake and use of glucose Glucagon: increases breakdown of glycogen	Diabetes

The Effects of Aging

The aging process affects hormone activity in one of three ways: their secretion can decrease, remain unchanged, or increase.

Hormones that decrease secretion include the following:

- Estrogen (in women)
- Testosterone (in men)
- Growth hormone
- Melatonin

In women, the decline in estrogen levels leads to menopause. In men, testosterone levels usually decrease gradually. Decreased levels of growth hormone may lead to decreased muscle mass and strength. Decreased melatonin levels may play an important role in the loss of normal sleep-wake cycles (circadian rhythms) with aging.

Hormones that usually remain unchanged or slightly decrease include the following:

- Cortisol
- Insulin
- Thyroid hormones

Hormones that may increase secretions levels include the following:

- Follicle-stimulating hormone
- Luteinizing hormone
- Norepinephrine
- Epinephrine, in the very old
- Parathyroid hormone

Example

Which of the following is an effect of aging on hormone secretion?

A. Weak teeth
B. Loss of appetite
C. Trouble sleeping
D. Loss of body hair

The correct answer is **C**. The reduction of melatonin can result in the inability to sleep.

Let's Review!

- The endocrine system functions with the nervous system to regulate the many activities critical to the maintenance of homeostasis.
- Chemical signals, or ligands, are molecules released from one location that move to another location to produce a response.
- Chemical signals bind to proteins or glycoproteins called receptor molecules to produce a response.
- A hormone is an intercellular chemical signal that is produced in minute amounts by collections of cells to influence the activity of those tissues in a specific way.
- Hormones are distributed in the blood to all parts of the body, but only certain tissues, called target tissues, respond to each type of hormone.
- Negative-feedback mechanisms control the secretion of hormones.
- The endocrine system consists of ductless glands that secrete hormones directly into the blood.
- The aging process affects hormone activity.

LESSON 9.3 THE LYMPHATIC SYSTEM

This lesson introduces the structure and function of the lymphatic system, which is commonly referred to as the immune system. It also examines the common diseases and disorders of this system.

The Key Players in the Lymphatic System

Components of the lymphatic system are the spleen, tonsils, adenoids, appendix, thymus gland, and lymph nodes. The **spleen** helps fight certain types of bacteria. The **tonsils**, **adenoids**, and **appendix** were once believed to be vestigial organs, meaning they are remnants left over from human evolution. Now, scientists have found they have active functions. The **thymus gland** is located directly above the heart. It secretes hormones that stimulate the maturation of killer T cells. This gland is only active from birth through puberty. After puberty, it decreases in size and functionality.

The body initiates a battle as soon as a **pathogen**, or a foreign body, enters. Two types of **lymphocytes**, B cells and T cells, are white blood cells that target the pathogen. Macrophages, another type of white blood cell, join in the invasion.

Killer T cells attack and kill infected cells. **B cells** label invaders for later destruction by macrophages. **Helper T cells** activate killer T cells and B cells. **Macrophages** consume pathogens and infected cells in a process known as **phagocytosis**. These four kinds of white blood cells exchange information and correlate their activities as an integrated system.

When someone comes down with the flu, influenza viruses enter the body in small water droplets inhaled into the respiratory system. If the mucous membranes do not ensnare them, they slip past patrolling macrophages and begin to infect and kill mucous membrane cells, which makes the person feel sick. Macrophages initiate an "alarm" signal that activates the helper T cells, which serve as the "generals" of the lymphatic system. Helper T cells activate killer T cells and B cells and produce defensive proteins.

The body now initiates a robust attack against the flu virus. Using a second chemical signal, the helper T cells call into action killer T cells, which recognize and destroy body cells that the virus has infected. The T cells have receptors that recognize tiny bits of the virus's proteins and release enzymes into the infected cells that encourage the cells to destroy themselves, a process known as **apoptosis**. This is when macrophages are actively working during the immune response to consume pathogens and infected cells.

The protein the helper T cells releases also activates the B cells. Like killer T cells, B cells have receptor proteins called **antibodies** on their surfaces. The B cells can release copies of these antibodies into the bloodstream or attach them directly to pathogens, marking pathogens for destruction. These B cells also secrete antibodies that attach to any invading pathogen into the bloodstream.

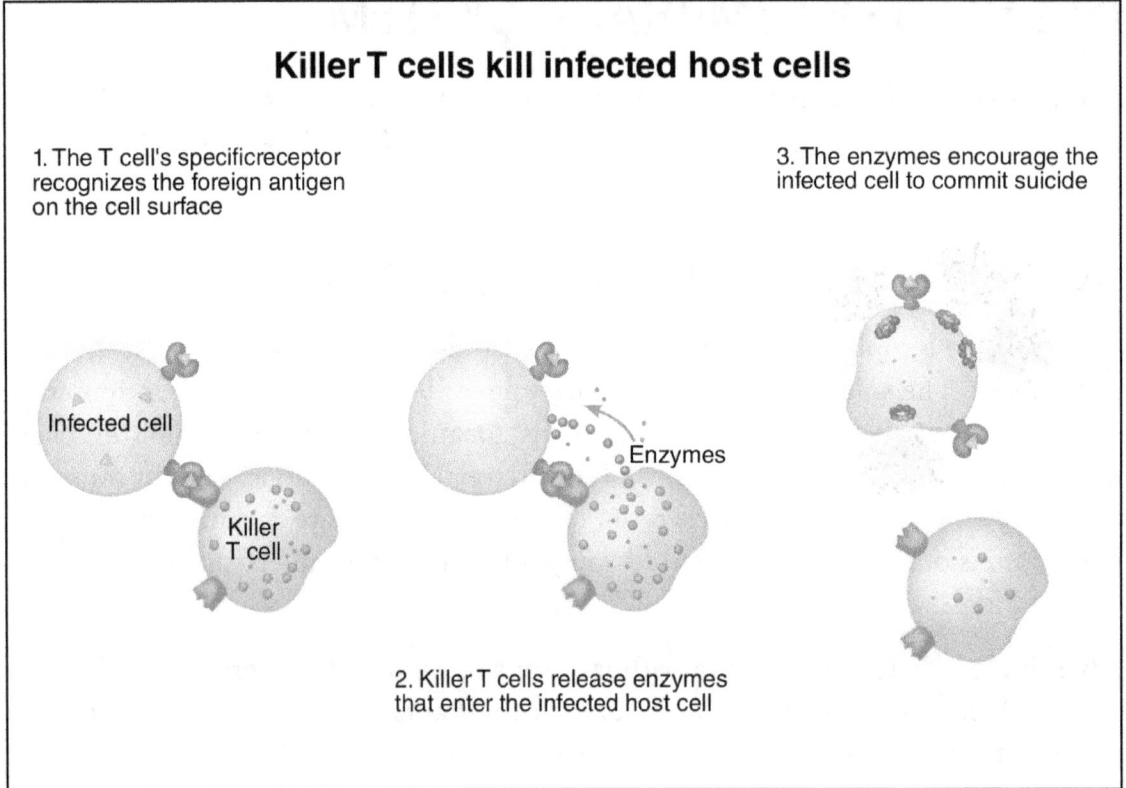

Examples

1. Which of the following is the correct series of the lymphatic system's defense mechanisms?

    A. B cell and T cell → Macrophage → Helper T cell

    B. Helper T cell → T cell → B cell → Macrophage

    C. Macrophage → Helper T cell → B cell → T cell

    D. Macrophage → Helper T cell → B cell and T cell

    The correct answer is **D**. Once the macrophages sound the alarm, the helper T cells simultaneously activate the B cells and T cells.

2. The B cells do not directly attack pathogens or infected cells. Instead, they

    A. mark the pathogens for destruction by macrophages and B cells.

    B. mark the antibodies for destruction by B cells and natural killer cells.

    C. mark the antibodies for destruction by macrophages and killer T cells.

    D. mark the pathogens for destruction by macrophages and natural killer cells.

    The correct answer is **D**. The B cells do not directly attack pathogens or infected cells. Instead, they mark the pathogens for destruction by macrophages and natural killer cells.

When a B cell encounters a foreign microbe with a surface protein that matches the shape of its antibodies, it attaches an antibody to the microbe.

Types of Immunity

The four types of immunity are natural/passive, natural/active, artificial/passive, and artificial/active. The following are examples of these types of immunities:

- Natural/passive – Babies receive immunities from breastmilk.
- Natural/active – The body produces antibodies to combat an illness when a person becomes sick.
- Artificial/passive – This immunity is temporary and requires doses of serum to maintain the immunity.
- Artificial/active – A vaccination provides artificial/active immunity.

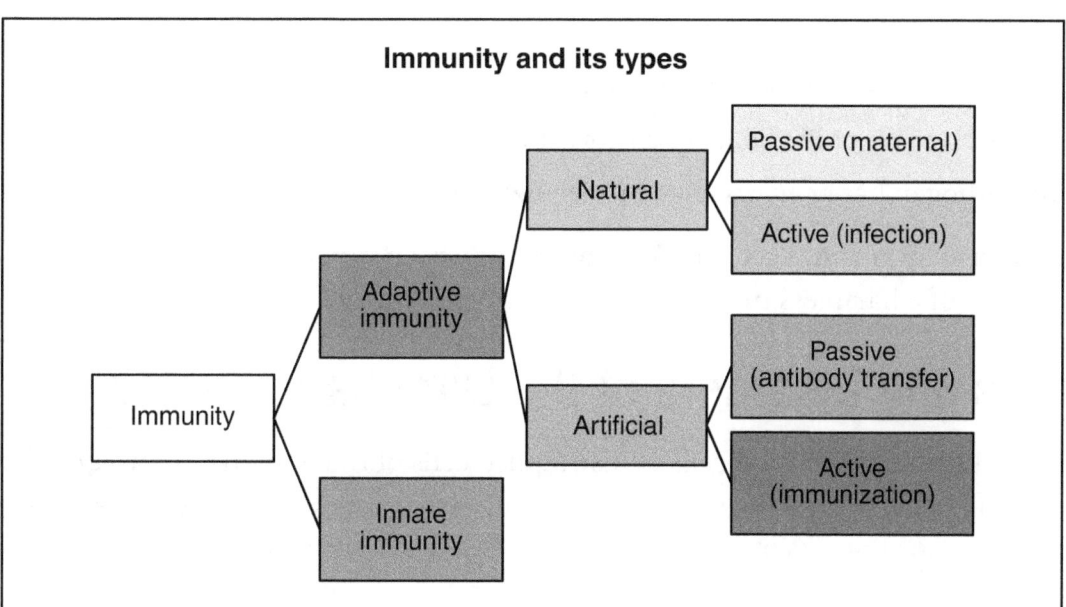

Example

When a child breastfeeds, that child is exposed to all the "germs" on the mother. As a result, what type of immunity is the child acquiring?

A. Artificial/active

B. Artificial/passive

C. Natural/active

D. Natural/passive

The correct answer is **D**. The child acquires this immunity without the baby's body experiencing an illness. The baby is not born with this immunity and does nothing to acquire it. Therefore, it is passive.

Vaccination Prepares the Lymphatic System

Vaccination is the introduction into the body of a dead or disabled pathogen or of a harmless microbe with the protein of a pathogen on its surface. Vaccination triggers the lymphatic system response against the pathogen without an infection occurring. Afterward, the bloodstream of the vaccinated person contains memory cells that are directed against the pathogen. The vaccinated person is immunized against the disease. Vaccinations have dramatically reduced the incidence of many bacterial and viral diseases, including polio, tetanus, and diphtheria. An intensive vaccination program led to the elimination of the deadly disease smallpox in the 1970s.

Example

Sometimes, people complain they have become sick because of a vaccination. Why is this impossible?

- A. The pathogen is dead.
- B. The pathogen was originally harmless.
- C. The pathogen is only viable for a short time.
- D. The pathogen has been disabled by sterilization.

The correct answer is **A**. Vaccination is the introduction into the body of a dead or disabled pathogen or of a harmless microbe with the protein of a pathogen on its surface.

Diseases and Disorders of the Lymphatic System

The ability of killer T cells and B cells to distinguish cells of the body from foreign cells is crucial to the fight against pathogens. In **autoimmune diseases**, this ability breaks down, causing the body to attack its own cells. The following chart gives examples of autoimmune conditions.

Diseases	Areas affected	Symptoms
Systemic Lupus Erythematosus	Connective tissue, joints, kidneys	Facial, skin rash; painful joints; fever; fatigue; kidney problems; weight loss
Type I Diabetes	Insulin-producing cells in the pancreas	Excessive urine production; blurred vision; weight loss; fatigue; irritability
Graves' Disease	Thyroid	Weakness; irritability; heat intolerance; increased sweating; weight loss; insomnia
Rheumatoid Arthritis	Joints	Crippling inflammation of the joints

Age

As people age, their bodies produce fewer B and T cells. As a result, their bodies' ability to defend themselves against viruses and bacteria lessens.

Allergies

Sometimes, the body's immune system works too well and attacks itself. This is known as an **allergy**. Hay fever is an example.

Mast cells, attached to white blood cells, line entrances to the body. When they encounter matching antibodies, they initiate an **inflammatory response**, which releases histamines. **Histamines** cause capillaries to swell and increase mucous membrane production.

HIV/AIDS: Lymphatic System Collapse

HIV/AIDS is a result of a mutation that occurred in a virus that affects chimpanzees. It destroys macrophages and helper T cells.

How Is HIV Transmitted?

Because there is no cure for AIDS, prevention is key. HIV/AIDS can only survive in blood or body fluids because macrophages are located there. The primary means of transmission is through sexual intercourse.

HIV is not transmitted through the air, on toilet seats, or by any other medium where a macrophage cannot survive. It cannot be transmitted through shaking hands, sharing food, or drinking from a water fountain because macrophages cannot be transmitted through casual contact.

Example

Why is AIDS a devastating disease?

A. It targets red blood cells.

B. It targets respiratory lining cells.

C. It targets many different types of cells.

D. It targets the cells in the lymphatic system that target pathogens.

The correct answer is **D**. A mutation arose in the chimpanzee virus that allowed it to recognize a human cell surface receptor on certain immune system cells, primarily the macrophages and helper T cells.

Let's Review!

- This lesson explored the lymphatic system's keys components and the major disease and disorders of the system.
- The lymphatic system provides immunity against pathogens.
- Several organs work together to make the lymphatic system efficient.
- Killer T cells recognize and destroy body cells that have been infected with a virus.

- B cells do not directly attack pathogens or infected cells.
- B cells have receptor proteins on their surface called antibodies.
- Vaccination is the introduction into the body of a dead or disabled pathogen or of a harmless microbe with the protein of a pathogen on its surface.
- In autoimmune diseases, the ability to distinguish cells of the body from foreign cells breaks down, causing the body to attack its own cells.
- Age has a negative effect on the lymphatic system.

Chapter 9 Human Anatomy and Physiology: Integration and Control Practice Quiz

1. Which of the following is a characteristic of an interneuron?
   A. Forms neural circuits
   B. Interacts with effectors
   C. Sends impulses to the CNS
   D. Functions as an efferent nerve cell

2. Nodes of Ranvier are
   A. spaces between myelin sheaths.
   B. cavities in the brain filled with fluid.
   C. dendrites that receive sensory inputs.
   D. chemical messages carried in vesicles.

3. Neurohormones are hormones secreted from cells of the _____ system.
   A. circulatory
   B. digestive
   C. integumentary
   D. nervous

4. The shape and chemical characteristics of each receptor site allow only certain chemical signals to bind to it. This is called _____.
   A. conductivity
   B. memory
   C. permeability
   D. specificity

5. Which of the following can transmit HIV?
   A. Air
   B. Toilet seats
   C. Water fountains
   D. Infected intravenous syringes

6. Why is sexual intercourse the most common method of spreading HIV?
   A. Because T cells are located in semen and vaginal secretions
   B. Because B cells are located in semen and vaginal secretions
   C. Because proteins are located in semen and vaginal secretions
   D. Because macrophages are located in semen and vaginal secretions

Chapter 9 Human Anatomy and Physiology: Integration and Control Practice Quiz — Answer Key

1. **A.** The interneuron is a type of nerve cell that bridges a connection between motor and sensory neurons to create neural circuits. This bridge facilitates communication between the neurons. **See Lesson: The Nervous System.**

2. **A.** Nodes of Ranvier are the gaps in myelin sheaths that increase the speed of an electrical neural signal down the axon of a neuron. **See Lesson: The Nervous System.**

3. **D.** Neurohormones are secreted by the nervous system. **See Lesson: Endocrine System.**

4. **D.** Specificity is the characteristic that causes chemical signals to connect only to the correct receptors. **See Lesson: Endocrine System.**

5. **D.** HIV can be transmitted through infected intravenous syringes, semen, vaginal secretions, and blood. **See Lesson: The Lymphatic System.**

6. **D.** Because semen and vaginal secretions are rich in macrophages, a person can become infected with HIV through sexual intercourse with an infected person. **See Lesson: The Lymphatic System.**

CHAPTER 10 LIFE AND PHYSICAL SCIENCES

LESSON 10.1 THE SCIENTIFIC METHOD AND DESIGNING AN EXPERIMENT

This lesson introduces the idea of experimental design and the factors one must consider to build a successful experiment.

Scientific Reasoning

When conducting scientific research, two types of scientific reasoning can be used to address scientific problems: inductive reasoning and deductive reasoning. Both forms of reasoning are also used to generate a hypothesis. **Inductive reasoning** involves drawing a general conclusion from specific observations. This form of reasoning is referred to as the "from the bottom up" approach. Information gathered from specific observations can be used to make a general conclusion about the topic under investigation. In other words, conclusions are based on observed patterns in data.

> **FOR EXAMPLE**
> Use your inductive reasoning to determine the next item in the sequence of events:
> 1. fall, winter, spring . . .
> 2. 4, 8, 12 . . .

Deductive reasoning is the logical approach of making a prediction about a general principle to draw a specific conclusion. It is recognized as the "from the top down" approach. For example, deductive reasoning is used to test a theory by collecting data that challenges the theory.

> **DID YOU KNOW?**
> While Francis Bacon was developing the scientific method, he advocated for the use of inductive reasoning. This is why inductive reasoning is considered to be at the heart of the scientific method.

Example

Which is an example of deductive reasoning?

    A. A scientist concludes that a plant species is drought resistant after watching it survive a hot summer.

    B. After a boy observes where the sun rises, he tells his mom that the sun will rise in the east in the morning.

    C. Since it is well established that noble gases are stable, scientists can safely say that the noble gas neon is stable.

    D. A state transportation department decides to use sodium road salt after studies show that calcium road salt is ineffective.

The correct answer is **C**. The statement that noble gases are stable is a general principle or well-accepted theory. Thus, the specific conclusion that the noble gas neon is stable can be drawn from this general principle.

Designing an Experiment

According to the **scientific method**, the following steps are followed after making an observation or asking a question: (1) conduct background research on the topic, (2) formulate a hypothesis, (3) test the hypothesis with an experiment, (4) analyze results, and (5) report conclusions that explain whether the results support the hypothesis. This means after using logical reasoning to formulate a hypothesis, it is time to design a way to test this hypothesis. This is where **experimental design** becomes a factor.

Experimental design is the process of creating a reliable experiment to test a hypothesis. It involves organizing an experiment that produces the amount of data and right type of data to answer the question. A study's validity is directly affected by the construction and design of an experiment. This is why it is important to carefully consider the following components that are used to build an experiment:

- **Independent variable:** This factor does not depend on what happens in the experiment. The independent variable has values that can be changed or manipulated in an experiment. Data from the independent variable is graphed on the x-axis.
- **Dependent variable:** This factor depends on the independent variable. Recognized as the outcome of interest, its value cannot change. It can only be observed during an experiment. Data from the dependent variable is graphed on the y-axis.
- **Treatment group:** This is the group that receives treatment in an experiment. It is the item or subject in an experiment that the researcher manipulates. During an experiment, treatment is directly imposed on a group and the response is observed.
- **Control group:** This is a baseline measure that remains constant. Used for comparison purposes, it is the group that neither receives treatment nor is experimentally manipulated. One type of control is a **placebo**. This false treatment is administered to a control group to

account for the placebo effect. This is a psychological effect where the brain convinces the body that a fake treatment is the real thing. Often, experimental drug studies use placebos.

TEST TIP

It can be hard to remember the differences between an independent and a dependent variable. Use the following mnemonic to help keep those differences clear:

D = dependent   **M** = manipulated variable   **Y** = y-axis
R = responding variable   **I** = independent variable   **X** = x-axis

Example

A control group

A. modifies the desired outcome of an experiment.

B. fluctuates in value if an experimental factor is manipulated.

C. establishes a baseline measure to compare dependent variables to.

D. depends on the type of independent variable chosen for an experiment.

The correct answer is **C**. A control group functions as a baseline measure or constant that is not influenced by experimental manipulations. It does not receive treatment in a study.

Data Analysis and Interpretation

When researchers test their hypotheses, the next step in the scientific method is to analyze the data and collect empirical evidence. **Empirical evidence** is acquired from observations and through experiments. It is a repeatable form of evidence that other researchers, including the researcher overseeing the study, can verify. Thus, when analyzing data, empirical evidence must be used to make valid conclusions.

While analyzing data, scientists tend to observe cause-and-effect relationships. These relationships can be quantified using correlations. **Correlations** measure the amount of linear association between two variables. There are three types of correlations:

- **Positive correlation:** As one variable increases, the other variable also increases. This is also known as a direct correlation.

FOR EXAMPLE

Studies have shown there is a positive correlation between smoking and lung cancer development. The more you smoke, the greater your risk of developing lung cancer. An example of a negative correlation is the relationship between speed and time when distance is kept constant. The faster a car travels, the amount of time to reach the destination decreases.

- **Negative correlation:** As one variable increases, the other decreases. The opposite is true if one variable decreases. A negative correlation is also known as an inverse correlation or an indirect correlation.
- **No correlation:** There is no connection or relationship between two variables.

From graphs to tables, there are many ways to visually display data. Typically, graphs are a powerful way to visually demonstrate the relationships between two or more variables. This is the case for correlations. A positive correlation is indicated as a positive slope in a graph, as shown below. Negative correlations are indicated as a negative slope in a graph. If there is no correlation between two variables, data points will not show a pattern.

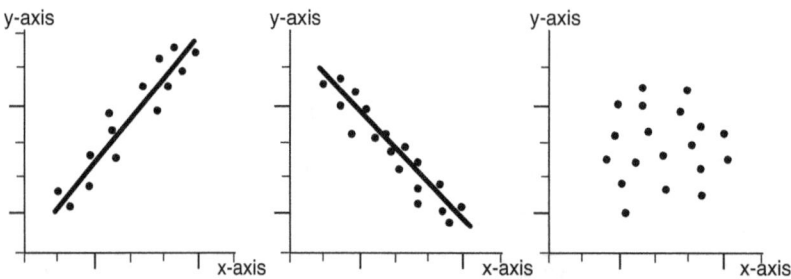

Examples

1. What is another term used to describe a direct correlation?

    A. Positive slope   B. Negative slope   C. Inverse correlation   D. Indirect correlation

    The correct answer is **A**. A direct correlation occurs when one variable increases as another increases. Graphically, this is shown as a positive slope.

2. If a researcher notices a negative slope while analyzing his data, what can he conclude?

    A. The variables exhibit no correlation.
    B. A different control group should be used.
    C. The variables exhibit a direct correlation.
    D. The variables exhibit an indirect correlation.

    The correct answer is **D**. A negative slope is indicative of an indirect, negative, or inverse correlation.

Lesson 10.1 The Scientific Method and Designing an Experiment

Scientific Tools and Measurement

Researchers use a wide variety of tools to collect data. The most common types of measuring tools are outlined below:

Barometer	Used to determines the air pressure in a space.
Clock or stopwatch	Used to record time.
Graduated cylinder	Used to measure the volume of liquid.
Ruler	Used to measure the length of an object.
Thermometer	Used to measure temperature. Measurement values may be expressed in degrees Celsius or Fahrenheit.
Triple beam balance	Used to measure the mass of an object or to determine the unit of mass. Electronic balances are used to measure very small masses.

Measured values are often associated with scientific units. Typically, the metric system is preferred when reporting scientific results. This is because nearly all countries use the metric system. Additionally, there is a single base unit of measurement for each type of measured quantity. For example, the base unit for length cannot be the same as the base unit for mass. The following base units are used:

Unit of Measurement	Base Unit Name	Abbreviation
Length	Meter	m
Mass	Gram	g
Volume	Liter	L

Another benefit of the metric system is that units are expressed in multiples of 10. This allows a researcher to express reported values that may be very large or small. This expression is facilitated by using the following metric prefixes, which are added to the base unit name:

Prefix	Abbreviation	Value	Description
kilo	k	1,000	thousand
hecto	h	100	hundred
deka	da	10	ten
BASE	N/A	1	one
deci	d	0.1	tenth
centi	c	0.01	hundredth
milli	m	0.001	thousandth

Example

What base measurement unit is associated with reported values measured by a graduated cylinder?

A. Celsius   B. Gram   C. Liter   D. Meter

The correct answer is **C**. Liter is a base unit for volume. Volume is measured using a graduated cylinder.

Let's Review!

- Formulating a hypothesis requires using either inductive or deductive reasoning.
- A good experimental design properly defines all variables and considers how data will be analyzed.
- Correlations illustrate the cause-and-effect relationships between two variables.
- Positive and negative correlations can be displayed graphically by analyzing the slope of a line.
- Different devices are used to measure objects in an experimental study.
- The metric system is usually used when expressing the units of measured values.

LESSON 10.2 THE FOUNDATIONS OF BIOLOGY

This lesson introduces the basics of biology, including the process researchers use to study science. It also examines the classes of biomolecules and how substances are broken down for energy.

Biology and Taxonomy

The study or science of living things is called **biology**. Some characteristics, or traits, are common to all living things. These enable researchers to differentiate living things from nonliving things. Traits include reproduction, growth and development, **homeostasis**, and energy processing. Homeostasis is the body's ability to maintain a constant internal environment despite changes that occur in the external environment. With so many living things in the world, researchers developed a **taxonomy** system, which is used for classification, description, and naming. As shown below, there are seven classification levels in the classical Linnaean system.

Specificity increases as the levels move from kingdom to species. For example, in the image the genus level contains two types of bears, but the species level shows one type. Additionally, organisms in each level are found in the level above it. For example, organisms in the order level are part of the class level. This classification system is based on physical similarities across living things. It does not account for molecular or genetic similarities.

> **DID YOU KNOW?**
> Carl Linnaeus only used physical similarities across organisms when he created the Linnaean system because technology was not advanced enough to observe similarities at the molecular level.

Example

A researcher classifies a newly discovered organism in the class taxonomy level. What other taxonomic level is this new organism classified in?

   A. Order   B. Family   C. Species   D. Kingdom

The correct answer is **D**. Each level is found in the level above it. The levels above class are phylum and kingdom.

Scientific Method

To develop the taxonomic system, researchers had to ask questions. Researchers use seven steps to answer science questions or solve problems. Recall that these make up the **scientific method**, described below:

1. Problem: The question created because of an observation. *Example: Does the size of a plastic object affect how fast it naturally degrades in a lake?*
2. Research: Reliable information available about what is observed. *Example: Learn how plastics are made and understand the properties of a lake.*
3. Hypothesis: A predicted solution to the question or problem. *Example: If the plastic material is small, then it will degrade faster than a large particle.*
4. Experiment: A series of tests used to evaluate the hypothesis. Experiments consist of an **independent variable** that the researcher modifies and a **dependent variable** that changes due to the independent variable. They also include a **control group** used as a standard to make comparisons. *Example: Collect plastic particles both onshore and offshore of the lake over time. Determine the size of the particles and describe the lake conditions during this time period.*
5. Observe: Analyze data collected during an experiment to observe patterns. *Example: Analyze the differences between the numbers of particles collected in terms of size.*
6. Conclusion: State whether the hypothesis is rejected or accepted and summarize all results.
7. Communicate: Report findings so others can replicate and verify the results.

Sometimes, just a few steps of the scientific method are necessary to research a question. At other times, several steps may be repeated as needed. The goal of this method is to find a reliable answer to the scientific question.

Lesson 10.2 The Foundations of Biology

> **TEST TIP**
> Using the first letter in each of the steps, you can create a mnemonic device to remember the steps. For example: "**P**eople **R**eally **H**ave **E**lephants **O**n **C**ompact **C**ars." Try creating your own mnemonic device!

Over the course of many years during which scientists are able to collect sufficient and reliable data, the scientific method can be used to create a law or theory. A **law** is a rule that describes patterns observed in nature. A **scientific theory** explains the how and why of things that happens in nature through observations and experiments. Scientists widely accept both laws and theories, but they can be modified over time.

Example

In a study, a researcher describes what happens to a plant following exposure to a dry and hot environment. What step of the scientific method does this most likely describe?

    A. Forming a hypothesis

    B. Making an observation

    C. Communicating findings

    D. Characterizing the problem

The correct answer is **B**. The researcher is collecting qualitative data by describing what happens to the plant under specific conditions. This data collection corresponds to the observation step of the scientific method.

Water and Biomolecule Basics

From oceans and streams to a bottle, water is fundamental for life. Without water, life would not exist. Because of water's unique properties, it plays a specific role in living things. The molecular structure of water consists of an oxygen atom bonded to two hydrogen atoms. The structure of water explains some of its properties. For example, water is polar. The oxygen atom is slightly negatively charged, while both hydrogen atoms are slightly positively charged.

As shown below, a single water molecule forms **hydrogen bonds** with nearby water molecules. This type of bonding creates a weak attraction between the water molecules. Hydrogen bonding contributes to water's high boiling point. Water is necessary for biochemical processes like photosynthesis and cellular respiration. It is also a universal solvent, which means water dissolves many different substances.

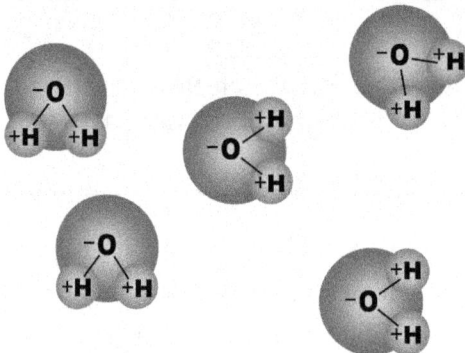

Only two water molecules are needed to show bonding. Remove the partial negative/positive signs and put a – sign next to the oxygen atom and a + sign next to each hydrogen (H) atom. Remove the solid lines between the H and O but keep the dashed line connecting one water molecule to the next.

> **KEEP IN MIND**
> It takes a lot of heat to create hot water. This is because of water's high specific heat capacity, which is the amount of heat required to raise the temperature of 1 kilogram of water by 1 degree Celsius. This property of water also makes it ideal for living things.

Biomolecules, or biological molecules, are found in living things. These organic molecules vary in structure and size and perform different functions. Researchers group the wide variety of molecules found in living things into four major classes for organizational purposes: proteins, carbohydrates, lipids, and nucleic acids. Each class of biomolecules has unique **monomers** and **polymers**. Monomers are molecules that covalently bond to form larger molecules or polymers.

Phospholipids, a class of lipids, are a structure with a phosphate "head" and a fatty acid "tail". The phosphate head is a molecule structure consisting of a phosphate atom and four oxygen atoms, making the head carry a polar charge to be soluble in water; hydrophilic. This is opposite the two fatty acid chains in the tail, which are nonpolar and water insoluble, or hydrophobic. This structure is important in creating the permeable, or semi-permeable membranes of cells, which help the flow of specific ions through designated channels of a cell.

The following table lists characteristics of each class of biomolecule.

Biomolecule	Monomer(s)	Function	Example
Protein	Amino acid	A substance that provides the overall basic structure and function for a cell	Enzymes
Carbohydrate	Monosaccharides	A form of storage for energy	Glucose Cellulose Starch Disaccharides
Lipid	Glycerol and fatty acids	A type of fat that provides a long-term storage for energy	Fats Steroids Oils Hormones
Nucleic acid	Nucleotides	A substance that aids in protein synthesis and transmission of genetic information	DNA RNA

Example

During protein synthesis in a cell, the primary structure of the protein consists of a linear chain of monomers. What is another way to describe this structure?

A. A linear chain of fatty acids that are hydrogen-bonded together

B. A linear chain of nucleotides that are hydrogen-bonded together

C. A linear chain of amino acids that are covalently bonded together

D. A linear chain of monosaccharides that are covalently bonded together

The correct answer is **C**. The monomers of proteins include amino acids, which are covalently bonded together to form a protein.

The Metabolic Process

Just like water, energy is essential to life. Food and sunlight are major energy sources. Metabolism is the process of converting food into usable energy. This refers to all biochemical processes or reactions that take place in a living thing to keep it alive.

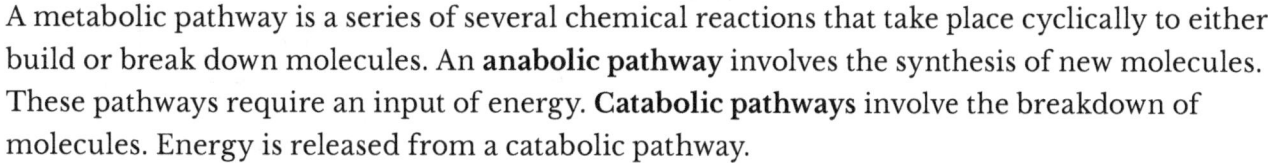

CONNECTIONS

Energy flows through living things. Energy from the sun is converted to chemical energy via photosynthesis. When living things feed on plants, they obtain this energy for survival.

A metabolic pathway is a series of several chemical reactions that take place cyclically to either build or break down molecules. An **anabolic pathway** involves the synthesis of new molecules. These pathways require an input of energy. **Catabolic pathways** involve the breakdown of molecules. Energy is released from a catabolic pathway.

Living things use several metabolic pathways. The most well-studied pathways include glycolysis, the citric acid cycle, and the electron transport chain. These metabolic pathways either release or add energy during a reaction. They also provide a continual flow of energy to living things.

1. **Glycolysis:** This is a catabolic pathway that uses several steps to break down glucose sugar for energy, carbon dioxide, and water. Energy that is released from this reaction is stored in the form of adenosine triphosphate (ATP). Two ATP molecules, two pyruvate molecules, and two NADH molecules are formed during this metabolic pathway.

> **BE CAREFUL!**
> Some of these metabolic pathways produce energy in different parts of the cell. Glycolysis takes place in the cytoplasm of the cell. But the citric acid cycle and oxidative phosphorylation occur in the mitochondria.

2. **Citric acid cycle:** The pyruvate molecules made from glycolysis are transported inside the cell's mitochondria. In this catabolic pathway, pyruvate is used to make two ATP molecules, six carbon dioxide molecules, and six NADH molecules.
3. **Electron transport chain and oxidative phosphorylation:** This also takes place in the cell's mitochondria. Many electrons are transferred from one molecule to another in this chain. At the end of the chain, oxygen picks up the electrons to produce roughly 34 molecules of ATP.

The following image provides an overview of **cellular respiration**. Glycolysis, the citric acid cycle, the electron transport chain, and oxidative phosphorylation collectively make up this process. Cellular respiration takes place in a cell and is used to convert energy from nutrients into ATP.

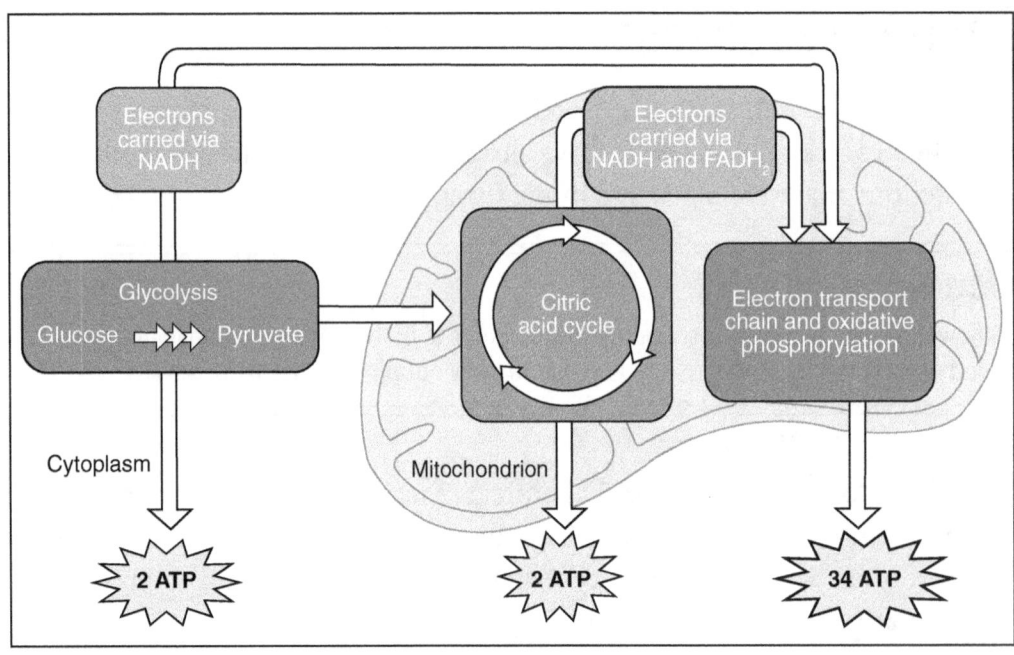

Example

Why are metabolic pathways cyclic?

A. Metabolic reactions generally take place one at a time.

B. All of the products created in metabolic reactions are used up.

C. The reactions are continuous as long as reactants are available.

D. Energy in the form of ATP is sent to different cells for various uses.

The correct answer is **C**. Metabolic reactions are cyclic, which means they keep occurring as long as enough starting materials are available to allow the reaction to proceed.

Let's Review!

- This lesson explored how living things are organized, what the scientific method is, and how biomolecules are classified. It also discussed how living things obtain energy via metabolism.
- Biology is the study of living things. Several characteristics distinguish living things from nonliving things.
- All living things are described, classified, and named using a taxonomic system.
- The scientific method uses seven steps to answer a question or solve a problem.
- Biomolecules are organic molecules that are organized into four classes: proteins, carbohydrates, lipids, and nucleic acids
- Living things rely on various metabolic pathways to produce energy and store it in the form of ATP.

LESSON 10.3 CELL STRUCTURE, FUNCTION, AND TYPE

This lesson describes the cell structure and two different types of cells. The lesson also explores the functions of various cell parts.

Cell Theory and Types

All living things are made of cells. **Cells** are the smallest structural units and basic building blocks of living things. Cells contain everything necessary to keep living things alive. Varying in size and shape, cells carry out specialized functions. Robert Hooke discovered the first cells in the mid-eighteenth century. Many years later, after advancements in microscopy, the cell theory was formed. This theory, or in-depth explanation, about cells consists of three parts:

1. All living things are composed of one or more cells.
2. Cells are alive and represent the basic unit of life.
3. All cells are produced from preexisting cells.

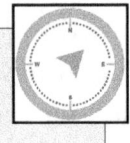

> **DID YOU KNOW?**
> More than a trillion cells and at least 200 different types of cells exist in the human body!

Many different types of cells exist. Because of this, cells are classified into two general types: prokaryotic cells and eukaryotic cells. The following comparison table lists key differences between prokaryotes and eukaryotes:

Characteristic	Prokaryote	Eukaryote
Cell size	Around 0.2–2.0 µm in diameter	Around 10–100 µm in diameter
Nucleus	Absent	True nucleus
Organelles	Absent	Several present, ranging from ribosomes to the endoplasmic reticulum
Flagella	Simple in structure	Complex in structure

Lesson 10.3 Cell Structure, Function, and Type

As shown in the image, prokaryotic cells lack nuclei. Their DNA floats in the **cytoplasm**, which is surrounded by a **plasma membrane**. Very simplistic in structure, these cells lack organelles but do have cell walls. **Organelles** are specialized structures with a specific cellular function. They also may have **ribosomes** that aid in protein synthesis. Also, these cells have a **flagellum** that looks like a tail attached to the cell. Flagella aid in locomotion. The **pili**, or hair-like structures surrounding the cells, aid in cellular adhesion. Bacteria and Archaea are the most common prokaryotes. Most prokaryotes are **unicellular**, or made of a single cell, but there are a few **multicellular organisms**.

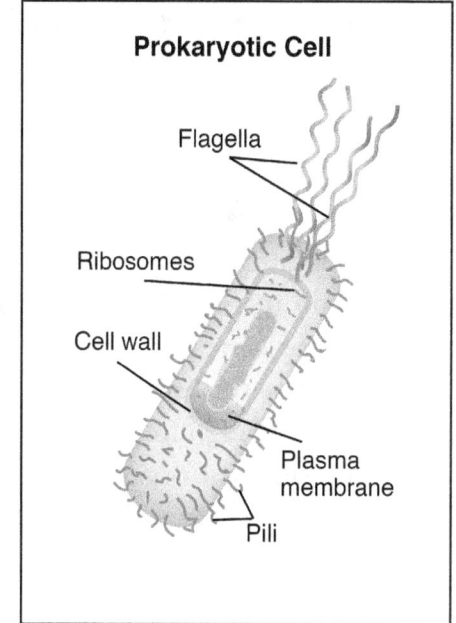

Eukaryotic cells contain a membrane-bound nucleus where DNA is stored. Membrane-bound organelles also exist in eukaryotic cells. Similar to prokaryotic cells, eukaryotic cells have cytoplasm, ribosomes, and a plasma membrane. Eukaryotic organisms can be either unicellular or multicellular. Much larger than prokaryotes, examples of eukaryotic organisms include fungi and even people.

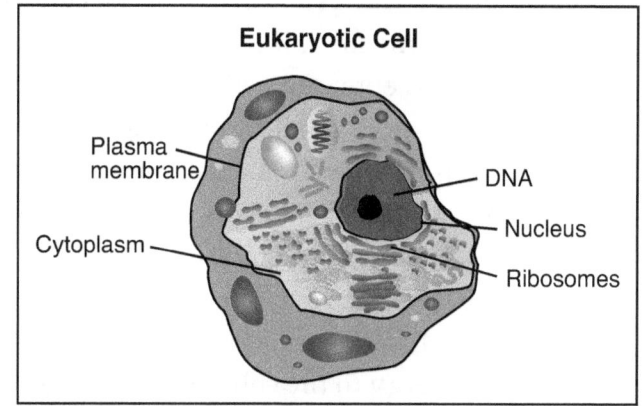

Example

What is an organelle?

- A. The building block of all living things
- B. A substance that is able diffuse inside a cell
- C. The specific receptor found on a cell's surface
- D. A membrane-bound structure with a special function

The correct answer is **D**. Organelles such as ribosomes and the nucleus are membrane-bound structures that have specific functions in a cell.

A Peek Inside the Animal Cell

Animal cells are eukaryotic cells. Cheek, nerve, and muscle cells are all examples of animal cells. Because there are many different types, each animal cell has a specialized function. But all animal cells have the same parts, or organelles. Use this image as a guide while going through following list, which describes the organelles found in a eukaryotic (or animal) cell.

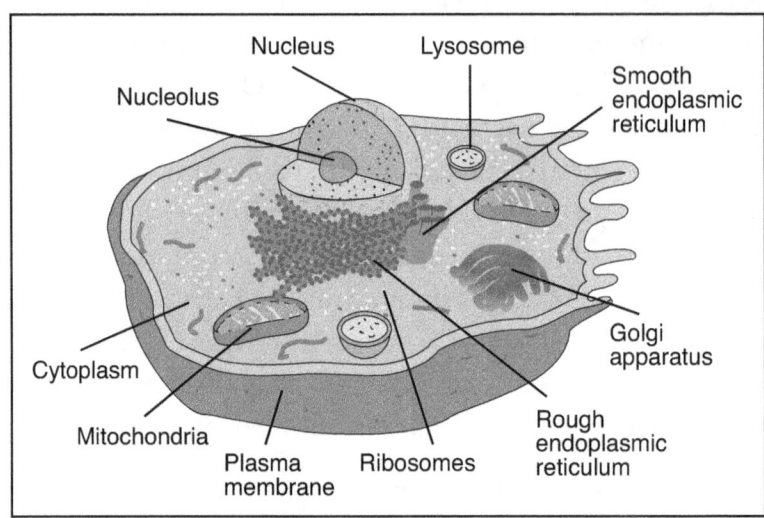

- **Cell membrane:** A double layer that separates the inside of the cell from the outside environment. It is semi-permeable, meaning it only allows certain molecules to enter the cell.
- **Nucleus:** A membrane-bound organelle that contains the genetic material, such as DNA, for a cell. Inside the nucleus is the **nucleolus** that plays a role in assembling subunits required to make ribosomes.
- **Mitochondria:** The cell's powerhouses that provide energy to the cell for it to function. Much of the energy in the form of ATP is produced here.
- **Ribosomes:** The cell's protein factories that can be found floating in the cytoplasm or attached to the endoplasmic reticulum.
- **Vacuoles:** Small sacs in a cell that store water and food for survival. This organelle also stores waste material that is mostly in the form of water.
- **Endoplasmic reticulum:** A network of membranes that functions as a cell's transportation system, shuttling proteins and other materials around the cell. The **smooth endoplasmic reticulum** lacks ribosomes, and the **rough endoplasmic reticulum** has ribosomes.
- **Lysosomes:** Sac-like structures that contain digestive enzymes that are used to break down food and old organelles.
- **Golgi apparatus:** A stack of flattened pouches that plays a role in processing proteins received from the endoplasmic reticulum. It modifies proteins from the endoplasmic reticulum and then packages them into a vesicle that can be sent to other places in the cell.

> **KEEP IN MIND!**
> Some of the organelles in animal cells are also present in plant cells. In addition, all organelles are found in the cytoplasm of the cell. The only exception is the nucleus, which it is separated from the cytoplasm because it has its own membrane.

Example

Which two organelles work together to facilitate protein synthesis?

A. Cytoplasm and lysosome

B. Vacuole and mitochondria

C. Nucleus and cell membrane

D. Ribosome and endoplasmic reticulum

The correct answer is **D**. After a protein is synthesized by ribosomes, it is shuttled to the endoplasmic reticulum, where it is further modified and prepared to be transported by vesicles to other places in the cell.

Plant Cells

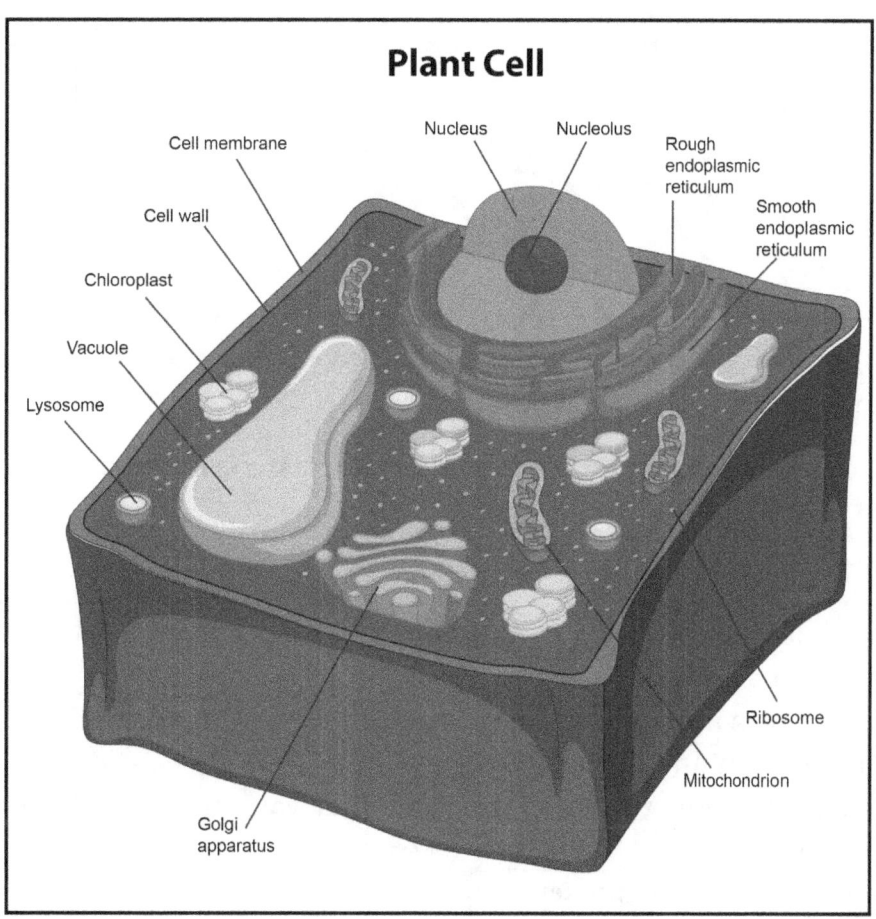

Recall that plant cells are also eukaryotic cells. Structurally, these cells are similar to animal cells because some of the parts in a plant cell are also found in an animal cell. However, there are some notable differences. The following image shows the structure of a plant cell.

First, only plant cells have a **cell wall**. The purpose of this structure is to provide protection and support to plant cells. The cell wall also enforces the overall structural integrity of the plant cell, and it is found outside the cell membrane. The next organelle is a chloroplast. It is found in the cytoplasm of only plant cells. **Chloroplasts** are photosynthetic compounds used to make food for plant cells by harnessing energy from the sun. These organelles play a role in photosynthesis.

Chloroplasts and mitochondria are both designed to collect, process, and store energy for the cell. Thus, organisms are divided into autotrophs or heterotrophs based on how they obtain energy. **Autotrophs** are organisms that make energy-rich biomolecules from raw material in nature. They do this by using basic energy sources such the sun. This explains why most autotrophs rely on photosynthesis to transform sunlight into usable food that can produce energy necessary for life. Plants and certain species of bacteria are autotrophs.

Animals are **heterotrophs** because they are unable to make their own food. Heterotrophs have to consume and metabolize their food sources to absorb the stored energy. Examples of heterotrophs include all animals and fungi, as well as certain species of bacteria.

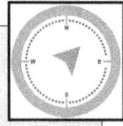

DID YOU KNOW?
More than 99% of all energy for life on Earth is provided through the process of photosynthesis.

Example

Kelp use chlorophyll to capture sunlight for food. What are these organisms classified as?

A. Autotrophs   B. Chemotrophs   C. Heterotrophs   D. Lithotrophs

The correct answer is **A**. Kelp is an autotroph because it uses chlorophyll to trap energy from the sun to make food.

Let's Review!

- This lesson focused on the cell theory, different cell types, and the various cell parts found in plant and animal cells.
- The cell theory is an in-depth explanation, supported with scientific data, to prove a cell is a living thing and has unique characteristics.
- Cells are the basic building blocks of life. Coming in various sizes and shapes, cells have specialized functions.
- Two broad types of cells are prokaryotic and eukaryotic cells.
- Prokaryotes are single-celled organisms that lack a nucleus, while eukaryotes are multicellular organisms that contain a nucleus.
- Chloroplasts and cell walls are only found in plant cells.
- Both animal and plant cells have similar organelles such as ribosomes, mitochondria, and an endoplasmic reticulum.
- Living things can be classified as autotrophs or heterotrophs based on how they obtain energy.

LESSON 10.4 | CELLULAR REPRODUCTION, CELLULAR RESPIRATION, AND PHOTOSYNTHESIS

This lesson introduces basic processes including cellular reproduction and division, cellular respiration, and photosynthesis. These processes provide ways for cells to make new cells and to convert energy to and from food sources.

Cell Reproduction

Cells divide primarily for growth, repair, and reproduction. When an organism grows, it normally needs more cells. If damage occurs, more cells must appear to repair the damage and replace any dead cells. During reproduction, this process allows all living things to produce offspring. There are two ways that living things reproduce: asexually and sexually.

Asexual reproduction is a process in which only one organism is needed to reproduce itself. A single parent is involved in this type of reproduction, which means all offspring are genetically identical to one another and to the parent. All prokaryotes reproduce this way. Some eukaryotes also reproduce asexually. There are several methods of asexual reproduction.

Binary fission is one method. During this process, a prokaryotic cell, such as a bacterium, copies its DNA and splits in half. Binary fission is simple because only one parent cell divides into two daughter cells (or offspring) that are the same size.

Sexual reproduction is a process in which two organisms produce offspring that have genetic characteristics from both parents. It provides greater genetic diversity within a population than asexual reproduction. Sexual reproduction results in the production of **gametes**. These are reproductive cells. Gametes unite to create offspring.

Example
Binary fission is a method

A. where one daughter cell is produced.
B. required to produce reproductive cells.
C. that represents a form of asexual reproduction.
D. where two parent cells interact with each other.

The correct answer is C. Binary fission is a method organisms use to reproduce asexually. It involves a single parent cell that splits to create two identical daughter cells.

When the Cell Cycle Begins

For a cell to divide into more cells, it must grow, copy its DNA, and produce new daughter cells. The **cell cycle** regulates cellular division. This process can either prevent a cell from dividing or trigger it to start dividing.

> **KEEP IN MIND**
> The cell cycle is a circular process. This means after two daughter cells are made, they can participate in the cell cycle process, starting it over from the beginning.

The cell cycle is an organized process divided into two phases: **interphase** and the **M (mitotic) phase**. During interphase, the cell grows and copies its DNA. After the cell reaches the M phase, division of the two new cells can occur. The G_1, S, and G_2 phases make up interphase.

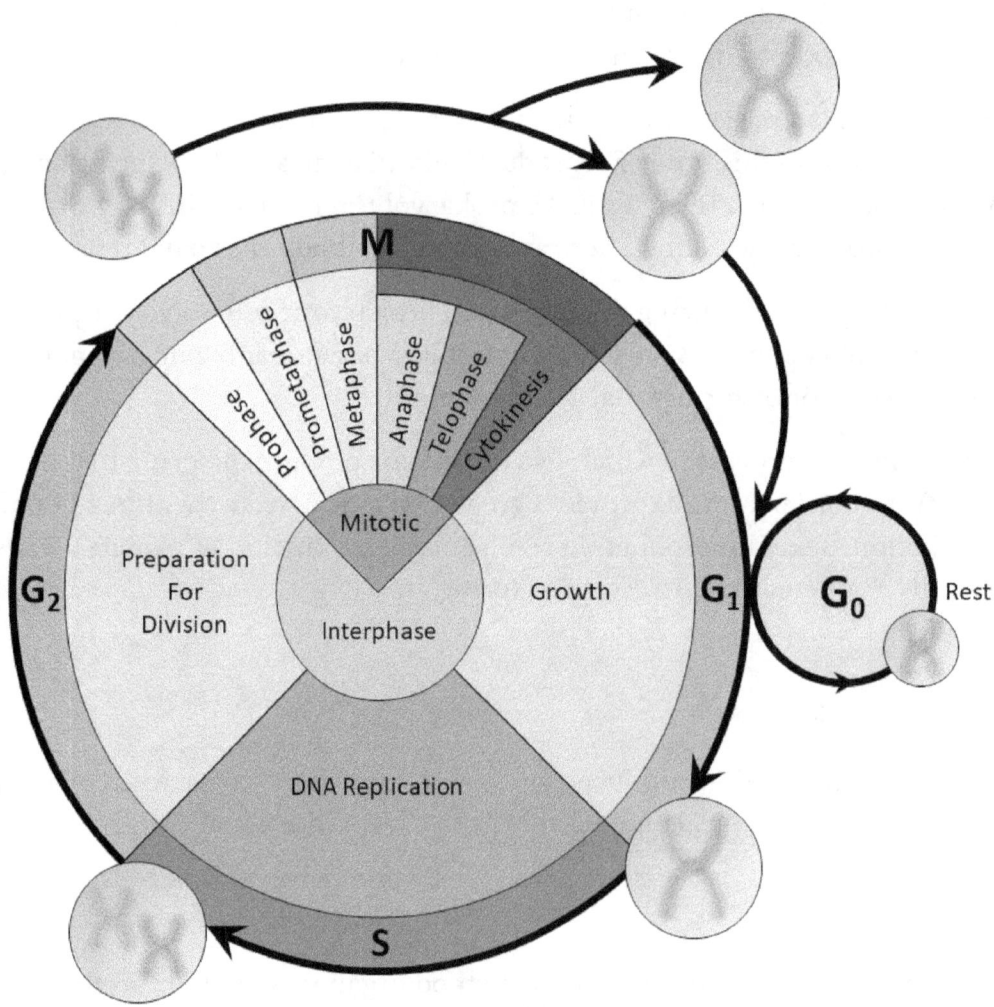

- G_1: The first gap phase, during which the cell prepares to copy its DNA
- **S**: The synthesis phase, during which DNA is copied
- G_2: The second gap phase, during which the cell prepares for cell division

It may appear that little is happening in the cell during the gap phases. Most of the activity occurs at the level of enzymes and macromolecules. The cell produces things like nucleotides for synthesizing new DNA strands, enzymes for copying the DNA, and tubulin proteins for building the mitotic spindle. During the S phase, the DNA in the cell doubles, but few other signs are obvious under the microscope. All the dramatic events that can be seen under a microscope occur during the M phase: the chromosomes move, and the cell splits into two new cells with identical nuclei.

Example

For an organism, the cell cycle is needed for

    A. competition.   B. dispersal.   C. growth.   D. parasitism.

The correct answer is **C**. The cell cycle is the process during which a cell grows, copies its own DNA, and physically separates into new cells. With help from the cell cycle, more cells can be provided to help an organism grow.

Mitosis

Mitosis is a form of cell division where two identical nuclei are produced from one nucleus. DNA contains the genetic information of the cell. It is stored in the nucleus. During mitosis, DNA in the nucleus must be copied, or replicated. Recall that this happens during the S phase of the cell cycle. During the M phase, this copied DNA is divided into two complete sets, one of which goes to a daughter cell.

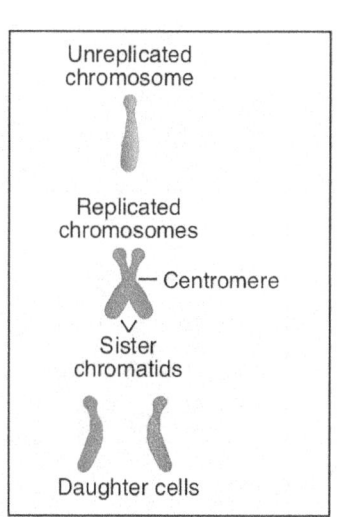

When DNA replicates, it condenses to form **chromosomes** that resemble an X. The DNA forms chromosomes by wrapping around proteins called histones. As shown below, it takes two identical sister chromatids to form a chromosome. A **centromere** holds the sister chromatids together.

Four phases take place during mitosis to form two identical daughter cells:

1. **Prophase:** The nuclear membrane disappears, and other organelles move out of the way. The spindle, made of microtubules, begins to form. During **prometaphase**, the microtubules begin to attach to the centromeres at the center of the chromosome.
2. **Metaphase:** Spindle fibers line the chromosomes at the center of the cell. This is because they are pulled equally by the spindle fibers, which are attached to the opposite poles of the cell.
3. **Anaphase:** The chromosomes are pulled to the opposite poles of the cell.
4. **Telophase:** The chromosomes de-condense, the nuclear membrane reappears, and other parts of the cell return to their usual places in the cell.

The cell divides into two daughter cells by way of **cytokinesis**. The illustration below demonstrates the process of mitosis.

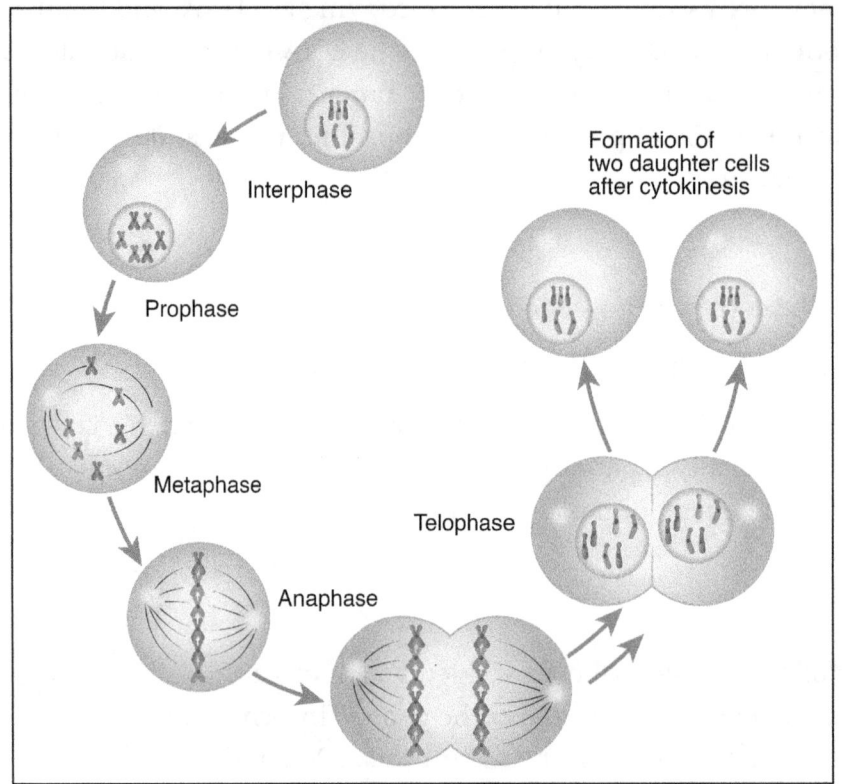

> **TEST TIP**
>
> There is a popular mnemonic to help remember the order of the phases for mitosis:
>
> *[Please] Pee on the MAT.*
>
> The "please" refers to prophase, while "pee" refers to prometaphase. MAT stands for metaphase, anaphase, and telophase, respectively.

Example

Before mitosis occurs

A. the spindle fibers must elongate.

B. DNA must wrap around histones.

C. chromosomes must split into chromatids.

D. the cell cycle process must be suspended.

The correct answer is **B**. After DNA replicates, it wraps around proteins called histones to form a chromosome. The chromosome must be formed for mitosis to occur.

Meiosis

Meiosis, sexual cell division in eukaryotes, involves two phases of mitosis that take place one after the other but without a second replication of DNA. This provides the reduction in chromosome number from $2n$ to n needed for fertilization to restore the normal $2n$ state.

Lesson 10.4 Cellular Reproduction, Cellular Respiration, and Photosynthesis

Diploid multicellular organisms use meiosis, which reduces the number of chromosomes by half. Then, when two haploid (*n*) sex cells (sperm, egg) unite, the normal number of chromosomes is restored. Diploid organisms, such as humans and oak trees, have two copies of every chromosome per cell (2*n*), as opposed to *n*, when one copy of every chromosome is present per cell.

DID YOU KNOW?
During prophase I of meiosis, **crossing over** occurs to increase genetic diversity. Corresponding chromosomes from the mother and the father of the organism undergoing meiosis are physically bound, and *X*-shaped structures called **chiasmata** form. These are where corresponding DNA from the different parental chromosomes are exchanged, resulting in increased diversity.

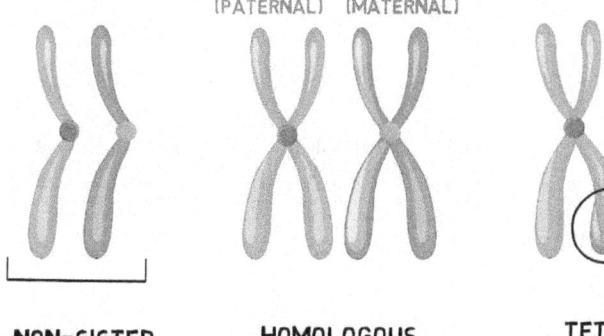

(PATERNAL) (MATERNAL)

NON-SISTER CHROMATIDS   HOMOLOGOUS CHROMOSOMES   TETRAD (4 CHROMATIDS)   GENETIC CROSSOVER

The process of meiosis is divided into two rounds of cell division: meiosis I and meiosis II. The phases that occur in mitosis (prophase, metaphase, anaphase, and telophase) also occur during each round of meiosis. Also, cytokinesis occurs after telophase during each round of cell division. However, DNA replication does not happen when meiosis I proceeds to meiosis II. The result of meiosis is one diploid cell that divides into four haploid cells, as shown in the following image.

Cytokinesis looks different in plant and animal cells. Plant cells build a new wall, or cell plate, between the two cells, while animal cells split by slowly pinching the membrane toward the center of the cell as the cell divides. Microtubules are more important for cytokinesis in plant cells, while the actin cytoskeleton performs the pinching-off operation during animal cytokinesis.

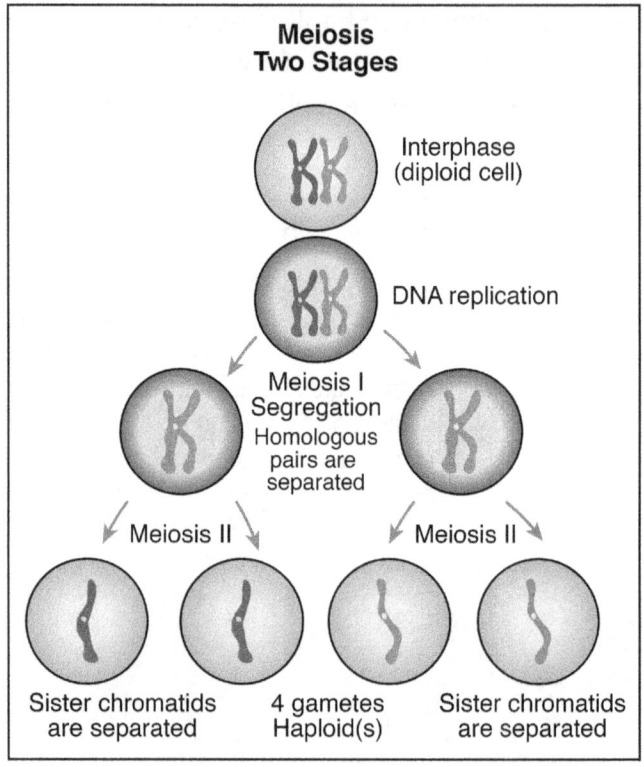

Example

How many rounds of cell division occur during meiosis?

A. 1
B. 2
C. 3
D. 4

The correct answer is **B**. A difference between mitosis and meiosis is that meiosis requires two rounds of cell division. At the end of both rounds, four haploid daughter cells have been produced.

> **KEY POINT**
>
> Meiosis and mitosis both require cytokinesis to physically separate a cell into daughter cells. Also, the sequence of events that occur in mitosis are the same in meiosis. However, there are two primary differences between the types of cell division: (1) meiosis has two rounds of cell division, and (2) daughter cells are genetically identical to the parent cell in mitosis but are not genetically identical in meiosis.

Cell Respiration

Once cells have been made, they need to be powered. Plants and some other cells can capture the energy of light and convert it into stored energy in ATP. However, most prokaryotic cells and all eukaryotic cells can perform a metabolic process called **cellular respiration**. Cellular respiration is the process by which the mitochondria of a cell break down glucose to produce energy in the form of ATP. The following is the general equation for cellular respiration:

$$O_2 + C_6H_{12}O_6 \rightarrow CO_2 + H_2O + ATP$$

Reactions during cellular respiration occur in the following sequence:

1. **Glycolysis:** One molecule of glucose breaks down into two smaller sugar molecules called **pyruvate**. This is an anaerobic process, which means it does not need oxygen to be present.

Glycolysis takes place in the cell's cytoplasm. End product yield from this reaction per one glucose molecule is

- two molecules of ATP
- two molecules of pyruvate
- two molecules of NADH

2. **Oxidation of pyruvate:** Pyruvate is converted into **acetyl coA** in the mitochondrial matrix. This transition reaction must happen for pyruvate to enter the next phase of cellular respiration. Pyruvate is **oxidized**, which means it loses two electrons and a hydrogen molecule. This results in the formation of NADH and loss of CO_2.

> **DID YOU KNOW?**
> The citric acid cycle is not identical for all organisms. Plants have some differences in terms of the enzymes used and energy carriers produced.

3. **Citric acid cycle:** Also called the **Krebs cycle**, during this cycle an acetyl group detaches from the coenzyme A in the acetyl coA molecule. This process is **aerobic**, which means it must occur in the presence of oxygen. The net yield per one glucose molecule is

- two molecules of ATP
- six molecules of NADH
- two molecules of $FADH_2$
- four molecules of CO_2

> **KEEP IN MIND**
> Cellular respiration requires oxygen, but there are forms of **fermentation** that extract energy from food without using oxygen. Fermentation can be either alcoholic (makes ethanol as an end product, like yeast in the brewing of beer) or lactic acid type. Lactic acid is produced in a person's muscles during strenuous activity when the body cannot move enough oxygen to the cells.

4. **Electron transport chain:** This process happens in the inner mitochondrial membrane. It consists of a series of enzymatic reactions. Both NADH and $FADH_2$ molecules are passed through a series of enzymes so that electrons and protons can be released from them. During this process, energy is released and used to fuel **chemiosmosis**. During chemiosmosis, protons are transported across the inner mitochondrial membrane to the outer mitochondrial compartment. This flow of protons drives the process of ATP synthesis. This step of cellular respiration creates an approximate net yield of 34 ATP per glucose molecule. Six molecules of water are also formed at the end of the electron transport chain.

Photosynthesis

Photosynthesis is the process plants use to make a food source from energy. This process can be thought of as the reverse of cellular respiration. Instead of glucose being broken down into carbon dioxide to create energy-containing molecules, energy is captured from the sun and used to turn carbon dioxide into glucose (and other organic chemicals the plant needs). The energy source is the sun. The reaction for photosynthesis is shown below:

$$CO_2 + H_2O \rightarrow C_6H_{12}O_6 + O_2$$

Energy is captured from the sun and used to turn carbon dioxide into glucose (and other organic chemicals). **Chloroplasts** are **organelles** in plants that contain green chlorophyll, which helps the plants absorb light from the sun.

The photosynthetic reaction involves two distinct phases: light reactions and dark reactions. Light-dependent reactions require light to produce ATP and NADPH. During dark reactions, also known as the **Calvin cycle**, light is not required. These reactions use ATP and NAPDH to produce sugar molecules like glucose.

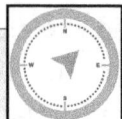

DID YOU KNOW?
Some plants skip photosynthesis! These plants are parasites. They lack chlorophyll, so they attach to nearby plants, stealing water and sugar from their hosts.

Let's Review!

- Cells are needed for growth, repair, and reproduction.
- Mitosis is a form of cell division where one parent cell divides into identical two daughter cells.
- Meiosis involves two rounds of cell division to divide two parent cells into four haploid cells.
- Cells are powered by cellular respiration and photosynthesis, which make ATP and organic chemicals.
- Cellular respiration goes from glycolysis to the citric acid cycle to the electron transport chain.
- Photosynthesis proceeds from the light reactions to the dark reactions, which are known as the Calvin cycle.

Genetics and DNA

The lesson introduces genetics, which is the study of heredity. Heredity is the characteristics offspring inherit from their parents. This lesson also examines Gregor Mendel's theories of heredity and how they have affected the field of genetics.

Gregor Mendel and Garden Peas

From experiments with garden peas, Mendel developed a simple set of rules that accurately predicted patterns of heredity. He discovered that plants either **self-pollinate** or **cross-pollinate**, when the pollen from one plant fertilizes the pistil of another plant. He also discovered that traits are either **dominant** or **recessive**. Dominant traits are expressed, and recessive traits are hidden.

Mendel's Theory of Heredity

To explain his results, Mendel proposed a theory that has become the foundation of the science of genetics. The theory has five elements:

1. Parents do not transmit traits directly to their offspring. Rather, they pass on units of information called **genes**.
2. For each trait, an individual has two factors: one from each parent. If the two factors have the same information, the individual is **homozygous** for that trait. If the two factors are different, the individual is **heterozygous** for that trait. Each copy of a factor, or **gene**, is called an **allele**.
3. The alleles determine the physical appearance, or **phenotype**. The set of alleles an individual has is its **genotype**.
4. An individual receives one allele from each parent.
5. The presence of an allele does not guarantee that the trait will be expressed.

Punnett Squares

Biologists can predict the probable outcomes of a cross by using a diagram called a **Punnett square**. In the Punnett square illustrated at the right, the yellow pea pods are dominant, as designated by a capital Y, and the green pea pods are recessive, as designated with a lowercase y. In a cross between one homozygous recessive (yy) parent and a heterozygous dominant parent (Yy), the outcome is two heterozygous dominant offspring (Yy) and two homozygous recessive offspring (yy), which gives a ratio of 2:2.

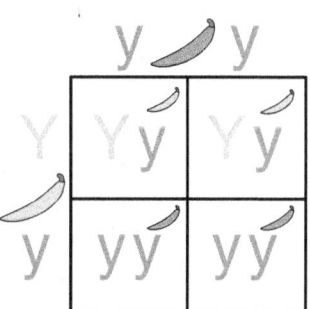

Example

In the Punnett square below, homozygous green pea pods are crossed with dominant yellow pea pods. What is the probability of a homozygous green pea pod?

A. 25%   C. 75%

B. 50%   D. 100%

The correct answer is **B**. There is a 2 out of 4, or 50%, chance of a homozygous green pea pod.

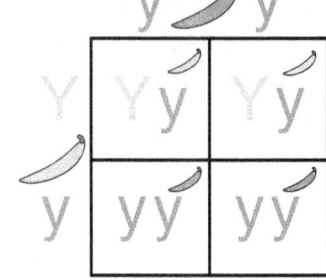

Chromosomes

A **gene** is a segment of DNA, deoxyribonucleic acid, which transmits information from parent to offspring. A single molecule of DNA has thousands of genes. A **chromosome** is a rod-shaped structure that forms when a single DNA molecule and its associated proteins coil tightly before cell division.

Chromosomes have two components:

- **Chromatids:** two copies of each chromosome
- **Centromeres:** protein discs that attach the chromatids together

Human cells have 23 sets of different chromosomes. The two copies of each chromosome are called **homologous** chromosomes, or homologues. An offspring receives one homologue from each parent. When a cell contains two homologues of each chromosome, it is termed **diploid (2n)**. A **haploid (n)** cell contains only one homologue of each chromosome. The only haploid cells humans have are the sperm and eggs cells known as **gametes**.

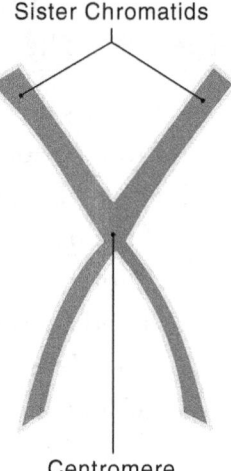

Example

What is the difference between a diploid cell and a haploid cell?

A. A haploid cell is only found in skin cells.

B. A diploid cell is only found in heart cells.

C. A diploid cell has a full number of chromosomes, and a haploid cell does not.

D. A haploid cell has a full number of chromosomes, and a diploid cell does not.

The correct answer is **C**. Diploid cells have a full number of chromosomes, and haploid cells have half the number of chromosomes.

Deoxyribonucleic Acid

The **DNA molecule** is a long, thin molecule made of subunits called **nucleotides** that are linked together in a **nucleic acid** chain. Each nucleotide is constructed of three parts: a **phosphate group**, **five-carbon sugar**, and **nitrogen base**.

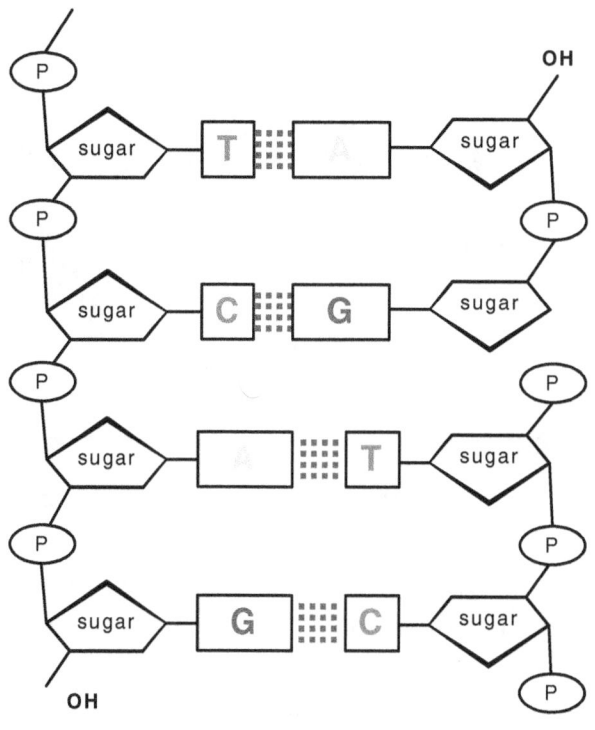

The four nitrogenous bases are

- adenine (A);
- guanine (G);
- thymine (T); and
- cytosine (C).

Adenine and guanine belong to a class of large, organic molecules called **purines**. Thymine and cytosine are **pyrimidines**, which have a single ring of carbon and nitrogen atoms. Base pairs are formed as adenine pairs with thymine and guanine pairs with cytosine. These are the only possible combinations.

DNA Replication

The process of synthesizing a new strand of DNA is called **replication**. A DNA molecule replicates by separating into two strands, building a complementary strand, and twisting to form a double helix.

Transcription

The first step in using DNA to direct the making of a protein is **transcription**, the process that "rewrites" the information in a gene in DNA into a molecule of messenger RNA. Transcription manufactures three types of RNA:

- Messenger RNA (mRNA)
- Transfer RNA (tRNA)
- Ribosomal RNA (rRNA)

Messenger RNA is an RNA copy of a gene used as a blueprint for a protein. In eukaryotes, transcription does not produce mRNA directly; it produces a pre-mRNA molecule. **Transfer RNA** translates mRNA sequences into amino acid sequences. **Ribosomal RNA** plays a structural role in ribosomes.

Transcription proceeds at a rate of about 60 nucleotides per second until the **RNA polymerase** (an enzyme) reaches a **stop codon** on the DNA called a **terminator** and releases the RNA molecule.

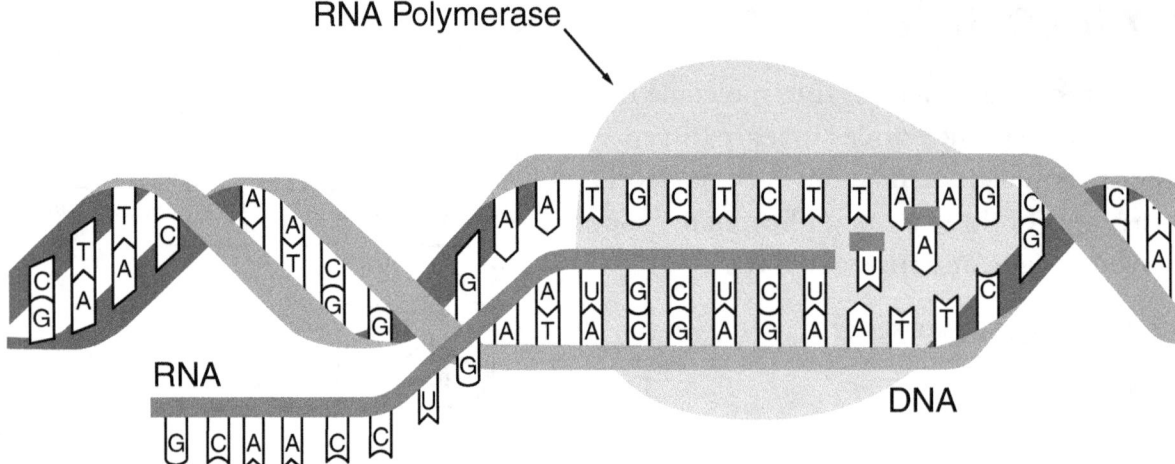

Translation

The components necessary for **translation** are located in the cytoplasm. Translation is the making of proteins by mRNA binding to a ribosome with the start codon that initiates the production of amino acids. A **peptide bond** forms and connects the amino acids together. The sequence of amino acids determines the protein's structure, which determines its function.

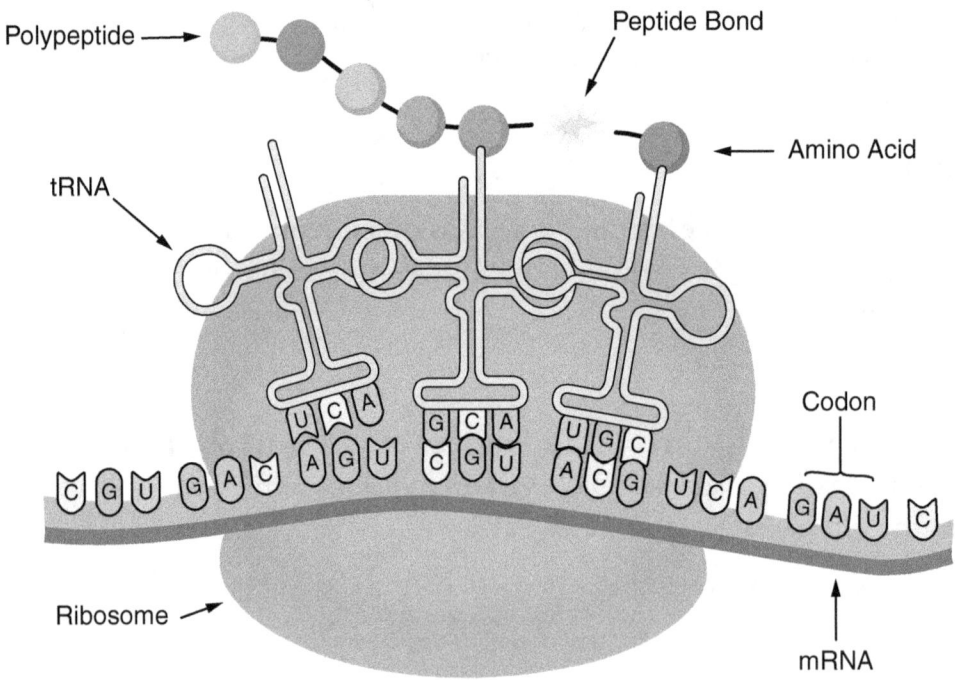

Example

Which type of RNA acts as an interpreter molecule?

A. mRNA B. pre-mRNA C. rRNA D. tRNA

The correct answer is **D**. Transfer RNA (tRNA) acts as an interpreter molecule, translating mRNA sequences into amino acid sequences.

Chapter 10 Life and Physical Sciences Practice Quiz

1. Fats and steroids belong to what biomolecule class?
   A. Lipids
   B. Proteins
   C. Nucleic acids
   D. Carbohydrates

2. How many hydrogen atoms are bonded to oxygen in water?
   A. 1
   B. 2
   C. 3
   D. 4

3. A protein is synthesized in the ribosome. Where does it travel next?
   A. Vacuole
   B. Lysosome
   C. Golgi apparatus
   D. Endoplasmic reticulum

4. Chromosomes contain all of the information necessary to run a cell and pass on a cell's hereditary traits to new cells. Where are these structures found in a cell?
   A. Nucleus
   B. Ribosome
   C. Cytoplasm
   D. Golgi apparatus

5. A chemist decides to study reactions occurring in a cell's cytoplasm. Which of the following reactions does she observe?
   A. Mitosis
   B. Cell cycle
   C. Glycolysis
   D. Carbon cycle

6. A scientist is watching a colony of bacteria on a plate, and the colony is growing. Which process is most likely responsible for this growth?
   A. Mitosis
   B. Binary fission
   C. Photosynthesis
   D. Sexual reproduction

7. Adenine and guanine belong to a class of organic molecules called _____.
   A. enzymes
   B. nucleotides
   C. purines
   D. pyrimidines

8. A _____ is a rod-shaped structure that forms when a single DNA molecule and its associated proteins coil tightly before cell division.
   A. centromere
   B. chromatid
   C. chromosome
   D. gene

Chapter 10 Life and Physical Sciences Practice Quiz — Answer Key

1. **A.** Lipids are a class of biomolecules that provide a long-term storage solution for energy in living things. Examples of lipids include fats, steroids, and oils. **See Lesson: An Introduction to Biology.**

2. **B.** In the molecular structure of water, a partially negative oxygen atom is bonded to two partially positive hydrogen atoms. **See Lesson: An Introduction to Biology.**

3. **C.** After a protein is synthesized, it goes to the Golgi apparatus where the protein is further modified and then packaged for transport in the cell. **See Lesson: Cell Structure, Function, and Type.**

4. **A.** The nucleus is where genetic information is found in a cell. This genetic information, or DNA, is packaged into chromosomes. **See Lesson: Cell Structure, Function, and Type.**

5. **C.** The first step of cellular respiration is glycolysis. This process happens in the cell's cytoplasm, where glucose is broken down to pyruvate, yielding two molecules of ATP. **See Lesson: Cellular Reproduction, Cellular Respiration, and Photosynthesis.**

6. **B.** Bacteria are able to reproduce asexually using binary fission. **See Lesson: Cellular Reproduction, Cellular Respiration, and Photosynthesis.**

7. **C.** Adenine and guanine belong to a class of organic molecules called purines, which are large molecules. **See Lesson: Genetics and DNA.**

8. **C.** A chromosome is a rod-shaped structure that forms when a single DNA molecule and its associated proteins coil tightly before cell division. **See Lesson: Genetics and DNA.**

CHAPTER 11 CHEMISTRY

LESSON 11.1 SCIENTIFIC NOTATION

This lesson begins by explaining how to convert measurements with very large or very small values into more manageable numbers using scientific notation. It then explores the structure of the atom and describes how to determine the number of protons, neutrons, and electrons in an atom of a specific element. Finally, it describes the relationship between isotopes of the same element and the effects that these isotopes have on the average atomic mass of an element.

Scientific Notation

Scientists often work with very large and very small numbers. For example, the radius of Earth's orbit around the sun is very large: 15,000,000,000,000 centimeters. On the other extreme, the radius of a hydrogen atom is very small: 0.00000000529 centimeters. To make these numbers more manageable, scientists write them using **scientific notation**. Scientific notation is a way to represent numbers and contains three components, which are shown in the diagram below.

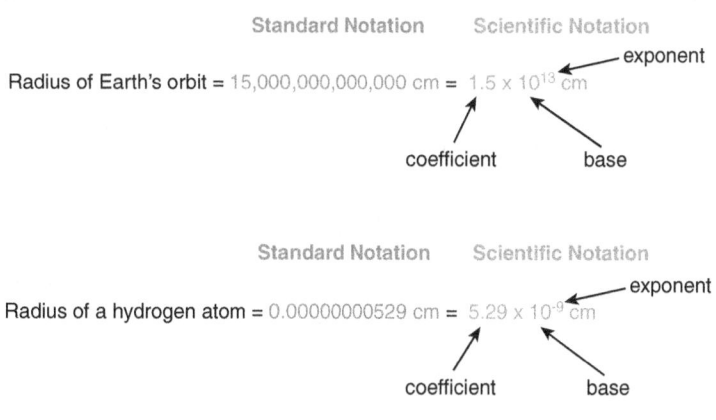

Understanding how these components relate to one another makes it possible to convert between standard notation and scientific notation. The coefficient is a number that has a value of at least 1 but less than 10 and includes all significant digits in the given value. Another way to think about this is that there should always be one non-zero digit before the decimal point.

In scientific notation, the base is always 10.

The exponent indicates the number of places the decimal point needs to move. Notice that when the exponent is positive, the decimal place moves to the right; this is how larger numbers are represented. When the exponent is negative, the decimal place moves to the left; this is how smaller numbers are represented. When the decimal must move beyond the digits that are in the measurement, the "empty" spaces are filled in with zeros.

> **KEY POINT**
> When converting from scientific notation to standard notation, a negative exponent requires the decimal point to move to the left, and a positive exponent requires the decimal point to move to the right.

Example

The length of a year is 31,560,000 seconds. What is this value in scientific notation?

A. 0.3156×10^{-6} s   B. 3.156×10^{-7} s   C. 3.156×10^{7} s   D. 31.56×10^{6} s

The correct answer is **C**. The coefficient is a value between 1 and 10 and includes all digits, which is 3.156. Starting with that coefficient, the decimal must be moved seven places to the right to get the value in standard notation, which means that the exponent is a positive seven.

The Atom

All matter is made of atoms. Every atom contains a dense core in the center called a **nucleus**. The nucleus is composed of subatomic particles called **protons** and **neutrons**. Surrounding this core is an area known as the **electron cloud**, in which smaller subatomic particles known as **electrons** are moving.

The Bohr model below shows these components of the atom. In the model, each subatomic particle is marked with a charge. Protons have a positive (+) charge, electrons have a negative (−) charge, and neutrons do not carry any charge; they are neutral. Therefore, the overall charge of an atom depends on the numbers of protons and electrons and is not influenced by the number of neutrons. An atom is neutral if the number of protons is equal to the number of electrons. If there are more protons than electrons, the atom will have an overall positive charge; if there are more electrons than protons, the atom will have an overall negative charge.

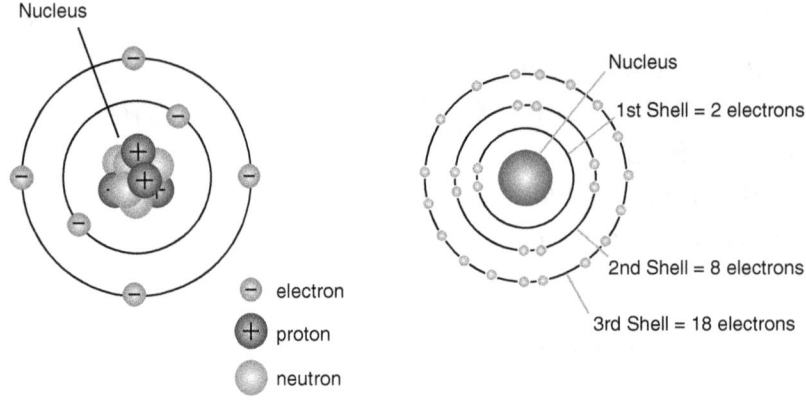

> **COMPARE THE BOHR MODEL TO A REAL ATOM.**
>
> Note that this model is not to scale. The nucleus should be much smaller because it is about 10,000 times smaller than the electron cloud in a real atom. Also, the space between the electrons a real atom is much greater than in the model. In a real atom, the electron cloud is mostly empty space.

To further compare these three subatomic particles, their locations, charges, and masses are shown in the table below. The unit used for mass is the **atomic mass unit (amu)**. The masses of a proton or neutron are considerably larger than the mass of an electron. This difference in mass has important implications. First, because the nucleus is so small relative to the overall size of the atom and contains the more massive protons and neutrons, it is extremely dense. Second, because the electrons are almost 2,000 times less massive than the other subatomic particles, they do not significantly influence the atom's mass.

Subatomic Particle	Symbol	Location	Charge	Mass (amu)
Proton	$p+$	Nucleus	+1	1.0
Neutron	n_0	Nucleus	0	1.0
Electron	$e-$	Electron cloud	−1	0.00054

One final note about the Bohr model of the atom is that the electrons lie on rings. These rings represent energy levels, sometimes referred to as electron "shells." Electrons that occupy energy levels that are closest to the nucleus have the least energy. Electrons found farther from the nucleus have more energy. A limited number of electrons can occupy each energy level. The first energy level can fit up to 2 electrons. The second energy level can fit up to 8 electrons. The third energy level can fit up to 18 electrons. An atom in its normal state will have electrons lying in the lowest possible energy levels.

While the Bohr model provides a good way to visualize the atom, its representation of the electron cloud is not completely accurate. Electrons move around the nucleus in different energy levels, but this movement is not restricted to specific circular orbits as the Bohr model indicates. The **quantum mechanical model** (also known as the electron cloud model) describes the probable locations of electrons because their exact pathways, locations, and speeds cannot be determined simultaneously.

Example

Which subatomic particles affect the overall charge of the atom?

A. Only protons

B. Protons and neutrons

C. Protons and electrons

D. Protons, neutrons, and electrons

The correct answer is **C**. Because protons are positively charged and electrons are negatively charged, they affect the overall charge of the atom. Neutrons do not affect the charge because they are uncharged.

The Periodic Table of the Elements

The atom is not only the basic building block of matter, but also the smallest unit of an element that can be defined as that element. All known elements are listed in the periodic table.

Periodic Table of Elements

[Periodic table of elements showing groups 1-18 and periods 1-7, with Lanthanides and Actinides displayed separately below. Legend indicates: Alkali Metal, Alkaline Earth Metal, Transition Metal, Halogen, Noble Gas, Lanthanide, Actinide.]

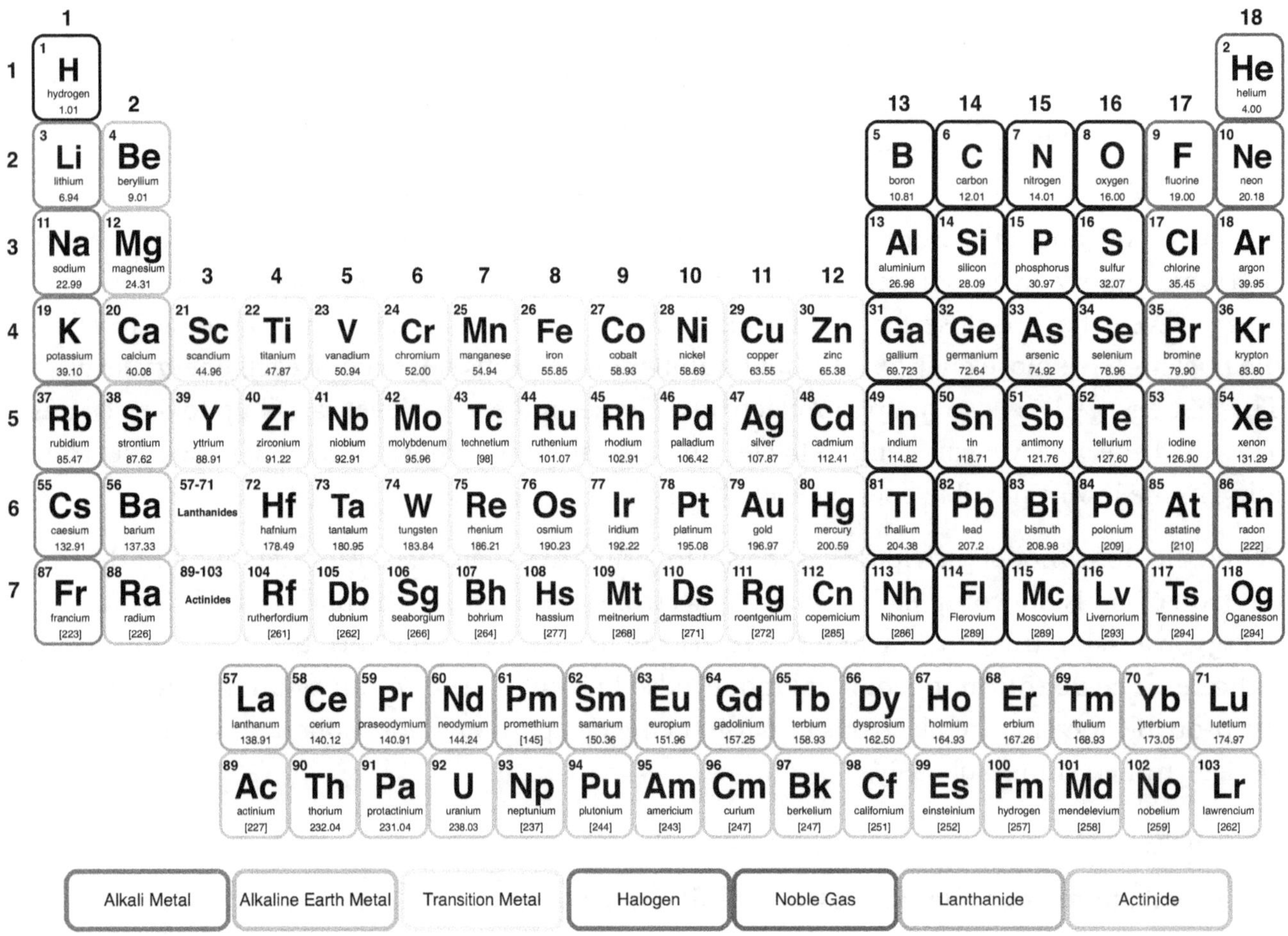

In the periodic table, elements are arranged in rows, also known as **periods**, and columns, also known as **groups**. Both the periods and the groups can be referred to by number. For example, argon is in period 3 and group 18.

Elements with similar properties are put into families that are outlined in different colors in the periodic table above. Note that these families generally correspond to the groups in the periodic table. For example, the elements in group 18 are in a family called the noble gases, while the elements in group 2 are all alkaline earth metals.

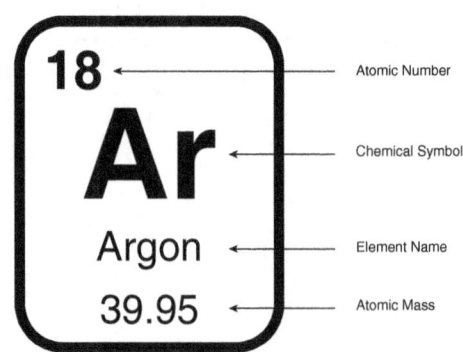

236

Lesson 11.1 Scientific Notation

Periodic tables differ in the information they provide, and an example of a block is shown above. This block shows the name of the element and its **chemical symbol**, which is an abbreviation for the name. The chemical symbol is one, two, or three letters with the first letter capitalized and all subsequent letters letter lowercase. The symbol for the element argon is Ar.

> **DID YOU KNOW?**
> While many elements have chemical symbols that resemble their names, like argon (Ar), some elements have chemical symbols that are different from their names. This is because the symbols are derived from either the Latin or the Greek names for the elements rather than the English names. The symbol for sodium is Na because the Latin name for the element is natrium.

Each element is assigned an **atomic number**. The atomic number is equal to the number of protons in a single atom of that element and is how an element is identified. Argon, for example, has an atomic number of 18. Therefore, every atom of argon has 18 protons, regardless of how many neutrons or electrons it has.

Example

Which of the following statements is true?

A. A tin atom has 22 protons.

B. An iron atom has 26 protons.

C. A sodium atom has 16 protons.

D. A potassium atom has 15 protons.

The correct answer is **B**. In the periodic table, iron has an atomic number of 26, which means it has 26 protons.

Average Atomic Mass and Mass Number

Some periodic tables also provide the **average atomic mass** of an element in atomic mass units (amu). Because not all atoms of argon have the same mass, the periodic table shows the average mass of all argon atoms. These forms of argon are differentiated based on their **mass numbers**, which are determined by adding the number of protons and neutrons. Argon has three stable forms, called isotopes, which are shown in the table below.

Name	Abundance	Mass (amu)	Mass Number	Number of protons	Number of neutrons
Argon-36	0.337%	35.97	36	18	18
Argon-38	0.063%	37.96	38	18	20
Argon-40	99.6%	39.96	40	18	22

The mass number can be used to determine the number of neutrons, as shown by the equation below. Argon-40 is the most abundant and has a mass number of 40. Its 18 protons contribute 18 to the mass number of the atom. The remaining mass is from the neutrons.

mass number = number of protons + number of neutrons

40 = 18 + number of neutrons

number of neutrons = 40 − 18 = 22 neutrons

To determine the number of electrons, the charge of the atom must be considered. If a charge is not indicated, it can be assumed that the atom in question is neutral. A neutral atom has an equal number of positively charged protons and negatively charged electrons. Therefore, a neutral atom of argon has 18 electrons that balance the charge of its 18 protons, given by the atomic number.

Example

> **CHECKLIST**
> Here are reminders for how to determine the numbers of subatomic particles using information found in the periodic table:
>
> Number of protons = atomic number
> Number of neutrons = mass number − number of protons (atomic number)
> Number of electrons = number of protons (atomic number) in a neutral atom

Using the periodic table, determine how many protons and electrons a neutral atom of potassium has.

   A. 19 protons, 19 electrons

   B. 19 protons, 20 electrons

   C. 19 protons, 39 electrons

   D. 39 protons, 39 electrons

The correct answer is **A**. The atomic number of potassium is 19, which means it has 19 protons. Because the atom is neutral, the number of electrons must equal the number of protons.

Isotopes

All atoms of an element have the same number of protons, but the number of neutrons may be different. Atoms that have the same number of protons but different numbers of neutrons are called **isotopes**. Because they have the same number of protons, they are the same element. However, because they contain different numbers of neutrons, their masses and mass numbers are different. The Bohr models for three isotopes of carbon are shown below.

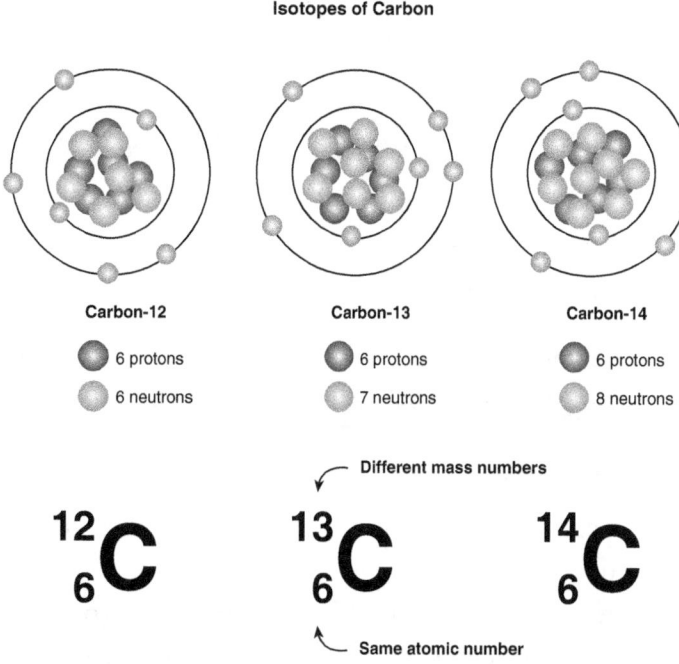

All three isotopes have 6 protons because they are all different forms of carbon. They all have 6 electrons because these are neutral atoms of carbon, which means that the positive and negative charges balance each other. The different numbers of neutrons and the different masses differentiate these isotopes.

The isotopes can be named according to their masses. Carbon-12 has a mass number of 12, with 6 protons and 6 neutrons. Carbon-13 has a mass number of 13, with 6 protons and 7 neutrons. Carbon-14 has a mass number of 14, with 6 protons and 8 neutrons. The figure above shows how isotopes can be represented using the element symbols.

Isotopes are present in varying amounts. Carbon-12 makes up 98.93% of all carbon on Earth, and carbon-13 makes up 1.07%. Although carbon-14 exists, its amount is negligible. When calculating the average atomic mass, all isotopes are taken into account. In the periodic table, carbon has an atomic mass of 12.01 amu, which is extremely close to the mass of the most abundant isotope, carbon-12. Though not always true, the average atomic mass of an element is often closest to the mass of the most common isotope.

Example

Atom X has 7 protons and 8 neutrons, and Atom Y has 7 protons and 7 neutrons. Which of the following statements describes the relationship between Atom X and Atom Y?

    A. They are different elements because they have different masses.

    B. They are different elements because they have different numbers of neutrons.

    C. They are isotopes because they have different atomic numbers but the same masses.

    D. They are isotopes because they have the same number of protons but different numbers of neutrons.

The correct answer is **D**. Atom X and Y are different isotopes of nitrogen. They both have 7 protons, but the different numbers of neutrons give them different masses.

Let's Review!

- Scientific notation is used to make very large numbers and very small numbers easier to use.
- An atom is composed of protons, neutrons, and electrons. Protons and neutrons are found in the nucleus, and electrons are found in the electron cloud that surrounds the nucleus.
- The number of protons in an atom determines its identity (which element it is).
- The mass number of an atom is determined by adding the number of protons and the number of neutrons.
- The charge of an atom is determined by the numbers of protons and electrons.
- Isotopes are atoms of the same element that have different numbers of neutrons and, therefore, different masses.

LESSON 11.2 STATES OF MATTER

This lesson explains the differences between solids, liquids, gases, and plasmas. It also describes how a sample can change from one state of matter to another.

States of Matter

On Earth, substances are found in four states of matter: solid, liquid, gas, and plasma. Many properties of these states of matter are familiar. For example, solids are rigid and hard, liquids can flow inside their containers, and gases can spread throughout an entire room. But what happens at the molecular level may not be as familiar. The differences among them can be explained by the amount of energy that the particles have and the strength of the cohesive forces that hold the particles together. **Cohesion** is the tendency of particles of the same kind to stick to each other and is an important property to consider when looking at states of matter. The motion and density of particles in a substance and the tendency of a substance to take the shape and volume of its container differentiate states of matter.

Solids have the lowest energy. The particles are packed close together, and their structure is relatively rigid. Strong cohesive forces prevent particles from moving very far or very fast. Therefore, both the shape and volume of a solid are fixed.

> **DID YOU KNOW?**
> While particles are generally more tightly packed in solids than in other states, water is an exception. When liquid water freezes, it expands. The molecules are pushed apart as strong intermolecular forces, known as hydrogen bonds, allow the particles to form crystals. This property of water is important in many processes on Earth.

In **liquids**, particles have more energy than in solids and can overcome the cohesive forces to some degree. Since particles can move more freely, they flow and take the shape of their container. However, cohesive forces are strong enough to somewhat restrict the movement of particles. While the shape of the liquid is not fixed, the volume is.

Gases have more energy than solids or liquids. In a gas, the cohesive forces are very weak because the particles move very quickly. Gas particles move more freely than liquids, which means that gas particles can not only take the shape of the container, but also spread to occupy the entire volume of the container.

> **CONNECTIONS**
> Gases and liquids are considered fluids because of their ability to "flow" and take the shape of their containers.

In **plasma**, the particles have so much energy that the electrons separate from their nuclei. The result is a substance composed of moving positively and negatively charged particles. Although plasmas are less common in everyday life than the other states of matter, there are a few familiar examples. First, the hottest parts of the sun are made of plasma because of the high temperature (up to 15,000,000 K). Also, neon signs glow when plasma is produced by passing an electric current through a gas.

> **DID YOU KNOW?**
> Not all neon signs contain neon. Other noble gases (helium, argon, and xenon) can be used to produce different colors of light.

Example

In which state of matter are particles moving slowest?

A. Solid   B. Liquid   C. Gas   D. Plasma

The correct answer is **A**. Because solid particles have less energy than particles in other states of matter, they have the most restricted movement.

Phase Changes

Whenever a substance transforms from one state of matter to another, it undergoes a phase change. These processes are physical changes because the chemical composition of the substance remains the same; only its appearance is different. The six most common phase changes are summarized in the diagram and chart below. Note that the states of matter are arranged in order of increasing energy from left to right.

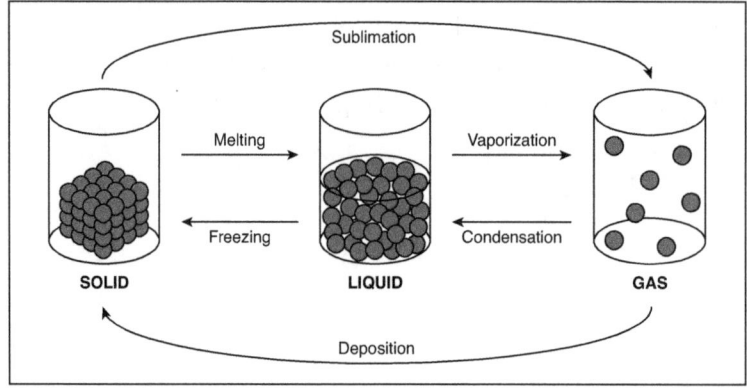

Lesson 11.2 States of Matter

Phase Change	Name	Absorb or Release Energy
solid to liquid	melting	absorb
liquid to gas	vaporization	absorb
solid to gas	sublimation	absorb
liquid to solid	freezing	release
gas to liquid	condensation	release
gas to solid	deposition	release

All phase changes require the system to either absorb or release energy. Any phase change that moves to the right in the diagram above requires energy to be added to the system because the substance has more energy at the end of the phase change. The phase changes are **melting**, **vaporization (boiling)**, and **sublimation**. When energy is added, particles move faster and can break away from each other more easily as they move to a state of matter with a higher amount of energy. This is most commonly done by heating the substance.

Any phase change that moves to the left in the diagram requires energy to be removed from the system because the substance has less energy at the end of the phase change. These phase changes are **freezing**, **condensation**, and **deposition**. When the particles release energy, they move more slowly. The cohesive forces bring these particles closer together as they move to a state of matter with a lower amount of energy. This is most commonly done by cooling the substance.

The temperatures at which phase changes occur depends the strength of the cohesive forces between particles. For substances like metals that have high melting and boiling points, it takes a relatively large amount of energy to overcome the intermolecular forces enough to change states of matter. Similarly, substances with low melting and boiling points, like the gases that make up Earth's atmosphere, do not require as much energy to overcome their intermolecular forces.

Example

Which of the following phase changes requires a substance to release energy?

    A. Boiling   B. Condensation   C. Melting   D. Sublimation

The correct answer is **B**. During condensation, a gas turns to a liquid. For this to occur, high-energy particles in the gas must release some energy for the cohesive forces to bring the particles closer together.

Heating and Cooling Curves

When studying phase changes, one can examine the heating or cooling curve of a substance. Heating and cooling curves are plots of temperature versus time that occur as energy is added to or removed from the system at a constant rate.

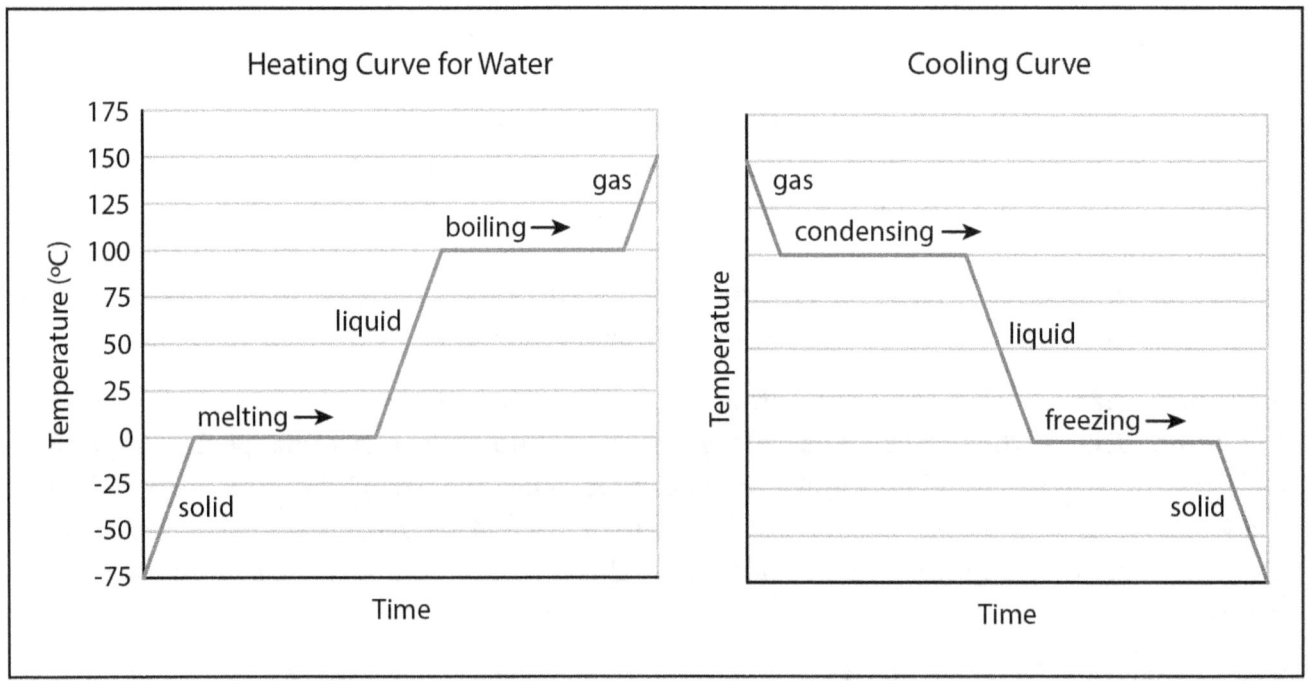

The heating curve for water is shown above. Notice that at the beginning of the experiment, the substance is a solid. As heat is added, the temperature of the solid increases until it reaches its melting point, 0°C. The temperature remains constant at the melting point until the entire sample has changed to a liquid. Note that even though heat is still being added, the temperature is not increasing. This is because the added energy is used to disrupt the cohesive forces in the solid, allowing the particles to move more freely as the substance changes to a liquid.

Once the sample is completely melted, the temperature increases again. It increases until the boiling point, 100°C, is reached. Heat is still being added, but the temperature remains constant as the substance boils. This time, the added energy is being used to break the intermolecular bonds in the liquid as the particles transform into a gas and move farther away from each other. It is not until the phase change is complete and the sample is entirely gas that the temperature starts increasing again.

KEEP IN MIND
The temperature of a substance is a measure of the kinetic energy of the particles that make up a substance. In other words, temperature is related to how fast the particles are moving.

A cooling curve has the opposite shape of a heating curve, as seen in the graph above. In these experiments, the sample starts as a high-temperature gas. As heat is removed, the temperature of the gas decreases to its boiling point. At this point, the temperature remains constant until the entire sample is liquid. The liquid then cools to a lower temperature until it reaches the freezing point. The temperature remains constant as the substance freezes, and once it is completely solid, the temperature decreases again.

> **KEY POINT!**
> As a substance undergoes a phase change, its temperature remains constant. The only time a substance experiences an increase or decrease in temperature is when it is entirely in one state of matter.

Example

If a sample of water is losing energy but its temperature is not changing, what may be happening?

A. Freezing   B. Melting   C. Sublimation   D. Vaporization

The correct answer is **A**. When a substance is freezing, the liquid particles lose enough energy to become a solid. The temperature will not change until the phase change is complete.

Let's Review!

- Solids, liquids, gases, and plasmas differ from one another in the amount of energy that the particles have and the strength of the cohesive forces that hold the particles together.
- A substance can undergo a phase change if it either absorbs or releases enough energy.
- Heating and cooling curves show the temperature of a substance as heat is consistently added or removed.
- As a substance changes states, its temperature remains constant. Any energy that is absorbed or released is used to change the way in which the particles interact with one another.

LESSON 11.3 PROPERTIES OF MATTER

This lesson introduces the properties of matter, which are fundamental to the understanding of chemistry.

Matter and Its Properties

Aluminum, clothing, water, air, and glass are all different kinds of matter. **Matter** is anything that takes up space and has mass. A golf ball contains more matter than a table-tennis ball. The golf ball has more mass. The amount of matter that an object contains is its **mass**.

Table sugar is 100 percent sugar. Table sugar (sucrose) is an example of a substance. A **substance** is matter that has a uniform and definite composition. Lemonade is not a substance because not all pitchers of lemonade are identical. Different pitchers of lemonade may have different amounts of sugar, lemon juice, or water and may taste different.

All crystals of sucrose taste sweet and dissolve completely in water. All samples of a substance have identical physical properties. A **physical property** is a quality or condition of a substance that can be observed or measured without changing the substance's composition. Some physical properties of matter are color, solubility, mass, odor, hardness, density, and boiling point.

Just as every substance has physical properties, every substance has chemical properties. For example, when iron is exposed to water and oxygen, it corrodes and produces a new substance called iron (III) oxide (rust). The chemical properties of a substance are its ability to undergo chemical reactions and to form new substances. Rusting is a chemical property of iron. **Chemical properties** are observed only when a substance undergoes a change in composition, which is a chemical change.

Physical vs. Chemical Properties

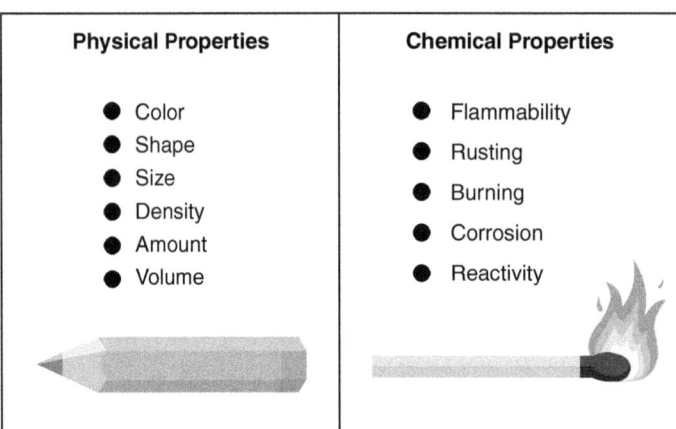

Lesson 11.3 Properties of Matter

Intensive and Extensive Properties

Intensive properties do not depend on the amount of matter that is present. Intensive properties do not change according to the conditions. They are used to identify samples because their characteristics do not depend on the size of the sample. In contrast, **extensive** properties do depend on the amount of a sample that is present. A good example of the difference between the two types of properties is that mass and volume are extensive properties, but their ratio (density) is an intensive property. Notice that mass and volume deal with amounts, whereas density is a physical property.

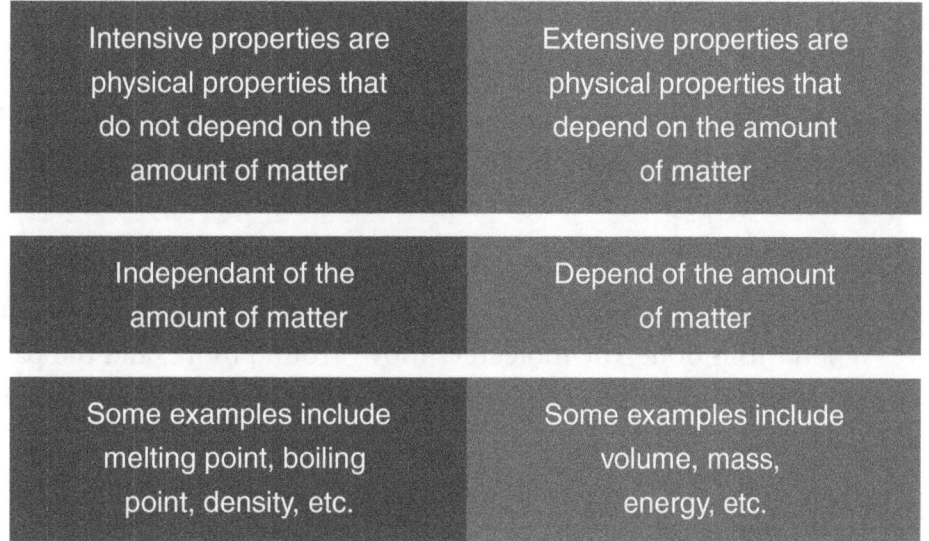

Example

Which of the following explains the difference between chemical and physical properties?

A. Physical properties can easily change, while chemical properties are constant.

B. Chemical properties always involve a source of heat, and physical properties always involve light.

C. Chemical properties involve a change in the chemical composition of a substance, while physical properties can easily be observed.

D. Physical properties involve a change in the chemical composition of a substance, while chemical properties can easily be observed.

The correct answer is **C**. A physical property is a quality or condition of a substance that can be observed or measured without changing the substance's composition, while a chemical property is one where a change in chemical composition has occurred.

Phase Changes

There are six phase changes: condensation, evaporation, freezing, melting, sublimation, and deposition.

Condensation is the change of a gas or vapor to a liquid. A change in the pressure and the temperature of a substance causes this change. The condensation point is the same as the boiling point of a substance. It is most noticeable when there is a large temperature difference between an object and the atmosphere. Condensation is also the opposite of evaporation.

Evaporation is the change of a liquid to a gas on the surface of a substance. This is not to be confused with boiling, which is a phase transition of an entire substance from a liquid to a gas. The evaporation point is the same as the freezing point of a substance. As the temperature increases, the rate of evaporation also increases. Evaporation depends not only on the temperature, but also on the amount of substance available.

Freezing is the change of a liquid to a solid. It occurs when the temperature drops below the freezing point. The amount of heat that has been removed from the substance allows the particles of the substance to draw closer together, and the material changes from a liquid to a solid. It is the opposite of melting.

Melting is the change of a solid into a liquid. For melting to occur, enough heat must be added to the substance. When this is done, the molecules move around more, and the particles are unable to hold together as tightly as they can in a solid. They break apart, and the solid becomes a liquid.

Sublimation is a solid changing into a gas. As a material sublimates, it does not pass through the liquid state. An example of sublimation is carbon dioxide, a gas, changing into dry ice, a solid. It is the reverse of deposition.

Deposition is a gas changing into a solid without going through the liquid phase. It is an uncommon phase change. An example is when it is extremely cold outside and the cold air comes in contact with a window. Ice will form on the window without going through the liquid state.

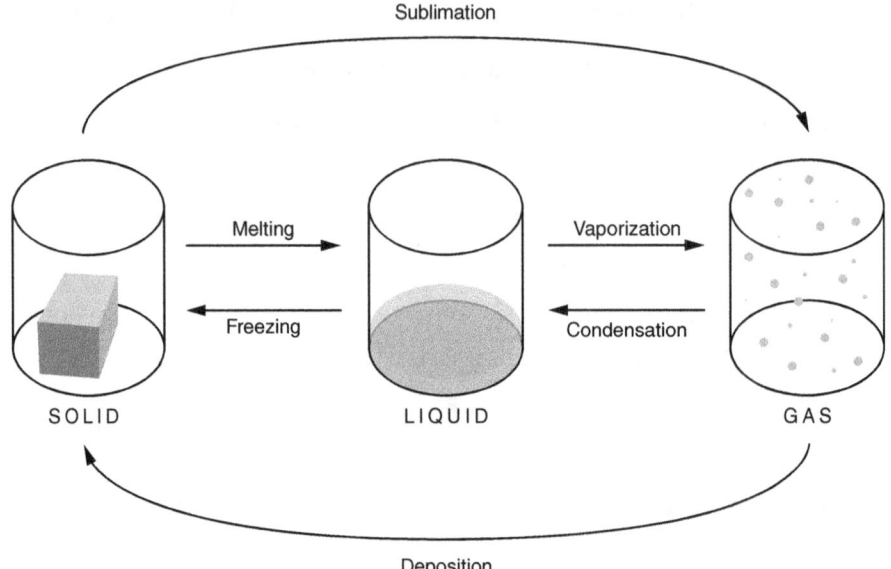

Example

Which of the six types of phase changes is the opposite of sublimation?

A. Condensation B. Deposition C. Evaporation D. Freezing

The correct answer is **B**. Sublimation is the changing of a solid to a gas, and deposition is the changing of a gas to a solid.

Adhesiveness and Cohesiveness

Because of polarity, water is attracted to water, a property called **cohesion**. The typical water molecule has a polar configuration, as seen below.

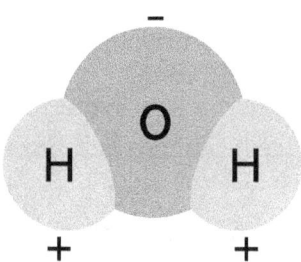

Notice that there is a negative end and a positive end. This means it is a polar molecule. In a **polar molecule**, one end of the molecule is slightly negative and one end is slightly positive.

Inside a plant, water has to travel up, against gravity, to reach all the leaves. Because the water molecules are attracted to each other, or demonstrate **cohesion**, they also adhere to the sides of the xylem vessels that transport water up to where it is needed in the plant. This is possible because of **adhesion**. Adhesion is water's ability to be attracted to other substances.

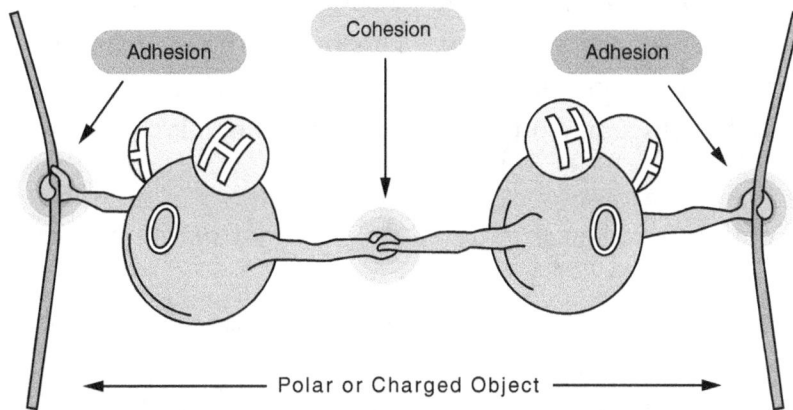

Example

What property allows water to flow against the force of gravity?

A. Adhesion B. Cohesion C. Polarity D. Xylem

The correct answer is **A**. Adhesion is water's ability to be attracted to other substances. Because of adhesion, water is able to move upward.

Diffusion and Osmosis

When a bottle of perfume is opened, perfume molecules diffuse throughout a room. **Diffusion** is the tendency of molecules and ions to move toward areas of lower concentrations until the concentration is uniform throughout the room (that is, it reaches equilibrium). This random movement of individual particles has an important consequence. Because the movement is random, a particle is more likely to move from an area where there are a lot of molecules (area of high concentration) to an area where there are fewer molecules (an area of lower concentration). In the human lungs, oxygen diffuses into the bloodstream because there is a higher concentration of oxygen molecules in the lungs' air sacs than there is in the blood.

Solute and solvent particles tend to diffuse from areas where their concentration is high to areas where their concentration is lower. Imagine that a membrane separates two regions of liquid. As long as solute particles and solvent (water) molecules can pass freely through the membrane, diffusion will equalize the amount of solute and solvent on the two sides. The sides will reach equilibrium.

But what if a polar solute that cannot pass through the membrane is added to one side? This situation is common in cells. An amino acid cannot cross a lipid bilayer, and neither can an ion or a sugar molecule. Unable to cross the membrane, the polar solute particles form hydrogen bonds with the water molecules surrounding them. These "bound" water molecules are no longer free to diffuse through the membrane. The polar solute has reduced the number of free water molecules on that side of the membrane. This means the opposite side of the membrane (without solute) has more free water molecules than the side with the polar solute. As a result, water molecules move by diffusion from the side without the polar solute to the side with the polar solute.

Eventually, the concentration of free water molecules will equalize on the sides of the membrane. At this point, however, there are more water molecules (bound and unbound) on the side of the membrane with the polar solute. Net water movement through a membrane in response to the concentration of a solute is called **osmosis**. Stated another way, osmosis is the diffusion of water molecules through a membrane in the direction of higher solute concentration.

OSMOSIS and DIFFUSION

Osmosis
Molecules go through a semipermeable membrane. Just water

Similarities
Molecules move around to create equilibrium

Diffusion
Molecules spread out over a large area. Everything but water

Example

What is the goal of osmosis?

    A. The water will equalize on both side of the semipermeable membrane.

    B. The concentration of solutes will diffuse through the semipermeable membrane.

    C. The concentration of free water molecules will equalize on both sides of the membrane

    D. The solute particles will flow from an area of high concentration to an area of lower concentration.

The correct answer is **C**. As a result of osmosis, the concentration of free water molecules will equalize on both sides of the membrane.

Let's Review!

- Matter is anything that takes up space and has mass.
- The difference between physical and chemical properties is that chemical properties involve a change in a substance's chemical composition and physical properties do not.
- The difference between extensive and intensive properties is based on whether the properties depend on the amount of substance that is present.
- Cohesiveness is the attraction of water to itself, and adhesiveness is the attraction of water to other substances.
- Osmosis is the diffusion of water and the movement of molecules from an area of high concentration to an area of lower concentration.

LESSON 11.4 CHEMICAL BONDS

This lesson introduces bonding and explains the three ways in which atoms can become stable. The rest of the lesson examines different types of bonds in more detail.

Introduction to Bonding

Chemical elements found in the periodic table have different levels of reactivity. The number of **valence electrons** in an atom is the most important factor in determining how an element will react. Valence electrons, which are found in an atom's outermost energy level, are involved in forming chemical bonds. The periodic table below shows the Bohr models of select elements. The valence electrons appear in red.

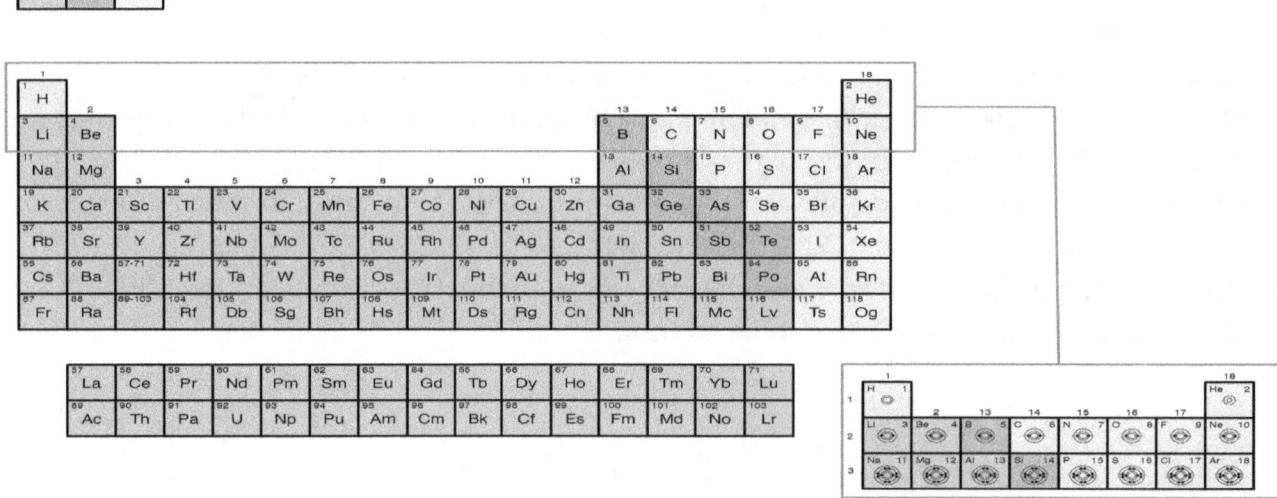

The **octet rule** states that atoms will lose, gain, or share electrons to obtain a stable electron configuration of eight valence electrons. In other words, if an atom needs to become stable, it will react with another atom, which can result in the formation of a chemical compound. Note that the elements in group 18, the noble gases, have eight valence electrons. Helium is an exception and is stable with two valence electrons. Because they have a stable electron configuration, the noble gases do not need to react with other elements to become stable. As a result, they are found in nature as single elements rather than in compounds.

> **KEY POINT!**
> The goal of forming chemical bonds is to become stable by having eight electrons in the outer shell. This is easy to remember because it is described in the *octet* rule. The prefix *octa-* means "eight," and it can be seen in other words, such as *octopus* and *octagon*.

Elements in other groups will react to become stable in predictable ways, depending on how many valence electrons they have. In the periodic table above, elements are classified as metals,

Lesson 11.4 Chemical Bonds

nonmetals, or metalloids. Compared to other elements, metals have fewer valence electrons and tend to lose them to become stable. Notice that removing the red valence electrons from the outermost energy level exposes another energy level. This becomes the valence shell, and the atom is stable because it has eight valence electrons.

Nonmetals and metalloids have a relatively high number of valence electrons. Except for the noble gasses, these elements tend to gain or share electrons to become stable.

Ionic compounds are formed when electrons are transferred from a metal (which loses one or more electrons) to a nonmetal (which gains one or more electrons). **Covalent compounds** are formed when two nonmetals or metalloids share electrons.

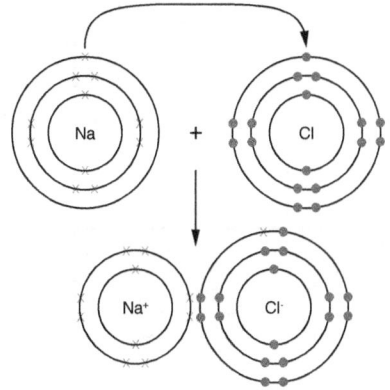

Ionic Bond

> **TEST TIP**
>
> A quick way to determine if atoms are held together by ionic or covalent bonds is to examine the types of elements involved. If a metal and a nonmetal bond, an ionic bond forms. If two nonmetals or metalloids bond, a covalent bond forms.

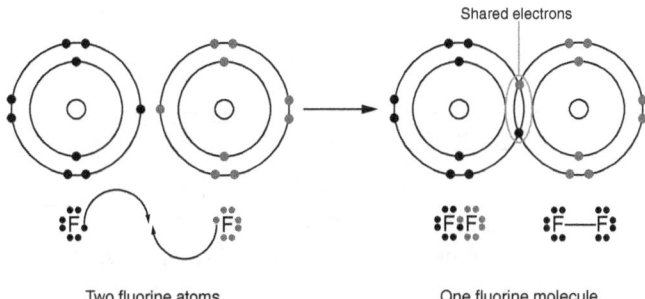

Covalent Bond

Example

In the compound sodium bromide (NaBr), electrons are _____. In the compound carbon tetrabromide (CBr_4), electrons are _____.

- A. shared, shared
- B. shared, transferred
- C. transferred, shared
- D. transferred, transferred

The correct answer is **C**. Electrons are transferred when an ionic compound like sodium bromide forms. Electrons are shared when a covalent compound like carbon tetrabromide forms.

Ion Formation

If an atom has an equal number of positively charged protons and negatively charged electrons, it is neutral and has no **net charge**. When electrons are transferred, atoms end up with either more protons than electrons or more electrons than protons. The atoms are considered **ions** because they have a net positive or negative charge.

> **KEEP IN MIND**
>
> Protons are positively charged subatomic particles and can be represented by the symbol $p+$. Electrons are negatively charged subatomic particles and can be represented by the symbol $e-$.

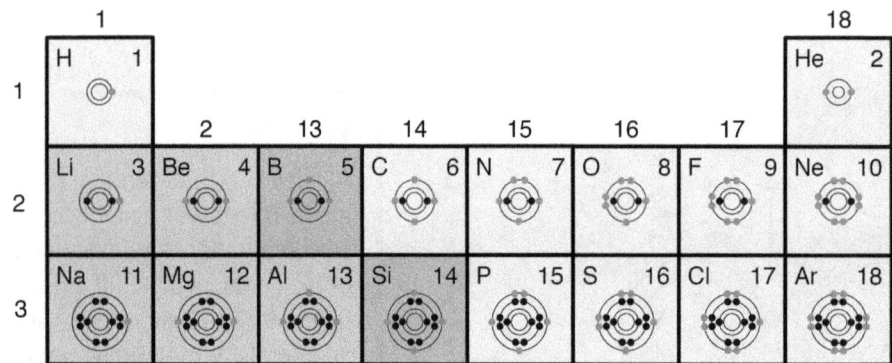

When a metal such as sodium reacts to become stable, it loses its valence electrons. At first, it is a neutral atom with 11 protons and 11 electrons. When it loses an electron, the number of protons does not change, and the atom has 11 protons and 10 electrons. Because there is one more positively charged proton, a **cation** forms. A cation is an ion with a net positive charge.

When a nonmetal such as chlorine reacts to become stable, it gains a valence electron. At first, it is a neutral atom with 17 protons and 17 electrons. When it gains an electron, the number of protons does not change, and the atom has 17 protons and 18 electrons. Because there is one more negatively charged electron, an **anion** forms. An anion is an ion with a net negative charge.

> **BE CAREFUL!**
>
> When an atom *gains* electrons, it has a net *negative* charge because it gains negatively charged particles. When an atom *loses* electrons, it has a net *positive* charge. After the loss, there are more protons than electrons, which means there are more positively charged particles.

The way in which an element reacts can be predicted based on that element's position in the periodic table. The table below summarizes the reactivity of elements according to their group number. Elements in each group have a specific number of valence electrons, which dictates what the atoms need to do to obtain a valence shell with eight electrons. Some will lose electrons, and others will gain electrons. This, along with the number of electrons that must be transferred, determines the charge of the stable ion that forms.

Lesson 11.4 Chemical Bonds

Group	1	2	13	14	15	16	17	18
Valence e-	1	2	3	4	5	6	7	8
Lose/Gain e-	Lose 1	Lose 2	Lose 3	Lose/Gain 4	Gain 3	Gain 2	Gain 1	N/A
Charge	+1	+2	+3	+/-4	-3	-2	-1	N/A

Example

What will strontium do to form a stable ion with a +2 charge?

A. Gain two protons
B. Lose two protons
C. Gain two electrons
D. Lose two electrons

The correct answer is **D**. Atoms gain or lose electrons, not protons, to form ions. Like other metals in group 2, strontium will lose its two valence electrons to become stable.

Ionic Bonding

An ionic compound is composed of a cation and an anion. An ionic bond is formed from the cation's attraction to the oppositely charged anion. The figure at the right shows how transferring an electron from sodium to chlorine results in the formation of an ionic bond.

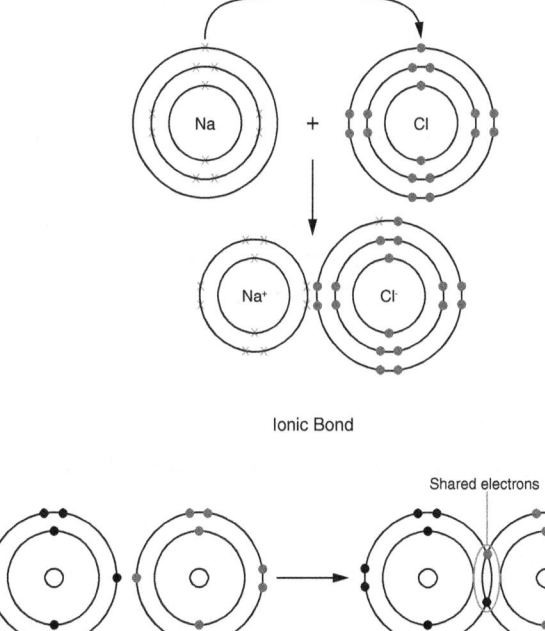

Ionic Bond

Two fluorine atoms → One fluorine molecule

Shared electrons

Covalent Bond

Notice that the charges on sodium (Na^+) and chlorine (Cl^-) ions have the same magnitude (they both have a value of 1). Therefore, the charge of one sodium ion balances the charge of one chlorine ion. When an ionic compound is formed from ions that have equal but opposite charges, the elements will be present in a 1:1 ratio. Examples are shown in the table below.

Compound Name	Cation	Anion	Compound Formula
Potassium fluoride	K^+	F^-	KF
Magnesium oxide	Mg^{2+}	O^{2-}	MgO
Aluminum nitride	Al^{3+}	N^{3-}	AlN

In some cases, atoms need to lose or gain two, three, or, in rare cases, four electrons to become stable. For example, magnesium must give up two electrons to become stable. Because chlorine only needs one electron, magnesium can give an electron to two different chlorine atoms. Then, one magnesium cation with a +2 charge (Mg^{2+}) bonds with two chloride anions (Cl^-) to form magnesium chloride, ($MgCl_2$). The subscript 2 indicates that there are two chloride ions in this compound.

Compound Name	Cation	Anion	Compound Formula
Calcium bromide	Ca^{2+}	Br^-	$CaBr_2$
Aluminum fluoride	Al^{3+}	F^-	AlF_3
Rubidium oxide	Rb^+	O^{2-}	Rb_2O
Sodium phosphide	Na^+	P^{3-}	Na_3P
Aluminum oxide	Al^{3+}	O^{2-}	Al_2O_3
Calcium phosphide	Ca^{2+}	P^{3-}	Ca_3P_2

Similarly, when oxygen and lithium react, the oxygen atom receives an electron from each of two lithium atoms. This transfer results in two lithium cations (Li^+) and an oxygen anion (O^{2-}). They attract each other to form the compound lithium oxide with a formula of Li_2O. Other examples are shown in the table below. Notice that in all ionic compounds, the total positive charge balances out the total negative charge, resulting in a neutral compound.

KEY POINT!
Regardless of how many electrons are transferred, ionic compounds have net charges of zero. They are all neutral because the positive cations attract as many anions as they need to balance their charges, and vice versa.

Example

What is the formula for the compound formed between calcium and oxygen?

A. CaO　　　　　B. CaO_2　　　　　C. Ca_2O　　　　　D. Ca_3O_2

The correct answer is **A**. Calcium is in group 2 and will lose its two valence electrons to become stable. Oxygen is in group 16 and, because it has six valence electrons, will gain two electrons to complete its octet. Therefore, one calcium ion requires one oxide ion to balance its charge to form a neutral ionic compound.

Covalent Bonding

When a nonmetal atom reacts with a nonmetal or metalloid, the atoms share electrons to obtain eight valence electrons each. An example can be seen in the model below. Both the Bohr models and the electron dot structures of the fluorine atoms show their seven valence electrons. After each atom shares an electron with the other, shown by the arrows, a covalent bond forms. In the newly formed fluorine molecule, both fluorine atoms have the stable electron configuration of eight valence electrons. The shared electrons can be represented by two dots or by a line in between the fluorine atoms.

Lesson 11.4 Chemical Bonds

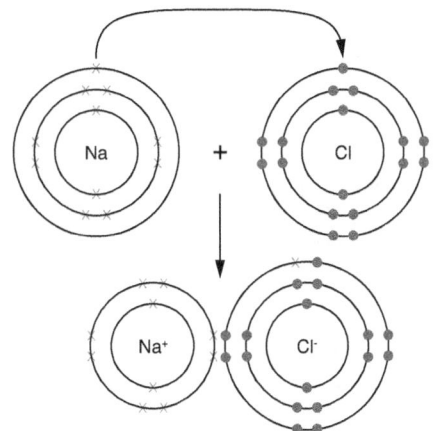

Ionic Bond

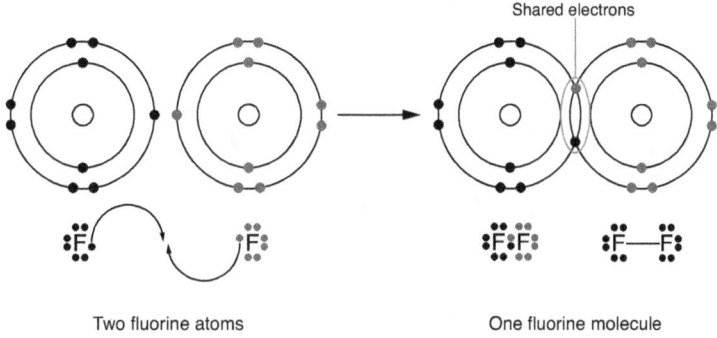

Covalent Bond

Covalent compounds can be modeled in **Lewis structures**. Lewis structures for methane, ammonia, and water are shown below. In a Lewis structure, covalent bonds, also called shared electrons, are represented by lines between two atoms. Valence electrons that are not involved in bonding, also called **lone-pair electrons**, are represented by dots.

KEEP IN MIND
Each line (bond) in a Lewis structure represents two electrons, one from each atom involved in the bond.

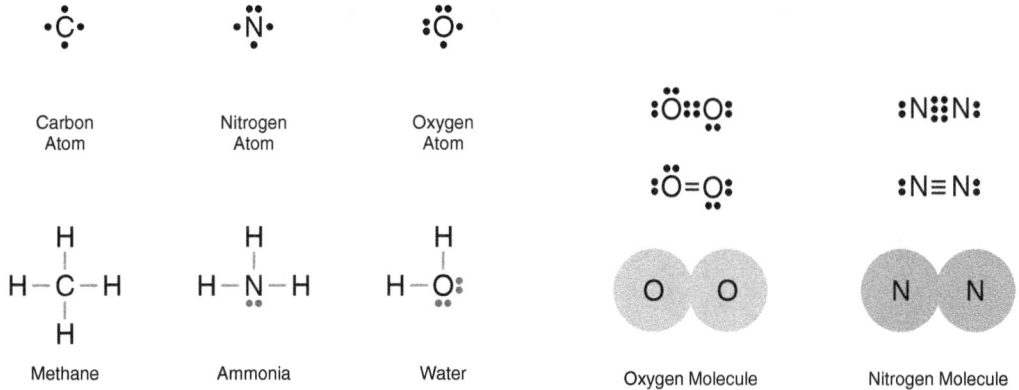

257

The number of bonds that an atom forms depends on the number of valence electrons that the atom has as a single atom. In a molecule of methane (CH_4), one carbon atom bonds to four hydrogen atoms. A single neutral carbon atom has four valence electrons and can share each one with a different hydrogen atom. In the end, it has four covalent bonds. Because each covalent bond involves two electrons, carbon has a total of eight valence electrons and is stable.

Similarly, in a molecule of ammonia (NH_3), one nitrogen atom bonds to three hydrogen atoms. Nitrogen shares six electrons total and has two remaining lone-pair electrons that are not involved in bonding for a total of eight. In a water molecule, an oxygen atom bonds to two hydrogen atoms. Oxygen has four shared electrons and four lone-pair electrons for a total of eight.

Example

In the Lewis structure of a fluorine molecule shown below, how are the eight valence electrons of each fluorine atom arranged?

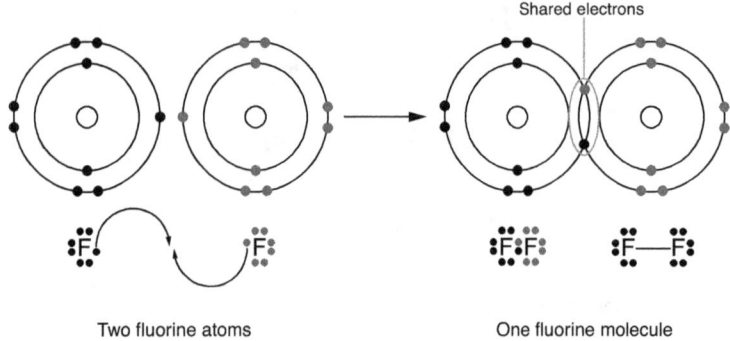

A. 2 are shared, 6 are lone-pair.

B. 4 are shared, 4 are lone-pair.

C. 6 are shared, 2 are lone-pair.

D. 8 are shared, none are lone-pair.

The correct answer is **A**. A fluorine atom forms a single covalent bond with another fluorine atom, which means that two electrons are being shared. The other six valence electrons are lone-pair electrons and are represented by dots around the atom.

Types of Covalent Bonds

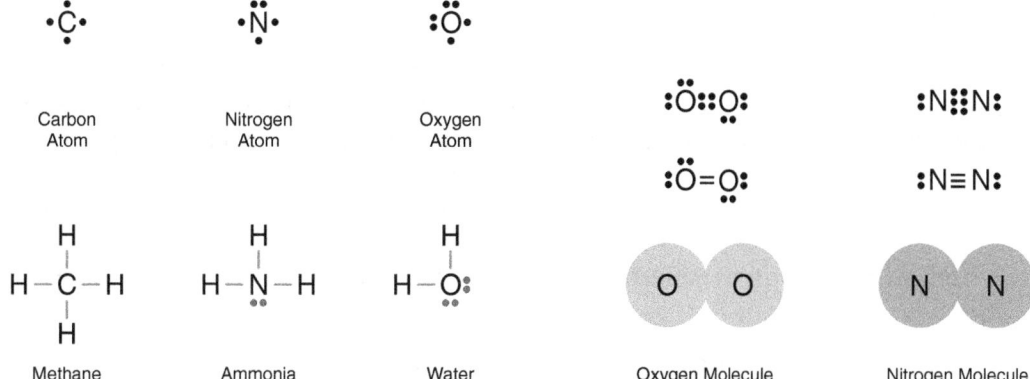

In methane, ammonia, and water, atoms are joined by **single covalent bonds** in which the atoms share two electrons. However, two atoms may need to share more than one pair of electrons to be stable. For example, two oxygen atoms form a **double bond**, in which two pairs of electrons (four electrons total) are shared. Similarly, two nitrogen atoms form a molecule with a **triple bond**, in which three pairs of electrons (six electrons total) are shared.

As more pairs of electrons are shared, the length of the bond decreases, and the bond strength increases. Single bonds are the longest and weakest bonds. They require the least energy to break because there is not as much energy stored in them.

> **CONNECTION**
> A pair of shared electrons between two atoms can be compared to a rubber band stretching between two objects. Having two or three rubber bands, rather than one, increases the strength of the "bond" that holds them together, making it harder to separate the objects.

Regardless of how many electrons are shared, the strength of a covalent bond comes from the positively charged nuclei of both atoms attracting the negatively charged electrons that are being shared. However, not all atoms attract shared electrons equally. This property is known as **electronegativity**, the tendency of an atom to attract shared electrons in a covalent bond. It is a measure of how hard an atom is pulling on shared electrons. Electronegativity increases going from left to right in the periodic table. Nonmetal atoms pull harder on electrons and do not tend to give them up. Therefore, the halogens in group 17 have the highest electronegativity of all elements.

If the two atoms share electrons equally, the bond is classified as **nonpolar covalent**. This occurs if the two atoms have similar electronegativities, which means that neither atom pulls significantly harder on the shared electrons than the other. If the two atoms share electrons unequally, the bond is **polar covalent**. This occurs if the electronegativity of one atom is significantly higher than the other, causing it to pull significantly harder on the shared electrons.

Example

> **CONNECTION**
> The sharing of electrons is like a game of tug-of-war in which two opposing teams are pulling on a rope in opposite directions. In a nonpolar bond, the opposing teams are pulling with the same force, and the rope is not moving toward one team or the other. In a polar bond, one team is winning by pulling the rope closer to its side.

An atom of which of the following elements has the strongest pull on shared electrons in a covalent bond?

A. Aluminum   B. Chlorine   C. Sodium   D. Sulfur

The correct answer is **B**. The element with the highest electronegativity will have the strongest pull on shared electrons in a covalent bond. Electronegativity increases moving from left to right across the periodic table, so the element farthest to the right in the period, chlorine, has the highest electronegativity.

Let's Review!

- As stated in the octet rule, any atom that does not have a stable electron configuration of eight valence electrons will lose, gain, or share electrons to become stable.
- Exceptions to the octet rule include hydrogen and helium, which are stable when they have two valence electrons.
- Ionic bonds are formed when electrons are transferred from a metal atom to a nonmetal atom.
- Covalent bonds are formed when two atoms share electrons. When two atoms need to share more than one pair of electrons, multiple bonds form. If two pairs are shared, a double bond forms. If three pairs are shared, a triple bond forms.
- The difference in the electronegativities of the two atoms determines if electrons are shared equally, forming a nonpolar covalent bond, or shared unequally, forming a polar covalent bond.

LESSON 11.5 CHEMICAL SOLUTIONS

This lesson discusses the properties of different types of mixtures, focusing on solutions. Then, it examines aspects of chemical reactions, including the components of the reactions and the types of changes that occur.

Solutions

When elements and compounds are physically (not chemically) combined, they form a **mixture**. When the substances mix evenly and it is impossible to see the individual components, the mixture is described as **homogeneous**. When the substances mix unevenly and it is possible to see the individual components, the mixture is described as **heterogeneous**.

Solubility is the ability of a substance to dissolve in another substance. For example, salt and sugar are both substances that can dissolve in water. They are **soluble**. In contrast, sand does not dissolve in water. It is **insoluble**. Individual particles of sand can be seen in water, but individual particles of salt are completely mixed in.

When one substance dissolves in the other, a type of homogeneous mixture called a **solution** forms. The substance that is being dissolved is the **solute**. The substance in which the solute is dissolved is the **solvent**, which makes up a greater percentage of the mixture than the solute. When salt dissolves in water, salt is the solute, and water is the solvent. Saltwater is an example of an **aqueous solution**, which forms when any substance dissolves in water.

The **concentration** of a solution is the amount of solute in a given volume of solution and can be expressed in several ways:

- **Molarity** (number of moles of a substance in one liter of solution)
- **Molality** (number of moles of a substance per kilogram of solvent)
- **Percent composition by mass** (mass of a solute per unit mass of the solution)
- **Mole fraction** (moles of a solute divided by the total number of moles in the solution)

Solubility can also refer to the *amount* of a substance that can dissolve. Even for soluble substances, there is a limit to how much of it can dissolve. The lines in the

Solubility Curves

Graph showing solubility (g of solute in 100 g H_2O) vs. Temperature (°C) for $CaCl_2$, NaCl, $KClO_3$, and $Ce_2(SO_4)_3$.

graph below show these limits for different substances at different temperatures in 100 grams of water. The area below a line represents masses of solute that dissolve in 100 grams of water. This type of solution is **unsaturated** because more solute can be dissolved. At the line, the solution is **saturated** because the limit has been reached. Any solute added above that mass will remain undissolved.

Example

> **CONNECTION**
> The term *saturated* is also used in everyday life to describe things, such as sponges or clothing that have soaked up all the water that they can absorb.

A beaker contains 50 mL of oil and 50 mL of water. No matter how much the mixture is stirred, the oil and the water still separate into two layers. Which statement accurately describes this mixture?

A. Oil is insoluble in water.

B. It is an unsaturated solution.

C. It is a homogeneous mixture.

D. Water is a good solvent for oil.

The correct answer is **A**. Because the oil will not mix into the water, it is insoluble.

Chemical Reactions

A chemical reaction involves elements and compounds that combine, break apart, rearrange, or change form in some way. **Reactants** are the substances that are present at the beginning of the reaction and undergo a change. **Products** are the substances that are formed from the reactants. Chemical reactions can be described by chemical equations, an example of which is shown below.

$$CH_4(g) + 2O_2(g) \longrightarrow CO_2(g) + 2H_2O(g)$$

Coefficient (on the 2 in $2O_2$ and $2H_2O$)

Reactant side | Product side

In this reaction, methane (CH_4) is burned in the presence of oxygen (O_2) to form carbon dioxide (CO_2) and water (H_2O). In the chemical equation, the formulas of the reactants (CH_4 and O_2) and

> **KEEP IN MIND**
> Reactants will always be on the left side of the arrow, and products will always be on the right side.

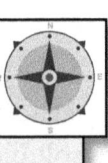

Lesson 11.5 Chemical Solutions

products (CO_2 and H_2O) are used. If there is more than one reactant or more than one product, their formulas are separated by a plus sign (+). The reactants and products are separated by an arrow.

The state of matter may also be shown in the chemical equation in parentheses after the substance formula. Substances can be solid, liquid, or gas, indicated by (*s*), (*l*), or (*g*), respectively. If a substance is dissolved in water, forming an aqueous solution, that state is indicated by (*aq*) in a chemical equation.

Finally, coefficients may appear in chemical equations. These coefficients indicate how many particles (atoms or molecules) of each substance react or form. When there is no coefficient present, only one particle is involved. In the example above, one molecule of methane (CH_4) reacts with two molecules of oxygen (O_2). One molecule of carbon dioxide (CO_2) is produced, along with two molecules of water (H_2O).

Example

The equation describing the formation of ammonia (NH3) from nitrogen and hydrogen is shown below. Which of the following statements is true?

$3H_2(g) + N_2(g)$ $2NH_3(g)$

A. NH_3 is the reactant, and H_2 and N_2 are products.

B. H_2 and N_2 are the reactants, and NH_3 is the product.

C. N and H_3 are the reactants, and H_2 and N_2 are products.

D. H_2 and N_2 are the reactants, and N and H_3 are the products.

The correct answer is **B**. Two reactants, H_2 and N_2, are found on the left side of the arrow. One product, NH_3, is found on the right side of the arrow.

Types of Reactions

Chemical reactions can be classified according to the reactants and products involved. This lesson will cover five types of reactions: synthesis, decomposition, single-replacement, double-replacement, and combustion. The first four types are outlined in the table below.

Type of Reaction	Model	Example
Synthesis	A + B AB	$2H_2(g) + O_2(g)$ $2H_2O(g)$
Decomposition	AB A + B	$2H_2O_2(aq)$ $2H_2O(l) + O_2(g)$
Single-Replacement	AB + C AC + B	$2HCl(aq) + Zn(s)$ $ZnCl_2(aq) + H_2(g)$
Double-Replacement	AB + CD AD + CB	$AgNO_3(aq) + NaCl(aq)$ $AgCl(s) + NaNO_3(aq)$

Synthesis reactions involve two or more reactants (A and B) combining to form one product (AB). In the example provided, hydrogen (H_2) and oxygen (O_2) begin as separate elements. At the end of the reaction, the hydrogen and oxygen atoms are bonded in a molecule of water (H_2O).

Decomposition reactions have only one reactant (AB) that breaks apart into two or more products (A and B). In the example above, hydrogen peroxide (H_2O_2) breaks apart into two smaller molecules: water (H_2O) and oxygen (O_2).

Single-replacement reactions involve two reactants, one compound (AB) and one element (C). In this type of reaction, one element replaces another to form a new compound (AC), leaving one element by itself (B). In the example, zinc replaces hydrogen in hydrochloric acid (HCl). As a result, zinc forms a compound with chlorine, zinc chloride ($ZnCl_2$), and hydrogen (H_2) is left by itself.

Double-replacement reactions involve two reactants, both of which are compounds made of two components (AB and CD). In the example, silver nitrate, composed of silver (Ag^{1+}) and nitrate (NO_3^{1-}) ions, reacts with sodium chloride, composed of sodium (Na^{1+}) and chloride (Cl^{1-}) ions. The nitrate and chloride ions switch places to produce two compounds that are different from those in the reactants.

Combustion reactions occur when fuels burn, and they involve specific reactants and products, as seen in the examples below. Some form of fuel that contains carbon and hydrogen is required. Examples of such fuels are methane, propane in a gas grill, butane in a lighter, and octane in gasoline. Notice that these fuels all react with oxygen, which is necessary for anything to burn. In all combustion reactions, carbon dioxide, water, and energy are produced. When something burns, energy is released, which can be felt as heat and seen as light.

Fuel	Reaction
Methane (CH_4)	$CH_4 + 2O_2 \rightarrow CO_2 + 2H_2O$ + energy
Propane (C_3H_8)	$C_3H_8 + 5O_2 \rightarrow 3CO_2 + 4H_2O$ + energy
Butane (C_4H_{10})	$2C_4H_{10} + 13O_2 \rightarrow 8CO_2 + 10H_2O$ + energy
Octane (C_8H_{18})	$2C_8H_{18} + 25O_2 \rightarrow 16CO_2 + 18H_2O$ + energy

> **DID YOU KNOW?**
> The fuels used in combustion reactions belong to a class of compounds called *hydrocarbons* because they are composed of hydrogen and carbon atoms. Hydrocarbons can be found in crude oil and include fossil fuels such as coal and natural gas. They are referred to as *fossil fuels* because they formed from the decomposition of organisms that died millions of years ago.

Example

Which of the following equations shows a decomposition reaction?

A. $3H_2 + N_2 \rightarrow 2NH_3$

B. $2KClO_3 \rightarrow 2KCl + 3O_2$

C. $2C_2H_2 + 5O_2 \rightarrow 4CO_2 + 2H_2O$

D. $2Na + ZnCl_2 \rightarrow Zn + 2NaCl$

The correct answer is **B**. This reaction starts with a single compound as a reactant that breaks down into two smaller products.

Energy Diagrams

Energy diagrams can be used to show how the energy of the species in a reaction changes over time. The reactants have a certain amount of energy stored in their bonds, and the products usually have a different amount of energy. If energy is released, the products have less energy than the reactants, and the reaction is **exothermic**. If energy is absorbed, the products have more energy than the reactants, and the reaction is **endothermic**. The shapes of the energy diagrams are shown below.

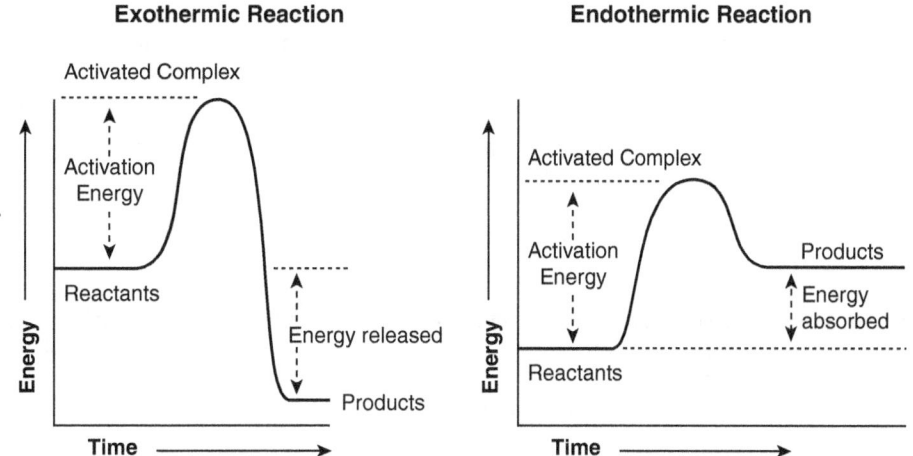

In every reaction, an **activated complex** must form between reactants. This complex can also be referred to as a transition state because it is required to convert, or provide a transition between, the reactants and products. In energy diagrams like the ones above, the activated complex has more energy than both the reactants and the products. The **activation energy** is the amount of energy required to transform the reactants into the activated complex, which then breaks apart to form the products.

> **CONNECTION**
>
> The difference between *endothermic* and *exothermic* reactions can be remembered by thinking about the meanings of the prefixes of these terms. In an *exothermic* reaction, energy is released or "exits" the system. In an *endothermic* reaction, energy "goes in."

The components of an energy diagram are as follows:

- Energy of reactants - energy of substances at the beginning of the reaction
- Energy of products - energy of substances at the end of the reaction
- Energy of the activated complex - energy of the substance represented by the maximum in the energy diagram
- Activation energy - difference in energy between the reactants and the activated complex
- Amount of energy released/absorbed - difference in energy between the reactants and products

Example

When iron reacts with oxygen, iron (III) oxide (Fe_2O_3), also known as rust, forms according to the equation below. The iron (III) oxide has less energy than the iron and oxygen. How is reaction classified, and why?

$$4Fe(s) + 3O_2(g) \; 2Fe_2O_3(s)$$

A. It is exothermic because energy is released.

B. It is exothermic because energy is absorbed.

C. It is endothermic because energy is released.

D. It is endothermic because energy is absorbed.

The correct answer is **A**. It is exothermic because the reactants must release energy to form a product that has less energy.

Let's Review!

- A solution is a type of homogeneous mixture that is formed when a solute dissolves in a solvent.
- The concentration of a solution is the amount of a substance in a given amount of solution.
- Chemical reactions occur when reactants combine, break apart, or rearrange to form products.
- Chemical equations represent chemical reactions using formulas and symbols.
- Chemical reactions can be classified as synthesis, decomposition, single-replacement, double-replacement, or combustion based on the reactants and products.
- Energy diagrams show how the energy of the species involved in the reaction changes as the reaction progresses.

LESSON 11.6 ACIDS AND BASES

This lesson introduces the properties of acids and bases, including the various theories that define them. It also covers acid-base reactions and the pH scale.

Nature of Acids and Bases

Acids are compounds that contain at least one hydrogen atom or proton (H^+), which, when dissolved in water, can form a hydronium ion (H_3O^+). Acids dissolved in water generally have the following properties:

- Taste sour
- Turn litmus red
- Act corrosive

Acids are found in a variety of substances, from vinegar to apple juice. The following table provides a list of common acids and their sources or applications.

Name of Acid	Chemical Formula	Sources or Applications
Citric acid	$C_6H_8O_7$	Citrus fruits such as oranges and lemons
Lactic acid	$C_3H_6O_3$	Yogurt and buttermilk
Acetic acid	$C_2H_4O_2$ or CH_3COOH	Nail polish remover and vinegar
Hydrochloric acid	HCl	Stomach
Phosphoric acid	H_3PO_4	Detergents and soft drinks
Nitric acid	HNO_3	Fertilizers

Bases are compounds that form hydroxide ions (OH^-) in a water solution. They also accept hydronium ions from acids. Bases dissolved in water generally have the following properties:

- Slippery in solution
- Very corrosive
- Turn litmus blue
- Taste bitter

Like acids, bases have many applications. The following table provides examples of common bases and how they are used.

Name of Base	Chemical Formula	Applications
Sodium hydroxide	NaOH	Soap, oven cleaners, and textiles
Potassium hydroxide	KOH	Soap and textiles
Ammonia	NH_3	Cleaning agents and fertilizers
Magnesium hydroxide	$Mg(OH)_2$	Laxatives and antacids

Acidic solutions have more hydrogen ions than hydroxide ions, whereas basic solutions have more hydroxide ions than hydrogen ions. All water solutions have both ion types, but the relative numbers dictate whether an aqueous solution is acidic, basic, or neutral. Anything that is dissolved in water is an **aqueous solution**. Neutral solutions are neither acidic nor basic, meaning that an equal number of hydrogen and hydroxide ions are present. Pure water is an example of a neutral solution.

Water is the primary solvent used to create an aqueous solution. Thus, it is important to understand how pure water behaves in solution. A small fraction of water molecules breaks down to form hydronium and hydroxide ions. When two water molecules interact, one water molecule gives up a positively charged hydrogen ion to form a hydroxide ion. A hydronium ion forms when a water molecule accepts a hydrogen ion. The following equation illustrates this reaction:

> **KEEP IN MIND**
> Substances that form ions in aqueous solutions are called **electrolytes**. As electrolytes, acids and bases are conductors of electricity in solution. This is because they contain dissolved ions.

$$2H_2O \rightarrow H_3O^+ + OH^-$$

Examples

1. Which of the following is an acid?

    A. KNO_3 B. $BaCl_2$ C. NaOH   D. H_3PO_4

    The correct answer is **D**. Phosphoric acid (H_3PO_4) is a common acid that is capable of donating one of its hydrogen atoms to form a hydronium ion.

2. Which is a characteristic of a basic solution?

    A. Tastes sour   C. Turns litmus blue

    B. Accepts OH^- ions   D. Contains a lot of H_3O^+ ions

    The correct answer is **C**. A basic solution is made using water as a solvent. Basic solutions turn litmus paper from red to blue.

Acid and Base Classification

Recall that an acid produces hydrogen ions, and a base produces hydroxide ions. These compounds are defined as **Arrhenius** acids and bases. The Arrhenius theory explains how acids and bases form ions when dissolved in water. Take, for example, the acid HCl, shown in the equation below. When forming an aqueous solution of HCl, this acid dissociates, or splits, into hydrogen ions and chloride ions in water.

$$HCl\,(g) \rightarrow H^+\,(aq) + Cl^-\,(aq)$$

An Arrhenius base dissociates into hydroxide ions (OH^-) in an aqueous solution. This is the case for sodium hydroxide, NaOH, as shown in the following equation:

$$NaOH\,(s) \rightarrow Na^+\,(aq) + OH^-(aq)$$

One limitation of this theory is that it does not account for acids and bases that lack a hydrogen or hydroxide ion in their molecular structure. Another way to define acids and bases is by using the Brønsted-Lowry theory. A Brønsted-Lowry **acid** is a hydrogen ion donor that increases the concentration of hydronium ions in solution. A Brønsted-Lowry **base** is a hydrogen ion acceptor that increases hydroxide ion concentration in solution. The term *proton* is used interchangeably with the term *hydrogen ion*.

> **BE CAREFUL!**
> Free H+ ions do not float in an aqueous solution. Rather, they bind with water to form H_3O^+. However, it is not uncommon to see the two formulas, H+ and H_3O^+, used interchangeably in chemical reactions.

When a base accepts a hydrogen ion, it produces a conjugate acid. When an acid donates a hydrogen ion, it produces a conjugate base. In the following example, ammonia is the base, but its conjugate acid is ammonium ion. What is the conjugate base for the acid?

$$NH_3 \text{ (base)} + H_2O \text{ (acid)} \longrightarrow NH_4^+ \text{ (conjugate acid)} + OH^- \text{ (conjugate base)}$$

> **KEEP IN MIND**
> When substances such as pure water act as an acid or a base, they are **amphoteric**.

The last theory about acids and bases is called the Lewis theory. This theory is based on electron movement during an acid-base reaction. A **Lewis acid** accepts a pair of electrons, while a **Lewis base** donates an electron pair.

Example

What is the conjugate acid in the following equation?

$$CH_3COOH + H_2O \rightleftharpoons H_3O^+ + CH_3COO^-$$

A. H_3O^+ B. H_2O C. CH_3COO^- D. CH_3COOH

The correct answer is **A**. A conjugate acid is a substance that accepts a proton from a base. In this case, the base H_2O accepts a proton to form the conjugate acid, hydronium ion (H_3O^+).

Acid-Base Reactions

In an aqueous solution, a base increases the hydroxide concentration (OH^-), while an acid increases the hydrogen ion (H^+) concentration. Sometimes, **neutralization reactions** also occur. This type of reaction happens when an acid and a base react with each other to form water and salt. Salt is typically defined as an **ionic compound** that includes any cation except H^+ and any anion except OH^-. Consider the following example of a neutralization reaction between hydrobromic acid (HBr) and potassium hydroxide (KOH).

$$HBr + KOH \longrightarrow KBr + H_2O$$

> **BE CAREFUL!**
> Not all neutralization reactions proceed in the manner where all reactants are in the aqueous phase. In some chemical reactions, one reactant may be a solid. The neutralization reaction can still proceed to completion.

In the above equation, one molecule of water forms in addition to the salt potassium bromide (KBr). There are instances where acid-base reactions must be balanced because more than one molecule of an acid or a base react to form products. This is the case for the reaction between hydrochloric acid and magnesium hydroxide, as shown below.

$$2HCl + Mg(OH)_2 \longrightarrow MgCl_2 + 2H_2O$$

When two molecules of hydrochloric acid react with magnesium hydroxide, two water molecules and one molecule of salt, $MgCl_2$, form.

Example

Which is a product of a neutralization reaction?

    A. Acid   B. Base   C. Proton   D. Salt

The correct answer is **D**. When an acid and a base react, they form a salt and water. This type of reaction is called a neutralization reaction.

Acid and Base Strength and pH

Acids and bases can be classified according to their strength. This strength refers to how readily an acid donates a hydrogen ion. The strength of a base is determined by how readily it removes a hydrogen ion from a molecule, or **deprotonates**. Strong acids are also known as strong electrolytes, which means that they completely ionize in solution. Weak acids are weak electrolytes because they partially ionize in solution. The following diagram shows what happens to a strong or weak acid in an aqueous solution.

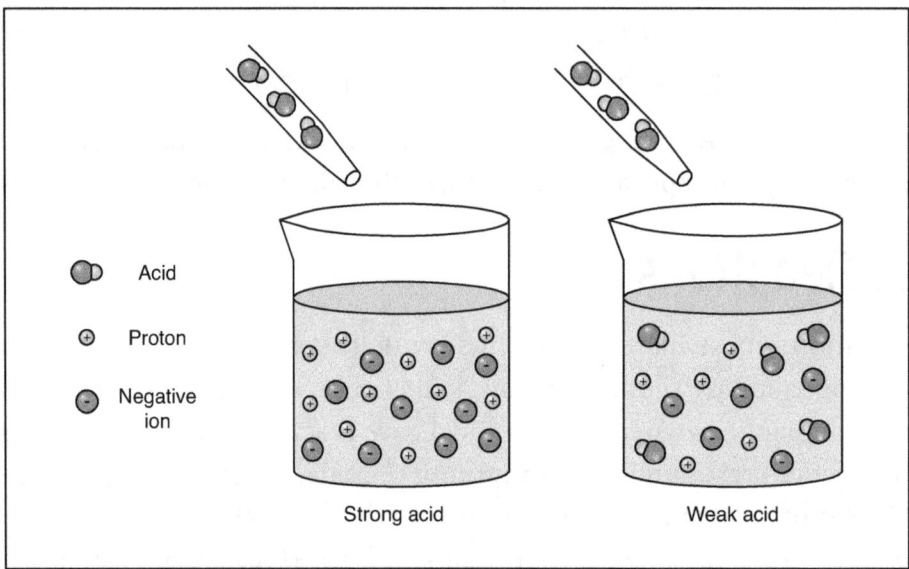

The maximum number of ions is produced when strong acids ionize. As shown in the following equations, the weak acid reaction is reversible (and incomplete) in aqueous solutions. This explains why weak acids produce fewer ions than strong acids.

Strong acid in solution

$$HNO_3 \longrightarrow H^+ + NO_3^-$$

Weak base in solution

$$NH_3 + H_2O \rightleftharpoons NH_4^+ + OH^-$$

Like strong acids, strong bases fully dissociate in solution. They produce metal ions and hydroxide ions. Like weak acids, weak bases partially dissociate and participate in reversible reactions. The following table provides a list of common strong acids and bases and common weak acids and bases.

BE CAREFUL!
Ammonia is a weak base even though it does not have a hydroxide ion (OH^-) in its chemical formula. It will accept a proton and form hydroxide ions in aqueous solutions.

Strong Acid	Weak Acid	Strong Base	Weak Base
Hydrochloric acid (HCl)	Hydrofluoric acid (HF)	Sodium hydroxide (NaOH)	Ammonia (NH_3)
Nitric acid (HNO_3)	Carbonic acid (H_2CO_3)	Potassium hydroxide (KOH)	Methylamine (CH_3NH_2)
Perchloric acid ($HClO_4$)	Phosphoric acid (H_3PO_4)	Calcium hydroxide ($Ca(OH)_2$)	Hydrazine (N_2H_4)
Sulfuric acid (H_2SO_4)	Acetic acid ($C_2H_4O_2$ or CH_3COOH)	Lithium hydroxide (LiOH)	Pyridine (C_5H_5N)

Researchers can determine the strength of an acid or a base by measuring the **pH** of a solution. The pH value describes how acidic or basic a solution is. On pH scale, shown below, if the number is less than 7 the solution is acidic. A pH greater than 7 means the solution is basic. When the pH is exactly 7, the solution is neutral.

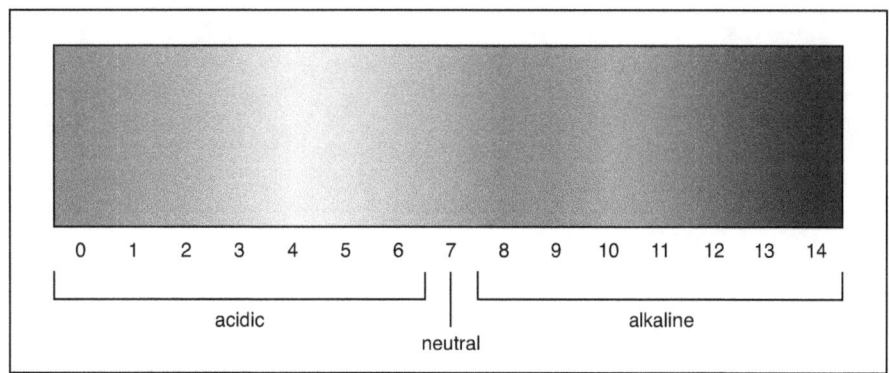

Example

Which of the following measured pH values means a solution is basic?

A. 2 B. 5 C. 7 D. 9

The correct answer is **D**. When the pH of an aqueous solution is greater than 7, which is the case for a solution that has a pH of 9, the solution is basic.

Let's Review!

- Acids and bases exhibit unique properties when dissolved in water.
- Arrhenius acids donate hydrogen ions, and Arrhenius bases accept hydrogen ions in solution.
- Brønsted-Lowry acids donate protons (or hydrogen ions), and Brønsted-Lowry bases accept protons (or hydrogen ions).
- Lewis acids are electron pair acceptors, and Lewis bases are electron pair donors.
- A neutralization reaction occurs when an acid and a base react to form a salt and water.
- Strong acids completely ionize in solution, and strong bases fully dissociate in solution.
- Weak acids and weak bases only partially dissociate in solution.
- The pH of a solution determines how acidic or basic it is.

Chapter 11 Chemistry Practice Quiz

1. Which subatomic particles affect the overall charge of the atom?

    A. Only protons

    B. Protons and neutrons

    C. Protons and electrons

    D. Protons, neutrons, and electrons

2. In which state of matter are particles moving slowest?

    A. Solid
    C. Gas

    B. Liquid
    D. Plasma

3. Which of the following explains the difference between chemical and physical properties?

    A. Physical properties can easily change, while chemical properties are constant.

    B. Chemical properties always involve a source of heat, and physical properties always involve light.

    C. Chemical properties involve a change in the chemical composition of a substance, while physical properties can easily be observed.

    D. Physical properties involve a change in the chemical composition of a substance, while chemical properties can easily be observed.

4. Which of the following statements is true regarding the number of valence electrons in different elements?

    A. The number of valence electrons increases going from left to right on the periodic table.

    B. The number of valence electrons decreases going from left to right on the periodic table.

    C. The number of valence electrons increases going from top to bottom on the periodic table.

    D. The number of valence electrons decreases going from top to bottom on the periodic table.

5. What type of reaction is described by the following equation?

    $2Mg(s) + O_2(g) \rightarrow 2MgO(s)$

    A. Synthesis

    B. Decomposition

    C. Single-replacement

    D. Double-replacement

6. Which is a product of a neutralization reaction?

    A. Acid
    C. Proton

    B. Base
    D. Salt

ATI TEAS: Full Study Guide, Test Strategies and Secrets

Chapter 11 Chemistry Practice Quiz – Answer Key

1. C. Because protons are positively charged and electrons are negatively charged, they affect the overall charge of the atom. Neutrons do not affect the charge because they are uncharged. **See Lesson: An Overview of Matter.**

2. A. Because solid particles have less energy than particles in other states of matter, they have the most restricted movement. **See Lesson: States of Matter.**

3. C. A physical property is a quality or condition of a substance that can be observed or measured without changing the substance's composition, while a chemical property is one where a change in chemical composition has occurred. **See Lesson: Properties of Matter.**

4. A. Group 1 elements all have one valence electron, and the number of valence electrons increases going across the periodic table, from left to right, to the group 18 elements, which all have eight valence electrons. **See Lesson: Chemical Bonds.**

5. A. In this reaction, two elements are combining to form one compound, which is a defining characteristic of synthesis reactions. **See Lesson: Chemical Solutions.**

6. D. When an acid and a base react, they form a salt and water. This type of reaction is called a neutralization reaction. **See Lesson: Acids and Bases.**

SECTION IV
ENGLISH AND LANGUAGE USAGE

English and Language Usage: 37 questions, 37 minutes, Conventions of standard English, Knowledge of language.

Areas assessed: Language, Conventions of Standard English, Knowledge of Language, Vocabulary Acquisition

ENGLISH TIPS

- Even if English is your first language, do not be overly confident.
- Rules of language arts and grammar may be explicitly asked.
- Know the eight parts of basic sentence: nouns, pronouns, verbs, adjectives, adverbs, conjunctions, prepositions, and interjections.
- Understand dependent and independent clauses of a complex sentence. Know how to join two independent clauses.
- Spelling: Important to remember how many repeated letters are in a word. For example, accommodate, foreign, appointments, necessary.
- Know subject-verb agreement.
- Learn the meaning of common prefixes and suffixes.
- Study terms and formal terms. Know what they are and how they work (e.g., coordinate conjunctions, sub conjunctions, subject verb agreement).
- Review basic rules of punctuation; e.g., semicolon and dash usage.
- If you are not sure about the meaning of the word, use context clues and process of elimination to come to a final answer.

CHAPTER 12 CONVENTIONS OF STANDARD ENGLISH

LESSON 12.1 SPELLING

Spelling correctly is important to accurately convey thoughts to an audience. This lesson will cover (1) vowels and consonants, (2) suffixes and plurals, (3) homophones and homographs.

Vowels and Consonants

Vowels and **consonants** are different speech sounds in English.

The letters A, E, I, O, U and sometimes Y are **vowels** and can create a variety of sounds. The most common are short sounds and long sounds. Long **vowel** sounds sound like the name of the letter such as the *a* in late. Short **vowel** sounds have a unique sound such as the *a* in cat. A rule for **vowels** is that when two vowels are walking, the first does the talking as in pain and meat.

Consonants include the other twenty-one letters in the alphabet. **Consonants** are weak letters and only make sounds when paired with **vowels**. That is why words always must have a **vowel**. This also means that **consonants** need to be doubled to make a stronger sound like sitting, grabbed, progress. Understanding general trends and patterns for **vowels** and **consonants** will help with spelling. The table below represents the difference between short and long **vowels** and gives examples for each.

	Symbol	Example Words
Short a	a	Cat, mat, hat, pat
Long a	ā	Late, pain, pay, they, weight, straight
Short e	e	Met, said, bread
Long e	ē	Breeze, cheap, dean, equal
Short i	i	Bit, myth, kiss, rip
Long i	ī	Cry, pie, high
Short o	o	Dog, hot, pop
Long o	ō	Snow, nose, elbow
Short u	u	Run, cut, club, gum
Long u	ū	Duty, rule, new, food
Short oo	oo	Book, foot, cookie
Long oo	ōō	Mood, bloom, shoot

Suffixes and Plurals

A **suffix** is a word part that is added to the ending of a root word. A **suffix** changes the meaning and spelling of words. There are some general patterns to follow with **suffixes**.

- Adding -er, -ist, or -or changes the root to mean *doer* or *performer*
  - Paint → Painter
  - Abolition → Abolitionist
  - Act → Actor

- Adding -ation or -ment changes the root to mean *an action* or *a process*
  - Ador(e) → Adoration
  - Develop → Development

- Adding -ism changes the root to mean *a theory or ideology*
  - Real → Realism

- Adding -ity, -ness, -ship, or -tude changes the root to mean *a condition, quality, or state*
  - Real → Reality
  - Sad → Sadness
  - Relation → Relationship
  - Soli(tary) → Solitude

- **Plurals** are similar to suffixes as letters are added to the end of the word to signify more than one person, place, thing, or idea. There are also general patterns to follow when creating **plurals**.

- If a word ends in -s, -ss, -z, -zz, -ch, or -sh, add -es.
  - Bus → Buses

- If a word ends in a -y, drop the -y and add -ies.
  - Pony → Ponies

- If a word ends in an -f, change the f to a v and add -es.
  - Knife → Knives

- For all other words, add an -s.
  - Dog → Dogs

Homophones and Homographs

A **homophone** is a word that has the same sound as another word, but does not have the same meaning or spelling.

- To, too, and two
- There, their, and they're
- See and sea

A **homograph** is a word that has the same spelling as another word, but does not have the same sound or meaning.

- Lead (to go in front of) and lead (a metal)
- Bass (deep sound) and bass (a fish)

Let's Review!

- Vowels include the letters A, E, I, O, U and sometimes Y and have both short and long sounds.
- Consonants are the other twenty-one letters and have weak sounds. They are often doubled to make stronger sounds.
- Suffixes are word parts added to the root of a word and change the meaning and spelling.
- To make a word plural, add -es, -ies, -ves, or -s to the end of a word.
- Homophones are words that have the same sound, but not the same meaning or spelling.
- Homographs are words that have the same spelling, but not the same meaning or sound.

LESSON 12.2 CAPITALIZATION

Correct capitalization helps readers understand when a new sentence begins and the importance of specific words. This lesson will cover the capitalization rules of (1) geographic locations and event names, (2) organizations and publication titles, (3) individual names and professional titles, and (4) months, days, and holidays.

Geographic Locations and Event Names

North, east, south, and west are not **capitalized** unless they relate to a **definite region**.

- Go north on I-5 for 200 miles.
- The West Coast has nice weather.

Words like northern, southern, eastern, and western are also not **capitalized** unless they describe **people or the cultural and political activities of people**.

- There is nothing interesting to see in eastern Colorado.
- Midwesterners are known for being extremely nice.
- The Western states almost always vote Democratic.

These words are not **capitalized** when placed before a name or region unless it is part of the **official name**.

- She lives in southern California.
- I loved visiting Northern Ireland.

Continents, countries, states, cities, and **towns** need to be **capitalized**.

- Australia has a lot of scary animals.
- Not many people live in Antarctica.
- Albany is the capital of New York.

Historical events should be **capitalized** to separate the specific from the general.

- The bubonic plague in the Middle Ages killed a large portion of the population in Europe.
- The Great Depression took place in the early 1930s.
- We are living in the twenty-first century.

Organizations and Publication Titles

The **names of national organizations** need to be **capitalized**. Short prepositions, articles, and conjunctions within the title are not **capitalized** unless they are the first word.

- The National American Woman Suffrage Association was essential in passing the Nineteenth Amendment.
- The House of Representatives is one part of Congress.
- The National Football League consists of thirty-two teams.

The **titles of books, chapters, articles, poems, newspapers, and other publications** should be **capitalized**.

- Her favorite book is *A Wrinkle in Time*.
- I do the crossword in *The New York Times* every Sunday.
- *The Jabberwocky* by Lewis Carroll has many silly sounding words.

Individual Names and Professional Titles

People's names as well as their **familial relationship title** need to be **capitalized**.

- Barack Obama was our first African American president.
- Uncle Joe brought the steaks for our Memorial Day grill.
- Aunt Sarah lives in California, but my other aunt lives in Florida.

Professional titles need to be **capitalized** when they precede a name, or as a direct address. If it is after a name or is used generally, titles do not need to be **capitalized**.

- Governor Cuomo is trying to modernize the subway system in New York.
- Andrew Cuomo is the governor of New York.
- A governor runs the state. A president runs the country.
- Thank you for the recommendation, Mr. President.
- I need to see Doctor Smith.
- I need to see a doctor.

Capitalize the **title of high-ranking government officials** when an individual is referred to.

- The Secretary of State travels all over the world.
- The Vice President joined the meeting.

With **compound titles**, the prefixes or suffixes do not need to be **capitalized**.

- George W. Bush is the ex-President of the United States.

Months, Days, and Holidays

Capitalize all months of the year (January, February, March, April, May, June, July, August, September, October, November, December) and **days of the week** (Sunday, Monday, Tuesday, Wednesday, Thursday, Friday, Saturday).

- Her birthday is in November.
- People graduate from college in May or June.
- Saturdays and Sundays are supposed to be fun and relaxing.

Holidays are also **capitalized**.

- Most kids' favorite holiday is Christmas.
- The new school year usually starts after Labor Day.
- It is nice to go to the beach over Memorial Day weekend.

The **seasons** are not **capitalized**.

- It gets too hot in the summer and too cold in the winter.
- The flowers and trees bloom so beautifully in the spring.

Let's Review!

- Only capitalize directional words like north, south, east, and, west when they describe a definite region, people, and their political and cultural activities, or when it is part of the official name.
- Historical periods and events are capitalized to represent their importance and specificity.
- Every word except short prepositions, conjunctions, and articles in the names of national organizations are capitalized.
- The titles of publications follow the same rules as organizations.
- The names of individual people need to be capitalized.
- Professional titles are capitalized if they precede a name or are used as a direct address.
- All months of the year, days of the week, and holidays are capitalized.
- Seasons are not capitalized.

LESSON 12.3 PUNCTUATION

Punctuation is important in writing to accurately represent ideas. Without correct punctuation, the meaning of a sentence is difficult to understand. This lesson will cover (1) periods, question marks, and exclamation points, (2) commas, semicolons, and colons, and (3) apostrophes, hyphens, and quotation marks.

Terminal Punctuation Marks: Periods, Question Marks, and Exclamation Points

Terminal punctuation are used at the end of a sentence. Periods, question marks, and exclamation points are the three types of terminal punctuation.

Periods (.) mark the end of a declarative sentence, one that states a fact, or an imperative sentence, one that states a command or request). Periods can also be used in abbreviations.

- Doctors save lives.
- She has a B.A. in Psychology.

Question Marks (?) signify the end of a sentence that is a question. Where, when, who, whom, what, why, and how are common words that begin question sentences.

- Who is he?
- Why is the sky blue?
- Where is the restaurant?

Exclamation Points (!) indicate strong feelings, shouting, or emphasize a feeling.

- Watch out!
- I hate you!
- That is incredible!

Internal Punctuation: Commas, Semicolons, and Colons

Internal punctuation is used within a sentence to help keep words, phrases, and clauses in order. These punctuation marks can be used to indicate elements such as direct quotations and definitions in a sentence.

A **comma (,)** signifies a small break within a sentence and separates words, clauses, or ideas.

Commas are used before conjunctions that connect two independent clauses.

- I ate some cookies, and I drank some milk.

Commas are also used to set off an introductory phrase.

- After the test, she grabbed dinner with a friend.

Short phrases that emphasize thoughts or emotions are enclosed by **commas**.

- The school year, thankfully, ends in a week.

Commas set off the words yes and no.

- Yes, I am available this weekend.
- No, she has not finished her homework.

Commas set off a question tag.

- It is beautiful outside, isn't it?

Commas are used to indicate direct address.

- Are you ready, Jack?
- Mom, what is for dinner?

Commas separate items in a series.

- We ate eggs, potatoes, and toast for breakfast.
- I need to grab coffee, go to the store, and put gas in my car.

Semicolons (;) are used to connect two independent clauses without a coordinating conjunction like *and* or *but*. A **semicolon** creates a bond between two sentences that are related. Do not capitalize the first word after the **semicolon** unless it is a word that is normally capitalized.

- The ice cream man drove down my street; I bought a popsicle.
- My mom cooked dinner; the chicken was delicious.
- It is cloudy today; it will probably rain.

Colons (:) introduce a list.

- She teaches three subjects: English, history, and geography.

At the end of a sentence, **colons** can create emphasis of a word or phrase.

- She had one goal: pay the bills.

More Internal Punctuation: Apostrophes, Hyphens, and Quotation Marks

Apostrophes (') are used to indicate possession or to create a contraction.

- Bob has a car - Bob's car is blue.
- Steve's cat is beautiful.

For plurals that are also possessive, put the **apostrophe** after the s.

- Soldiers' uniforms are impressive.

Make contractions by combining two words.

- I do not have a dog - I don't have a dog
- I can't swim.

Its and it's do not follow the normal possessive rules. Its is possessive while it's means it is.

- It's a beautiful day to be at the park.
- The dog has many toys, but its favorite is the rope.

Hyphens (-) are mainly used to create compound words.

- The documentary was a real eye-opener for me.
- We have to check-in to the hotel before midnight.
- The graduate is a twenty-two-year-old woman.

Quotation Marks (") are used when directly using another person's words in your own writing. Commas and periods, sometimes question marks and exclamation points, are placed within **quotation marks**. Colons and semicolons are placed outside of the **quotation marks**, unless they are part of the quoted material. If quoting an entire sentence, capitalize the first word. If it is a fragment, do not capitalize the first word.

- Ernest Hemingway once claimed, "There is nothing noble in being superior to your fellow man; true nobility is being superior to your former self."
- Steve said, "I will be there at noon."

An indirect quote which paraphrases what someone else said does not need **quotation marks**.

- Steve said he would be there at noon.

Quotation marks are also used for the titles of short works such as poems, articles, and chapters. They are not italicized.

- Robert Frost wrote "The Road Not Taken."

Let's Review!

- **Periods (.)** signify the end of a sentence or are used in abbreviations.
- **Question Marks (?)** are also used at the end of a sentence and distinguish the sentence as a question.
- **Exclamation Points (!)** indicate strong feelings, shouting, or emphasis and are usually at the end of the sentence.
- **Commas (,)** are small breaks within a sentence that separate clauses, ideas, or words. They are used to set off introductory phrases, the words yes and no, question tags, indicate direct address, and separate items in a series.
- **Semicolons (;)** connect two similar sentences without a coordinating conjunctions such as and or but.
- **Colons (:)** are used to introduce a list or emphasize a word or phrase.
- **Apostrophes (')** indicate possession or a contraction of two words.
- **Hyphens (-)** are used to create compound words.
- **Quotation Marks (")** are used when directly quoting someone else's words and to indicate the title of poems, chapters, and articles.

Chapter 12 Conventions of Standard English Practice Quiz

1. Fill in the blank with the correctly capitalized form.

   My favorite book in the Harry Potter series is _____.

   A. *harry potter and the prisoner of azkaban*
   B. *Harry Potter and the prisoner of azkaban*
   C. *Harry Potter And The Prisoner Of Azkaban*
   D. *Harry Potter and the Prisoner of Azkaban*

2. Choose the correct sentence.

   A. Arnold Schwarzenegger was the governor of California.
   B. Arnold Schwarzenegger was the Governor of California.
   C. Arnold Schwarzenegger was the governor of california.
   D. arnold schwarzenegger was the governor of california.

3. What is the correct use of a period in the following sentence?

   A. She had a bad day
   B. She had a bad day.
   C. She had. a bad day.
   D. She. had. a. bad. day.

4. What is the sentence with the correct use of punctuation?

   A. The bookstore has three types of books: fiction, nonfiction, and biography.
   B. The bookstore has three types of books, fiction, nonfiction, and biography.
   C. The bookstore: has three types of books fiction, nonfiction, and biography.
   D. The bookstore has three: types of books fiction, nonfiction, and biography.

5. Which of the following spellings is correct?

   A. Argument
   B. Arguemint
   C. Arguement
   D. Arguemant

6. Which of the following spellings is correct?

   A. Acomodation
   B. Accomodation
   C. Accomudation
   D. Accommodation

Chapter 12 Conventions of Standard English
Practice Quiz – Answer Key

1. **D.** *Harry Potter and the Prisoner of Azkaban.* Short prepositions, conjunctions, and articles are not capitalized in publication titles. **See Lesson: Capitalization.**

2. **A.** Arnold Schwarzenegger was the governor of California. Individual names and states are always capitalized. Professional titles are capitalized when they precede a name or are part of a direct address. **See Lesson: Capitalization.**

3. **B.** *She had a bad day.* A period is only used at the end of a sentence, and not anywhere in between. **See Lesson: Punctuation.**

4. **A.** *The bookstore has three types of books: fiction, nonfiction, and biography.* Colons are used after the last word before introducing a list. **See Lesson: Punctuation.**

5. **A.** *Argument* is the only correct spelling. **See Lesson: Spelling.**

6. **D.** *Accommodation* is the only correct spelling. **See Lesson: Spelling.**

CHAPTER 13 PARTS OF SPEECH

LESSON 13.1 NOUNS

In this lesson, you will learn about nouns. A noun is a word that names a person, place, thing, or idea. This lesson will cover (1) the role of nouns in sentences and (2) different types of nouns.

Nouns and Their Role in Sentences

A **noun** names a person, place, thing, or idea.

Some examples of nouns are:

- Gandhi
- New Hampshire
- garden
- happiness

A noun's role in a sentence is as **subject** or **object**. A subject is the part of the sentence that does something, whereas the object is the thing that something is done to. In simple terms, the subject acts, and the object is acted upon.

Look for the nouns in these sentences.

1. The Louvre is stunning. (subject noun: The Louvre)
2. Marco ate dinner with Sara and Petra. (subject noun: Marco; object nouns: dinner, Sara, Petra)
3. Honesty is the best policy. (subject noun: honesty; object noun: policy)
4. After the election, we celebrated our new governor. (object nouns: governor, election)
5. I slept. (0 nouns)

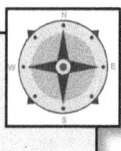

KEEP IN MIND...
The subjects *I* and *we* in the two sentences to the left are pronouns, not nouns.

Look for the nouns in these sentences.

1. Mrs. Garcia makes a great pumpkin pie. (subject noun: Mrs. Garcia; object noun: pie)
2. We really need to water the garden. (object noun: garden)
3. Love is sweet. (subject noun: love)
4. Sam loves New York in the springtime. (subject noun: Sam; object nouns: New York, springtime)
5. Lin and her mother and father ate soup, fish, potatoes, and fruit for dinner. (subject nouns: Lin, mother, father; object nouns: soup, fish, potatoes, fruit, dinner)

Why isn't the word *pumpkin* a noun in the first sentence? *Pumpkin* is often a noun, but here it is used as an adjective that describes what kind of *pie*.

Why isn't the word *water* a noun in the second sentence? Here, *water* is an **action verb**. To *water the garden* is something we do.

How is the word *love* a noun in the third sentence and not in the fourth sentence? *Love* is a noun (thing) in sentence 3 and a verb (action) in the sentence 4.

How many nouns can a sentence contain? As long as the sentence remains grammatically correct, it can contain an unlimited number of nouns.

> **BE CAREFUL!**
> Words can change to serve different roles in different sentences. A word that is usually a noun can sometimes be used as an adjective or a verb. Determine a word's function in a sentence to be sure of its part of speech.

Types of Nouns

A. Singular and Plural Nouns

Nouns can be **singular** or **plural**. A noun is singular when there is only one. A noun is plural when there are two or more.

- The book has 650 pages.

Book is a singular noun. *Pages* is a plural noun.

Often, to make a noun plural, we add *-s* at the end of the word: *cat/cats*. This is a **regular** plural noun. Sometimes we make a word plural in another way: *child/children*. This is an **irregular** plural noun. Some plurals follow rules, while others do not. The most common rules are listed here:

> **KEEP IN MIND . . .**
> **Some nouns are countable,** and others are not. For example, we eat *three blueberries*, but we **do not** drink *three milks*. Instead, we drink *three glasses of milk* or *some milk*.

Singular noun	Plural noun	Rule for making plural
star	stars	for most words, add *-s*
box	boxes	for words that end in *-j, -s, -x, -z, -ch* or *-sh*, add *-es*
baby	babies	for words that end in *-y*, change *-y* to *-i* and add *-es*
woman	women	irregular
foot	feet	irregular

B. Common and Proper Nouns

Common nouns are general words, and they are written in lowercase. **Proper nouns** are specific names, and they begin with an uppercase letter.

Examples:

Common noun	Proper noun
ocean	Baltic Sea
dentist	Dr. Marx
company	Honda
park	Yosemite National Park

C. Concrete and Abstract Nouns

Concrete nouns are people, places, or things that physically exist. We can use our senses to see or hear them. *Turtle, spreadsheet,* and *Australia* are concrete nouns.

Abstract nouns are ideas, qualities, or feelings that we cannot see and that might be harder to describe. *Beauty, childhood, energy, envy, generosity, happiness, patience, pride, trust, truth,* and *victory* are abstract nouns.

Some words can be either concrete or abstract nouns. For example, the concept of *art* is abstract, but *art* that we see and touch is concrete.

- We talked about *art*. (abstract)
- She showed me the *art* she had created in class. (concrete)

Let's Review!

- A noun is a person, place, thing, or idea.
- A noun's function in a sentence is as subject or object.
- Common nouns are general words, while proper nouns are specific names.
- Nouns can be concrete or abstract.

LESSON 13.2 PRONOUNS

A pronoun is a word that takes the place of or refers to a specific noun. This lesson will cover (1) the role of pronouns in sentences and (2) the purpose of pronouns.

Pronouns and Their Role in Sentences

A **pronoun** takes the place of a noun or refers to a specific noun.

Subject, Object, and Possessive Pronouns

A pronoun's role in a sentence is as **subject**, **object**, or **possessive**.

Subject Pronouns	Object Pronouns	Possessive Pronouns
I	me	my, mine
you	you	your, yours
he	him	his
she	her	her, hers
it	it	its
we	us	ours
they	them	their, theirs

In simple sentences, subject pronouns come before the verb, object pronouns come after the verb, and possessive pronouns show ownership.

Look at the pronouns in these examples:

BE CAREFUL!
It is easy to make a mistake when you have multiple words in the role of subject or object.

- She forgot her coat. (subject: she; possessive: her)
- I lent her mine. (subject: I; object: her; possessive: mine)
- She left it at school. (subject: she; object: it)
- I had to go and get it the next day. (subject: I; object: it)
- I will never lend her something of mine again! (subject: I; object: her; possessive: mine)

Correct	Incorrect	Why?
John and I went out.	*John and me* went out.	*John and I* is a subject. *I* is a subject pronoun; *me* is not.
Johan took *Sam and me* to the show.	Johan took *Sam and I* to the show.	*Sam and me* is an object. *Me* is an object pronoun; *I* is not.

Relative Pronouns

Relative pronouns connect a clause to a noun or pronoun.

These are some relative pronouns:

who, whom, whoever, whose, that, which

- Steve Jobs, <u>who founded Apple</u>, changed the way people use technology.

The pronoun *who* introduces a clause that gives more information about Steve Jobs.

- This is the movie <u>*that* Emily told us to see</u>.

The pronoun *that* introduces a clause that gives more information about the movie.

Other Pronouns

Some other pronouns are:

this, that, what, anyone, everything, something

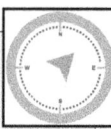

DID YOU KNOW?
Pronouns can sometimes refer to general or unspecified things.

Look for the pronouns in these sentences.

- What is that?
- There is something over there!
- Does anyone have a pen?

Pronouns and Their Purpose

The purpose of a pronoun is to replace a noun. Note the use of the pronoun *their* in the heading of this section. If we did not have pronouns, we would have to call this section *Pronouns and Pronouns' Purpose*.

What Is an Antecedent?

A pronoun in a sentence refers to a specific noun, and this noun called the **antecedent**.

- John Hancock signed the Declaration of Independence. <u>He</u> signed <u>it</u> in 1776.

The antecedent for *he* is John Hancock.
The antecedent for *it* is the Declaration of Independence.

BE CAREFUL!
Look out for unclear antecedents, such as in this sentence:

- Take the furniture out of the room and paint *it*.

What needs to be painted, the furniture or the room?

Find the pronouns in the following sentence. Then identify the antecedent for each pronoun.

Erin had an idea *that she* suggested to Antonio: "*I*'ll help *you* with *your* math homework if *you* help *me* with *my* writing assignment."

Pronoun	Antecedent
that	idea
she	Erin
I	Erin
you	Antonio
your	Antonio's
you	Antonio
me	Erin
my	Erin's

What Is Antecedent Agreement?

A pronoun must agree in **gender** and **number** with the antecedent it refers to. For example:

- Singular pronouns *I, you, he, she,* and *it* replace singular nouns.
- Plural pronouns *you, we,* and *they* replace plural nouns.
- Pronouns *he, she,* and *it* replace masculine, feminine, or neutral nouns.

Correct	Incorrect	Why?
Students should do their homework every night.	A student should do their homework every night.	The pronoun *their* is plural, so it must refer to a plural noun such as *students*.
When an employee is sick, he or she should call the office.	When an employee is sick, they should call the office.	The pronoun *they* is plural, so it must refer to a plural noun. *Employee* is not a plural noun.

Let's Review!

- A pronoun takes the place of or refers to a noun.
- The role of pronouns in sentences is as subject, object, or possessive.
- A pronoun must agree in number and gender with the noun it refers to.

LESSON 13.3 ADJECTIVES AND ADVERBS

An **adjective** is a word that describes a noun or a pronoun. An **adverb** is a word that describes a verb, an adjective, or another adverb.

Adjectives

An **adjective** describes, modifies, or tells us more about a **noun** or a **pronoun**. Colors, numbers, and descriptive words such as *healthy, good,* and *sharp* are adjectives.

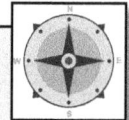

> **KEEP IN MIND . . .**
> Adjectives typically come **before the noun** in English. However, with **linking verbs** (non-action verbs such as *be, seem, look*), the adjective may come **after the verb** instead. Think of it like this: a linking verb **links** the adjective to the noun or pronoun.

Look for the adjectives in the following sentences:

	Adjective	Noun or pronoun it describes
I rode the blue bike.	blue	bike
It was a long trip.	long	trip
Bring two pencils for the exam.	two	pencils
The box is brown.	brown	box
She looked beautiful.	beautiful	she
That's great!	great	that

Multiple adjectives can be used in a sentence, as can multiple nouns. Look at these examples:

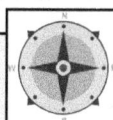

	Adjectives	Noun or pronoun it describes
The six girls were happy, healthy, and rested after their long beach vacation.	six, happy, healthy, rested; long, beach	girls; vacation
Leo has a good job, but he is applying for a better one.	good; better	job; one

> **KEEP IN MIND . . .**
> Note comparative and superlative forms of adjectives, such as:
>
> fast, faster, fastest
> far, farther, farthest
> good, better, best
> bad, worse, worst

Articles:  *A, An, The*

Articles are a unique part of speech, but they work like adjectives. An article tells more about a noun. *A* and *an* are **indefinite** articles. Use *a* before a singular **general** noun. Use *an* before a singular general noun that begins with a vowel.

The is a **definite** article. Use *the* before a singular or plural **specific** noun.

Look at how articles are used in the following sentences:

- I need *a* pencil to take *the* exam. (any pencil; specific exam)

- Is there *a* zoo in town? (any zoo)
- Let's go to *the* zoo today. (specific zoo)
- Can you get me *a* glass of milk? (any glass)
- Would you bring me *the* glass that's over there? (specific glass)

Adverbs

An **adverb** describes, modifies, or tells us more about a **verb**, an **adjective**, or another **adverb**. Many adverbs end in *-ly*. Often, adverbs tell when, where, or how something happened. Words such as *slowly*, *very*, and *yesterday* are adverbs.

Adverbs that Describe Verbs

Adverbs that describe verbs tell something more about the action.

Look for the adverbs in these sentences:

	Adverb	Verb it describes
They walked quickly.	quickly	walked
She disapproved somewhat of his actions, but she completely understood them.	somewhat; completely	disapproved; understood
The boys will go inside if it rains heavily.	inside; heavily	go; rains

Adverbs that Describe Adjectives

Adverbs that describe adjectives often add intensity to the adjective. Words like *quite*, *more*, and *always* are adverbs.

Look for the adverbs in these sentences:

	Adverb	Adjective it describes
The giraffe is very tall.	very	tall
Do you think that you are more intelligent than them?	more	intelligent
If it's really loud, we can make the volume slightly lower.	really; slightly	loud; lower

Adverbs that Describe Other Adverbs

Adverbs that describe adverbs often add intensity to the adverb.

Look for the adverbs in these sentences:

	Adverb	Adverb it describes
The mouse moved too quickly for us to catch it.	too	quickly
This store is almost never open.	almost	never
Those women are quite fashionably dressed.	quite	fashionably

Adjectives vs. Adverbs

Not sure whether a word is an adjective or an adverb? Look at these examples.

	Adjective	Adverb	Explanation
fast	You're a *fast* driver.	You drove *fast*.	The adjective *fast* describes *driver* (noun); the adverb *fast* describes *drove* (verb).
early	I don't like *early* mornings!	Try to arrive *early*.	The adjective *early* describes *mornings* (noun); the adverb *early* describes *arrive* (verb).
good/well	They did *good* work together.	They worked *well* together.	The adjective *good* describes *work* (noun); the adverb *well* describes *worked* (verb).
bad/badly	The dog is *bad*.	The dog behaves *badly*.	The adjective *bad* describes *dog* (noun); the adverb *badly* describes *behaves* (verb).

Let's Review!

- An **adjective** describes, modifies, or tells us more about a **noun** or a **pronoun**.
- An **adverb** describes, modifies, or tells us more about a **verb**, an **adjective**, or another **adverb**.

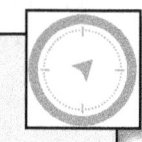

BE CAREFUL!

When an adverb ends in *-ly*, add *more* or *most* to make comparisons.

Correct: The car moved *more slowly*.

Incorrect: The car moved *slower*.

LESSON 13.4   CONJUNCTIONS AND PREPOSITIONS

A **conjunction** is a connector word; it connects words, phrases, or clauses in a sentence. A **preposition** is a relationship word; it shows the relationship between two nearby words.

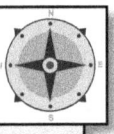

Conjunctions

A **conjunction** connects words, phrases, or clauses.

And, so, and *or* are conjunctions.

Types of Conjunctions

> **KEEP IN MIND...**
> A clause is a phrase that has a subject and a verb.
> Some clauses are **independent**. An independent clause can stand alone.
> Some clauses are **dependent**. A dependent clause relies on another clause in order to make sense.

- **Coordinating** conjunctions connect two words, phrases, or independent clauses. The full list of coordinating conjunctions is: *and, or, but, so, for, nor, yet.*
- **Subordinating** conjunctions connect a main (independent) clause and a dependent clause. The conjunction may show a relationship or time order for the two clauses. Some subordinating conjunctions are: *after, as soon as, once, if, even though, unless.*
- **Correlative** conjunctions are pairs of conjunctions that work together to connect two words or phrases. Some correlative conjunctions are: *either/or, neither/nor, as/as.*

Example	Conjunction	What it is connecting
Verdi, Mozart, **and** *Wagner* are famous opera composers.	and	three nouns
Would you like *angel food cake, chocolate lava cake,* **or** *banana cream pie* for dessert?	or	three noun phrases
I took the bus to work, **but** *I walked home.*	but	two independent clauses
It was noisy at home, **so** *we went to the library.*	so	two independent clauses
They have to clean the house **before** *the realtor shows it.*	before	a main clause and a dependent clause
Use **either** hers **or** mine.	either/or	two pronouns
After everyone leaves, make sure you lock up.	after	a main clause and a dependent clause
I'd **rather** *fly* **than** *take the train.*	rather/than	two verb phrases
As soon as they announced the winning number, she looked at her ticket and shouted, "Whoopee!"	as soon as	a main clause and a dependent clause

> **DID YOU KNOW?**
> In the last example above, "*Whoopee!*" is an interjection. An **interjection** is a short phrase or clause that communicates emotion.
>
> Some other interjections are:
> - *Way to go!*
> - *Yuck.*
> - *Hooray!*
> - *Holy cow!*
> - *Oops!*

Prepositions

A **preposition** shows the relationship between two nearby words. Prepositions help to tell information such as direction, location, and time. *To, for,* and *with* are prepositions.

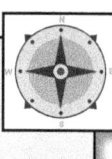

KEEP IN MIND . . .
Some prepositions are more than one word. *On top of* and *instead of* are prepositions.

Example	Preposition	What it tells us
The desk is in the classroom.	in	location
We'll meet you at 6:00.	at	time
We'll meet you at the museum.	at	place
The book is on top of the desk.	on top of	location

Prepositional Phrases

A preposition must be followed by an **object of the preposition**. This can be a noun or something that serves as a noun, such as a pronoun or a gerund.

DID YOU KNOW?
A gerund is the *-ing* form of a verb that serves as a noun. *Hiking* is a gerund in this sentence:

   I wear these shoes for *hiking*.

A **prepositional phrase** is a preposition plus the object that follows it.

Look for the prepositional phrases in the following examples. Note that a sentence can have more than one prepositional phrase.

Example	Preposition	Object of the preposition
The tiny country won the war *against all odds*.	against	all odds
Look *at us*!	at	us
Why don't we go swimming *instead of sweating in this heat*?	instead of; in	sweating; this heat
Aunt Tea kept the trophy *on a shelf of the cabinet between the sofas in the living room*.	on; of; between; in	a shelf; the cabinet; the sofas; the living room

BE CAREFUL!
Sometimes a word looks like a preposition but is actually part of the verb. In this case, the verb is called a phrasal verb, and the preposition-like word is called a particle. Here is an example:

- Turn *on* the light. (*Turn on* has a meaning of its own; it is a phrasal verb. *On* is a particle here, rather than a preposition.)
- Turn *on that street*. (*On that street* shows location; it is a prepositional phrase. *On* is a preposition here.)

Let's Review!

- A **conjunction** connects words, phrases, or clauses. *And, so,* and *or* are conjunctions.
- A **preposition** shows the relationship between two nearby words. *To, for,* and *with* are prepositions.
- A **prepositional phrase** includes a preposition plus the object of the preposition.

Lesson 13.5 Verbs and Verb Tenses

A **verb** is a word that describes a **physical or mental action** or a **state of being**. This lesson will cover the role of verbs in sentences, verb forms and tenses, and helping verbs.

The Role of Verbs in Sentences

A verb describes an action or a state of being. A complete sentence must have at least one verb.

Verbs have different tenses, which show time.

Verb Forms

Each verb has three primary forms. The **base form** is used for simple present tense, and the **past form** is used for simple past tense. The **participle form** is used for more complicated time situations. Participle form verbs are accompanied by a helping verb.

Base Form	Past Form	Participle Form
end	ended	ended
jump	jumped	jumped
explain	explained	explained
eat	ate	eaten
take	took	taken
go	went	gone
come	came	come

Some verbs are **regular**. To make the **past** or **participle** form of a regular verb, we just add *-ed*. However, many verbs that we commonly use are **irregular**. We need to memorize the forms for these verbs.

In the chart above, *end, jump,* and *explain* are regular verbs. *Eat, take, go,* and *come* are irregular.

Using Verbs

A simple sentence has a **subject** and a **verb**. The subject tells us who or what, and the verb tells us the action or state.

Example	Subject	Verb	Explanation/Time
They ate breakfast together yesterday.	They	ate	*happened yesterday*
I walk to school.	I	walk	*happens regularly*
We went to California last year.	We	went	*happened last year*
She seems really tired.	She	seems	*how she seems right now*
The teacher is sad.	teacher	is	*her state right now*

You can see from the examples in this chart that **past tense verbs** are used for a time in the past, and **present tense verbs** are used for something that happens regularly or for a state or condition right now.

Lesson 13.5 Verbs and Verb Tenses

Often a sentence has more than one verb. If it has a connector word or more than one subject, it can have more than one verb.

- The two cousins <u>live</u>, <u>work</u>, and <u>vacation</u> together. (3 verbs)
- The girls <u>planned</u> by phone, and then they <u>met</u> at the movies. (2 verbs)

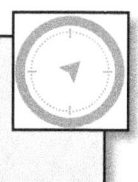

BE CAREFUL!
When you have more than one verb in a sentence, make sure both verb tenses are correct.

Helping Verbs and Progressive and Perfect Tenses

Helping Verbs

A **helping verb** is a supporting verb that accompanies a main verb.

Questions, negative sentences, and certain time situations require helping verbs.

forms of helping verb "to be"	forms of helping verb "to have"	forms of helping verb "to do"	some modals (used like helping verbs)
am, are, is, was, were, be, being, been	have, has, had, having	do, does, did, doing	will, would, can, could, must, might, should

Here are examples of helping verbs in questions and negatives.

- Where *is* he *going*?
- *Did* they *win*?
- I *don't* *want* that.
- The boys *can't* go.

Progressive and Perfect Tenses

Helping verbs accompany main verbs in certain time situations, such as when an action is or was ongoing, or when two actions overlap in time. To form these tenses, we use a **helping verb** with the **base form plus -*ing*** or with the **participle form** of the main verb.

The **progressive tense** is used for an action that is or was ongoing. It takes base form of the main verb plus -*ing*.

Example sentence	Tense	Explanation/Time
I <u>am taking</u> French this semester.	Present progressive	*happening now, over a continuous period of time*
I <u>was working</u> when you stopped by.	Past progressive	*happened over a continuous period of time in the past*

The **perfect tense** is used to cover two time periods. It takes the *participle* form of the main verb.

Example sentence	Tense	Explanation/Time
I have lived here for three years.	Present perfect	*started in the past and continues to present*
I had finished half of my homework when my computer stopped working.	Past perfect	*started and finished in the past, overlapping in time with another action*

Sometimes we use both the **progressive** and **perfect** tenses together.

Example sentence	Tense	Explanation/Time
I have been walking for hours!	Present perfect progressive	*started in the past, took place for a period of time, and continues to present*
She had been asking for a raise for months before she finally received one.	Past perfect progressive	*started in the past, took place for a period of time, and ended*

Let's Review!

- A verb describes an action or state of being.
- Each verb has three primary forms: base form, past form, and participle form.
- Verbs have different tenses, which are used to show time.
- Helping verbs are used in questions, negative sentences, and to form progressive and perfect tenses.

Chapter 13 Parts of Speech Practice Quiz

1. How many adjectives are in the following sentence?

   The new building is tall and modern.

   A. 1
   B. 2
   C. 3
   D. 4

2. Select the musical title that contains an adverb.

   A. *Follies*
   B. *West Side Story*
   C. *Into the Woods*
   D. *Merrily We Roll Along*

3. Identify the preposition in the following sentence.

   It's really hot in that room.

   A. It
   B. hot
   C. in
   D. that

4. Identify the prepositional phrase in the following sentence.

   The show got great reviews, so we plan to see it on Saturday.

   A. got great reviews
   B. so we plan
   C. see it
   D. on Saturday

5. Select the sentence that has a noun as its subject.

   A. Whose turn is it?
   B. Susan made dinner.
   C. I walked to the bus stop.
   D. They didn't know the answer.

6. What part of speech is the underlined word in the following sentence?

   Lincoln was elected <u>president</u> in 1860.

   A. Noun
   B. Verb
   C. Pronoun
   D. Preposition

7. Which word in the following sentence is a pronoun?

   The driver checked her side mirror.

   A. The
   B. her
   C. side
   D. driver

8. How many pronouns are in the following sentence?

   I called her, but she didn't return my call.

   A. 1
   B. 2
   C. 3
   D. 4

9. How many verbs are in the following sentence?

   They toured the art museum and saw the conservatory.

   A. 0
   B. 1
   C. 2
   D. 3

10. How many verbs are in the following sentence?

    We read about World War I, World War II, and the Korean War in my history class.

    A. 0
    B. 1
    C. 2
    D. 3

Chapter 13 Parts of Speech Practice Quiz – Answer Key

1. **C.** The adjectives *new, tall,* and *modern* describe the noun *building.* **See Lesson: Adjectives and Adverbs**

2. **D.** *Merrily* is an adverb that describes the verb *roll.* **See Lesson: Adjectives and Adverbs.**

3. **C.** *In* is a preposition. **See Lesson: Conjunctions and Prepositions.**

4. **D.** *On Saturday* is a prepositional phrase. **See Lesson: Conjunctions and Prepositions.**

5. **B.** *Susan* is a noun; the other answers have pronouns as their subjects. **See Lesson: Nouns.**

6. **A.** *President* is a noun. **See Lesson: Nouns.**

7. **B.** *Her* is a possessive pronoun. **See Lesson: Pronouns.**

8. **D.** *I, her, she,* and *my* are pronouns. **See Lesson: Pronouns.**

9. **C.** *Toured* and *saw* are verbs. **See Lesson: Verbs and Verb Tenses.**

10. **B.** *Read* is the only verb in the sentence. **See Lesson: Verbs and Verb Tenses.**

CHAPTER 14 KNOWLEDGE OF LANGUAGE

LESSON 14.1 SUBJECT AND VERB AGREEMENT

Every sentence must include a **subject** and a **verb**. The subject tells **who or what**, and the verb describes an **action or condition**. Subject and verb agree in number and person.

Roles of Subject and Verb

A complete sentence includes a **subject** and a **verb**. The verb is in the part of the sentence called the **predicate**. A predicate can be thought of as a verb phrase.

Simple Sentences

A sentence can be very simple, with just one or two words as **subject** and one or two words as **predicate**.

Sometimes, in a command, a subject is "understood," rather than written or spoken.

BE CAREFUL!
It's is a contraction of *it is*.
Its (without an apostrophe) is the possessive of the pronoun *it*.

Look at these examples of short sentences:

Sentence	Subject	Predicate, with main verb(s) underlined
I ate.	I	ate
They ran away.	They	ran away
It's OK.	It	is OK
Go and find the cat!	(You)	go and find the cat

More Complex Sentences

Sometimes a subject or predicate is a long phrase or clause.

Some sentences have more than one subject or predicate, or even a predicate within a predicate.

Sentence	Subject(s)	Predicate(s), with main verb(s) underlined
My friend from work had a bad car accident.	My friend from work	had a bad car accident
John, his sister, and I plan to ride our bikes across the country this summer.	John, his sister, and I	plan to ride our bikes across the country this summer
I did so much for them, and they didn't even thank me.*	I; they	did so much for them; didn't even thank me
She wrote a letter that explained the problem.**	She	wrote a letter that explained the problem

*This sentence consists of two clauses, and each clause has its own subject and its own predicate.

**In this sentence, *that explained the problem* is part of the predicate. It is also a type of subordinate clause, called a relative clause, with its own subject and predicate.

Subject and Verb Agreement

Subjects and verbs must agree in **number** and **person**. This means that different subjects take different forms of a verb.

KEEP IN MIND . . .
The third person singular subject takes a different verb form than other subjects.

With **regular** verbs, simply add *-s* to the singular third person verb, as shown below:

	Singular		Plural	
	Subject	Verb	Subject	Verb
(first person)	I	play	we	play
(second person)	you	play	you	play
(third person)	he/she/it	plays	they	play

Some verbs are **irregular**, so simply adding *-s* doesn't work. For example:

verb	form for third person singular subject
have	has
do	does
fix	fixes

BE CAREFUL!
The verbs *be*, *have*, and *do* can be either main verbs or helping verbs.

Look for subject-verb agreement in the following sentences:

- *I* usually <u>eat</u> a banana for breakfast.
- *Marcy* <u>does</u> well in school.
- The *cat* <u>licks</u> its fur.

Subject-Verb Agreement for the Verb *Be*

Present		Past	
I am	we are	I was	we were
you are	you are	you were	you were
he/she/it is	they are	they were	they were

BE CAREFUL!
The verb *be* is very irregular. Its forms change with several subjects, in both present and past tense.

Things to Look Out For

Subject-verb agreement can be tricky. Be careful of these situations:

- **Sentences with more than one subject:** If two subjects are connected by *and,* the subject is **plural**. When two singular subjects are connected by *neither/nor,* the subject is **singular**.

    Sandra and Luiz shop. (plural)
    Neither Sandra nor Luiz has money. (singular)

- **Collective nouns:** Sometimes a noun stands for a group of people or things. If the subject is **one group**, it is considered **singular**.

    Those students are still on chapter three. (plural)
    That class is still on chapter three. (singular)

- ***There is*** **and** ***there are:*** With pronouns such as *there, what,* and *where,* the verb agrees with the noun or pronoun that follows it.

    There's a rabbit! (singular)
    Where are my shoes? (plural)

- **Indefinite pronouns:** Subjects such as *everybody, someone,* and *nobody* are **singular**. Subjects such as *all, none,* and *any* can be either **singular or plural**.

    Everyone in the band plays well. (singular)
    All of the students are there. (plural)
    All is well. (singular)

Let's Review!

- Every sentence has a subject and a verb.
- The predicate is the part of the sentence that contains the verb.
- The subject and verb must agree in number and person.
- The third person singular subject takes a different verb form.

LESSON 14.2 TYPES OF SENTENCES

Sentences are a combination of words that communicate a complete thought. Sentences can be written in many ways to signal different relationships among ideas. This lesson will cover (1) simple sentences (2) compound sentences (3) complex sentences (4) parallel structure.

Simple Sentences

A **simple sentence** is a group of words that make up a **complete thought**. To be a complete thought, simple sentences must have one **independent clause.** An independent clause contains a single **subject** (who or what the sentence is about) and a **predicate** (a **verb** and something about the subject).

Let's take a look at some simple sentences:

Simple Sentence	Subject	Predicate	Complete Thought?
The car was fast.	car	was fast (verb = was)	Yes
Sally waited for the bus.	Sally	waited for the bus (verb = waited)	Yes
The pizza smells delicious.	pizza	smells delicious (verb = smells)	Yes
Anton loves cycling.	Anton	loves cycling (verb = loves)	Yes

It is important to be able to recognize what a simple sentence is in order to avoid **run-ons** and **fragments**, two common grammatical errors.

A **run-on** is when two or more independent clauses are combined without proper punctuation:

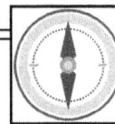

> **FOR EXAMPLE**
>
> *Gregory is a very talented actor he was the lead in the school play.*
>
> If you take a look at this sentence, you can see that it is made up of 2 independent clauses or simple sentences:
>
> 1. *Gregory is a very talented actor*
> 2. *he was the lead in the school play*
>
> You <u>cannot</u> have two independent clauses running into each other without proper punctuation.
>
> You can fix this run-on in the following way:
>
> **Gregory is a very talented actor. He was the lead in the school play.**

A **fragment** is a group of words that looks like a sentence. It starts with a capital letter and has end punctuation, but when you examine it closely you will see it is not a complete thought.

Let's put this information all together to determine whether a group of words is a simple sentence, a run-on, or a fragment:

Group of Words	Category
Mondays are the worst they are a drag.	Run-On: These are two independent clauses running into one another without proper punctuation. FIX: *Mondays are the worst. They are a drag.*
Because I wanted soda.	Fragment: This is a dependent clause and needs more information to make it a complete thought. FIX: *I went to the store because I wanted soda.*
Ereni is from Greece.	Simple Sentence: YES! This is a simple sentence with a subject (*Ereni*) and a predicate (*is from Greece*), so it is a complete thought.
While I was apple picking.	Fragment: This is a dependent clause and needs more information to make it a complete thought. FIX: *While I was apple picking, I spotted a bunny.*
New York City is magical it is my favorite place.	Run-On: These are two independent clauses running into one another without proper punctuation. FIX: *New York City is magical. It is my favorite place.*

Compound Sentences

A **compound sentence** is a sentence made up of two independent clauses connected with a **coordinating conjunction**.

Let's take a look at the following sentence:

Joe waited for the bus, but it never arrived.

If you take a close look at this compound sentence, you will see that it is made up of two independent clauses:

1. *Joe waited for the bus*
2. *it never arrived*

The word *but* is the coordinating conjunction that connects these two sentences. Notice that the coordinating conjunction has a comma right before it. This is the proper way to punctuate compound sentences.

Here are other examples of compound sentences:

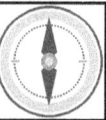

> **FOR EXAMPLE**
>
> *I want to try out for the baseball team, and I also want to try out for track.*
>
> *Sally can play the clarinet in the band, or she can play the violin in the orchestra.*
>
> *Mr. Henry is going to run the half marathon, so he has a lot of training to do.*
>
> All these sentences are compound sentences since they each have two independent clauses joined by a comma and a coordinating conjunction.

The following is a list of **coordinating conjunctions** that can be used in compound sentences. You can use the mnemonic device "FANBOYS" to help you remember them:

For

And

Nor

But

Or

Yet

So

Think back to Section 1: Simple Sentences. You learned about run-ons. Another way to fix run-ons is by turning the group of words into a compound sentence:

RUN-ON: *Gregory is a very talented actor he was the lead in the school play.*

FIX: *Gregory is a very talented actor,* **so** *he was the lead in the school play.*

Complex Sentences

A **complex** sentence is a sentence that is made up of an independent clause and one or more dependent clauses connected to it.

Think back to Section 1 when you learned about fragments. You learned about a **dependent clause**, the part of a sentence that cannot stand by itself. These clauses need other information to make them complete.

You can recognize a dependent clause because they always begin with a **subordinating conjunction**. These words are a key ingredient in complex sentences.

Here is a list of **subordinating conjunctions**:

after	although	as	because	before
despite	even if	even though	if	in order
that	once	provided that	rather than	since
so that	than	that	though	unless
until	when	whenever	where	whereas
wherever	while	why		

Let's take a look at a few complex sentences:

> **FOR EXAMPLE**
>
> *Since the alarm clock didn't go off, I was late for class.*
>
> This is an example of a complex sentence because it contains:
>
> | | |
> |---|---|
> | A dependent clause: | Since the alarm clock didn't go off |
> | An independent clause: | I was late for class |
> | A subordinating conjunction: | since |
>
> *Sarah studied all night for the exam even though she did not receive an A.*
>
> This is an example of a complex sentence because it contains:
>
> | | |
> |---|---|
> | A dependent clause: | even though she did not receive an A |
> | An independent clause: | Sarah studied all night |
> | A subordinating conjunction: | even though |
>
> ***NOTE:*** *To make a complex sentence, you can either start with the dependent clause or the independent clause. When beginning with the dependent clause, you need a comma after it. When beginning with an independent clause, you do not need a comma after it.*

Parallel Structure

Parallel structure is the repetition of a grammatical form within a sentence to make the sentence sound more harmonious. Parallel structure comes into play when you are making a list of items. Stylistically, you want all the items in the list to line up with each other to make them sound better.

Let's take a look at when to use parallel structure:

1. Use parallel structure with verb forms:

   In a sentence listing different verbs, you want all the verbs to use the same form:

   Manuel likes hiking, biking, and mountain climbing.

   In this example, the words *hiking, biking* and *climbing* are all gerunds (having an -ing ending), so the sentence is balanced since the words are all using the gerund form of the verb.

   Manuel likes to hike, bike, and mountain climb.

   In this example, the words *hike, bike* and *climb* are all infinitives (using the basic form of the verb), so the sentence is balanced.

   You do not want to mix them up:

   Manuel likes, hiking, biking, and to mountain climb.

   This sentence **does not** use parallel structure since *hiking* and *biking* use the gerund form of the verb and *to mountain climb* uses the infinitive form.

2. Use parallel structure with active and passive voice:

    In a sentence written in the **active voice**, the subject performs the action:

    Sally kicked the ball.

    Sally, the subject, is the one doing the action, kicking the ball.

    In a sentence written in the **passive voice**, the subject is acted on by the verb.

    The ball was kicked by Sally.

    When using parallel structure, you want to make sure your items in a list are either all in **active voice**:

    Raymond baked, frosted, and decorated the cake.

    Or all in **passive voice**:

    The cake was baked, frosted, and decorated by Raymond.

    You do not want to mix them up:

    The cake was baked, frosted, and Raymond decorated it.

    This sentence **does not** use parallel structure because it starts off with passive voice and then switches to active voice.

3. Use parallel structure with the length of terms within a list:

    When making a list, you should either have all short individual terms or all long phrases.

    Keep these consistent by either choosing short, individual terms:

    Cassandra is bold, courageous, and strong.

    Or longer phrases:

    Cassandra is brave in the face of danger, willing to take risks, and a force to be reckoned with.

    You do not want to mix them up:

    Cassandra is bold, courageous, and a force to be reckoned with.

    This sentence **does not** use parallel structure because the first two terms are short, and the last one is a longer phrase.

Let's Review!

- A simple sentence consists of a clause, which has a single subject and a predicate.
- A compound sentence is made up of two independent clauses connected by a coordinating conjunction.
- A complex sentence is made up of a subordinating conjunction, an independent clause and one or more dependent clauses connected to it.
- Parallel structure is the repetition of a grammatical form within a sentence to make the sentence sound more harmonious.

LESSON 14.3 TYPES OF CLAUSES

There are four types of clauses that are used to create sentences. Sentences with several clauses, and different types of clauses, are considered complex. This lesson will cover (1) independent clauses, (2) dependent clauses and subordinate clauses, and (3) coordinate clauses.

Independent Clause

An **independent clause** is a simple sentence. It has a subject, a verb, and expresses a complete thought.

- Steve went to the store.
- She will cook dinner tonight.
- The class was very boring.
- The author argues that listening to music helps productivity.

Two **independent clauses** can be connected by a semicolon. There are some common words that indicate the beginning of an **independent clause** such as: moreover, also, nevertheless, however, furthermore, consequently.

- I wanted to go to dinner; however, I had to work late tonight.
- She had a job interview; therefore, she dressed nicely.

Dependent and Subordinate Clauses

A **dependent clause** is not a complete sentence. It has a subject and a verb but does not express a complete thought. **Dependent clauses** are also called **subordinate clauses**, because they depend on the **independent or main clause** to complete the thought. A sentence that has both at least one **independent clause** and one **subordinate clause** are considered complex.

Subordinate clauses can be placed before or after the **independent clause**. When the **subordinate clause** begins the sentence, there should be a comma before the **main clause**. If the **subordinate clause** ends the sentence, there is no need for a comma.

Dependent clauses also have common indicator words. These are often called **subordinating conjunctions** because they connect a **dependent clause** to an **independent clause**. Some of these include: although, after, as, because, before, if, once, since, unless, until, when, whether, and while. Relative pronouns also signify the beginning of a **subordinate clause**. These include: that, which, who, whom, whichever, whoever, whomever, and whose.

- When I went to school...
- Since she joined the team...
- After we saw the play...
- *Because she studied hard*, she received an A on her exam.
- *Although the professor was late*, the class was very informative.
- I can't join you unless I finish my homework.

Coordinate Clause

A **coordinate clause** is a sentence or phrase that combines clauses of equal grammatical rank (verbs, nouns, adjectives, phrases, or independent clauses) by using a coordinating conjunction (and, but, for, nor, or so, yet). **Coordinating conjunctions** cannot connect a **dependent or subordinate clause** and an **independent clause.**

- She woke up, and he went to bed.
- We did not have cheese, so I went to the store to get some.
- Ice cream and candy taste great, but they are not good for you.
- Do you want to study, or do you want to go to Disneyland?

Let's Review!

- An independent clause is a simple sentence that has a noun, a verb, and a complete thought. Two independent clauses can be connected by a semicolon.
- A dependent or subordinate clause depends on the main clause to complete a thought. A dependent or subordinate clause can go before or after the independent clause and there are indicator words that signify the beginning of the dependent or subordinate clause.
- A coordinate clause connects two verbs, nouns, adjectives, phrases, or independent clauses using a coordinating conjunction (and, but, for, nor, or, so, yet).

LESSON 14.4 — FORMAL AND INFORMAL LANGUAGE

In English, there is formal language that is used most often in writing, and informal language that is most often used in speaking, but there are situations where one is more appropriate than the other. This lesson will cover differentiating contexts for (1) formal language and (2) informal language.

Formal Language

Formal language is often associated with writing for professional and academic purposes, but it is also used when giving a speech or a lecture. An essay written for a class will always use **formal language**. **Formal language** is used in situations where people are not extremely close and when one needs to show respect to another person. Certain qualities and contexts differentiate **formal language** from informal language.

Formal language does not use contractions.

- It doesn't have that - It does not have that.
- He's been offered a new job - He has been offered a new job.

Formal language also uses complete sentences.

- So much to tell you - I have so much to tell you.
- Left for the weekend - We left for the weekend.

Formal language includes more formal and polite vocabulary.

- The class starts at two - The class commences at two.
- I try to be the best person I can be I endeavor to be the best person I can be.

Formal language is not personal and normally does not use the pronouns "I" and "We" as the subject of a sentence.

- I argue that the sky is blue - This essay argues that the sky is blue.
- We often associate green with grass - Green is often associated with grass.

Formal language also does not use slang.

- It's raining cats and dogs It is raining heavily.
- Patients count on doctors to help them - Patients expect doctors to help them.

Informal Language

Informal language is associated with speaking, but is also used in text messages, emails, letters, and postcards. It is the language a person would use with their friends and family.

Informal language uses contractions.

- I can't go to the movie tomorrow.
- He doesn't have any manners.

Informal language can include sentence fragments.

- See you
- Talk to you later

Informal language uses less formal vocabulary such as slang.

- The dog drove me up the wall.
- I was so hungry I could eat a horse.
- I can always count on you.

Informal language is personal and uses pronouns such as "I" and "We" as the subject of a sentence.

- I am in high school.
- We enjoy going to the beach in the summer.

Let's Review!

- **Formal language** is used in professional and academic writing and talks. It does not have contractions, uses complete sentences, uses polite and formal vocabulary, not slang, and is not personal and does not use the pronouns "I" and "We" as the subject of a sentence.
- **Informal language** is used in daily life when communicating with friends and family through conversations, text messages, emails, letters, and postcards. It uses contractions, can be sentence fragments, uses less formal vocabulary and slang, and is personal and uses pronouns such as "I" and "We" as the subject of a sentence.

Chapter 14 Knowledge of Language Practice Quiz

1. Which of the following sentences uses the MOST formal language?

   A. I'm sorry to tell you you haven't been accepted.

   B. We regret that you haven't been accepted.

   C. We're sorry that you haven't been accepted.

   D. We regret to inform you that you have not been accepted.

2. Which of the following sentences uses the MOST informal language?

   A. I dislike the dentist.

   B. The dentist scares me.

   C. I don't wanna go to the dentist.

   D. I only go to the dentist when I have to.

3. Select the correct verbs to complete the following sentence.

   We _____ she will fall in love with the puppy the first time she _____ him.

   A. know, see
   C. knows, see

   B. know, sees
   D. knows, sees

4. Which of the following is an example of a compound sentence?

   A. Monte cannot run in the race tomorrow, he injured his ankle.

   B. Monte injured his ankle and cannot run in the race tomorrow.

   C. Monte injured his ankle, so he cannot run in the race tomorrow.

   D. Monte cannot run in the race tomorrow since he injured his ankle.

5. Select the correct verb to complete the following sentence.

   The news I got ____ not the news I was expecting.

   A. are
   C. were

   B. was
   D. being

6. Identify the independent clause in the following sentence.

   Although most people understand the benefits of exercise, people do not exercise as much as they should.

   A. Although most people understand

   B. The benefits of exercise

   C. People do not exercise as much as they should

   D. People do not exercise

7. Identify the type of clause.

   When she went to the movie.

   A. Main clause

   B. Coordinate clause

   C. Independent clause

   D. Dependent or subordinate clause

8. Which of the following is an example of a simple sentence?

   A. Tamara's sporting goods store.

   B. Tamara has a sporting goods store in town.

   C. Tamara has a sporting goods store it is in town.

   D. Tamara's sporting goods store is in town, and she is the owner.

Chapter 14 Knowledge of Language Practice Quiz – Answer Key

1. **D.** We regret to inform you that you have not been accepted. The sentence does not have any contractions and uses formal vocabulary such as *regret* and *inform*. **See Lesson: Formal and Informal Language.**

2. **C.** I don't wanna go to the dentist. It is the sentence that uses the most slang. **See Lesson: Formal and Informal Language.**

3. **B.** *We know* and *she sees* have the correct subject-verb agreement. **See Lesson: Subject and Verb Agreement.**

4. **C.** This is a compound sentence joining two independent clauses with a comma and the conjunction *so*. **See Lesson: Types of Sentences.**

5. **B.** The subject *news* is third person singular, so it takes the verb *was*. **See Lesson: Subject and Verb Agreement.**

6. **C.** People do not exercise as much as they should. It is independent because it has a subject, verb, and expresses a complete thought. **See Lesson: Types of Clauses.**

7. **D.** Dependent or subordinate clause. The clause does not express a complete thought. When is also a common indicator word that begins a dependent or subordinate clause. **See Lesson: Types of Clauses.**

8. **B.** This is a simple sentence since it contains one independent clause consisting of a simple subject and a predicate. **See Lesson: Types of Sentences.**

CHAPTER 15 VOCABULARY ACQUISITION

LESSON 15.1 ROOT WORDS, PREFIXES, AND SUFFIXES

A root word is the most basic part of a word. You can create new words by: adding a prefix, a group of letters placed before the root word; or a suffix, a group of letters placed at the end of a root word. In this lesson you will learn about root words, prefixes, suffixes, and how to determine the meaning of a word by analyzing these word parts.

Root Words

Root words are found in everyday language. They are the most basic parts of words. Root words in the English language are mostly derived from Latin or Greek. You can add beginnings (prefixes) and endings (suffixes) to root words to change their meanings. To discover what a root word is, simply remove its prefix and/or suffix. What you are left with is the root word, or the core or basis of the word.

At times, root words can be stand-alone words.

Here are some examples of stand-alone root words:

STAND-ALONE ROOT WORDS	MEANINGS
dress	*clothing*
form	*shape*
normal	*typical*
phobia	*fear of*
port	*carry*

Most root words, however, are **not** stand-alone words. They are not full words on their own, but they still form the basis of other words when you remove their prefixes and suffixes.

Here are some common root words in the English language:

ROOT WORDS	MEANINGS	EXAMPLES
ami, amic	*love*	amicable
anni	*year*	anniversary
aud	*to hear*	auditory
bene	*good*	beneficial
biblio	*book*	bibliography
cap	*take, seize*	capture
cent	*one hundred*	century
chrom	*color*	chromatic
chron	*time*	chronological

319

ROOT WORDS	MEANINGS	EXAMPLES
circum	*around*	circumvent
cred	*believe*	credible
corp	*body*	corpse
dict	*to say*	dictate
equi	*equal*	equality
fract; rupt	*to break*	fracture
ject	*throw*	eject
mal	*bad*	malignant
min	*small*	miniature
mort	*death*	mortal
multi	*many*	multiply
ped	*foot*	pedestrian
rupt	*break*	rupture
sect	*cut*	dissect
script	*write*	manuscript
sol	*sun*	solar
struct	*build*	construct
terr	*earth*	terrain
therm	*heat*	thermometer
vid, vis	*to see*	visual
voc	*voice; to call*	vocal

Prefixes

Prefixes are the letters added to the **beginning** of a root word to make a new word with a different meaning.

Prefixes on their own have meanings, too. If you add a prefix to a root word, it can change its meaning entirely.

Here are some of the most common prefixes, their meanings, and some examples:

PREFIX	MEANING	EXAMPLE
auto	*self*	autograph
con	*with*	conclude
hydro	*water*	hydrate
im, in, non, un	*not*	unimportant
inter	*between*	international
mis	*incorrect, badly*	mislead
over	*too much*	over-stimulate
post	*after*	postpone

Lesson 15.1   Root Words, Prefixes, and Suffixes

PREFIX	MEANING	EXAMPLE
pre	*before*	preview
re	*again*	rewrite
sub	*under, below*	submarine
trans	*across*	transcribe

Let's look back at some of the root words from Section 1. By adding prefixes to these root words, you can create a completely new word with a new meaning:

ROOT WORD	PREFIX	NEW WORD	MEANING
dress (*clothing*)	un (*remove*)	**un**dress	*remove clothing*
sect (*cut*)	inter (*between*)	**inter**sect	*cut across or through*
phobia (*fear*)	hydro (*water*)	**hydro**phobia	*fear of water*
script (*write*)	post (*after*)	**post**script	*additional remark at the end of a letter*

Suffixes

Suffixes are the letters added to the **end** of a root word to make a new word with a different meaning.

Suffixes on their own have meanings, too. If you add a suffix to a root word, it can change its meaning entirely.

Here are some of the most common suffixes, their meanings, and some examples:

SUFFIX	MEANING	EXAMPLE
able, ible	*can be done*	agreeable
an, ean, ian	*belonging or relating to*	European
ed	*happened in the past*	jogged
en	*made of*	wooden
er	*comparative (more than)*	stricter
est	*comparative (most)*	largest
ful	*full of*	meaningful
ic	*having characteristics of*	psychotic
ion, tion, ation, ition	*act, process*	hospitalization
ist	*person who practices*	linguist
less	*without*	artless
logy	*study of*	biology

Let's look back at some of the root words from Section 1. By adding suffixes to these root words, you can create a completely new word with a new meaning:

ROOT WORD	SUFFIX	NEW WORD	MEANING
aud (*to hear*)	logy (*study of*)	audio**logy**	*the study of hearing*
form (*shape*)	less (*without*)	form**less**	*without a clear shape*
port (*carry*)	able (*can be done*)	port**able**	*able to be carried*
normal (*typical*)	ity (*state of*)	normal**ity**	*condition of being normal*

Determining Meaning

Knowing the meanings of common root words, prefixes, and suffixes can help you determine the meaning of unknown words. By looking at a word's individual parts, you can get a good sense of its definition.

If you look at the word *transportation*, you can study the different parts of the word to figure out what it means.

If you were to break up the word you would see the following:

| PREFIX: *trans = across* | ROOT: *port = carry* | SUFFIX: *tion = act or process* |

If you put all these word parts together, you can define transportation as: *the act or process of carrying something across*.

Let's define some other words by looking at their roots, prefixes and suffixes:

WORD	PREFIX	ROOT	SUFFIX	WORKING DEFINITION
indestructible	in (*not*)	struct (*build*)	able (*can be done*)	Not able to be "un" built (torn down)
nonconformist	non (*not*) con (*with*)	form (*shape*)	ist (*person who practices*)	A person who can not be shaped (someone who doesn't go along with the norm)
subterranean	sub (*under, below*)	terr (*earth*)	ean (*belonging or relating to*)	Relating or belonging to something under the earth

Let's Review!

- A root word is the most basic part of a word.
- A prefix is the letters added to beginning of a root word to change the word and its meaning.
- A suffix is the letters added to the end of a root word to change the word and its meaning.
- You can figure out a word's meaning by looking closely at its different word parts (root, prefixes, and suffixes).

LESSON 15.2 — Context Clues and Multiple Meaning Words

Sometimes when you read a text, you come across an unfamiliar word. Instead of skipping the word and reading on, it is important to figure out what that word means so you can better understand the text. There are different strategies you can use to determine the meaning of unfamiliar words. This lesson will cover (1) how to determine unfamiliar words by reading context clues, (2) multiple meaning words, and (3) using multiple meaning words properly in context.

Using Context Clues to Determine Meaning

When reading a text, it is common to come across unfamiliar words. One way to determine the meaning of unfamiliar words is by studying other context clues to help you better understand what the word means.

Context means the other words in the sentences around the unfamiliar word.

You can look at these other words to find **clues** or **hints** to help you figure out what the word means.

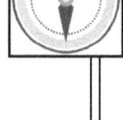

> **FOR EXAMPLE**
>
> Look at the following sentence:
>
> Some of the kids in the cafeteria *ostracized* Janice because she dressed differently; they never allowed her to sit at their lunch table, and they whispered behind her back.
>
> If you did not know what the word *ostracized* meant, you could look at the **other words** for **clues** to help you.
>
> Here is what we know based on the clues in the sentence:
>
> - Janice dressed differently
> - Some kids did not allow her to sit at their table
> - They whispered behind her back
>
> We know that the kids **never allowed her to sit at their lunch** table and that they **whispered behind her back**. If you put all these clues together, you can conclude that the other students were **mistreating** Janice by **excluding** her.
>
> Therefore, based on these context clues, *ostracized* means "excluded from the group."

323

Here's another example:

> **EXAMPLE 2**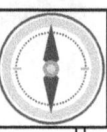
>
> Look at this next sentence:
>
> Louis's teacher was offended because after she called on him he gave a *flippant* response instead of a serious answer.
>
> If you did not know what the word *flippant* meant, you could look at the **other words** for **clues** to help you.
>
> Here is what we know based on the clues in the sentence:
>
> - Louis's teacher was offended
> - He gave a flippant response instead of a serious answer
>
> We know that Louis said something that **offended** his teacher. Another keyword in this sentence is the word **instead**. This means that **instead of a serious answer** Louis gave the **opposite** of a serious answer.
>
> Therefore, based on these context clues, *flippant* means "lacking respect or seriousness."

Multiple Meaning Words

Sometimes when we read words in a text, we encounter words that have **multiple meanings**.

Multiple meaning words are words that have **more than one definition** or meaning.

> **FOR EXAMPLE**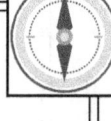
>
> The word **current** is a multiple meaning word. Here are the different definitions of *current*:
>
> CURRENT:
>
> 1. adj: happening or existing in the present time
>
>   Example: *It is important to keep up with current events so you know what's happening in the world.*
>
> 2. noun: the continuous movement of a body of water or air in a certain direction
>
>   Example: *The river's current was strong as we paddled down the rapids.*
>
> 3. noun: a flow of electricity
>
>   Example: *The electrical current was very weak in the house.*

Lesson 15.2 Context Clues and Multiple Meaning Words

Here are some other examples of words with multiple meanings:

Multiple Meaning Word	Definition #1	Definition #2	Definition #3
Buckle	noun: a metal or plastic device that connects one end of a belt to another	verb: to fasten or attach	verb: to bend or collapse from pressure or heat
Cabinet	noun: a piece of furniture used for storing things	noun: a group of people who give advice to a government leader	-
Channel	noun: a radio or television station	noun: a system used for sending something	noun: a long, narrow place where water flows
Doctor	noun: a person skilled in the science of medicine, dentistry, or one holding a PhD	verb: to change something in a way to trick or deceive	verb: to give medical treatment
Grave	noun: a hole in the ground for burying a dead body	adj: very serious	-
Hamper	noun: a large basket used for holding dirty clothes	verb: to slow the movement, action, or progress of	-
Plane	noun: a mode of transportation that has wings and an engine and can carry people and things in the air	noun: a flat or level surface that extends outward	noun: a level of though, development, or existence
Reservation	noun: an agreement to have something (such as a table, room, or seat) held for use at a later time	noun: a feeling of uncertainty or doubt	noun: an area of land kept separate for Native Americans to live an area of land set aside for animals to live for protection
Season	noun: one of the four periods in which a year is divided (winter, spring, summer, and fall)	noun: a particular period of time during the year	verb: to add spices to something to give it more flavor
Sentence	noun: a group words that expresses a statement, question, command, or wish	noun: the punishment given to someone by a court of law	verb: to officially state the punishment given by a court of law

From this chart you will notice that words with multiple meanings may have different **parts of speech**. A part of speech is a category of words that have the same grammatical properties. Some of the main parts of speech for words in the English language are: nouns, adjectives, verbs, and adverbs.

Part of Speech	Definition	Example
Noun	a person, place, thing, or idea	*Linda, New York City, toaster, happiness*
Adjective	a word that describes a noun or pronoun	*adventurous, young, red, intelligent*
Verb	an action or state of being	*run, is, sleep, become*
Adverb	a word that describes a verb, adjective, or other adverb	*quietly, extremely, carefully, well*

For example, in the chart above, *season* can be a **noun** or a **verb**.

Using Multiple Meaning Words Properly in Context

When you come across a **multiple meaning word** in a text, it is important to discern which meaning of the word is being used so you do not get confused.

You can once again turn to the **context clues** to clarify which meaning of the word is being used.

Let's take a look at the word *coach*. This word has several definitions:

COACH:
1. noun: a person who teaches and trains an athlete or performer
2. noun: a large bus with comfortable seating used for long trips
3. noun: the section on an airplane with the least expensive seats
4. verb: to teach or train someone in a specific area
5. verb: to give someone instructions on what to do or say in a certain situation

Since *coach* has so many definitions, you need to look at the **context clues** to figure out which definition of the word is being used:

The man was not happy that he had to sit in <u>coach</u> on the 24-hour flight to Australia.

In this sentence, the context clues **sit in** and **24-hour flight** help you see that *coach* means the least expensive seat on an airplane.

Let's look at another sentence using the word *coach*:

The lawyer needed to <u>coach</u> her witness so he would answer all the questions properly.

In this sentence, the context clues **so he would answer all the questions properly** help you see that the lawyer was giving the witness instructions on what to say.

Let's Review!
- When you come across an unfamiliar word in a text you can use context clues to help you define it.
- Context clues can also help you determine which definition of a multiple meaning word to use.

LESSON 15.3 THE WRITING PROCESS

Effective writers break the writing task down into steps to tackle one at a time. They allow a certain amount of room for messiness and mistakes in the early stages of writing but attempt to create a polished finished product in the end.

> **KEEP IN MIND . . .**
>
> If your writing process varies from the steps outlined below, that's okay—as long as you can produce a polished, organized text in the end. Some writers like to write part or all of the first draft before they go back to outline and organize. Others make a plan in the prewriting phase, only to change the plan when they're drafting. It is not uncommon for writers to compose the body of an essay before the introduction, or to change the thesis statement at the end to make it fit the essay they wrote rather than the one they intended to write.
>
> The point of teaching the writing process is not to force you to follow all the steps in order every time. The point is to give you a sense of the mental tasks involved in creating a well-written text. If you are drafting and something is not working, you will know you can bounce back to the prewriting stage and change your plan. If you are outlining and you end up fleshing out one of your points in complete sentences, you will realize you still need to go back to finish the rest of the plan before you continue drafting.
>
> In other words, it is fine to change the order of steps from the writing process,* or to jump around between them. Published writers do it all the time, and you can too.
>
> *But almost everyone really does benefit from saving the editing until the end.

The Writing Process

A writer goes through several discrete steps to transform an idea into a polished text. This series of steps is called the **writing process**. Individual writers' processes may vary somewhat, but most writers roughly follow the steps below.

Prewriting is making a plan for writing. Prewriting may include brainstorming, free writing, outlining, or mind mapping. The prewriting process can be messy and include errors. Note that if a writing task requires research, the prewriting process is longer because you need to find, read, and organize source materials.

Writing/Drafting is getting the bulk of the text down on the page in complete sentences. Although most writers find drafting difficult, two things can make it easier: 1) prewriting to make a clear plan, and 2) avoiding perfectionism. Drafting is about moving ideas from the mind to the page, even if they do not sound right or the writer is not sure how to spell a word. For writing tasks that involve research, drafting also involves making notes about where the information came from.

Conferencing/Revising is making improvements to the content and structure of a draft. Revising may involve moving ideas around, adding information to flesh out a point, removing chunks of text that are redundant or off-topic, and strengthening the thesis statement. Revising may also mean improving readability by altering sentence structure, smoothing transitions, and improving word choice.

Editing is fixing errors in spelling, grammar, and punctuation. Many writers feel the urge to do this throughout the writing process, but it saves time to wait until the end. There is no point perfecting the grammar and spelling in a sentence that is going to get cut later.

For research projects, you also need to craft **citations,** or notes that tell readers where you got your information. If you noted this information while working on your prewriting and first draft, all you need to do now is format it correctly. (If you did not make notes as you worked, you will have to search laboriously through all your research materials again.) If you are using MLA or APA styles, citations are included in parentheses at the ends of sentences. If you are using Chicago style, citations appear in footnotes or endnotes.

Prewriting Techniques

Prewriting encompasses a wide variety of tasks that happen before you start writing. Many new writers skip or skimp on this step, perhaps because a writer's prewriting efforts are not clearly visible in the final product. But writers who spend time gathering and organizing information tend to produce more polished work.

Thinking silently is a valid form of prewriting. So is telling someone about what you are planning to write. For very short pieces based on your prior knowledge, it may be enough to use these—but most long writing tasks go better if you also use some or all of the strategies below.

Gathering Information

- **Conducting research** involves looking for information in books, articles, websites, and other sources. Internet research is almost always necessary, but do not overlook the benefits of a trip to a library, where you can find in-depth printed sources and also get help from research librarians.
- **Brainstorming** is making a list of short phrases or sentences related to the topic. Brainstorming works best if you literally write down every idea that comes to mind, whether or not you think you can use it. This frees up your mind to find unconscious associations and insights.
- **Free writing** is writing whatever comes to mind about your topic in sentences and paragraphs. Free writing goes fast and works best if you avoid judging your ideas as you go.

Organizing information

- **Mind mapping** arranges ideas into an associative structure. Write your topic, main idea, or argument in a circle in the middle of the page. Then draw lines and make additional circles for supporting points and details. You can combine this step with brainstorming to make a big mess of ideas, some of which you later cross out if you decide not to use them. Or you can do this after brainstorming, using the ideas from your brainstormed list to fill in the bubbles.

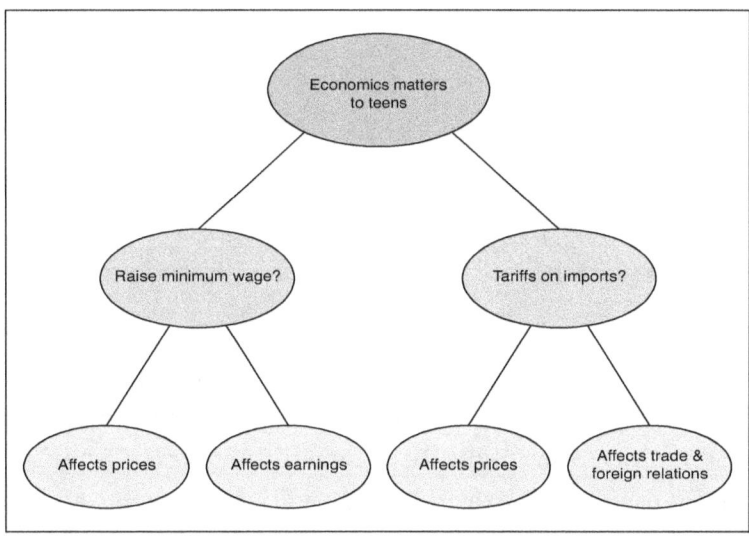

- **Outlining** arranges ideas into a linear structure. It starts with an introduction, includes supporting points and details to back them up, and ends with a conclusion. Traditionally, an outline uses Roman numerals for main ideas and letters for minor ideas.

Example:
I. Introduction - Economics should be a required subject in high school because it affects political and social issues that matter to students.
II. Domestic Issues - Minimum wage
   a. How do people decide if the minimum wage should be raised?
   b. They need to know how changes to the minimum wage affect workers, businesses, and prices.
III. Foreign Issues - Tariffs
   a. How do people decide if they favor taxes on imports?
   b. They need to know how tariffs affect prices and trade.
IV. Conclusion – These issues affect how much money high school graduates can earn and what they can afford to buy.

Paragraph Organization

Paragraphs need to have a clear, coherent organization. Whether you are providing information, arguing a point, or entertaining the reader, the ultimate goal is to make it easy for people to follow your thoughts.

Introductions

The opening of a text must hook the reader's interest, provide necessary background information on the topic, and state the main point. In an academic essay, all of this typically happens in a single paragraph. For instance, an analytical paper on the theme of unrequited love in a novel might start with a stark statement about love, a few sentences identifying the title and author of the work under discussion, and a thesis statement about the author's apparently bleak outlook on love.

Body Paragraphs

In informational and persuasive writing, body paragraphs should typically do three things:

1. Make a point.
2. Illustrate the point with facts, quotations, or examples.
3. Explain how this evidence relates to the point.

Body paragraphs need to stay on topic. That is, the point needs to relate clearly to the thesis statement or main idea. For example, in an analytical paper about unrequited love in a novel, each body paragraph should say something different about the author's bleak outlook on love. Each paragraph might focus on a different character's struggles with love, presenting evidence in the form of an example or quotation from the story and explaining what it suggests about the author's outlook. When you present evidence like this, you must introduce it clearly, stating where it came from in the book. Don't assume readers understand exactly what it has to do with your main point; spell it out for them with a clear explanation.

The structure above is useful in most academic writing situations, but sometimes you need to use other structures:

Chronological – Describe how events happen in order.
Sequential – Present a series of steps.
Descriptive – Describe a topic in a coherent spatial order, e.g. from top to bottom.
Cause/Effect – Present an action and its results.
Compare/Contrast – Describe the similarities and differences between two or more topics.

Conclusions

Like introductions, conclusions have a unique structure. A conclusion restates the thesis and main points in different words and, ideally, adds a bit more. For instance, it may take a broader outlook on the topic, giving readers a sense of why it matters or how the main point affects the world. A text should end with a sentence or two that brings the ideas together and makes the piece feel finished. This can be a question, a quotation, a philosophical statement, an intense image, or a request that readers take action.

Let's Review!

- The writing process includes prewriting, drafting, revision, and editing.
- For projects that involve research, writers must include the creation of citations within the writing process.
- Effective writers spend time gathering and organizing information during the prewriting stage.
- Writers must organize paragraphs coherently so that readers can follow their thoughts.

Chapter 15 Vocabulary Acquisition Practice Quiz

1. Select the word from the following sentence that has more than one meaning.

   It was a grave situation, and many people had given up hope.

   A. Hope
   B. Grave
   C. People
   D. Situation

2. Select the word from the following sentence that has more than one meaning.

   The teacher was content with the quality of her students' work on their math exam.

   A. Teacher
   B. Content
   C. Quality
   D. Math

3. Select the correct definition of the underlined word that has multiple meanings in the sentence.

   Sandra needed to crop the photograph to make it fit into the frame.

   A. To cut off a part of
   B. To bite off and eat the tops of
   C. To produce or make a plant grow
   D. To come on or appear unexpectedly

4. Which of the following prefixes means incorrect?

   A. un-
   B. non-
   C. mis-
   D. over-

5. Which of the following suffixes means capable of?

   A. -ful
   B. -tion
   C. -ous
   D. -ible

6. Which of the following root words means to break?

   A. ject
   B. dict
   C. rupt
   D. struct

Chapter 15 Vocabulary Acquisition Practice Quiz – Answer Key

1. **B.** The word "grave" has more than one meaning. **See Lesson: Context Clues and Multiple Meaning Words.**

2. **B.** The word "content" has more than one meaning. **See Lesson: Context Clues and Multiple Meaning Words.**

3. **A.** The meaning of <u>crop</u> in the context of this sentence is "to cut off a part of." **See Lesson: Context Clues and Multiple Meaning Words.**

4. **C.** The prefix that means "incorrect" is *mis*. **See Lesson: Root Words, Prefixes, and Suffixes.**

5. **D.** The suffix that means "capable of" is *ible*. **See Lesson: Root Words, Prefixes, and Suffixes.**

6. **C.** The root that means "to break" is *rupt*. **See Lesson: Root Words, Prefixes, and Suffixes.**

SECTION V
FULL-LENGTH
PRACTICE EXAMS

TEAS Practice Exam 1 Answer Sheet

Reading

1. _____   24. _____
2. _____   25. _____
3. _____   26. _____
4. _____   27. _____
5. _____   28. _____
6. _____   29. _____
7. _____   30. _____
8. _____   31. _____
9. _____   32. _____
10. _____ 33. _____
11. _____ 34. _____
12. _____ 35. _____
13. _____ 36. _____
14. _____ 37. _____
15. _____ 38. _____
16. _____ 39. _____
17. _____ 40. _____
18. _____ 41. _____
19. _____ 42. _____
20. _____ 43. _____
21. _____ 44. _____
22. _____ 45. _____
23. _____

Mathematics

1. _____   20. _____
2. _____   21. _____
3. _____   22. _____
4. _____   23. _____
5. _____   24. _____
6. _____   25. _____
7. _____   26. _____
8. _____   27. _____
9. _____   28. _____
10. _____ 29. _____
11. _____ 30. _____
12. _____ 31. _____
13. _____ 32. _____
14. _____ 33. _____
15. _____ 34. _____
16. _____ 35. _____
17. _____ 36. _____
18. _____ 37. _____
19. _____ 38. _____

Science

1. _____   26. _____
2. _____   27. _____
3. _____   28. _____
4. _____   29. _____
5. _____   30. _____
6. _____   31. _____
7. _____   32. _____
8. _____   33. _____
9. _____   34. _____
10. _____ 35. _____
11. _____ 36. _____
12. _____ 37. _____
13. _____ 38. _____
14. _____ 39. _____
15. _____ 40. _____
16. _____ 41. _____
17. _____ 42. _____
18. _____ 43. _____
19. _____ 44. _____
20. _____ 45. _____
21. _____ 46. _____
22. _____ 47. _____
23. _____ 48. _____
24. _____ 49. _____
25. _____ 50. _____

English and Language Usage

1. _____   20. _____
2. _____   21. _____
3. _____   22. _____
4. _____   23. _____
5. _____   24. _____
6. _____   25. _____
7. _____   26. _____
8. _____   27. _____
9. _____   28. _____
10. _____ 29. _____
11. _____ 30. _____
12. _____ 31. _____
13. _____ 32. _____
14. _____ 33. _____
15. _____ 34. _____
16. _____ 35. _____
17. _____ 36. _____
18. _____ 37. _____
19. _____

TEAS Practice Exam 1

Section I. Reading

Please read the text below and answer questions 1-5.

A global temperature change of a few degrees is more significant than it may seem at first glance. This is not merely a change in weather in any one location. Rather, it is an average change in temperatures around the entire surface of the planet. It takes a vast amount of heat energy to warm every part of our world—including oceans, air, and land—by even a tiny measurable amount. Moreover, relatively small changes in the earth's surface temperatures have historically caused enormous changes in climate. In the last ice age 20,000 years ago, when much of the northern hemisphere was buried under huge sheets of ice, mean global temperatures were only about five degrees Celsius lower than they are now. Scientists predict a temperature rise of two to six degrees Celsius by 2100. What if this causes similarly drastic changes to the world we call home?

1. Which sentence is the topic sentence?
   A. What if this causes similarly drastic changes to the world we call home?
   B. A global temperature change of a few degrees is more significant than it may seem at first glance.
   C. It takes a vast amount of heat energy to warm every part of our world—including oceans, air, and land—by even a tiny measurable amount.
   D. In the last ice age 20,000 years ago, when much of the northern hemisphere was buried under huge sheets of ice, mean global temperatures were only about five degrees Celsius lower than they are now.

2. In the paragraph global temperature change is:
   A. the topic.
   B. the main idea.
   C. a supporting detail.
   D. the topic sentence.

3. Which sentence summarizes the main idea of the paragraph?
   A. A small change in weather at any one location is a serious problem.
   B. The author is manipulating facts to make global warming sound scary.
   C. People should be concerned by even minor global temperature change.
   D. It takes an enormous amount of energy to warm the earth even a little.

4. What function does the information about temperature differences in the last ice age play in the paragraph?

   A. Topic
   B. Opinion
   C. Main idea
   D. Supporting detail

5. Which sentence would *best* function as a supporting detail in this paragraph?

   A. Electricity and heat production create one quarter of all carbon emissions globally.
   B. The world was only about one degree cooler during the Little Ice Age from 1700 to 1850.
   C. China has surpassed the United States as the single largest producer of carbon emissions.
   D. Methane emissions are, in some ways, more concerning than carbon dioxide emissions.

Please read the text below and answer questions 6-8.

Publishers typically pay male authors slightly higher advances than female authors. They also price men's books higher, which results in higher royalty payments for male creators. Male authors are more likely than female authors to win literary awards, receive speaking invitations, and gain attention from major reviewers, all of which drive sales.

6. Which phrase best describes the topic of the group of sentences above?

   A. An analysis of literary award winners
   B. Gender differences in author income
   C. A description of a book reviewer's day
   D. Resources for increasing author income

7. Which of the following sentences would best function as a topic sentence to unite the information above?

   A. Gender differences in author pay primarily result from the fact that male authors appeal to a broader audience base.
   B. Although writers do not have fixed salaries, entrenched stereotyping results in a substantial pay gap between male and female authors.
   C. Authors can access a wide variety of income streams including fees for new work, royalties, speaking fees for public appearances, and more.
   D. Substantial evidence suggests that female authors simply do not produce work with the same impressive visionary quality as their greatest male peers.

8. Which sentence provides another supporting detail to address the topic of the sentences above?

   A. Many young people dream of being famous writers, but authors face a difficult path to financial success with their work.
   B. Many female authors have recently come forward with alarming stories of sexual harassment and assault by powerful members of their industry.
   C. Very few contemporary authors are able to earn a living solely off their published works, so most rely on other sources of income to pay the bills.
   D. Numerous studies show that both publishers and readers are more likely to buy the same book if the author has a male name rather than a female name.

Read the following sentence and answer questions 9-10.

Numerous robotic missions to Mars have revealed tantalizing evidence of a planet that may once have been capable of supporting life.

9. Imagine this sentence is a *supporting detail* in a well-developed paragraph. Which of the following sentences would best function as a *topic sentence*?

    A. Venus is an intensely hot planet surrounded by clouds full of drops of sulfuric acid.

    B. Of all the destinations within human reach, Mars is the planet most similar to Earth.

    C. Liquid water—a necessary ingredient of life—may once have flowed on the planet's surface.

    D. Space research is a costly, frivolous exercise that brings no clear benefit to people on Earth.

10. Imagine this sentence is the *topic sentence* of a well-developed paragraph. Which of the following sentences would best function as a *supporting detail*?

    A. Of all the destinations within human reach, Mars is the planet most similar to Earth.

    B. Venus is an intensely hot planet surrounded by clouds full of drops of sulfuric acid.

    C. Space research is a costly, frivolous exercise that brings no clear benefit to people on Earth.

    D. Liquid water—a necessary ingredient of life—may once have flowed on the planet's surface.

Read the paragraph below and answer questions 11-15.

Until about 1850, few people living in temperate climates had ever had the opportunity to taste a banana. Only after the invention of the steamship could importers and exporters reliably transport this fruit to North America and Europe. Railways and refrigeration were two other vital components in the development of the banana trade. Today, bananas are a major export in several Central and South American countries as well as the Philippines. Around the world, people in climates that cannot support banana production now have access to plentiful inexpensive bananas.

11. Which sentence provides an effective summary of the text above?

    A. The author of this paragraph really likes bananas and researched them thoroughly.

    B. Shipping and refrigeration technology helped bananas become a major export crop.

    C. This paragraph should include more detail about the development of the banana trade.

    D. Before 1850, most Americans and Europeans had never had the opportunity to taste a banana.

12. Read the following summary of the paragraph.

According to John K. Miller, the invention of shipping and refrigeration technology helped bananas become a major export crop. The banana trade is an important source of income for many countries around the world, and consumers can buy bananas easily even in places where bananas do not grow.

What makes this summary effective?

A. It makes a judgment on the original text without being unfair.

B. It restates the ideas of the original text in completely new words.

C. It rearranges the ideas of the original text into a different sequence.

D. It highlights ideas from the original text that were not stated explicitly.

13. Which summary sentence retains language too close to the original text?

A. The author of this paragraph really likes bananas and researched them thoroughly.

B. This paragraph should include more detail about the development of the banana trade.

C. Before 1850, most Americans and Europeans had never had the opportunity to taste a banana.

D. The technological developments of the Industrial Revolution helped create a global banana trade.

14. Which summary sentence fails to be objective?

A. The author of this paragraph really likes bananas and researched them thoroughly.

B. This paragraph should include more detail about the development of the banana trade.

C. Before 1850, most Americans and Europeans had never had the opportunity to taste a banana.

D. The technological developments of the Industrial Revolution helped create a global banana trade.

15. Read the following sentence.

Nobody would eat bananas today if modern shipping and refrigeration technology had never been invented.

Why doesn't this sentence belong in a summary of the paragraph?

A. It concerns supporting details and not main ideas.

B. It adheres too closely to the original author's language.

C. It fails to make a clear judgment about the original text.

D. It does not accurately state an idea from the original text.

Read the following passages and answer questions 16-21.

As a parent, I find television and movie rating systems unhelpful. Ratings systems are not human. Their scores are based on numbers: how many bad words, how many gory scenes. To me, that makes no sense. Nobody else knows my kids like I do, so nobody else can say what's okay for them to watch.

In my experience, the content a government organization rates as PG or PG-13 may or may not be appropriate for my 9-, 14-, and 16-year-olds. My youngest is quite mature for his age, and I'm fine with him hearing a bad word or two as a part of a meaningful story.

Violence concerns me more. I won't let even my 16-year-old watch frivolous violence or horror. But I don't shelter him from realistic violence. My little guy still has to stay out of the room for the bloody stuff. But eventually, kids need to know what's out there.

16. **The primary purpose of this passage is to:**
    A. decide.
    B. inform.
    C. persuade.
    D. entertain.

17. **The author of this passage would be most likely to agree that:**
    A. kids should not watch television or movies at all until they are in their teens.
    B. government rating systems should have more levels to make them more useful.
    C. it is never appropriate to prevent any human being from watching any show or movie.
    D. another parent should have the right to let her own kids watch extremely violent movies.

18. **The author of this passage would be likely to support an effort to:**
    A. create a government system to recommend ages for reading children's books.
    B. prevent kids from attending movies in the theater without their parents' presence.
    C. provide parents more information about the content of children's shows and movies.
    D. change the age for watching PG-13 movies down to 10 because today's kids are more savvy.

19. **What is the most likely reason for the author's decision to include the phrase "as a parent" at the beginning?**
    A. This phrase provides a reason to support her opinion.
    B. She is implying that non-parents cannot know what kids need.
    C. This phrase provides a transition from the points she made earlier.
    D. She is establishing herself as a knowledgeable source on this topic.

20. **When the author says ratings systems are "based on numbers," she is developing the point that:**
    A. logic and reasoning have no place in parenting.
    B. the only numbers that matter are her children's ages.
    C. some decisions should be made on a case-by-case basis.
    D. she is not good enough at math to rely on ratings systems.

21. Which of the following would serve as a suitable title to the above passage? (select all that apply)

   A. *My Mature Son*
   B. *Movie Ratings Systems are Unhelpful*
   C. *Sheltering Children from Movie Violence*
   D. *Improving Movie Rating Systems*
   E. *The Problem with Movie Ratings*

22. What is the most likely purpose of a popular science book describing recent advances in genetics?

   A. To decide
   B. To inform
   C. To persuade
   D. To entertain

Study the following label and answer questions 23-27.

Nutrition Facts

Serving Size 20 crackers (38g)
Servings Per Container 5

Amount Per Serving

Calories 150   Calories from Fat 45

	% Daily Value*
Total Fat 9g	12%
Saturated Fat 4g	20%
Trans Fat 0g	
Cholesterol 0mg	0%
Sodium 160mg	7%
Total Carbohydrate 16g	6%
Dietary Fiber Less than 1g	2%
Sugars Less than 1g	0%
Protein 1g	
Vitamin D	0%
Calcium	5%
Iron	20%
Potassium	8%

* Percent Daily Values are based on a 2,000 calorie diet. Your Daily Values may be higher or lower depending on your calorie needs:

		Calories:	2,000	2,500
Total Fat		Less than	65g	80g
Saturated Fat		Less than	20g	25g
Cholesterol		Less than	300mg	300mg
Sodium		Less than	2,400mg	2,400mg
Total Carbohydrate			300g	375g
Dietary Fiber			25g	30g

23. How many calories are in one serving of this product?
    A. 5
    B. 20
    C. 150
    D. 3750

24. Germain ate 60 crackers out of this box. How many servings did he consume?
    A. 1
    B. 3
    C. 5
    D. 10

25. The product in this package is considered high in:
    A. sodium.
    B. trans fat.
    C. cholesterol.
    D. saturated fat.

26. Fatima is attempting to confine her diet to products low in sodium. How much of this product should she eat?
    A. None; the product is not low in sodium.
    B. One serving; the amount of sodium is reasonable.
    C. The whole package; the contents are appropriate for a low-sodium diet.
    D. Less than three servings; she needs to keep her sodium intake below 20%.

27. The product in this package is a good source of:
    A. iron.
    B. fiber.
    C. calcium.
    D. vitamin D.

Read the following passage and answer questions 28-29.

Overworked public school teachers are required by law to spend extra time implementing Individual Educational Plans for students with learning and attention challenges. This shortchanges children who are actually engaged in their education by depriving them of an equal amount of individualized attention.

28. What assumption behind this passage reflects negative stereotypical thinking?
    A. Public school teachers are generally overworked and underpaid.
    B. Students with learning disabilities are not engaged in their education.
    C. Laws require teachers to provide accommodations to certain students.
    D. Teachers have a finite amount of attention to divide between students.

29. The above argument is invalid because the author:
    A. suggests that some students do not need as much attention because they learn the material more quickly.
    B. uses derogatory and disrespectful word choice to describe people who think, learn, and process information differently.
    C. describes public school teachers in a negative way that makes it seem as though they have no interest in helping students.
    D. professes an interest in equality for all students while simultaneously suggesting some students are more worthy than others.

30. Which statement is an opinion?
    A. Freshman Anita Jones states that excessive homework requirements cause her undue stress.
    B. Students reported symptoms such as headaches, anxiety attacks, and difficulty sleeping.
    C. Excessive homework requirements causes students undue stress and harm their quality of life.
    D. Students who do homework more than three hours per day show elevated cortisol levels compared to students who do no homework.

Read the following passage and answer questions 31-35.

A growing focus on STEM—science, technology, engineering, and math—has brought funding and excitement for these subjects into schools. Meanwhile, the push for standardized testing is requiring teachers to devote a large proportion of class time to reading and math test preparation. One consequence of these dual trends is that schools are skimping on social studies instruction.

Mindful world citizens need, at a minimum, a general awareness of foreign cultures, a passing familiarity with geography, and a basic understanding of history. If you're not sure your child's school is instilling these basic foundations of knowledge, you need to support your kids' learning yourself. Daunting as this may sound, it doesn't need to take an inordinate amount of time and effort.

A good first step is to keep a globe or world map in a prominent location in your home. Whenever possible, refer to this resource in conversation. For instance, if your child is interested in a particular animal, point out where in the world it lives. If older children ask questions about the news, show them where current events are happening. If your budget allows it, keep a good children's atlas handy too. This will allow your conversations to go into greater depth if your children show interest.

Children have ever-greater access to high-quality fiction about people and cultures around the world. If you're reading together about a foreign place or time—or if you see your older child picking up a historical or multicultural book—take a moment to find a children's nonfiction book on the same subject. If you don't have time to do this research during a family library trip, most libraries allow patrons to browse and order books online.

31. This article is written for:
    A. parents.   C. teachers.
    B. children.   D. policymakers.

32. The author of this article assumes that:
    A. parents are eager to support their children's education.
    B. parents have unlimited time to support their kids' education.
    C. teachers do not like helping children learn about social studies.
    D. teachers all prefer STEM subjects and reading over social studies.

33. A careful reader of this article can infer that the author wants children to grow up to become:
    A. STEM employees.
    B. successful teachers.
    C. multicultural patrons.
    D. mindful world citizens.

34. Which conclusion is not supported by the article?
    A. The author thinks teachers have limited time and energy.
    B. The author thinks people benefit from understanding history.
    C. The author thinks many parents read regularly with their kids.
    D. The author thinks STEM instruction is a waste of children's time.

35. Which sentence from the article shows the author's awareness that modern parents are often busy people?

    A. A good first step is to keep a globe or world map in a prominent location in your home.

    B. If you don't have time to do this research during a family library trip, most libraries allow patrons to browse and order books online.

    C. If you're not sure your child's school is instilling these basic foundations of knowledge, you need to support your kids' learning yourself.

    D. A growing focus on STEM—science, technology, engineering, and math—has brought funding and excitement for these subjects into schools.

36. Which of the following is an example of a secondary source?

    A. A diary of a politician
    B. A biography of a politician
    C. A study guide on a politician's speech
    D. An encyclopedia article about a politician

37. Which of the following is not a primary source on Charles Darwin?

    A. Charles Darwin's field notes from his travels
    B. *On the Origin of Species* by Charles Darwin
    C. An online database of Charles Darwin's writings
    D. A blog post about Charles Darwin's contributions

Read the following passage and answer questions 38-40.

There is inherent risk associated with the use of Rip Gym facilities. Although all Rip Gym customers sign a Risk Acknowledgment and Consent Form before gaining access to our grounds and equipment, litigation remains a possibility if customers suffer injuries due to negligence. Negligence complaints may include either staff mistakes or avoidable problems with equipment and facilities. It is therefore imperative that all Rip Gym employees follow the Safety Protocol in the event of a customer complaint.

Reports of Unsafe Equipment and Environs

Rip Gym employees must always respond promptly and seriously to any customer report of a hazard in our equipment or facilities, even if the employee judges the complaint frivolous. **Customers may not use rooms or equipment that have been reported unsafe until the following steps have been taken, in order, to confirm and/or resolve the problem.**

1. Place "Warning," "Out of Order," or "Off Limits" signs in the affected area or on the affected equipment, as appropriate. **Always follow this step first, before handling paperwork or attempting to resolve the reported problem.**

2. Fill out a Hazard Complaint Form. Include the name of the customer making the complaint and the exact wording of the problems being reported.

3. Visually check the area or equipment in question to verify the problem.

   a) If the report appears to be **accurate** and a resolution is necessary, proceed to step 4.

   b) If the report appears to be **inaccurate**, consult the manager on duty.

4. Determine whether you are qualified to correct the problem. Problems **all** employees are qualified to correct are listed on page 12 of the Employee Handbook.

   a) Employees who have **not** undergone training for equipment repair and maintenance must....

38. This passage is best described as a(n):

    A. narrative text.
    B. technical text.
    C. expository text.
    D. persuasive text.

39. Which term best describes the structure of the opening paragraph?

    A. Sequence
    B. Description
    C. Problem-solution
    D. Compare/Contrast

40. Which term best describes the structure of the section under the subheading "Reports of Unsafe Equipment and Environs"?

    A. Sequence
    B. Description
    C. Cause/effect
    D. Compare/contrast

41. **What is the difference between expository and technical writing?**

    A. Expository writing is always fiction, and technical writing is always nonfiction.
    B. Expository writing is often academic, and technical writing is usually practical.
    C. Expository writing is meant to persuade, and technical writing is meant to inform.
    D. Expository writing is dry and impersonal, and technical writing is often entertaining.

The bar graph below provides information about book sales for a book called *The Comings*, which is the first book in a trilogy. Study the image and answer questions 42-43.

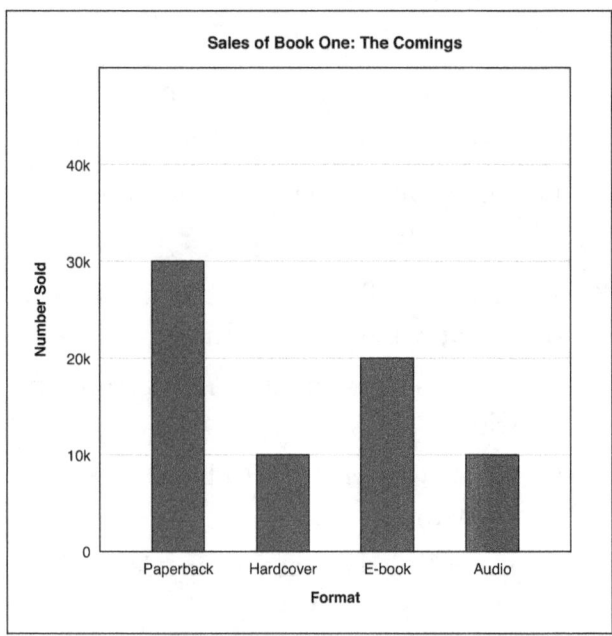

42. Which type of book has sold the most copies?

    A. E-book   C. Paperback
    B. Hardcover   D. Audio book

43. The marketing director for *The Comings* wants to use a different strategy for publishing book two in the series. Which argument does the bar graph *best* support?

   A. The first book in the trilogy has only sold 10,000 copies.

   B. The second book in the trilogy should not be released in hardcover.

   C. The second book in the trilogy should only be released as an e-book.

   D. The second and third books in the trilogy should be combined into one.

The diagram below provides information about the parts of a neuron (brain cell). Study the image and answer questions 44-45.

45. Which question can be answered by consulting this diagram?

   A. Why does the brain contain neurons?

   B. Where is a nucleus located in a neuron?

   C. What is the function of a myelin sheath?

   D. How does a neuron interact with other cells?

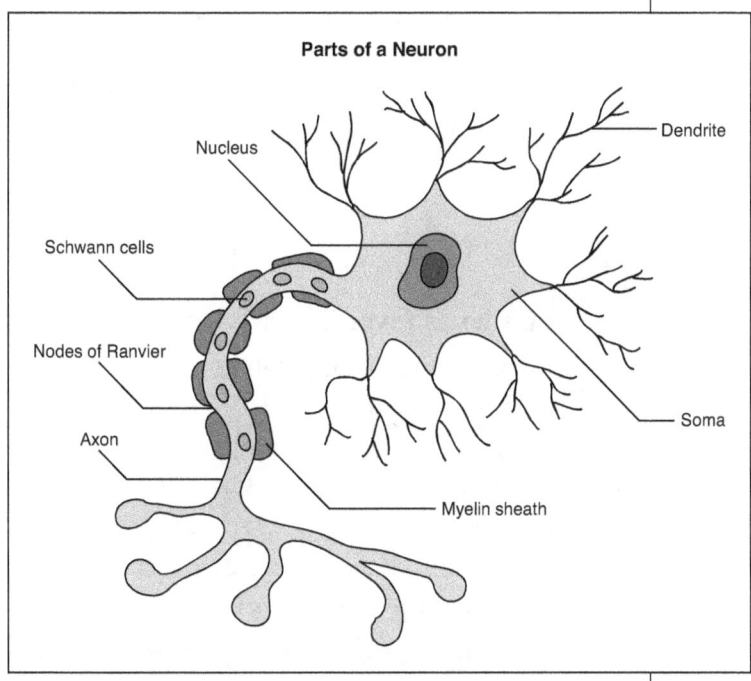

44. What is the small, root-like part of the neuron on the top right called?

   A. Axon
   B. Nucleus
   C. Dendrite
   D. Myelin sheath

Section II. Mathematics

1. The graph shows the amount of rainfall in inches for 12 days. Which statement is true for the line graph?

   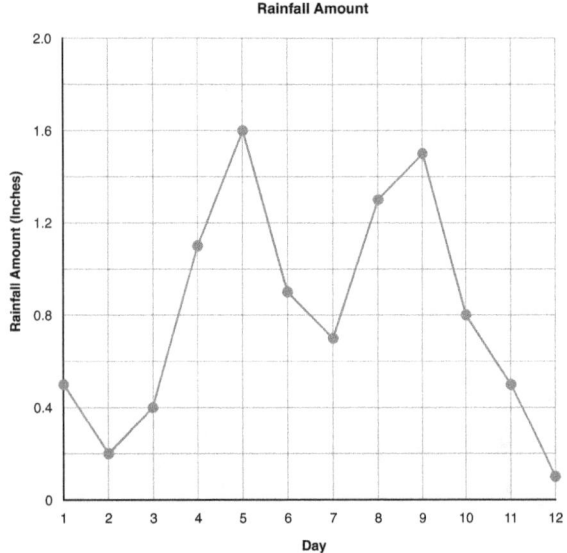

   A. It rained more than 1.5 inches more than half of the days.
   B. The average amount of rainfall was 1 inch.
   C. It rained every day.
   D. The amount of rainfall steadily increased throughout the days.

2. Megan served a dinner party while at work and earned a 22% tip from the customers. If Megan received $16.50 as her tip, what was the customer's bill?

   A. $66.75
   B. $363
   C. $75
   D. $82.50

3. The number 20 is approximately 15% of what value?

   A. 133
   B. 120
   C. 140
   D. 127

4. Convert 2.5 miles to feet. (Note: 1 mile is equal to 5,280 feet).

   A. 2,112 feet
   B. 2,640 feet
   C. 10,560 feet
   D. 13,200 feet

5. A doctor writes a prescription for 0.5 liters of liquid medicine to a patient. How many milliliters (mL) will the medicine bottle be filled with?

   A. 500 mL
   B. 5 mL
   C. 5,000 mL
   D. 50 mL

6. Perform the operation.

   $(8x^2 - 6x - 3) - (4x^2 - 5x + 4)$

   A. $4x^2 - 11x - 7$
   B. $4x^2 - 11x + 1$
   C. $4x^2 - x - 7$
   D. $4x^2 - x + 1$

7. Convert $\frac{1}{8}$ to a decimal. Round to the nearest hundredth.

   A. 0.18
   B. 0.13
   C. 0.018
   D. 0.12

8. A patient's fever is 102°F. Convert the temperature to the Celsius scale. (Note: °C = $\frac{5}{9}$(°F − 32)).

   A. 39°C
   B. 25°C
   C. 24°C
   D. 18°C

9. A pizza shop sells individual pizza slices throughout the day in addition to whole pizza orders. The shop sells $\frac{3}{8}$ of a cheese pizza, $\frac{3}{8}$ of a pepperoni pizza, and $\frac{2}{5}$ of a specialty pizza. How many pizzas did they sell in individual slices?

   A. $1\frac{1}{4}$
   B. $1\frac{3}{20}$
   C. $\frac{8}{21}$
   D. $1\frac{1}{2}$

10. What is 32 out of 160 as a percent?

    A. 12%   C. 50%

    B. 20%   D. 22%

11. Two friends got the same percentage of math questions right on their tests. One friend got 96 questions correct out of 120 questions. If the second friend took an exam with only 75 questions, how many did she answer correctly?

    A. 56   C. 60

    B. 63   D. 58

12. Solve the equation for the unknown.

    $4x + 3 = 8$

    A. -2 C. $\frac{5}{4}$

    B. $-\frac{5}{4}$ D. 2

13. $\frac{4}{5} \times \frac{1}{5}$

    A. $\frac{4}{25}$ C. $\frac{3}{5}$

    B. $\frac{2}{5}$ D. $\frac{16}{25}$

14. A yield sign in the shape of a triangle has a base length of 90 centimeters and a height of 80 centimeters. What is the area in square centimeters?

    (Note: $A = bh/2$).

    A. 1,800   C. 5,400

    B. 3,600   D. 7,200

15. Trisha put $1800 down on a new car and paid $375 a month for 6 years. How much did Trisha spend in total for her car?

    A. $28,800   C. $27,000

    B. $4,050   D. $25,200

16. A nurse provides 0.25 liters of fluid to a recovering patient every 4 hours. The doctor wants to restrict the fluid intake and says to stop it after 1,500 milliliters, and then the doctor will check on the patient. How many times will the patient receive fluid before the doctor checks on him?

    A. 5   C. 3

    B. 6   D. 8

17. Change 0.89 to a fraction.

    A. $\frac{9}{10}$ C. $\frac{8}{10}$

    B. $\frac{89}{100}$ D. $\frac{45}{100}$

18. If $5 - x \leq 2$, then

    A. $x \geq 7$ C. $x \geq 3$

    B. $x \geq -7$ D. $x \geq -3$

19. $\frac{2}{7} + \frac{1}{10}$

    A. $\frac{27}{70}$ C. $\frac{3}{8}$

    B. $\frac{21}{70}$ D. $\frac{3}{17}$

20. A circular dinner plate has a diameter of 13 inches. A ring is placed along the edge of the plate. Find the circumference of the ring in inches. Use 3.14 for π.

    A. 31.4   C. 62.8

    B. 40.82   D. 81.64

21. $\frac{3}{10} \times \frac{1}{7}$

    A. $\frac{3}{70}$ C. $\frac{2}{7}$

    B. $\frac{3}{17}$ D. $\frac{2}{3}$

22. Solve the equation for the unknown.

    $a - 10 = -20$

    A. -30 C. 2

    B. -10 D. 200

23. The following circle graph shows what a family spends their income on each month. If the family earns $6,500 a month, how much money are they spending on their bills?

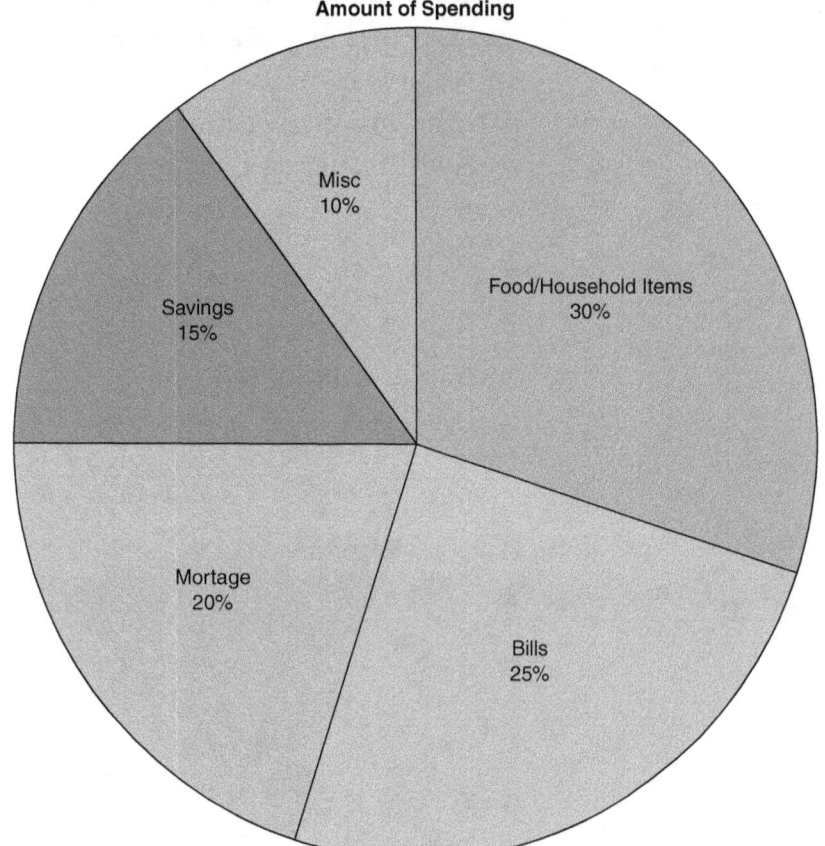

A. $975
B. $1,950
C. $1,300
D. $1,625

24. A right triangular prism has a triangular base with legs of 5 centimeters and 12 centimeters and a hypotenuse of 13 centimeters. What is the surface area in square centimeters if the height is 2 centimeters?

A. 60
B. 120
C. 180
D. 240

25. A candy shop charges $0.50 a piece, knowing it costs 22 cents to make. The shop also has other costs to the business that total $4,200 a month. Select the equation that would represent how many pieces of candy (C) the shop would make if the candy shop were to break even in operational costs for a month.

A. $0.22C - $4,200 = $0
B. $0.28C + $4,200 = $0
C. $0.28C - $4,200 = $0
D. $0.50C - $4,200 = $0

26. Students were surveyed about their favorite pet and the bar graph shows the results. Select the best statement for the bar graph.

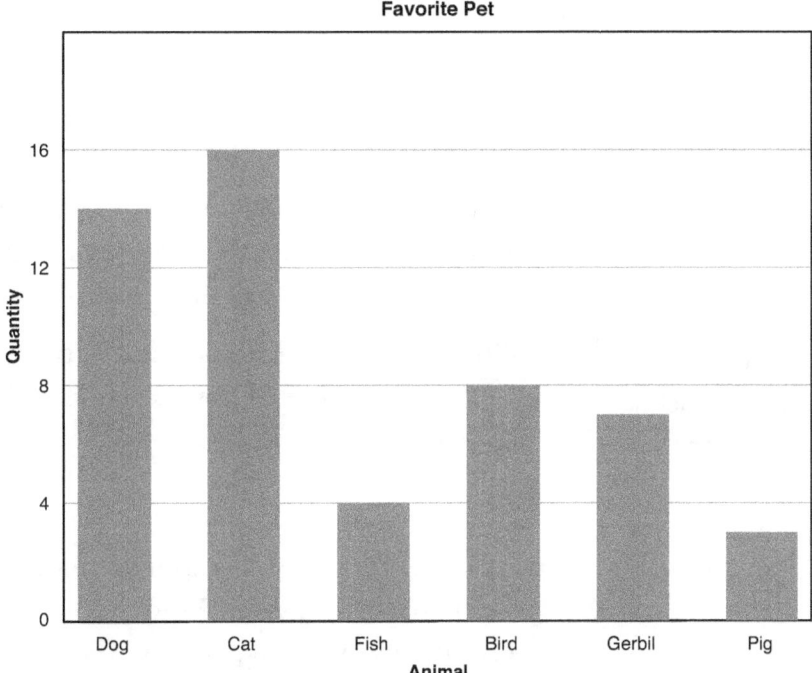

A. The most number of students consider dogs their favorite pet.

B. The total number of students who prefer fish and pigs is equal to the number of students who prefer gerbils.

C. The total number of students who prefer fish and pigs is equal to the number of students who prefer birds.

D. Fish are the least preferred pet among the students surveyed.

27. For a recent mending a seamstress used buttons from two seperate boxes. After completing the job she had $\frac{3}{5}$ of a box of buttons left from one box, while she used $\frac{1}{4}$ of the other box. If both boxes contained 200 buttons each when they were originally bought, how many buttons did the seamstress use for her recent mending?

   A. 120   C. 225
   B. 130   D. 90

28. A doctor writes a prescription for his patient for 200 milligrams (mg), but the pharmacy technician only has the medicine available in grams. How many grams (g) will the pharmacy technician need to fill the order?

   A. 20   C. 0.2
   B. 2   D. 0.02

29. Solve for the value of y when x = 3.
   $y = (x^2 + 4) - 2$

   A. 11   C. 15
   B. 8   D. 10

30. $\frac{3}{4} \div \frac{1}{2}$

   A. $\frac{1}{4}$　　　　C. $1\frac{1}{5}$

   B. $\frac{3}{8}$　　　　D. $1\frac{1}{2}$

31. Find the median for the data set 20, 22, 23, 24, 25, 21, 20, 22, 24, 25, 23, 22, 25, 26, 22, and 20.

   A. 22　　　　C. 22.5

   B. 22.25　　　D. 22.75

32. A homeowner is renovating their kitchen and needs 75 square feet of tile for the backsplash. The tile contractor requires a 15% overage of tiles to complete the job. How many square feet of tile does the homeowner need to purchase? (Fill in the blank)

   _____

33. Order all of the numbers from least to greatest.

   $\frac{4}{12}$

   $\frac{2}{8}$

   $-\frac{4}{5}$

   $\frac{15}{16}$

   $-\frac{1}{8}$

34. A teacher buys 4 bottles of water for class. Each bottle of water contains 3 liters. Each cup holds 2/5 of a liter. How many cups can be filled?

   A. 12　　　　C. 42

   B. 30　　　　D. 60

35. A service group collects trash from area roadways for four straight weeks. The amount of trash they pick up is about $19\frac{1}{2}$, $15\frac{1}{3}$, $20\frac{7}{10}$, and $16\frac{3}{5}$ pounds. Estimate the total number of pounds collected.

   A. 70　　　　C. 72

   B. 71　　　　D. 73

36. The area of a penny is approximately 11 square millimeters. Find the circumference of a penny to the nearest tenth of a millimeter. Use 3.14 for π.

   A. 1.8　　　　C. 11.9

   B. 5.7　　　　D. 17.0

37. Convert 8 liters to quarts.

   A. 6.94 quarts　　C. 8.48 quarts

   B. 7.55 quarts　　D. 9.06 quarts

38. The line chart shows the number of cars sold each month. Which statement is true?

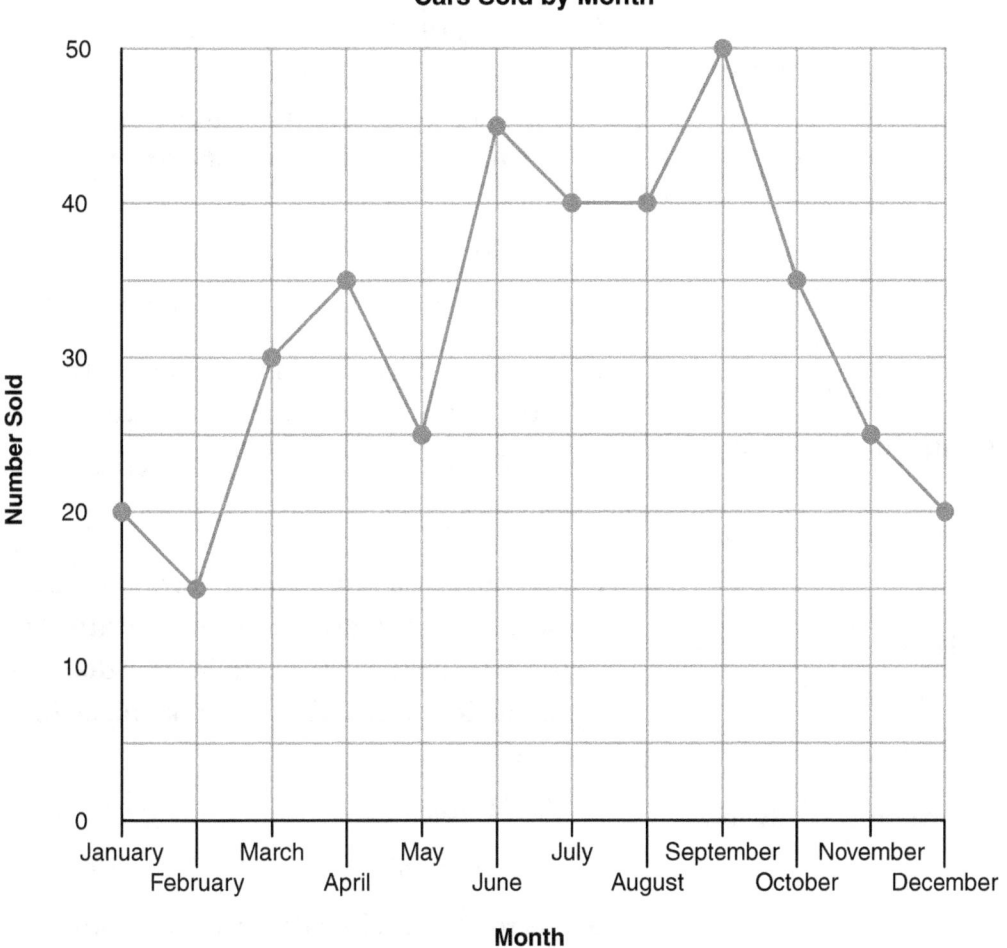

A. June had the most cars sold.

B. There were two months where 30 cars were sold.

C. The months with the smallest decreases all sold 5 fewer cars.

D. The difference between the highest and lowest month is 30 cars.

Section III. Science

1. Which of the following types of tissues include cells of the immune system and of the blood?
   A. Connective
   B. Epithelial
   C. Muscle
   D. Neural

2. Which best describes homeostasis?
   A. A functional system of the body
   B. Blood flow to every cell in the body
   C. A relatively constant environment within the body
   D. Neural pathways that have integrated into the body

3. Which blood group is a universal donor?
   A. A
   B. B
   C. AB
   D. O

4. Blood oxygen levels are most likely low when blood
   A. leaves the aorta.
   B. fills the right atrium.
   C. reaches body tissues.
   D. flows through arteries.

5. An intracellular chemical signal can be produced in the cell membrane. Once it is produced, where does it go?
   A. To a different cell
   B. To another part of the same cell
   C. To a region right outside the cell
   D. To an area with a high ion concentration

6. During the aging process, not all hormone levels decrease; some actually increase. Which of the following is a hormone that may increase as a person ages?
   A. Cortisol
   B. Insulin
   C. Luteinizing
   D. Thyroid

7. After food has been masticated in the oral cavity, where does it go next?
   A. Colon
   B. Liver
   C. Pancreas
   D. Pharynx

8. The diffusion of nutrients through the walls of the digestive system is critical to homeostasis in the body. Where does the majority of this diffusion take place in the digestive system?
   A. Stomach
   B. Esophagus
   C. Oral cavity
   D. Small intestine

9. As soon as an invader, known as a(n) _____, enters the body, the body begins to fight.
   A. antibody
   B. pathogen
   C. trigger
   D. vaccination

10. Where is skeletal muscle found?
    A. Inside the heart
    B. Attached to bone
    C. Lining the walls of the bladder
    D. Within the gastrointestinal tract

11. If a person smells something sweet, what form of information is this initially perceived as in the nervous system?
    A. Cognitive
    B. Integrative
    C. Motor
    D. Sensory

12. While hiking, a person is startled after encountering a bear. Her palms get sweaty and her heart starts racing. Which part of her nervous system was directly stimulated?

    A. Central

    B. Parasympathetic

    C. Somatic

    D. Sympathetic

13. Which of the following are included in the male reproductive system?

    A. the penis and epididymis

    B. the vas deferens and uterus

    C. the penis and Fallopian tube

    D. the penis, scrotum, and cervix

14. Fertilization (the fusing of one sperm and an ovum) results in a(n) _____.

    A. embryo   C. infant

    B. fetus   D. zygote

15. What structure channels food to the esophagus and air to the trachea?

    A. Bronchiole   C. Larynx

    B. Capillary   D. Lung

16. What structure plays a role in air conduction?

    A. Alveolus   C. Lung

    B. Capillary   D. Trachea

17. What body system is the skeletal system most closely associated with when hematopoiesis happens?

    A. Urinary system

    B. Digestive system

    C. Muscular system

    D. Cardiovascular system

18. What is the final structure through which urine must travel to empty out of the body?

    A. Bladder   C. Ureter

    B. Kidney   D. Urethra

19. Which sequence describes the hierarchy level of biological organization?

    A. Kingdom, phylum, class, order, family, genus, and species

    B. Genus, class, kingdom, species, order, phylum, and family

    C. Family, species, genus, order, kingdom, class, and phylum

    D. Species, kingdom, genus, class, family, phylum, and order

20. Which example is part of the scientific method?

    A. A student reads about a new way to harness energy from the sun.

    B. A researcher studies the effects of car exhaust on how people breathe.

    C. A researcher analyzes how many plants respond well to a new fertilizer.

    D. A student discovers how insulin plays a role in the development of diabetes.

21. Why did it take many years for the cell theory to be developed?

    A. Advancements in microscopy took place slowly.

    B. Cells were difficult to isolate for experimental analysis.

    C. Researchers believed a cell formed from preexisting cells.

    D. Scientists already proved that cells were essential for life.

22. What organelle is only associated with plant cells?
    A. Cell wall
    B. Ribosome
    C. Cytoplasm
    D. Golgi apparatus

23. What phase is the cell cycle part of?
    A. Interphase
    B. Metaphase
    C. Prophase
    D. Telophase

24. What is the correct order of the stages of the cell cycle?
    A. G_1, S, G_2, M
    B. G_2, S, G_1, M
    C. M, S, G_2, G_1
    D. S, M, G_1, G_2

25. When would a cell most likely contain the most nucleotides?
    A. S
    B. G_1
    C. M
    D. G_2

26. The sequence of amino acids in a gene determines
    A. the primary structure of a codon.
    B. the primary structure of a protein.
    C. the primary structure of a nucleotide.
    D. the primary structure of a nucleic acid.

27. Which statement best represents Mendel's experiments with garden peas?
    A. As a result, Mendel developed several theories that have since been disproved.
    B. Mendel realized he was on an incorrect track, which led him to other experimental media.
    C. As a result, Mendel developed foundational conclusions that are still valued and followed today.
    D. Mendel collaborated with others interested in genetics to develop heredity guidelines we still use today.

28. Mendel discovered the pattern associated with _____ after developing a series of rules in genetics.
    A. epigenetics
    B. heredity
    C. heterogeneity
    D. taxonomy

29. A student notices a pattern of stripes on five tigers. Each of the five tigers has the same stripe pattern. Using his inductive reasoning, what does he logically assume based on this information?
    A. The pattern continues to change over time.
    B. Natural adaptations cause this pattern to occur.
    C. Each offspring will have the same stripe pattern.
    D. Ancestors of the tigers have different stripe patterns.

30. A spoonful of sugar is added to a hot cup of tea. All the sugar dissolves. How can the resulting solution be described?

    A. Saturated and homogeneous

    B. Saturated and heterogeneous

    C. Unsaturated and homogeneous

    D. Unsaturated and heterogeneous

31. A researcher notices a positive correlation between the height of a plant and nutrient concentration over time. Based on this observation, what conclusion does he reach?

    A. The height of a plant increases in the absence and presence of the nutrients.

    B. When the amount of nutrients available to the plant decreases, its height increases.

    C. The amount of nutrients available to a plant is independent of how tall the plant gets.

    D. When the amount of nutrients available to the plant increases, its height also increases.

32. In the following single-replacement reaction, _____ replaces _____.

    $Cl_2 + 2NaI \rightarrow 2NaCl + I_2$

    A. sodium, iodine

    B. chlorine, iodine

    C. chlorine, sodium

    D. sodium, chlorine

33. What type of bond forms between nitrogen and oxygen, and why?

    A. Ionic, because electrons are shared

    B. Covalent, because electrons are shared

    C. Ionic, because electrons are transferred

    D. Covalent, because electrons are transferred

34. In which state of matter are the intermolecular forces between particles in a substance the strongest?

    A. Gas   C. Plasma

    B. Liquid   D. Solid

35. Which of the following atoms is a cation?

    A. 14 protons, 14 neutrons, 18 electrons

    B. 34 protons, 45 neutrons, 36 electrons

    C. 35 protons, 44 neutrons, 35 electrons

    D. 82 protons, 125 neutrons, 78 electrons

36. In which state of matter do the particles of iron have the lowest amount of cohesion?

    A. Solid iron particles have the lowest amount of cohesion.

    B. Liquid iron particles have the lowest amount of cohesion.

    C. Gaseous iron particles have the lowest amount of cohesion.

    D. The particles have the same amount of cohesion in all states of matter.

37. What type of reaction is described by the following equation?

    $ZnBr_2(aq) + 2KOH(aq) \rightarrow Zn(OH)_2(s) + 2KBr(aq)$

    A. Synthesis
    B. Decomposition
    C. Single-Replacement
    D. Double-Replacement

38. An intracellular chemical signal can be produced in the cell membrane. Once it is produced, where does it go?

    A. To a different cell
    B. To another part of the same cell
    C. To a region right outside the cell
    D. To an area with a high ion concentration

39. What standard is used to make comparisons in experiments?

    A. Sample size
    B. Control group
    C. Dependent variable
    D. Independent variable

40. Which of the following is supported by the cell theory?

    A. Cells are alive and recognized as the building blocks for life.
    B. Scientists can identify and differentiate cells by using a microscope
    C. Cells are produced from existing cells using meiosis instead of mitosis.
    D. Living things are composed of a single cell that remains undifferentiated.

41. What raw inorganic material would an autotroph most likely use to create chemical energy for growth?

    A. carbon dioxide
    B. minerals in soil
    C. decaying matter
    D. sugar molecules

42. Which of the following is a component of a chromosome?

    A. Centromere
    B. Gamete
    C. Homologue
    D. Ribose

43. What solution has a pH of 7?

    A. Aniline
    B. Pyridine
    C. Pure water
    D. Sodium hydroxide

44. Which is classified as a type of acid-base reaction that produces a salt?

    A. Combination
    B. Decomposition
    C. Hydrolysis
    D. Neutralization

45. Which of the following determines the strength of an acidic solution?

    A. Litmus paper that turns red
    B. Litmus paper that turns blue
    C. Measured pH value equal to 7
    D. Measured pH value less than 7

46. _____ is dependent not only on the temperature, but also on the amount of substance available.

    A. Condensation   C. Evaporation
    B. Deposition   D. Melting

47. During which of the following phase changes will the cohesion between the particles in a substance decrease?

   A. Condensation
   C. Freezing
   B. Deposition
   D. Vaporization

48. Which is true regarding the Urinary system? (Select all that apply.)

   A. Kidneys makes urine
   B. As a person ages, kidney tissue and filtration capacity increase
   C. Kidney help regulate water balance
   D. Regulates levels of electrolytes such as sodium and potassium
   E. Eliminates metabolic wastes.

49. An atom has 28 protons, 32 neutrons, and 28 electrons. What is the name of this isotope?

   A. Nickel-32
   B. Nickel-60
   C. Germanium-56
   D. Germanium-60

50. Arrange the steps of external respiration in the correct sequential order. (Use all the steps.)

   A. Gases are transported by circulation of the blood, with help from the heart.
   B. Gases are exchanged between air and blood in the lungs by diffusion.
   C. Gases are exchanged by diffusion between blood and tissues throughout the body.
   D. Air moves in and out of the lungs, which is called pulmonary ventilation.

Section IV. English and Language Usage

1. Read the following sentence from the passage:

   "Don't hit me with arguments about grater (sic) freedom for workers."

   Which of the following would be a more formal way to rewrite the sentence?

   A. I disagree with the argument about contract workers having greater freedom.
   B. Stop telling me that freelancers have more freedom!
   C. Is there actually greater freedom for workers?
   D. I've already heard arguments about greater freedom for workers.

2. Which of the following prefixes means with?

   A. bio-   C. con-
   B. per-   D. trans-

3. Select the context clue from the following sentence that helps you define the word <u>emulate</u>.

   Felicia always tried to emulate her big sister, so she would often imitate the way she spoke, moved, and how she dressed.

   A. "tried"   C. "imitate"
   B. "often"   D. "way"

4. Which of the following spellings is correct?

   A. Depindant   C. Dependunt
   B. Dependint   D. Dependent

5. Select a verb that correctly completes the following sentence.

   ___ not worry about it.

   A. Is   C. You
   B. Do   D. Was

6. What is the correct plural of chair?

   A. Chair   C. Chaires
   B. Chairs   D. Chairies

7. Which word in the following sentence is an adverb?

   We should go outside.

   A. We   C. go
   B. should   D. outside

8. Identify the independent clause in the following sentence.

   You need to call your mother as soon as you get home.

   A. You need to call your mother
   B. As soon as you get home
   C. You get home
   D. You need to call

9. Which of the following spellings is correct?

   A. Posibility   C. Possibilitie
   B. Possibility   D. Possibillity

10. Select the meaning of the underlined word in the sentence based on the context clues.

    If you wake up outside in your pajamas in the middle of the night, you may be a <u>somnambulist</u>.

    A. Explorer   C. Insomniac
    B. Magician   D. Sleepwalker

11. Which is the sentence with the correct use of punctuation?
    A. I cooked so I could eat dinner.
    B. I cooked so, I could eat dinner.
    C. I cooked so I, could eat dinner.
    D. I cooked, so I could eat dinner.

12. Which strategy is recommended during the drafting phase?
    A. List all ideas that come to mind without worrying whether they're good or on-topic.
    B. Don't worry about noting where you got your information; save that step for the end.
    C. Stop writing frequently to look up grammar rules and words you don't know how to spell.
    D. Get the ideas down on paper, even if some sentences sound awkward or contain errors.

13. Select the pronoun that could be used in the following sentence.
    Mrs. Sato, _____ lives down the street, is 99 years old.
    A. she   C. which
    B. who   D. whom

14. Which of the following is an example of a complex sentence?
    A. Timothy got a massage after running.
    B. After running, Timothy got a massage.
    C. Since Timothy went running he got a massage.
    D. Timothy went running, and then he got a massage.

15. Which of the following suffixes means person who practices?
    A. -en   C. -logy
    B. -ist   D. -able

16. Which of the following prefixes means self?
    A. con-   C. auto-
    B. man-   D. post-

17. Which of the following is an example of a simple sentence?
    A. Although termites are insects.
    B. Termites are very industrious insects.
    C. Termites are insects, and they are very industrious.
    D. Because termites are insects, they are very industrious.

18. Which of the following spellings is correct?
    A. Judgmant   C. Judgement
    B. Judgment   D. Judgemant

19. Select the meaning of the underlined word in the sentence. Jolie's has remained intransigent in her stance on the issue.
    A. Stubborn
    B. Indefinite
    C. Passionate
    D. Outspoken

20. Select the correct verb to complete the following sentence.
    I _____ about it for a long time before I decided to major in criminal justice.
    A. think   C. thinked
    B. thank   D. thought

21. Select the word that is a possessive pronoun
    A. It's
    B. Who
    C. That
    D. Ours

22. Which of the following sentences uses the MOST formal language?
    A. What's up?
    B. How are you?
    C. How's it going?
    D. How's your day?

23. What is the sentence with the correct use of punctuation?
    A. Offcampus apartments are nicer.
    B. Off campus apartments are nicer.
    C. Off-campus apartments are nicer.
    D. Off-campus-apartments are nicer.

24. Why is it not recommended to edit while you write your first draft?
    A. It is prewriting.
    B. It wastes effort.
    C. It clouds the judgment.
    D. It changes the organization.

25. Identify the preposition in the following sentence.
    It's really hot in that room.
    A. It
    B. hot
    C. in
    D. that

26. Which is the sentence with the correct use of punctuation?
    A. The book was amazing she couldn't put it down;
    B. The book was amazing; she couldn't put it down.
    C. The book was amazing; so she couldn't put it down.
    D. The book was amazing so; she couldn't put it down.

27. What is the correct plural of century?
    A. Centurys
    B. Centures
    C. Centuries
    D. Centuryies

28. Select the sentence that correctly answers the following question.
    What were you doing when the thunderstorm started?
    A. I mowed the lawn.
    B. I am mowing the lawn.
    C. I was mowing the lawn.
    D. I have mowed the lawn.

29. Apparently in order to acheive success across multiple subjects when learning, a student basically must be agressive with the amount of time they spend studying.

    Which of the following words are misspelled in the sentence above? (select all that apply)
    A. Apparently
    B. Achieve
    C. Across
    D. Basically
    E. Agressive

30. The tone of a text is _____ if the words say the opposite of what they really mean.
    A. ironic   C. confused
    B. earnest   D. unambiguous

31. Which term refers to the feelings a text creates in the reader?
    A. Tone   C. Mood
    B. Irony   D. Theme

32. In literature, a genre is a:
    A. moral   C. category
    B. theme   D. narrative

33. Which term describes the most likely structure of an essay about the similarities and differences between World War I and World War II?
    A. Technical
    B. Expository
    C. Cause/effect
    D. Compare/contrast

34. Select the correct verb to complete the following sentence.

    Our family _____ staying home for the holidays this year.
    A. is   C. am
    B. be   D. are

35. Select the correct verbs to complete the following sentences.

    Where ___ everyone? What ___ they doing?
    A. is, is   C. are, is
    B. is, are   D. are, are

36. Which of the following movie titles contains a pronoun?
    A. *Rear Window*
    B. *North by Northwest*
    C. *The Trouble with Harry*
    D. *The Man Who Knew Too Much*

37. Select the correct words to complete the following sentence.

    I have _____ due tomorrow.
    A. many homework
    B. many homeworks
    C. a lot of homework
    D. a lot of homeworks

TEAS Practice Exam 1
Answer Key with Explanatory Answers

Section I. Reading

1. **B.** The first sentence of this paragraph expresses the main idea that people should be concerned by even a small amount of climate change. This makes it the topic sentence. **See Lesson: Main Ideas, Topic Sentences, and Supporting Details.**

2. **A.** The topic of a sentence is a word or phrase that describes what the text is about. **See Lesson: Main Ideas, Topic Sentences, and Supporting Details.**

3. **C.** This paragraph argues that a small change in global temperatures could have a major result. This idea is expressed in a topic sentence at the beginning of the paragraph. **See Lesson: Main Ideas, Topic Sentences, and Supporting Details.**

4. **D.** The information about temperature differences in the last ice age supports the main idea that people should be concerned by global climate change. This makes it a supporting detail. **See Lesson: Main Ideas, Topic Sentences, and Supporting Details.**

5. **B.** All of the above sentences relate to the topic of global climate change, but only the sentence about the Little Ice Age relates directly to the main idea that a small amount of climate fluctuation is cause for concern. **See Lesson: Main Ideas, Topic Sentences, and Supporting Details.**

6. **B.** All of the above sentences relate to author income, and particularly to differences in income for male and female authors. **See Lesson: Main Ideas, Topic Sentences, and Supporting Details.**

7. **B.** The sentences above discuss pay differences between male and female authors but not differences in the quality or appeal of their work, so the best topic sentence would relate to gender stereotyping and author pay. **See Lesson: Main Ideas, Topic Sentences, and Supporting Details.**

8. **D.** The collection of sentences above all relate to gender differences in author income, so the best fit for the topic is a statement about people's likelihood of purchasing books by men and women. **See Lesson: Main Ideas, Topic Sentences, and Supporting Details.**

9. **B.** The sentence above conveys factual information about Mars in an excited tone that suggests a positive interest in the subject. This makes it most likely to fit into an informational paragraph sharing facts about Mars. **See Lesson: Main Ideas, Topic Sentences, and Supporting Details.**

10. **D.** If the above sentence were a topic sentence, its supporting details would likely share information to develop the idea that Mars may have supported life in the past. **See Lesson: Main Ideas, Topic Sentences, and Supporting Details.**

11. B. A summary must restate the ideas of the original text, not comment on them with judgments or speculation, and without adhering too closely to the wording of the original. This paragraph explains how shipping and refrigeration technology helped bananas become a major export crop. **See Lesson: Summarizing Text and Using Text Features.**

12. B. These sentences, like all effective summaries, restate the ideas of the original text in different words. Although a summary can sometimes state an implicit idea from the original text, this one does not need to do so. **See Lesson: Summarizing Text and Using Text Features.**

13. C. The structure and word choice of this sentence are so close to the original that it qualifies as plagiarism. **See Lesson: Summarizing Text and Using Text Features.**

14. B. This sentence comments on the original text rather than summarizing it. Some types of writing allow this, but it is not a summary. **See Lesson: Summarizing Text and Using Text Features.**

15. D. It would be inaccurate to say that nobody would eat bananas if modern shipping and refrigeration technology had never been invented. This is not in the original text, and logically speaking, bananas would still be eaten in the tropics regardless of changes in technology. **See Lesson: Summarizing Text and Using Text Features.**

16. C. This passage shares the author's opinions about television and movie rating systems. This makes it a persuasive piece. **See Lesson: The Author's Purpose and Point of View.**

17. D. The author of the passage says that only she knows her kids well enough to be able to decide what they can watch. She would likely agree that other parents are the best people to make similar choices for their own kids. **See Lesson: The Author's Purpose and Point of View.**

18. C. The author of this passage suggests that parents should decide for themselves whether or not kids should watch certain shows or movies. She would likely agree with an effort to provide parents more information for making these choices. **See Lesson: The Author's Purpose and Point of View.**

19. D. The author includes her credentials as a parent to establish that she is a trustworthy authority on this subject. **See Lesson: The Author's Purpose and Point of View.**

20. C. The author uses the phrase "based on numbers" in a negative way, she is implying that some decisions need to be based on more nuanced positions. **See Lesson: The Author's Purpose and Point of View.**

21. A. *My Mature Son* **is incorrect.** This title refers only to the 2nd paragraph, rather than the entire passage

B. *Movie Rating Systems are Unhelpful* **is correct.** A passage title should refer to the overall theme or topic of the passage. Throughout the passage the author explains why they find the rating system unhelpful.

C. *Sheltering Children from Movie Violence* **is incorrect.** This title only refers to the 3rd paragraph rather than the entire content of the passage

D. *Improving Movie Rating Systems* **is incorrect.** This title does not refer to the overall theme or topic of the passage and the author makes no mention of how to improve the ratings system.

E. *The Problem with Movie Ratings* **is correct.** A passage title should refer to the overall theme or topic of the passage. This title describes the passage's primary topic of identifying in the author's opinion the problem with movie ratings.

22. B. If a book is describing information, its purpose is to inform. **See Lesson: The Author's Purpose and Point of View.**

23. C. The label shows the number of calories per serving: 150. **See Lesson: Evaluating and Integrating Data.**

24. B. The label shows that there are 20 crackers per serving. 60 crackers would be three servings. **See Lesson: Evaluating and Integrating Data.**

25. D. Although the sodium content is not low, only the saturated fat value is considered particularly high. **See Lesson: Evaluating and Integrating Data.**

26. A. Products are considered low in a nutrient if the Daily Value is below 5%. This product does not meet that criterion. **See Lesson: Evaluating and Integrating Data.**

27. A. Although this product would not be considered healthy by most standards, it is a good source of iron. **See Lesson: Evaluating and Integrating Data.**

28. B. The writer of this passage suggests implicitly that only students without learning and attention challenges are engaged in their education. This assumption reflects a negative stereotype that renders the entire argument faulty. **See Lesson: Facts, Opinions, and Evaluating an Argument.**

29. B. The author of the passage uses the phrase "students with learning and attention challenges" to refer to students who think and learn differently. This is not derogatory, but even so, the passage implies that people who experience these differences are less engaged in their education. **See Lesson: Facts, Opinions, and Evaluating an Argument.**

30. C. Words like *excessive* and *undue* are subject to interpretation and reflect beliefs rather than verifiable facts. However, words like these may appear in factual statements about what people said they felt or believed. **See Lesson: Facts, Opinions, and Evaluating an Argument.**

31. A. From phrases like "your child," you can infer that the intended audience of this passage is parents. **See Lesson: Understanding Primary Sources, Making Inferences, and Drawing Conclusions.**

32. A. The author makes several references to time constraints but assumes that parents want their children to be well educated. **See Lesson: Understanding Primary Sources, Making Inferences, and Drawing Conclusions.**

33. D. The author of this article assumes that all children should grow up to become mindful world citizens. **See Lesson: Understanding Primary Sources, Making Inferences, and Drawing Conclusions.**

34. D. The author does not suggest that STEM instruction is unimportant. The article says only that increased time spent on STEM instruction is often made at the expense of other subjects, like social studies. **See Lesson: Understanding Primary Sources, Making Inferences, and Drawing Conclusions.**

35. B. The line about online library databases shows that the author understands that parents may need a convenient way to follow the article's advice. **See Lesson: Understanding Primary Sources, Making Inferences, and Drawing Conclusions.**

36. B. A biography of a politician would be a historical or analytical account that adds insight on the topic. This makes it a secondary source. **See Lesson: Understanding Primary Sources, Making Inferences, and Drawing Conclusions**

37. D. An online database of writings by a historical figure is primary, but a blog post reflecting on his contributions is secondary. **See Lesson: Understanding Primary Sources, Making Inferences, and Drawing Conclusions.**

38. B. This is a technical text written to inform the reader about a complex process. **See Lesson: Types of Passages, Text Structures, Genre and Theme.**

39. C. The opening paragraph has a problem-solution structure. The problem it describes involves risks of injury and litigation, and the solution is that employees follow a process designed to minimize those risks. **See Lesson: Types of Passages, Text Structures, Genre and Theme.**

40. A. The step-by-step instructions under the subheading follow a sequential structure. Note key words and phrases such as "first" and "in order." **See Lesson: Types of Passages, Text Structures, Genre and Theme.**

41. B. Expository writing explores academic questions and may be written in an entertaining style. Technical writing explains complex processes or mechanism and is usually written in an impersonal style. **See Lesson: Types of Passages, Text Structures, Genre and Theme.**

42. C. Larger bars in a bar graph indicate higher numbers. This book has sold more paperback copies than any other. **See Lesson: Summarizing Text and Using Text Features.**

43. B. The bar graph shows fewer hardcover sales than any other kind. This could help support an argument that later books should only be released in electronic and paperback forms. **See Lesson: Summarizing Text and Using Text Features.**

44. C. Labels name parts of the diagram and indicate them with lines pointing to the part of the picture to which they correspond. The small, root-like part of the neuron on the top right is a dendrite. **See Lesson: Summarizing Text and Using Text Features.**

45. B. A diagram illustrates what complex things look like and provides information about their parts. It cannot explain exactly what things do. **See Lesson: Summarizing Text and Using Text Features.**

ATI TEAS: Full Study Guide, Test Strategies and Secrets

Section II. Mathematics

1. C. According to the graph, it rained every day for the 12 days because the line never crosses 0 inches of rainfall. **See Lesson: Interpreting Graphics.**

2. C. The customer's bill was $75 because ($16.50 × 100) ÷ 22 = $75. **See Lesson: Ratios, Proportions, and Percentages.**

3. A. Divide 20 by the decimal equivalent of 15% to solve for the value. 20 ÷ 0.15 = 133.33 which can be rounded to 133. **See Lesson: Ratios, Proportions, and Percentages.**

4. D. The correct solution is 13,200 feet. $2.5\ mi \times \frac{5280\ ft}{1\ m} = 13,200\ ft$. **See Lesson: Standards of Measure.**

5. A. The medicine bottle will have 500 mL of liquid medicine because 1 liter is equal to 1,000 mL. **See Lesson: Solving Real World Mathematical Problems.**

6. C. The correct solution is $4x^2 - x - 7$.

$(8x^2 - 6x - 3) - (4x^2 - 5x + 4)$
$= (8x^2 - 6x - 3) + (-4x^2 + 5x - 4)$
$= (8x^2 - 4x^2) + (-6x + 5x) + (-3 - 4)$
$= 4x^2 - x - 7$

See Lesson: Powers & Exponents, Roots & Radicals, with Polynomials.

7. B. The fraction converts to 0.125 as a decimal. The hundredths place is two place values to the right of the decimal and the 5 value in the thousandths place makes the decimal round up to 0.13. **See Lesson: Decimals and Fractions.**

8. A. The patient has a fever of 39°C because using the conversion equation $\frac{5}{9}(°F - 32)$ = $\frac{5}{9}(70)$ = 38.8°C ≈ 39°C. **See Lesson: Standards of Measure.**

9. B. The pizza shop sold $1\frac{3}{20}$ pizzas because the lowest common denominator is 20. By adding $\frac{3}{8}$ of both pizzas, they sold $\frac{3}{4}$, and converting the fractions to have the LCD, $\frac{3}{4} = \frac{15}{20}$ and $\frac{2}{5} = \frac{8}{20}$, and $\frac{23}{20} = 1\frac{3}{20}$. **See Lesson: Addition and Subtraction of Fractions.**

10. B. The solution is 20% because $\frac{32}{160} = \frac{x}{100}$ and x solves out to be 20. **See Lesson: Ratios, Proportions, and Percentages.**

11. C. A proportion may be used to solve the problem which would be set up as $\frac{96}{120} = \frac{x}{75}$ and x= 60. Alternatively, 96 ÷ 120 = 0.8 or 80%. Multiplying 0.8 by 75 = 60. **See Lesson: Ratios, Proportions, and Percentages.**

12. **C.** The correct solution is $\frac{5}{4}$.

$4x = 5$ Subtract 3 from both sides of the equation.

$x = \frac{5}{4}$ Divide both sides of the equation by 4.

See Lesson: Equations with One Variable.

13. **A.** The correct solution is $\frac{4}{25}$ because $\frac{4}{5} \times \frac{1}{5} = \frac{4}{25}$. **See Lesson: Multiplication and Division of Fractions.**

14. **B.** The correct solution is 3,600. Substitute the values into the formula and simplify using the order of operations, $A = \frac{1}{2}bh = \frac{1}{2}(90)(80) = 3{,}600$ square centimeters. **See Lesson: Similarity, Right Triangles, and Trigonometry.**

15. **A.** Trisha paid $375 for 72 months because there are 12 months in a year. The cost of Trisha's car can be written as an equation $1800 + ($375 x 72) = $1800 + $ 27,000 = $28,800. **See Lesson: Solving Real World Mathematical Problems.**

16. **B.** The patient will receive fluids 6 times because each dose is ¼ a liter, or 250 mL. 1,500 mL ÷ 250 mL = 6 doses. **See Lesson: Solving Real World Mathematical Problems.**

17. **B.** The answer is $\frac{89}{100}$ and cannot be reduced any further. **See Lesson: Decimals and Fractions.**

18. **C.** The correct solution is x ≥ 3 because subtracting 5 from each side of the inequality reveals that −x ≤ −3. By dividing each side of the inequality by −1 requires a sign flip. **See Lesson: Equations with One Variable.**

19. **A.** The correct solution is $\frac{27}{70}$ because $\frac{2}{7} + \frac{1}{10} = \frac{20}{70} + \frac{7}{70} = 20 + \frac{7}{70} = \frac{27}{70}$. **See Lesson: Addition and Subtraction of Fractions.**

20. **B.** The correct solution is 40.82 because $C = \pi d \approx 3.14(13) \approx 40.82$ inches. **See Lesson: Circles.**

21. **A.** The correct solution is $\frac{3}{70}$ because $\frac{3}{10} \times \frac{1}{7} = \frac{3}{70}$. **See Lesson: Multiplication and Division of Fractions.**

22. **B.** The correct solution is −10 because 10 is added to both sides of the equation. **See Lesson: Equations with One Variable.**

23. **D.** The family spends $1,625 a month on their bills because $6,500 × 0.25 = $1,625. **See Lesson: Interpreting Graphics.**

24. **B.** The correct solution is 120. Substitute the values into the formula and simplify using the order of operations, $SA = (2)(\frac{1}{2})(5)(12) + (2)(5) + 2(12) + 2(13) = 60 + 10 + 26 + 24 = 120$ square centimeters. **See Lesson: Similarity, Right Triangles, and Trigonometry.**

25. C. The candy shop makes 28 cents of profit for each piece of candy after accounting for the cost to make them. Since the business has $4,200 worth of operational costs, $0.28C - $4,200 = $0, or the break-even point for the company. **See Lesson: Solving Real World Mathematical Problems.**

26. B. The survey reveals that a total number of 7 students prefer fish and pigs as pets, and 7 students prefer gerbils. **See Lesson: Interpreting Graphics.**

27. B. The seamstress used 130 buttons because $\frac{3}{5}$ of a box of 200 buttons is 120 which means she used 80 buttons from that box and $\frac{1}{4}$ of a box of 200 is 50. Altogether the seamstress used 80 + 50 = 130 buttons. **See Lesson: Addition and Subtraction of Fractions.**

28. C. The pharmacy technician will need 0.2 grams to fill the order because 1,000 mg is equal to 1 gram. **See Lesson: Solving Real World Mathematical Problems.**

29. A. The correct solution is 11 because $3^2 = 9 + 4 = 13 - 2 = 11$. **See Lesson: Equations with One Variable.**

30. D. The correct solution is $1\frac{1}{2}$ because $\frac{3}{4} \times \frac{2}{1} = \frac{6}{4} = 1\frac{2}{4} = 1\frac{1}{2}$. **See Lesson: Multiplication and Division of Fractions.**

31. C. The correct solution is 22.5. The data set written in order is 20, 20, 20, 21, 22, 22, 22, 22, 23, 23, 24, 24, 25, 25, 25 and 26. The middle two numbers are 22 and 23, and the mean of these numbers is 22.5. **See Lesson: Interpreting Graphics.**

32. Calculate the overage by multiplying the required amount of tile by the overage amount of tile: 0.15 x 75 = 11.25. Then add the overage amount to the required about: 11.25 + 75 = 86.25 square feet. **See Lesson: Solving Real World Mathematical Problems**

33. The best way to compare rational numbers is often to convert them to the equivalent decimal using a calculator.

$\frac{4}{12} = 0.3333$

$\frac{2}{8} = 0.25$

$-\frac{4}{5} = -0.8$

$\frac{15}{16} = 0.93$

$-\frac{1}{8} = -0.125$

$-0.8 < -0.125 < 0.25 < 0.33 < 0.93$

After converting the fractions to decimals, the correct order from least to greatest is $-\frac{4}{5}, -\frac{1}{8}, \frac{2}{8}, \frac{4}{12}, \frac{15}{16}$. **See Lesson: Decimals and Fractions.**

34. B. The correct solution is 30 because $4(3) \div \frac{2}{5} = 12 \div \frac{2}{5} = \frac{12}{1} \times \frac{5}{2} = \frac{60}{2} = 30$ cups of water. **See Lesson: Solving Real World Mathematical Problems.**

35. D. The correct solution is 73. The estimated weights are 20, 15, 21, and 17 pounds, and the total weight is about 73 pounds. **See Lesson: Solving Real World Mathematical Problems.**

36. C. The correct solution is 11.9. millimeters. millimeters. **See Lesson: Circles.**

37. C. The correct solution is 8.48 quarts. **See Lesson: Standards of Measure.**

38. C. The correct solution is the months with the smallest decreases all sold 5 fewer cars. There was a decline of 5 cars from January to February, June to July, and from November to December. **See Lesson: Interpreting Graphics.**

Section III. Science

1. **A.** Connective tissue includes cells of the immune system and cells of the blood. **See Lesson: Organization of the Human Body.**

2. **C.** Homeostasis the existence and maintenance of a relatively constant environment within the body. **See Lesson: Organization of the Human Body.**

3. **D.** Blood group O is a universal blood donor, which means a person with this blood type can donate blood to people who have a different blood type. **See Lesson: Cardiovascular System.**

4. **B.** Deoxygenated blood that leaves tissues by way of capillaries flows through veins before reaching the right atrium. **See Lesson: Cardiovascular System.**

5. **B.** Intracellular chemical signals are only sent to other components of the same cell. **See Lesson: Endocrine System.**

6. **C.** Luteinizing hormone production can increase with age. **See Lesson: Endocrine System.**

7. **D.** Once the food has been masticated in the oral cavity, or mouth, it is then swallowed by the pharynx. **See Lesson: Gastrointestinal System.**

8. **D.** The majority of diffusion occurs in the duodenum, which is the first section of the small intestine. **See Lesson: Gastrointestinal System.**

9. **B.** As soon as an invader, known as a pathogen, enters the body, the body begins to fight. **See Lesson: The Lymphatic System.**

10. **B.** There are three types of muscles in the body: cardiac, smooth, and skeletal. Smooth muscles line the walls of internal organs, and cardiac is found inside the heart. Skeletal muscles are attached to bone and aid in body movement. **See Lesson: Muscular System.**

11. **D.** Sensory nerves are responsible for receiving information from the external environment and sending that information to the CNS. Sensory nerves can collect this information using the senses like smelling. **See Lesson: The Nervous System.**

12. **D.** The sympathetic nervous system is part of the autonomic system. It is activated during periods of stress or emergencies, such as when the body responds to external stimuli related to fear. **See Lesson: The Nervous System.**

13. **A.** The penis, epididymis, scrotum, and vas deferens are components of the male reproductive system; the Fallopian tube, cervix, and uterus are components of the female reproductive system. **See Lesson: Reproductive System.**

14. **D.** Fertilization results in a zygote (a fertilized egg); a zygote develops into an embryo, the embryo into a fetus, and the fetus into an infant. **See Lesson: Reproductive System.**

15. **C.** The larynx contains the voice box. It funnels air to the trachea and food past the epiglottis and down the esophagus. **See Lesson: The Respiratory System.**

16. D. The air-conducting portion of the respiratory system consists of the upper and lower respiratory tract, which includes the trachea. The trachea delivers air to the lungs. **See Lesson: The Respiratory System.**

17. D. During hematopoiesis, bones generate red blood cells. These cells are associated with various functions in the cardiovascular system. **See Lesson: Skeletal System.**

18. D. The final body structure through which urine travels to exit the body is the urethra. After collecting in the bladder, the sphincter pushes the urine into the urethra. A different sphincter, under voluntary control, pushes the urine from the urethra out of the body. **See Lesson: The Urinary System.**

19. A. Taxonomy is the process of classifying, describing, and naming organisms. There are seven levels in the Linnaean taxonomic system, starting with the broadest level, kingdom, and ending with the species level. **See Lesson: An Introduction to Biology.**

20. C. One step of the scientific method is to analyze information or data collected from the experiment to conclude whether the hypothesis is supported. **See Lesson: An Introduction to Biology.**

21. A. The cell theory is a theory because it is supported by a significant number of experimental findings. The cell theory took many years to be developed because microscopes were not powerful enough to make such observations. **See Lesson: Cell Structure, Function, and Type.**

22. A. Only plant cells have cell walls, which help protect the cell and provide structural support. **See Lesson: Cell Structure, Function, and Type.**

23. A. Before mitosis or meiosis occurs, interphase must happen. This is when the cell cycle takes place. **See Lesson: Cellular Reproduction, Cellular Respiration, and Photosynthesis.**

24. A. During interphase, the cell undergoes an initial gap phase called G_1 before its DNA is copied in the S phase. After the DNA is copied, the cell undergoes a second gap phase called G_2. Then, the cell is ready to enter the mitotic phase, during which it divides into daughter cells. **See Lesson: Cellular Reproduction, Cellular Respiration, and Photosynthesis.**

25. B. A cell copies its DNA during the S phase, and nucleotides are the building blocks of DNA. Thus, the step preceding the S phase, the G_1 phase, is the phase of the cell cycle when the cell would contain the most nucleotides. **See Lesson: Cellular Reproduction, Cellular Respiration, and Photosynthesis.**

26. B. The sequence of amino acids in a gene determines the primary structure of a protein. **See Lesson: Genetics and DNA.**

27. D. Mendel developed theories of genetics that scientists around the world use today. **See Lesson: Genetics and DNA.**

28. B. Mendel was accurately able to predict the patterns of heredity by studying rules related to genetics. These rules helped shape his theory of heredity. **See Lesson: Genetics and DNA.**

29. C. Inductive reasoning involves making specific observations and using them to make broad statements. The student observes that all of the tigers have the same stripe pattern. He can use this observation to make the broad statement that all the tigers' offspring will have the same stripe pattern. **See Lesson: Designing an Experiment.**

30. C. Because more solute could be added and dissolve, the solution has not yet reached its limit and is considered unsaturated. Because all the solute dissolves, the particles in the mixture are evenly distributed as a homogenous mixture. **See Lesson: Chemical Solutions.**

31. D. Because this is a positive correlation, if the nutrient concentration increases or decreases, plant height will either increase or decrease accordingly. **See Lesson: Designing an Experiment.**

32. B. In this reaction, chlorine (Cl_2) is an element in the reaction that replaces iodine in the compound sodium iodide (NaI). This allows chlorine to form a compound with sodium (NaCl) and leaves iodine (I_2) as an element. **See Lesson: Chemical Solutions.**

33. B. Nitrogen and oxygen are both nonmetals, which means they will share electrons in a covalent bond. **See Lesson: Chemical Bonds.**

34. D. In solids, particles are usually closer together than in other states of matter because of the strong cohesive forces between the particles. **See Lesson: States of Matter.**

35. D. Because it has more protons than electrons, this atom has a positive charge and can be classified as a cation. **See Lesson: Chemical Bonds.**

36. C. The particles in a sample of gas are farther apart than in solids or liquids and therefore have the lowest amount of cohesion. **See Lesson: States of Matter.**

37. D. In this reaction, two elements are trading places. In the reactants, zinc and bromide ions are together, and potassium and hydroxide ions are together. In the products, zinc and hydroxide ions are together, and potassium and bromide ions are together. **See Lesson: Chemical Solutions.**

38. B. Intracellular chemical signals are only sent to other components of the same cell. There are two major types of receptor molecules that respond to an intercellular chemical signal:

- **Intracellular receptors:** These receptors are located in either the cytoplasm or the nucleus of the cell. Signals diffuse across the cell membrane and bind to the receptor sites on intracellular receptors, of the same cell.
- **Membrane-bound receptors:** These receptors extend across the cell membrane, with their receptor sites on the outer surface of the cell membrane. They respond to intercellular chemical signals that are large, water-soluble molecules that do not diffuse across the cell membrane.

See Lesson: Endocrine System.

39. B. A control group is a factor that does not change during an experiment. Due to this, it is used as a standard for comparison with variables that do change such as a dependent variable. **See Lesson: An Introduction to Biology.**

40. A. After scientists were able to view cells under the microscope they formulated the cell theory. One part of this theory concluded that all cells are alive. They also represent the basic unit of life. **See Lesson: Cell Structure Function and Type.**

41. B. Autotrophs are organisms that use basic raw materials in nature, like the sun, to make energy-rich biomolecules. Minerals are naturally inorganic. **See Lesson: Cell Structure Function and Type.**

42. A. The protein disc that holds two sister chromatids together is what collectively makes a chromosome. **See Lesson: Genetics and DNA.**

43. C. A pH of 7 is a neutral solution, which is how pure water is classified. **See Lesson: Acids and Bases.**

44. D. A neutralization reaction is a type of acid-base reaction where an acid and base react to form a salt and water. **See Lesson: Acids and Bases.**

45. D. Both litmus paper and a pH scale can be used to indicate whether a solution is acidic. However, a pH scale can also determine the strength of an acid. **See Lesson: Acids and Bases.**

46. C. Unlike condensation, deposition, and melting, evaporation is dependent not only on the temperature, but also on the amount of a substance available. **See Lesson: Properties of Matter.**

47. D. If the cohesion between particles decreases, then the particles must be undergoing a phase change that allows particles to move farther apart. This happens when a substance vaporizes and turns from liquid to gas. **See Lesson: States of Matter.**

48. C, D, E. Kidneys makes urine is incorrect. Kidneys do not make urine. They help regulate water balance, regulate levels of electrolytes such as sodium and potassium, and eliminate metabolic wastes. Urine is a byproduct of these functions.

As a person ages, kidney tissue and filtration capacity increase is incorrect. As a person ages, the kidneys and bladder change. This can affect functions such as bladder control and how well the kidneys filter blood. Kidney changes range from a decrease in kidney tissue to decreased filtration capacity.

Kidneys help regulate water balance is correct. Kidneys help regulate water balance, regulate levels of electrolytes such as sodium and potassium, and eliminate metabolic wastes. Urine is a byproduct of these functions.

Regulates levels of electrolytes such as sodium and potassium is correct. There must be a continual balance of water and salt in the blood. The urinary system, specifically the kidneys, help maintain this balance. It also balances levels of metabolites or electrolytes such as sodium, potassium, and calcium.

Eliminates metabolic wastes is correct. Urea, creatinine, uric acid, and ammonium are the primary types of nitrogenous wastes excreted from the body. The urinary system also detects and excretes excess water from the blood and out of the body. **See Lesson: Urinary System.**

49. B. The number of protons, 28, gives the atomic number, which identifies this atom as nickel. The mass is the number after the dash in the isotope name, which is determined by adding the numbers of protons and neutrons (28 + 32 = 60). **See Lesson: Scientific Notation.**

50. D, B, A, C.

- D. Air moves in and out of the lungs, which is called pulmonary ventilation.
- B. Gases are exchanged between air and blood in the lungs by diffusion.
- A. Gases are transported by circulation of the blood, with help from the heart.
- C. Gases are exchanged by diffusion between blood and tissues throughout the body.

Section IV. English and Language Usage

1. A. Throughout the passage, the author is sharing personal opinions without many facts to show their reasoning. Stating "I disagree" is a more formal way to share that concluded opinion. **See Lesson: Formal and Informal Language.**

2. C. The prefix that means "with" is *con*. **See Lesson: Root Words, Prefixes, and Suffixes.**

3. C. The meaning of <u>emulate</u> in this context is "to try to be like someone you admire." The word "imitate" helps you figure out the meaning of <u>emulate</u>. **See Lesson: Context Clues and Multiple Meaning Words.**

4. D. Dependent is the only correct spelling. **See Lesson: Spelling.**

5. B. The helping verb do should be used to make a negative statement with the main verb worry. **See Lesson: Verbs and Verb Tenses.**

6. B. For words ending in most consonants, add -s. **See Lesson: Spelling.**

7. D. Outside is an adverb that describes the verb go. **See Lesson: Adjectives and Adverbs**

8. A. You need to call your mother. It is independent because it has a subject, verb, and expresses a complete thought. **See Lesson: Types of Clauses.**

9. B. Possibility is the only correct spelling. **See Lesson: Spelling.**

10. D. The meaning of <u>somnambulist</u> in the context of this sentence is "sleepwalker." **See Lesson: Context Clues and Multiple Meaning Words.**

11. D. I cooked, so I could eat dinner. Commas are placed before coordinating conjunctions. **See Lesson: Punctuation.**

12. D. Drafting is about getting ideas down on paper. You can reread later to fix awkward sentences and errors. **See Lesson: The Writing Process.**

13. B. The relative pronoun who introduces a clause that gives more information about the noun Mrs. Sato. **See Lesson: Pronouns.**

14. B. This is a complex sentence because it starts with a subordinating conjunction, *after*, has a dependent clause followed by a comma, and then has an independent clause. **See Lesson: Types of Sentences.**

15. B. The suffix that means "person who practices" is *ist*. **See Lesson: Root Words, Prefixes, and Suffixes.**

16. C. The prefix that means "self" is *auto*. **See Lesson: Root Words, Prefixes, and Suffixes.**

17. B. This is a simple sentence since it contains one independent clause consisting of a simple subject and a predicate. **See Lesson: Types of Sentences.**

18. B. Judgment is the correct answer. Alternative standards allow for a spelling option of judgement, but American standards state that when adding a suffix such as "-ment" to a word ending with a silent sounding "-e" as in the word judge, the mute "-e" is dropped, making judgment the only correct option. **See Lesson: Spelling.**

19. A. The prefix *in* means "not," and the root word "trans" means across. So an intransigent person is not willing to cross or bend, so this would be a stubborn person. **See Lesson: Root Words, Prefixes, and Suffixes.**

20. D. Thought is the correct past tense of the verb think. **See Lesson: Verbs and Verb Tenses.**

21. D. Ours is a possessive pronoun. It's is a contraction of it is. Who and That are relative pronouns. See Lesson: Pronouns.

22. B. How are you? It is the only sentence that does not have a contraction and does not use slang. **See Lesson: Formal and Informal Language.**

23. C. Off-campus apartments are nicer. Hyphens are often used for compound words that are placed before the noun to help with understanding. **See Lesson: Punctuation.**

24. B. Editing as you write wastes effort because you may need to change your work drastically in revision. You may end up polishing a sentence you don't end up using later. **See Lesson: The Writing Process.**

25. C. *In* is a preposition. **See Lesson: Conjunctions and Prepositions.**

26. B. The book was amazing; she couldn't put it down. Semicolons are used to connect two related sentences without using a coordinating conjunction. **See Lesson: Punctuation.**

27. C. With a word ending in -y, you drop the -y and add -ies. **See Lesson: Spelling.**

28. C. The verb tense was mowing is past progressive, which matches the tense used in the question (were doing). **See Lesson: Verbs and Verb Tenses.**

29. Apparantly is correct: This correct spelling is apparently.
Acheive is correct: This correct spelling is achieve.
Across is incorrect: This word is spelled correctly.
Basically is incorrect: This word is spelled correctly.
Agressive is correct: This correct spelling is aggressive.

See Lesson: Spelling

30. A. Words that say the opposite of what they really mean are ironic. Irony can be confusing to the reader at times, but it is not confused (which would imply that the writer does not know what he or she means). **See Lesson: Tone and Mood, Transition Words.**

31. C. Mood is the feeling a text creates in a reader; tone is the author's attitude toward the subject. **See Lesson: Tone and Mood, Transition Words.**

32. C. The word genre is synonym of category. We use the word genre to discuss categories of literature. **See Lesson: Types of Passages, Text Structures, Genre and Theme.**

33. D. The structure of a text is its organizational scheme, not its category. Of the options above, a compare/contrast structure is most likely. **See Lesson: Types of Passages, Text Structures, Genre and Theme.**

34. A. The subject family is singular and takes the verb is. **See Lesson: Subject and Verb . Agreement.**

35. B. In questions with pronouns where and what, the verb agrees with the noun or pronoun that follows it. Everyone is the subject of the first sentence. It is third person singular, so it takes the verb form is. They is the subject of the second sentence, and it takes the verb form are. **See Lesson: Subject and Verb Agreement.**

36. D. Who is a pronoun. A pronoun is a type of word that replaces a noun (reminder, a noun is a person, place, or thing). Pronouns are words like she, you, him, them, this, and who, to name a few. **See Lesson: Pronouns.**

37. C. a lot of homework. Homework is a non-count noun and cannot be made plural by adding -s. **See Lesson: Nouns.**